W9-CKF-966

INTERNATIONAL LAW
a text

THE DORSEY SERIES IN POLITICAL SCIENCE

EDITOR NORTON E. LONG *Brandeis University*

MACRIDIS & BROWN *The De Gaulle Republic*

MACRIDIS & BROWN (eds.) *Comparative Politics: Notes and Readings* rev. ed.

DRAGNICH *Major European Governments* rev. ed.

ROBINSON *Congress and Foreign Policy-Making: A Study in Legislative Influence and Initiative* rev. ed.

JACOBINI *International Law: A Text* rev. ed.

MANGONE *The Elements of International Law* rev. ed.

GRIPP *Patterns of Soviet Politics* rev. ed.

MINAR *Ideas and Politics: The American Experience*

MEEHAN *The Theory and Method of Political Analysis*

EDELMANN *Latin American Government and Politics*

JACOB & ATHERTON *The Dynamics of International Organization: The Making of World Order*

SPIRO *World Politics: The Global System*

BROWN & WAHLKE *The American Political System: Notes and Readings*

ROELOFS *The Language of Modern Politics: An Introduction to the Study of Government*

MEEHAN *Contemporary Political Thought: A Critical Study*

FROHOCK *The Nature of Political Inquiry*

MEEHAN *Explanation in Social Science: A System Paradigm*

International Law
a text

H. B. JACOBINI

Professor of Government
Southern Illinois University

Revised Edition · 1968
THE DORSEY PRESS, Homewood, Illinois
IRWIN–DORSEY LIMITED, Nobleton, Ontario

REVISED EDITION

First Printing, March 1968

Library of Congress Catalog Card No. 68–17045
PRINTED IN THE UNITED STATES OF AMERICA

To
the Memory of My Father
and
to My Mother

Preface

TEXTS in international law follow one of three main forms:
(1) casebooks, (2) commentaries, and (3) combinations. Most
cover both peace and war, but some are concerned only with the
law of peace.

The present volume represents an attempt to develop a relatively brief text which is nevertheless comprehensive. It is recognized that in so doing some topics must be dealt with crypti-
cally, but this seems better than to leave them untouched on
the one hand, or to try to exhaust every topic on the other. If
this study can provide a useful theoretical framework and a
comprehensive substantive outline for the study of international law, its objectives will have been largely achieved.

As a text it is geared primarily to the liberal arts offerings
in international law, normally given in government or political
science departments. In this context it is as important for the
student to see how the law emerges and what social function it
performs as it is to assimilate its substance. Accordingly, an attempt has been made to balance these considerations.

Since it is assumed that many instructors may wish to have
their classes undertake research projects, an attempt has been
made throughout to cite, in addition to many highly specialized
sources, the sort of reference works which one might expect to
find in small college libraries as well as in the great university
collections. Thus, while a vast number of specialized mono-
graphs and articles are cited, much use has been made of
Moore's and Hackworth's Digests and the works of Hyde and
Oppenheim.

This work is primarily a text, but it is hoped that it may serve
as an introduction for the general reader as well. It is thought
that the brevity of the work will contribute to a wider famili-
arity with the law of nations. In this connection it should be
emphasized that the laws of war and neutrality were included
in this treatment because—however unsatisfactory these matters may be from a great many standpoints—they are fundamental parts of the international relationship. Moreover, an

attempt to see international law divorced entirely from its wartime aspects would no doubt convey a seriously distorted picture.

International law, as defined later in this work, is that body
of rules or laws which is binding upon states and other international persons in their mutual relations. Much has been written
about the foundation of the system, and these matters will be
noted in a subsequent chapter. It seems important, however,
to briefly note two matters here: (1) something about what international law is not; and (2) the pertinent theoretical foundations subscribed to in this book.

With reference to the first of these it is necessary to note that,
as a survey of international law, this is not a substitute for international politics. Rather, it must be stressed that international
law is concerned only with a part of the overall international
relationship. Nor is it held here that it is necessarily the most
important part—only that it *is a* part, and that it *is* important.
Indeed, an attempt has been made to portray international law
in proper perspective and, in the fortuitous words of Brierly,
to emphasize that international law ". . . is neither a myth on
the one hand, nor a panacea on the other, but just one institution among others which we can use for the building of a better international order."

With reference to the second matter mentioned above, the
theoretical framework within which this volume was written
can be categorized as a political conception of law. Thus law is
seen as a sort of formalized derivative of the political forces in
a society. Accordingly, it cannot necessarily be equated with
justice or wisdom or with any other virtue or vice, but it must
be equated with political forces, and this relationship is even
clearer—though no more fundamental—in international law
than in municipal law. Thus Judge Alvarez of the World
Court has written that "international law not only takes into
account politics and the psychology of peoples but . . . it has
essentially these qualities. Furthermore . . . said elements,
united to the exigencies of social life, *form or constitute* this
law; from these it is born spontaneously and directly." Since
it is especially useful for the student of political science to un-
derstand this relationship, considerable attention has been
given to stressing it at opportune points throughout the work.

Finally, it remains to be stressed that while the author must accept full responsibility for the present work, he is nevertheless deeply in the debt of a large number of persons for assistance of various sorts both directly and indirectly connected with this volume. Most such debts must necessarily go without specific recognition here, but a few must be singled out for special mention.

Among those who have read parts or all of the manuscript and who have contributed helpful comments and suggestions are Professor Llewellyn Pfankuchen of the University of Wisconsin; and the author's colleagues at Southern Illinois University, Professor Clarence A. Berdahl, Professor Frank L. Klingberg, and Professor Randall H. Nelson. Departmental and University encouragement of this undertaking of various sorts, including typing assistance from the Research Committee of the Graduate School and from the Department of Government, and the splendid assistance rendered by personnel of the University library, particularly Dr. John Clifford, Miss Ruby Kerley, and Mr. Harold F. Smith, are all very much appreciated. The author's students—particularly those in international law at Southern Illinois University, The Citadel, and the University of Alabama—have contributed much to this work. Indeed, it is in a sense essentially an attempt to come to grips with many of the questions which they have raised.

Many academic experiences prior to the development of this volume are nevertheless reflected in it or have had an impact upon it. An early introduction to the field of international law under Professor William D. Moreland at Fort Hays Kansas State College, and exploration of the diverse theoretical aspects of the field under the superb guidance of Professor Walter E. Sandelius and in seminar with Professor Francis H. Heller at the University of Kansas are particularly cherished experiences.

Finally, as in almost all matters, the author is indebted to his wife, Billie Connelley Jacobini, not only for patiently reading the manuscript and offering useful criticisms, but for helping willingly with that most dreadful of all academic processes, proofreading.

H. B. JACOBINI

Carbondale, Illinois
April, 1962

Preface to Revised Edition

This edition is designed to alter the original one in several ways. It seeks to update wherever necessary, to expand a few sections, to add explanations of terms, to expand some of the documentation, to correct errors, and to add commentary on a few matters which were not treated in the first edition. Finally, an appendix detailing accessions to major conventions has been added.

The goal, however, remains the same. The volume is an attempt to present a comprehensive, brief, and readable account of the law of nations, and in so doing to emphasize a political interpretation of law.

In the revision, the author has been aided by the solicited criticisms of students (given anonymously) and by the cooperation of the Dorsey Press in bringing the comments of colleagues at other institutions to his attention. Especially appreciated, moreover, are suggestions from Professor H. Kent Schellenger of San Jose State College; Professor John T. Everett, Jr., of Texas Christian University; Professor E. C. Buell of Memphis State University; and Professor Abdul Majid Abbass, the writer's colleague at Southern Illinois University. A sabbatical leave and assistance from the Office of Research and Projects at Southern Illinois University have greatly facilitated this work. Moreover, encouragement, useful comments, and cooperation by the writer's family are deeply appreciated. The foregoing represent debts and obligations which, however, do not absorb responsibility. The last remains entirely the author's.

H. B. Jacobini

Carbondale, Illinois
February, 1968

Table of Contents

CHAPTER 1

Definition, Sources, and History of International Law

INTERNATIONAL LAW, like all law, must be studied as part of a political-legal system. The circumstances of its development partially parallel the evolution of municipal law, but to some extent its origins are unique. There is a transcendent parallel in the fact that both systems derive directly from their respective political settings, but since those political settings differ widely the clarity of parallel on this point is often obscured. It is the principle and not the details of political derivation which links the systems as separate or divergent segments of encompassing law.

DEFINITION AND VALIDATION OF THE LAW OF NATIONS

Before undertaking to discuss the meaning, scope, and ramifications of the law of nations, it is useful to delineate the subject and to note something about its substantiation.

Definition

International law or the law of nations may be defined as that body of rules or laws which is binding on states and other international persons in their mutual relations.[1] This legal

---

[1] See John Bassett Moore, *A Digest of International Law* (Washington, D.C.: U.S. Government Printing Office, 1906), Vol. 1, p. 2 (hereafter cited as Moore,

system, while in part one of the oldest in existence, is at the same time less perfect in many ways than most of the municipal systems in operation today.

It has been emphasized by a number of modern writers that the law of nations is a developing thing,[2] and indeed that it is becoming part of a common law of mankind.[3] These developments are indeed real and will be considered at appropriate points in this volume. It must be emphasized, however, that the segment of law being considered here, international law or the law of nations, is concerned primarily with the legal relationships of states and to a lesser extent with the other entities which enjoy varying degrees of international personality.

Validity

There remains some argument as to whether international law is true law, but it is generally conceded today that, except in the narrowest Austinian usage of the term, the law of nations is true law.[4] Modern international law has been theoretically validated and substantiated in a variety of ways. To illustrate, it is seen by Kelsen as being established by custom at the pinnacle of a worldwide legal system. Thus international law is valid because customarily it has been and continues to be followed. Thinkers such as Leon Duguit have emphasized social solidarity as the essential underpinning of law. In this view international law is valid because it represents a socially derived sanction or pressure for adherence. Hugo Krabbe saw the validity of international law as stemming from a worldwide conception of what is just. Louis Le Fur and others of this tradition have seen it as being valid because it embraces the

---

Digest I) ; Green Haywood Hackworth, *Digest of International Law* (Washington, D.C.: U.S. Government Printing Office, 1940–44) , Vol. I, pp. 1–3 (hereafter cited as Hackworth, *Digest* I) . Marjorie M. Whiteman, *Digest of International Law* (Washington, D.C.: U.S. Government Printing Office, 1963) , Vol. I, pp. 1, 2. (hereafter cited as Whiteman, *Digest* I) .

2 Whiteman, *Digest* I, p. 1.

3 C. W. Jenks, *The Common Law of Mankind* (New York: Frederick A. Praeger, Inc., 1958) , *passim.*

4 See Hackworth, *Digest* I, pp. 5–6; J. L. Brierly, *The Law of Nations* (5th ed.; Oxford: The Clarendon Press, 1955) , pp. 69–71.

natural law. The mainstream of modern tradition is characterized by James Garner's emphasis on the consent of states as
validating international law.[5] These are some of the theoretical
approaches to an explanation of the validity of contemporary
international law. Brierly perhaps sums up the matter best,
however, when he says that:

> The ultimate explanation of the binding force of all law is that
> man, whether he is a single individual or whether he is associated
> with other men in a state, is constrained, insofar as he is a reasonable
> being, to believe that order and not chaos is the governing principle
> of the world in which he has to live.[6]

This attitude translated into political terms means that
states find it more convenient to follow certain rules than to
live in utter anarchy. Hence such laws have come into being
and continue to exist.

The fact of the matter is that the law of nations is generally
followed by most nations in most matters and therefore from a
very pragmatic standpoint it is validated. John Bassett Moore
observed, for example, that it is probably less violated in peacetime than is municipal law.[7] This, of course, is a difficult judgment to appraise, but if it has validity, it serves to illustrate the
point that most of the specific rules of international law are
followed.

It should be added that a somewhat fuller inquiry into the
foundations and nature of international law will be found in

---

[5] Hans Kelsen, *General Theory of Law and State* (Cambridge, Mass.: Harvard
University Press, 1945), pp. 369–70 *et passim;* Leon Duguit, "Objective Law,"
trans. Margaret Grandgent and Ralph W. Gifford, *Columbia Law Review,* Vol.
XX (December, 1920), pp. 817–31; Vol. XXI (January, 1921), pp. 17–34; Vol.
XXI (February, 1921), pp. 126–43; Vol. XXI (March, 1921), pp. 242–56; Hugo
Krabbe, *The Modern Idea of the State* (New York: D. Appleton & Co., 1922),
pp. 83–90, 236; See reference in Charles G. Fenwick, *International Law* (3d ed.;
New York: Appleton-Century-Crofts, Inc., 1948), p. 64; James W. Garner, *Recent
Developments in International Law* (Calcutta: The University of Calcutta,
1925), p. 7.

[6] Brierly, *op. cit.,* p. 57.

[7] John Bassett Moore, *International Law and Some Current Illusions and
Other Essays* (New York: The Macmillan Co., 1924), p. 300. See a similar
observation by Leo Gross in G. A. Lipsky (ed.), *Law and Politics in the World
Community* (Berkeley, Calif.: University of California Press, 1953), p. 64.

the following chapter. Brief mention is made here only to give a theoretical foundation for the contents of this chapter.

SOURCES OF INTERNATIONAL LAW

There are several meanings attached to the term "sources" of international law. Some writers apparently use it to mean theoretical foundations of international law in general, a matter appraised in this volume under the headings of nature or foundations. Others employ the term in the sense of the immediate source of particular rules, and in a related sense it embraces "evidences" of international law. It should be pointed out, however, that the concepts of "source" and "evidence" are often different in that the former may refer to an original establishment of a rule while the latter suggests proof that the rule exists and is valid. That the two merge is evident, and it is useful for one to speculate upon the character of the sources discussed below. Thus, for example, he may reflect upon when a court decision is more properly to be considered a "source" and when it should be considered merely an "evidence."

Political Factors

In the general sense it may be briefly stated that international law, like all juridical law, stems from a political consensus. Specifically, however, it is not sufficient to point broadly to "a political consensus" as the basis for a rule in dispute. Within the main outlines of the political consensus, there are five primary sources from which international law is gleaned. These are (1) customs, (2) treaties, (3) national and international court decisions, (4) the writings of the authorities and specialists, and (5) general principles. There are, in addition, a number of other related sources.[8]

Custom

Customary international law consists of rules which began as usages or practices and which have been so firmly accepted and

---

[8] Brierly, *op. cit.*, pp. 57–69; Hackworth, *Digest* I, pp. 15–24, 6–12; Fenwick, *op. cit.*, pp. 69–86; *Statute of the International Court of Justice,* Article 38.

are so generally applicable that they have ultimately emerged as rules of law. Such customary principles usually come to be recognized subsequently in treaties or court decisions and are thereby put on an even more secure basis.

Customary law ordinarily has the disadvantage of developing slowly. Rules thus emerge over a fairly long period of time. On the other hand, the principle of national sovereignty over superjacent airspace is a good example of a rule which solidified rather quickly after there was occasion to apply any rule at all and which was soon written into conventional law. Another somewhat similar principle which can be said to be in the process of firming up is that of national sovereignty over the so-called continental shelf. In both of these instances, simultaneous interest in the same objectives occurred broadly in the community of nations. These interests resulted in various national pronouncements, together with little or no protest on the part of other nations. The result in the former instance is a matter of history; the latter, on the other hand, may be observed both by way of noting its important substance and in regard to the procedure of customary enactment.

One most important rule which is certainly, at least in part, one of customary origin is that known as *pacta sunt servanda*. This principle means that there is a long-standing recognized customary obligation to adhere to the terms of agreements. In other words treaties are based on the *customary rule* that once enacted they are to be observed. The "pure theory of law," which will be noted in a later chapter, is largely based on this relationship.

There are, of course, innumerable cases in which the force of custom has been judicially recognized. Among these *The Paquete Habana* and *The Lola*[9] is perhaps the most widely cited. In this case Mr. Justice Gray wrote that where there are no treaties or national rules declarative of international law "resort must be had to the customs and usages of civilized nations."

---

[9] 175 U.S. 677 (1900). For a useful survey of evidence of custom and related matters see "United Nations, Report of the International Law Commission Covering Its Second Session, June 5—July 29, 1950," *American Journal of International Law*, Official Documents section, Vol. XLIV (October, 1950), especially pp. 111–25.

Treaties

Treaties or conventions constitute a second major source of modern international law.[10] They are, of course, merely formal agreements among nations setting down rules and obligations which are to govern their mutual relationships. Treaties may be between two or a few states (resulting in what is called particular international law) or among quite a number of states (resulting in general international law) and they may and do cover a wide variety of subjects. Treaty law is sometimes referred to as conventional law, and multilateral treaties are sometimes called lawmaking treaties because of their relatively wide application.[11]

Treaty law is binding only upon signatory states, but when a great number of states have agreed to similar stipulations, a general rule may often be said to have emerged. Furthermore, especially as in the laws of war, a convention may be temporarily adhered to by a number of nonsignatory states partly perhaps because it is merely declaratory of customary law, and also no doubt because it is to the adhering states' interests to do so.

Treaties fall into two broad categories: (1) those declaratory of broad political principles, and (2) those setting forth relatively specific rules. While a clear line cannot always be drawn between the two, the former may be considered as part of the constitutional law of international affairs, while the latter may

---

10 The validity of the making of law by treaty is virtually taken for granted by the courts. Various cases allude to it, however, and various other indications also obtain. See *e.g.,* U.S. Constitution, Art. III, Sec. 2 which states that "The judicial power of the United States shall extend to all Cases in Law and Equity, arising under the Constitution, the Laws of the United States, and Treaties made, or which shall be made, under their Authority;" In the *Paquete Habana* and *Lola,* there are many references to treaties with the clear assumption of the validity of the process. In the case of the Wimbledon, the Court stated "No doubt any convention creating an obligation of this kind places a restriction upon the exercise of the sovereign rights of the states, in the sense that it requires them to be exercised in a certain way. But the right of entering into international engagements is an attribute of state sovereignty." (P.C.I.J., Pub. of the Court, Series A, No. 1, 1923) In *Taylor* v. *Morton* (23 Fed. Cases 784) the Court said "The foreign sovereign between whom and the United States a treaty has been made, has a right to expect and require its stipulations to be kept with scrupulous good faith." Similar examples could be cited *ad infinitum.*

11 See discussion of treaties in Hackworth, *Digest V,* pp. 1–5 f.; also Sir Ernest Satow, *A Guide to Diplomatic Practice* (4th ed., rev. by Sir Nevile Bland; London: Longmans, Green & Co., Inc., 1957), pp. 324–89.

be considered as the administrative law of the international community. A treaty of peace and the United Nations Charter are examples of the first category while a consular agreement and an extradition treaty are suggestive of the latter group.

Treaties are perhaps the best device for keeping the law of nations up to date for, unlike customary law or court decisions, they can be enacted somewhat like domestic laws when the need arises. They constitute, therefore, together with custom, one of the two most important sources of modern international law.[12]

Court Decisions

Court decisions constitute a third major source of international law. Such decisions are ordinarily binding only in the case in question and rarely if ever binding in the sense of *stare decisis*.[13] Some cases are settled in international courts of adjudication, a few are resolved in arbitration tribunals, and many are the products of national courts. Nevertheless, they may serve to crystallize customary law and occasionally to help formulate new rules.[14] Indeed the International Court of Justice appears to be utilizing its prior decisions as bases for contemporary views to a considerable extent.

Court decisions fall naturally into the two categories of (1) decisions of national courts and (2) decisions of international tribunals.

The first of these types arises from a wide variety of circumstances but all have in common the fact that some element of the case turns on the interpretation of a point in international

---

[12] Fenwick, *op. cit.*, p. 69.

[13] *Stare decisis* means that in subsequent cases a court should adhere to the precedents set in earlier cases. Some judicial systems conform rather closely to this principle while others do not.

[14] See Hackworth, *Digest V*, pp. 22–24; *Statute of the International Court of Justice*, Articles 38, 59; Hersh Lauterpacht, *The Development of International Law by the International Court* (rev. ed.; New York: Frederick A. Praeger, Inc., 1958), pp. 3–25; see also comment and references in John H. Wigmore, *A Guide to American International Law and Practice* (New York: Matthew Bender & Co., 1943), pp. 271–366. See also *Thirty Hogsheads of Sugar, Bentzon, Claimant v. Boyle,* 9 Cranch 191, 198 (1815). Also see *The Lotus,* P.C.I.J. Reports, Series A, No. 9 (1927–28).

law. The Anglo-American casebook method of teaching international law is based rather largely on appraisal of such cases. While such cases may have persuasive influence in other countries, there is, of course, no legal requirement that they be followed (except within the country where the case was decided, and there only if the principle of *stare decisis* applies) and court interpretations in different nations often diverge noticeably. They are, nevertheless, among the available guideposts.

International court decisions are also *ad hoc* affairs. They fall into the two major categories of (1) adjudication and (2) arbitration. In both types, states agree in advance to allow the case to be tried, and the decisions are applicable only to the case in question. They may, nevertheless, have persuasive influence and such influence is often of considerable importance. There is a growing body of this type of case law.

Writers

Writers have exerted considerable influence on judicial matters of all sorts, and in international law their judgments have had pronounced effect. Like court decisions, however, such statements are essentially a form of persuasive evidence. Students of international law have written widely on topics affecting their discipline. Their opinions are quoted in court cases as pertinent evidence, and in the diplomatic discussions of governments as being descriptive of correct international usage and as authoritative scholarly judgment.

Often the scholarly accounts merely confirm customary law or attempt to give interpretation to treaties or court decisions. On other occasions, however, they may break new ground.

In the previously cited case of *The Paquete Habana* and *The Lola,* Mr. Justice Gray in speaking of the methods of ascertaining what binding rules and customs obtain, stated that it was necessary to resort

. . . to the works of jurists and commentators, who by years of labor, research, and experience, have made themselves peculiarly well acquainted with the subjects of which they treat. Such works are resorted to by judicial tribunals, not for the speculations of their authors concerning what the law ought to be, but for trustworthy evidence of what the law really is.[15]

Principles of Right

Early in the history of modern international law there was pronounced reliance upon principles as the underlying source of law. Among these were the principles of natural law believed to be concepts of basic justice and right implicit in the nature of things and, according to some, understandable by the use of right reason. Even one of the early advocates of legal positivism, Alberico Gentili, while making a brief for reliance upon such sources as the consent of states, observes, nevertheless, that one who transgressed the natural law "would desire to conceal the act through very shame."[16] These principles played a very important part in the great work of Hugo Grotius and have been relied upon—decreasingly to be sure but somewhat nevertheless—down through the centuries.[17]

Principles of Law

Another use of the term "principles" which is more concrete than that just discussed concerns principles of law. One of the methodological fundamentals of early modern international law centered upon the adaptation of concrete tenets of Roman law to the exigencies of international society. This was not too difficult to rationalize because international society needed rules, the principles of Roman law had achieved a pronounced degree of perfection, and the Roman law was believed to be almost synonymous with the principles of natural law. Thus principles of Roman law came to underlie much of international law, and other private law sources have had influence as well.

---

[15] 175 U.S. 677 (1900).

[16] Alberico Gentili, *De iure belli libri tres*, 1612 edition (*The Classics of International Law*, trans. J. C. Rolf; 2 vols; Oxford: The Clarendon Press, 1933), Vol. I, p. 10.

[17] In *U.S.* v. *Schooner La Jeune Eugenie*, 2 Mason 409 (1822), Mr. Justice Story in indicting the slave trade stated "Now the law of nations may be deduced, first from the general principles of right and justice, applied and the concerns of individuals, and thence to the relations and duties of nations."

Aspects of international law are still argued in terms of underlying principles and in terms of understood principles of law. There are many examples of recognized rules of international law which have these origins. One such rule of Roman origin concerns prescriptive rights, that is, the principle that a ✓ state which has entertained certain claims indisputably for a protracted period of time establishes thereby a legal right to the substance of the claim. Another example is evident in the following quotation from the *Chorzow Factory* case:

> It is moreover, a principle generally accepted in the jurisprudence of international arbitration, as well as by municipal courts, that one Party cannot avail himself of the fact that the other has not fulfilled some obligation or has not had recourse to some means of redress, if the former Party has, by some illegal act, prevented the latter from fulfilling the obligations in question, or from having recourse to the tribunal which would have been open to him.[18]

Many such rules may now be considered to be based on customary law as well as upon the initial principle, but principle as a basic source of law must be recognized as such.[19]

Other Sources

There are a number of other sources and evidences of international law which should also be briefly mentioned here. Official government documents, such as explanatory papers ("white papers" and the like), diplomatic correspondence, decisions of the attorney general, rulings of the Judge Advocate General, and other statements of official views have a definite bearing on the formulation of rules. If in correspondence and communications, papers, speeches, and so on, the same view is enunciated by several governments, the political effect is to tend toward its tacit acceptance and its ultimate recognition.[20]

---

[18] *Chorzow Factory* case, P.C.I.J. Reports, Series A, No. 9 (1927), p. 31.

[19] See comments in Brierly, *op. cit.*, pp. 16–25, 63–64; Hersh Lauterpacht, *Private Law Sources and Analogies of International Law* (New York: Longmans, Green & Co., Inc., 1927), *passim*.

[20] The reader is invited to peruse virtually any part of Hackworth's *Digest of International Law* for evidence of these matters. See also William G. Downey, Jr., "The Law of War and Military Necessity," *American Journal of International Law*, Vol. XLVII (April, 1953), pp. 251–52; also D. R. Deener, *The United States*

Scientific societies and organizations and individual writers occasionally draw up so-called draft conventions, that is, proposed new rules or organized expressions of what is believed to be customary law stated in treaty form.[21] Also conferences of states occasionally draw up multilateral treaties which, for one reason or another, are never ratified.[22]

These draft and unratified conventions are not of course law per se. Yet they may be the best available current expressions of customary law and if so they may have persuasive influence.[23] In this connection it should be noted that there are technicalities in the Hague warfare conventions which render them legally inapplicable if any one of the belligerents is not a party to them.[24] Yet on the outbreak of war belligerents ordinarily express their basic adherence to them as expressive of the customary rules of warfare.[25]

Political Acceptability

It should be remembered that although the technical sources of law are of several sorts, a basic fact underlying their applica- ⌐

Attorneys General and International Law (The Hague: Martinus Nijhoff, 1957), *passim*.

[21] See, *e.g.*, the draft conventions prepared by the Harvard Law School's Program of Research in International Law in *American Journal of International Law*, Vol. XXIII (Special Supplement; April, 1929) ; Vol. XXVI (Supplement; January and April, 1932) ; Vol. XXIX (Supplement; 1935) ; Vol. XXXIII (Supplement; 1939). See also Leone Levi, *International Law with Materials for a Code of International Law* (New York: D. Appleton & Co., 1888) ; for a code achieving considerable influence see that of Francis Lieber as issued by the U.S. War Department as "General Orders 100," cited conveniently in George Grafton Wilson, *International Law* (9th ed.; New York: Silver Burdett & Co., 1935), pp. vi–xxxvi; see also the *Yearbooks of the International Law Commission* (published since 1949).

[22] See for example the Declaration of London (1909) cited conveniently in Wilson, *op. cit.*, pp. lxxxvi–c.

[23] In this connection see citation of "General Report of the Commission of the Jurists of the Hague, 1923," on the use of aircraft and radio in war in Llewellyn Pfankuchen, *A Documentary Textbook in International Law* (New York: Farrar & Rinehart, Inc., 1940), pp. 781–99.

[24] For the extent of this situation in World War I, see Pfankuchen, *op. cit.*, p. 754, fn. 1. Since the U.S.S.R. did not honor the ratification by the Czarist regime, the technical inapplicability in World War II apparently came with its entry into the conflict.

[25] For evidence of such action in the Korean War, see *New York Times,* July 14, 1950, p. 3.

tion is that rules must be politically acceptable. This may involve the special acceptance of a treaty, the tacit or express acquiescence in a principle, a custom, or the contents of a scholarly treatise, or it may be represented by a willingness to accept the dictates of a court decision. This last would include the constitutional necessity to do so in some jurisdictions as well as the overt willingness to do so in cases of international arbitration and adjudication. The political source of law may sometimes be minimized if one is viewing law in its more technical aspects, but even the technical aspects must be viewed in terms of the political context in which they are operative. Thus, as was noted in the Introduction, the illustrious Chilean judge, Alejandro Alvarez, has stated very plainly that:

. . . international law *not only takes into account* politics and the psychology of peoples but . . . it has essentially these qualities (*characteres*). Furthermore, . . . [these] elements, united to the exigencies of social life, *form or constitute* this law; from these it is born spontaneously and directly.[26]

HISTORY OF INTERNATIONAL LAW

The history of international law is long and varied.[27] It has many facets and many merging and divergent threads. Often a review of the history of international law becomes a history of the philosophy of international law, for that aspect sometimes appears to be the only one that can be meaningfully portrayed. This brief survey will be directed insofar as possible toward a portrayal of the politico-legal development, however, leaving the philosophical aspects for a later treatment.

Ancient Concepts and Influences

There is evidence that many peoples outside the stream of Western civilization possessed systems resembling international

---

[26] Alejandro Alvarez, *Despues de la guerra* (Buenos Aires: Imprenta de la Universidad, 1943), p. 288; excerpt translated in H. B. Jacobini, *A Study of the Philosophy of International Law as Seen in Works of Latin American Writers* (The Hague: Martinus Nijhoff, 1954), p. 107.

[27] See in particular, Arthur Nussbaum, *A Concise History of the Law of Nations* (rev. ed.; New York: The Macmillan Co., 1954).

law, and treaties are recorded embodying agreements between sovereignties in very ancient times.[28]

Within the mainstream of Western civilization the Greeks, whose political organization was characterized by the sovereign city-state, had international legal arrangements which parallel many modern attitudes. Thus, for example, there seem to have been certain general principles and rules governing the treatment to be accorded diplomats, and there were agreements among the municipal sovereignties.[29]

The Romans too possessed practices which are closely related to the modern law of nations.[30] The Roman institution of the *jus fetiale* concerned the legal requirements attending a declaration of war. Their attitude on the sanctity of diplomats is still another case in point.

At the height of its power Rome considered itself to be coextensive with civilization itself and there was therefore no place for international law per se. The Roman *jus gentium*, a system of intergroup law and a sort of private international law emerged, however, within the Roman Empire. It involved the utilization of an official known as the *praetor peregrinus* whose function was to know and apply the proper rules in commercial and other private conflicts between persons from different nations within the Roman Empire.[31]

The Roman Empire engendered an attitude of universality which had been unknown before. This means that where the

---

[28] *Ibid.*, pp. 1–5. For excerpts from Egyptian, Indian, and Chinese ancient accords and commentary and for other interesting texts, see Louis Le Fur and George Chklaver, *Recueil de textes de droit international public,* Deuxième edition (Paris: Librairie Dalloz, 1934), *passim;* see Tshu Cheng, "International Law in Ancient China (1122–249 B.C.)," *Chinese Social and Political Science Review* XI (1927), pp. 38 ff., 251–70; for a comprehensive treatment of international law in ancient and medieval India see the series of articles by C. J. Chacko and Nagendra Singh entitled collectively, "International Law in India," *Indian Journal of International Law,* Vol. I (1960–61), pp. 184–92, 589–98; Vol. II (1962), pp. 48–64, 65–82, 143–63, 318–55; Vol. III (1963), pp. 44–62; also see C. J. Chacko, "India's Contribution to the Field of International Law Concepts," 93 *Recueil des cours* (1958) I, especially pp. 121–43; for description of Muslim practices, see Majid Khadduri, War and Peace in the Law of Islam (Baltimore: The Johns Hopkins Press, 1955), especially pp. 42–48; also *passim.*

[29] Coleman Phillipson, *The International Law and Custom of Ancient Greece and Rome* (2 vols.; London: Macmillan & Co., Ltd., 1911), *passim.*

[30] *Ibid.*

[31] *Ibid.*, Vol. 1, pp. 267–301.

Greeks emphasized their municipal sovereignties, the Romans were able to transcend provincialities, and people throughout the Empire emphasized their status as citizens of Rome. Probably one of the major reasons for this pattern of willingness to be Roman was due to the remarkably enlightened Roman policy of imposing only slight restraints on conquered peoples together with the fact that Roman civilization was incomparably higher and more satisfying than those of the peoples who lived in the outlying areas. These elements together with Roman might made the Roman way seem the right way.

The result was that Roman civilization, administration, law, language, and general culture came to prevail widely, and a common set of attitudes based on Roman culture grew up throughout Eruope.

When the Roman Empire crumbled, a certain basic unity of culture continued to persist, based on these common features further solidified by the common religion which had gradually grown out of the teachings of the early Christians together with the Greek and Roman attitudes on natural law.

Middle Ages

While through religion, legal background, and language of the elite, the pattern of the Middle Ages may have represented a continuation of Roman universalism, the political ethos of post-Roman international society was characterized by a fragmentation in which real authority reposed in relatively small political units. The Church and the Holy Roman Empire exerted considerable influence, however, and these together with the concept of Roman universalism perpetuated the idea of one god and one law. The fact remains, nevertheless, that small political units came to be the real seat of political dominance in much of Europe, and international law tended to become *inter* again. Various rules were applied during this era, such as church edicts which prescribed the times when fighting could take place, and rules designed to protect noncombatants. The fact that the church was a very real temporal power together with its influence through threats of excommunication lent weight to its demands and to the rules that it supported.[32]

During this period systems of private law also developed as seen in such codes as those of Rhodes, Amalfi, Barcelona, and the Hanseatic League. These were concerned mostly with the private international law of the sea.[33] Also, rules of diplomatic conduct came into use during this time as did other principles which emerged ultimately as general international usages.[34]

During the later phases of the Middle Ages states began to emerge in Italy and elsewhere in Europe. These states owed no allegiance to the Holy Roman Empire and were therefore *de jure* as well as *de facto* sovereignties. Their separateness was even more emphasized by the religious split of the Reformation. The religious wars and the Thirty Years' War showed a bitterness and a ruthlessness which appalled humanitarians and suggested to some that man was forsaking principles of right in the conduct of wars for postures of expediency and attitudes of brutality.[35]

Early Modern Era

By the middle of the 17th century the forces of medievalism were well along toward decay, and the modern era of sovereign states was being launched. The treaties of Osnabrück and Münster, better known as the Peace of Westphalia, ending the

---

[32] Nussbaum, *op. cit.*, pp. 17–60.

[33] See John H. Wigmore, *A Panorama of the World's Legal Systems*, Vol. III (St. Paul, Minn.: West Publishing Co., 1928), pp. 875–929. The term public law refers to those rules of law which involve the relations, status or rights and duties of the state or its subdivisions. The term private law on the other hand, refers to those laws which operate primarily between individual persons. Accordingly, laws which define the role of the state in controlling public utilities and which describe the obligations of a state in relation to soldiers of another state are public laws. Laws which concern the way in which one individual may be entitled to damages for violation of his property by another, or a law which describes the respective commerical rights of citizens of different countries vis-à-vis one another are examples of private law.

[34] Graham H. Stuart, *American Diplomatic and Consular Practice* (2d ed.; New York: Appleton-Century-Crofts, Inc., 1952), pp. 118–23 *et passim*.

[35] Grotius himself was apparently much concerned along this line. See Hugo Grotius, *De jure belli ac pacis libri tres*, 1645 edition (*The Classics of International Law*, trans. F. W. Kelsey; 2 vols.; Oxford: The Clarendon Press, 1925), prolegomena.

Thirty Years' War in 1648, is usually cited as the historical point when modern national Europe emerged from feudal Europe. At this point, too, international law ceased to function as an arm of an ossified universalism and emerged as a truly international legal system.

During the century preceding the Peace of Westphalia, a number of writers began to catch the essence of internationalism (as contrasted with universalism). The Spanish clerics, Vitoria and Suarez, and the Italo-English Protestant, Gentili, stressed various phases of the emerging pattern, but undoubtedly the most important publicist of all was the Hollander, Hugo Grotius, who has come to be called the father of modern international law.[36]

Grotius' major contribution to international law was his book published first in 1625 and again in 1648, *De jure belli ac pacis* (On the Laws of War and Peace) in which he laid the foundations for the modern study of the law of nations. This work depicted nations as sovereign bodies but subject in some sense to the laws of nature which were embodied in certain practices, the Roman law, and other legal, scriptural, and classical maxims. Grotius' book, coming as it did at the dawn of the modern period and grasping its essence, fitted into a real need and came to play an important part in determining the legal relationships among states.

Grotius and those who adhered most closely to his views saw international law as emanating both from the law of nature and from international agreements. Certain other scholars and writers like Zouche came to see it as deriving largely or entirely from treaties, and a few such as Pufendorf claimed that it was merely a reflection of the laws of nature.[37] These three views have come to be called the Grotian, positivist, and naturalist conceptions respectively and with varying intensity they have been carried down through the 18th and 19th centuries, and on into the 20th. These views together with other doctrinal aspects will be considered more fully in the following chapter.

During the 17th and 18th centuries the European political

---

[36] See Nussbaum, *op. cit.*, pp. 71–74; also Jacobini, *op. cit.*, pp. 12–15.

[37] Nussbaum, *op. cit.*, pp. 135–74.

scene was dominated by France, Spain, Austria and England. The end of the 18th and the beginning of the 19th centuries witnessed the French Revolution and the Napoleonic era, while the latter part of the 19th century saw the Western power balance altered by the emergence of a unified Germany and Italy, and by the increased importance of Russia and the United States.

During these centuries the interplay of political pressures, especially as exerted by the great powers, determined the emergence of new facets of international law.

Rules governing colonial claims and holdings were derived from the attitudes and potentialities of the major colonial powers. General claims to ownership of the seas were pressed and countered with the effect that only England—which in reality ruled the seas throughout much of the modern era—continued to exert significant claims for any considerable length of time. Later, when England followed the lead of some other states including the United States and pressed for freedom of the seas, that rule came to be accepted.[38]

The Napoleonic era witnessed the destruction of most of the old feudal entities in the Germanies, but remnants of the earlier era were salvaged for a time by the conservative Congress of Vienna. Of more immediate importance to international law, that Congress established a number of new rules among which was the crystallization of the law governing diplomatic ranks. It also gave birth to a concert of great powers which dominated the European scene and may be viewed as a forerunner of the League of Nations.[39] Several decades later, in 1856, the Declaration of Paris provided for certain property rights at sea and had the effect of outlawing privateers.[40]

With the widening of international horizons the new states of the western hemisphere came to have a voice in international affairs and were recognized as new entities, as had been

[38] See A. Pearce Higgins and C. John Colombos, *The International Law of the Sea* (London: Longmans, Green & Co., Inc., 1943), pp. 37–57.

[39] See Nussbaum, *op. cit.*, pp. 186–88.

[40] See conveniently in Pfankuchen, *op. cit.*, pp. 891–92, and in Wilson, *op. cit.*, pp. iv–v.

the situation earlier regarding such states as Russia and Turkey. Eventually (though to a considerable extent in the 20th century) a large number of Asian and African states attained full membership in the family of nations and the once parochial international law of Europe thus came to embrace the world.

The latter part of the 19th century witnessed a shake up of the power balance with the emergence of unified Germany and Italy and of the Balkan states together with a renewed colonialism on the part of all the major and some of the minor powers.

The rules of warfare were somewhat crystallized toward the end of the 19th and beginning of the 20th centuries. This was seen especially in the Geneva Convention of 1864 and the Hague Conventions of 1899 and 1907.

20th Century

The late 19th and early 20th centuries also witnessed a new interest in arbitration with the establishment of the Permanent Court of Arbitration and many arbitral agreements, but the major issues continued to be "decided by a weapon longer than a pen." World War I saw the laws of warfare strained but also saw the clear emergence of the rule of national control over the airspace. Following the war, a new attempt at international cooperation was launched through a formal League of Nations, and the famous Paris Peace Pact was signed which legally abolished war as an instrument of national policy. Adjudication was advanced by the creation of the Permanent Court of International Justice in conjunction with the League of Nations.

The efforts of the League to maintain peace were destined to failure, however, because men and nations had not yet realized that justice needs immediate defenders as well as the long perspective of history. Political, economic, and social dissatisfaction on the part of Germany, Italy, and Japan and a lack of willingness to take a clear stand on the part of the United States, Great Britain, and France, led to World War II, a struggle which ultimately revived and made respectable the realization and doctrine that international stability can be maintained only if there is a stable balance among the world powers.[41]

World War II witnessed a greater strain on the laws of war than had the previous conflagration; but after the war's end a renewed effort was made to put responsibility for acts of war on a legal basis, and, as a consequence, known war criminals were tried with the subsequent conviction of many.[42] Subsequently, in 1949, revised conventions were drawn up covering prisoners of war, civilians in wartime, and wounded, sick, and ship-wrecked military and naval personnel.[43]

A renewed effort to stabilize the world through organization led to the creation of the United Nations organization, this time stressing the need for unity among the great powers. General inability of the great powers to agree on matters of importance, however, has led to new approaches to the problem based largely on a naked balance of power relationship. The International Court of Justice, as a unit within the United Nations, continues the tradition of the old Permanent Court of International Justice.

Another aspect of the recent history of international law concerns the impact of the U.S.S.R. In the early years of the Soviet regime, the United States and some other nations refused to recognize the new Russian government on the grounds that it was not prepared to assume its normal obligations under international law. It was also contended, however, that the U.S.S.R. did in fact exist and that failure to recognize it was reminiscent of the ostrich. As a consequence of this political reality, recognition followed, but a similar problem persists with reference to Red China. The earlier reservation as to Russia's responsibility proved to be valid at least in part, for the U.S.S.R. has developed a consistent disregard for many established rules of international procedure, a glaring example

---

[41] See comments in Winston S. Churchill, *The Gathering Storm* (Boston: Houghton Mifflin Co., 1948), p. v, and elsewhere particularly in Book I.

[42] See *e.g.*, "International Military Tribunal (Nuremberg), Judgment and Sentences," *American Journal of International Law*, Vol. XLI (January, 1947), pp. 172–333.

[43] See *Geneva Conventions of 12 August, 1949 for the Protection of War Victims* (Department of the Army Pamphlet No. 20–150 [Washington, D.C.: U.S. Government Printing Office, 1950]).

of which has been its treatment of prisoners of war, and its refusal to return such personnel after the termination of war.

This attitude of the U.S.S.R. and the Russian bloc has led to a persistent feeling in the West that bad faith is an integral part of the Soviet system. This sentiment has mellowed somewhat in the mid-1960's, however and Soviet truculence in treaty making sometimes has been interpreted as reflecting a growing respect for the sanctity of agreements. Indeed there is increasing evidence of a growing reproachment in Soviet and Western views on international law. One interesting indication of this normalization is to be seen in the scope of an official Soviet textbook on international law which appears to parallel non-Soviet summaries of the subject to a very high degree.[44] Nevertheless, there has also been much variation in doctrine. While present positions appear to be relatively close to those of the West, the fluctuations have contributed to overall vagueness and impreciseness.[45]

If there has been a lessening of tension on this level, it has in no sense been reflected in relations between the United States and the People's Republic of China. Indeed, that relationship has become so irregular that little or no approximation of mutual legalism seems to exist. At present writing it may be conjectured that Chinese truculence, and seeming emphasis on fomenting conflict and revolt wherever possible represent a particularly self-centered phase of Marxist evolution not unlike some past aspects of Russian development.

In view of what has been suggested regarding the political nature of law, it is useful to reflect upon the content of international law when important members of the society of nations assume positions which impair its stature. Clearly in time the law emerges with a changed quality which reflects a measure of these deviations. Accordingly, while from a value-oriented position one may deplore undesirable changes, from a jurisprudential standpoint, it is necessary merely to see the impact of these alterations.

---

[44] Academy of Sciences of the U.S.S.R., Institute of State and Law, *International Law* (Moscow: Foreign Languages Publishing House, c. 1961), *passim* (hereafter cited as *Soviet textbook*).

[45] J. J. G. Syatauw, *Some Newly Established Asian States and the Development of International Law* (The Hague: Martinus Nijhoff, 1961), pp. 206–12.

Another source of impact, jurisprudentially similar but ideologically different in character, is that of the new states upon the development of international law. More than 50 new states have emerged in the past two decades,[46] and most represent peoples whose independence has in one way or another been the object of colonial repression. Moreover the peoples represented, while often having Western educations, represent traditional cultures with internal traditions, customs, and legal norms which are not of European origin. Moreover, the focus which they bring to the international scene is often different from that of their European brethren.[47] It may be conjectured that the differing impact may be more effective in those areas where existing rules lack definiteness.[48]

The period dating from the last third of the 19th century has witnessed not only what might be called a constitutional struggle in the international community, but it has also seen the emergence of a growing body of limited treaty law of enormous scope. Commercial agreements, trade pacts, extradition treaties, arbitration accords, and police agreements, to mention only a few, now blanket the globe, and a body of case law exists within national states and within the international community as a whole which further helps to spell out the scope of the law of nations. Much of this newer treaty law is essentially limited in character and represents an administrative (as contrasted with broadly political) type of activity and organization which is perhaps the most concrete nondiplomatic accomplishment of the League and the United Nations.

International Law: Constitutional and Administrative

Throughout the history of international law there have really been two major threads, one of which might be called international constitutional law and the other of which may be described as a sort of international administrative law. The

---

[46] Whiteman, *Digest* II, pp. 133–467.

[47] This subject is well developed in Rupert Emerson, "Self-Determination Revisited in the Era of Decolonization," Occasional Papers in International Affairs, No. 9, (Cambridge, Mass.: Center for International Affairs, Harvard University Press, 1964), especially pp. 1–24.

[48] Syatauw, *op. cit.*, p. 200 *et passim*.

former is a highly political thing which concentrates upon matters of major concern to the balance of power and hence to the political structure of international society.

Rules of less political import and rules within the accepted political pattern constitute the bulk of practical international jurisprudence, but international constitutional law and international administrative law go hand in hand just as do national constitutional and national administrative rules.

SUMMARY

International law is dependent upon the political context of the community of nations, but within that context the main sources of international law are (1) customs, (2) treaties, (3) scholarly writings, (4) court decisions, (5) principles of justice and law, and (6) other sources such as government documents, judge advocate general rulings and draft conventions.

In the sense of having its roots in the ancient past, the history of international law covers a great span of time. However, modern international law may be said to have begun with the Peace of Westphalia in 1648. It has been closely related to the main political threads of Western civilization. Now it is dependent upon world politics as a whole. The political orientation of the great powers and of the new powers as well as other political threads are reflected in it, and it is responsive to new concepts which originate from these sources.

Modern international law may be viewed in two main segments: (1) the broadly political or constitutional aspects, and (2) the more technical aspects. The body of the latter group especially has grown with the use of treaties enacted over the past 75 years.

CHAPTER 2

The Nature of International Law and Its Relation to Municipal Law

INTERNATIONAL LAW was defined in the first chapter as "that body of rules or laws which is binding on states and other international persons in their mutual relations." It is necessary to go beyond this formal definition, however, and to inquire somewhat more deeply into its real substance and foundation.

The fact that rules do exist and that they are generally followed should not obscure the fact that the structure of international society differs materially from its nation state counterpart. It is, therefore, worthwhile to inquire into the nature of law in general as well as into the nature of international law per se.

THE NATURE OF INTERNATIONAL LAW

What is law? At first glance this may not seem to be at all complex, for law appears to be simply the enactments of the Congress, the state legislature, the city council, and other similar bodies. Yet what does all this imply?

What the Existence of Law Implies

In the first place, it means that there is some entity which by law, custom, belief, or other force is recognized as having the political authority to make law. If there is no such body, then law must evolve in some other way if it is to evolve at all.

In the second place, it means that once enacted, the rules will be enforced or at least that there is some suitable redress for harmful violations, and that in general the law will be obeyed.

Fact and Law Are Often Disparate

From another standpoint the existence of enacted law must be viewed in relation to the practical reality of the law. Thus a careful appraisal of governmental procedures will reveal a startling number of cases in which the "law" as enacted does not describe the action as it really occurs or the procedure as it is carried out. Furthermore, the case of the 18th Amendment to the United States Constitution or the inoperative second sentence of the Second Section of the 14th Amendment, point to another problem, that of the duly enacted law—indeed constitutional stipulation—which is not taken very seriously. Still another related phenomenon is seen in the areas where allegedly a court conviction under a valid law cannot be obtained because of locally prevailing political attitudes or public opinion.

The Courts as Factors in Law

Still another approach to the question of what is law may be seen in the view that law is the result of careful judicial scrutiny and precedent, whereby—under the principle *stare decisis*—permanent rules of law emerge and remain. Yet here too courts change their minds from time to time and in these instances do not follow precedent.

Political Nature of Law

It may be suggested here that for the student of political science, law, including international law, can most accurately be viewed as an essentially political phenomenon.[1] In the first place political bodies enact it. In the second place it is submit-

---

[1] See comments in Francis H. Heller, *Introduction to American Constitutional Law* (New York: Harper & Bros., 1952), pp. vii–viii. On this whole subject see

ted that "technical" decisions contrary to strong public desire almost invariably fall—eventually; and in the third place those that are sustained conform within the prevailing political context. While the science of technical law is not to be disparaged, the important thing to realize is that a change in political context can destroy the technical developments almost overnight. Hence a moderate change in the 1930's in the United States witnessed a significant change in the interpretation of the contract clause of the Constitution,[2] and in a more radical instance, civil rights became nonexistent in Germany. Finally, in the United States, certain constitutional guarantees often have meant one thing in one region and something quite different in another.

Technical Rules a Science, but within Political Framework

Within the broad outlines laid down by the political context, a wealth of technical and administrative law develops and grows. Many of these detailed matters may partake of the political, but they tend to do so less obviously than do the broad constitutional and political enactments. Thus, within the established political framework, the development of technical rules can and does become highly scientific and detailed.

Political and Technical Dichotomy Also Valid for International Law

Within the scope of international law this same dichotomy of the political and the technical must also be recognized. While much of international law operates on a highly political and changeable plane, within established areas there are stable bodies of technical rules, these not only persist from year to year and decade to decade, but in some instances last from century to century.[3]

---

treatment in M. A. Kaplan and N. de B. Katzenback, *The Political Foundations of International Law* (New York: John Wiley & Sons, Inc., 1961), pp. 5–11 *et passim*.

[2] *Home Building and Loan Association* v. *Blaisdell,* 290 U.S. 398 (1934).

[3] See for example the rules governing diplomatic immunities; see Chapter Seven of this work.

SCHOOLS OF INTERNATIONAL LAW

Within the scope of international law itself there has been much speculation and inquiry into the broadly philosophical and the more narrowly theoretical bases of the law of nations.[4] These foundations for international law may be discussed in three categories which, it should be pointed out, are not altogether mutually exclusive. The first of these may be termed the broadly philosophical schools. They are concerned with the relation of international law to universals and to first principles. In this connection the classic trinity of naturalists, positivists, and Grotians or eclectics will be surveyed, and in addition a fourth grouping which may be called the social naturalists will also be mentioned.

The second category of theories may be classed as the juridical schools which, though not to be entirely divorced in treatment from the more classic conceptions, are more modern in origin and are concerned less with universals and first principles than with law per se. In this category mention will be made of Austinianism, the historical school, the pure theory of law, and social solidarity as well as several other approaches.

The third category of theories, again not wholly separate from the others, is concerned primarily with fairly modern specialized national and regional conceptions of international law. In this group mention will be made of the Italian, German, Soviet, and American schools.

The Philosophical Schools

These four theoretical persuasions have in common the assumption that international law is a valid legal factor in international affairs. They differ on the question of how law is constituted and these differences represent important philo-

---

4 See discussion in H. B. Jacobini, *A Study of the Philosophy of International Law as Seen in Works of Latin American Writers* (The Hague: Martinus Nijhoff, 1954), Chapter I particularly *et passim;* see also Arthur Nussbaum, *A Concise History of the Law of Nations* (rev. ed.; New York: The Macmillan Co., 1954), *passim.*

sophical cleavages which in some instances have existed throughout the modern history of international law.

Naturalism. Naturalism, though stemming out of the medieval era, was expressed most absolutely in the works of Samuel Pufendorf[5] who was of the opinion that divinely ordained rules were the only rules having bona fide force of law, and that laws not in conformity with the law of nature were not binding. While the term has had and still retains divergent meanings, it has generally suggested the existence of principles of justice which can be applied to the affairs of men and of nations. It embraces those mandates which are believed to represent the dictates of the Diety, as well as other insights into the character of eternal truth. It postulates that man can perceive the enduring and applicable principles by the use of right reason.

It is probably correct to state that while this view has a limited importance in its relatively pure form, it has played a more significant role as a segment of Grotian or eclectic thinking about the nature of the law of nations.

A somewhat confusing variant of the term suggests that there are social or cosmic laws of behavior which are viewed as "natural." This meaning is described elsewhere in this chapter.[6]

Positivism. Positivism in international law, contrasted with naturalism, stresses human action as the font of law. The difficulty in reaching agreement upon precisely what is or is not innately and naturally just has led many students to the conclusion that the importance of naturalism should be minimized or disregarded altogether. As a consequence such men as Gentili and Zouche, early in the history of international law, stressed customs and treaties as the important sources of law.[7] Thus

---

[5] Samuel von Pufendorf, *De jure naturae et gentium libri octo,* 1688 edition (*The Classics of International Law,* trans. C. H. and W. A. Oldfather; 2 vols.; Oxford: The Clarendon Press, 1934), p. 266 *et passim.*

[6] See below, this chapter, "Social Naturalism."

[7] Alberico Gentili, *De iure belli libri tres,* 1612 edition (*The Classics of International Law,* trans. J. C. Rolf; 2 vols.; Oxford: The Clarendon Press, 1933), p. 8 *et passim;* Richard Zouche, *Juris et judicii feciales, sive juris inter gentes, et quaestionum de eodem explicatio,* 1650 edition, Vol. II (*The Classics of International Law,* trans. J. L. Brierly; 2 vols.; Baltimore, Md.: The Lord Baltimore Press, 1911), p. 1 *et passim.*

positivists are those who see international law as stemming from the tacit or specific actions of men.

Grotians or Eclectics. The Grotian conception of international law, often called eclectic, derives its name from the legal theories of Hugo Grotius. Grotius and many who have followed him, stressed two major sources of international law: (1) the natural law and (2) rules of positive origin.[8] While the former would take precedence over the latter in cases of direct conflict, it was realized that in a great many cases no clear conflict would exist and such a system would merge nicely with popular beliefs. Through the centuries perhaps most of the writers on international law have been eclectics at least to a degree.[9]

Social Naturalism. A fourth general view may be called social naturalism. A great many writers through the ages have spoken of natural law not in the sense of innate justice but rather in the sense of patterns of action which naturally emerge from a certain set of circumstances, that is, laws of cause and effect. The expressions of this persuasion vary widely and it may appear a misnomer to classify them together, especially since some are avowedly positivist. Yet there are certain underlying similarities which induce this classification.

Hobbes,[10] as an example, believed that man in a state of nature was pitted against all other men and that states in international society were of like status. The sole natural rule in his view was therefore the law of survival. On the other hand a great number of writers have seen law as stemming naturally from the existence of society.[11] International law in this view

---

[8] Hugo Grotius, *De jure belli ac pacis libri tres,* 1645 edition (*The Classics of International Law,* trans. F. W. Kelsey; 2 vols.; Oxford: The Clarendon Press, 1925) ; see Thomas J. Lawrence, *Essays on Some Disputed Questions in International Law* (Cambridge, Mass.: Deighton Bell & Co., 1885) , p. 196; see also Nussbaum, *op. cit.,* pp. 108–9.

[9] See comments in Jacobini, *op. cit.,* p. 139 *et passim;* For an interesting contemporary example of grounding the modern law of nations partially in the law of nature, see W. V. O'Brien, "Legitimate Military Necessity in Nuclear War," *World Polity,* Vol. II (1960) , pp. 35–120.

[10] Thomas Hobbes, *Philosophical Rudiments Concerning Government and Society,* in William Molesworth (ed.) , *The English Works of Thomas Hobbes* (11 vols.; London: John Bohn, 1839–45) , Vol. II, pp. 8–9, 21–22, 187, *et passim.*

[11] See e.g., D. Simon Planas Suarez, *Tratado de derecho internacional publico,* Vol. I (Madrid: Hijos de Reus, 1916) , pp. 5–6.

derives from the existence of the community of nations, *ubi societas ibi jus,* (that is, where there is a society there is also law). Many moderns such as Leon Duguit and Hugo Krabbe have felt that law stems more or less naturally from the social complexion of society.[12] While these ends might or might not be "just" in the view of traditional ethical naturalism, they were conceived of as natural in the sense of being the logical consequence of certain causal actions.

Juridical Schools

The four basic concepts just reviewed have a scope reminiscent of the broader interpretations of history, but there are some other pointedly juridical schools of thought with which it is equally important for the student to be familiar.

Austinianism. The English jurist, John Austin, was of the opinion that all law stems from a sovereign will, that international law could not be so derived because there were several sovereignties concerned and therefore that international law was not true law but rather a useful sort of "positive morality."[13] This was the view of the Austinians (sometimes called the analytical school) on the legal nature of international law.

Austinianism is an important view not only because of its unfortunate conclusion concerning the law of nations, but also because of its antinatural law focus and perhaps most of all because of its relentless emphasis on clarity of reasoning. Its real shortcoming, however, lies not so much in what it states as in what it fails to perceive. In its relatively narrow conception of the sovereign, it leaves untouched the political essence of sovereignty. If, as must be argued, the law giving sovereign is merely the composite political power from which law emerges, then it is most difficult to draw a meaningful philosophical distinction between the legal character of municipal law on the one hand and of international law on the other. Certainly both

---

12 Leon Duguit, "Objective Law," *Columbia Law Review,* Vols. XX, XXI (1920, 1921); for full citations see above, Chapter One, fn. 5; Hugo Krabbe, *The Modern Idea of the State* (New York: D. Appleton & Co., 1922).

13 John Austin, *Lectures on Jurisprudence* (2 vols.; New York: James Crockcroft & Co., 1875), Vol. I, pp. 121–22, Vol. II, p. 177.

stem from political complexes, and although the patterns of these complexes vary notably, their theoretical essentials do not.

If this lesser quality of Austinianism must be noted, it is also necessary to recognize that Austin's focus was on internal, legal, and social improvement and not on international affairs. In terms of legal analysis he contributed greatly to careful and methodical thinking about law.

The pure theory of law is not unlike Austinianism in its effort to see law in a rigidly logical hierarchy which functions independently of moral and political considerations. Unlike Austinianism, however, international law is true law in the view of Kelsen and his followers.

Historical School. An early view which somewhat offset the influence of Austinianism was that of the historical school of international law. According to its chief proponents, Savigny and Maine, the essence of law was seen in the customary acceptance and adherence to a rule, not its legalistic enactment. Hence, certain established customs were to be considered as law. With special reference to international law, the historical school was not bothered by the seeming nonexistence of a sovereign lawgiver, and further, it has had the effect of reminding students of law generally that there is infinitely more to law than the mere legislative function of enacting it.[14]

Pure Theory of Law. Hans Kelsen, the founder of the pure theory of law, argues that international law is based on the fundamental postulate that international legal customs are binding. Not only is this true for general international law, but it is the basic factor under which the validity of treaties is ultimately brought about. It is the customary maxim, *pacta sunt servanda,* which postulates that treaties are binding.

International law, in Kelsen's view, validates national constitutional systems through recognition. These systems in turn validate national laws. Regional and local laws are in turn validated by higher national norms. From this relationship

---

[14] Friedrick K. von Savigny, *Of the Vocation of Our Age for Legislation and Jurisprudence,* trans. A. Hayward (London: Littlewood & Co., 1831) ; Henry Sumner Maine, *International Law* (New York: Henry Holt & Co., 1888) .

there emerges a seamless web of law with international norms in the superior position.

It is important to see the rigorously logical quality of these relationships. In method there is a close parallel between Austin and Kelsen, and many of the same virtues and shortcomings are to be attributed to both.[15]

Social and Moral Solidarity. A number of modern theorists stress the social aspects of legal formulation.[16] Hugo Krabbe saw law, including international law, as representing a consensus of justice, with international law superior to municipal law because of its wider scope. Leon Duguit viewed law, including international law, as stemming from a sentiment of social solidarity, that is, rules and their enforcement derive from the social complex and not from sovereignty as such. Jean Spiropoulos stresses that the acceptability of a school of law is not based on its logical or intrinsic merits, but rather upon the dominant opinion, that is, upon human attitudes regarding it. Scelle stressed the character of law as deriving from the necessities of the social situation.[17]

These theorists and others of essentially a sociological bent are concerned with the almost organic relationship between society (including its beliefs, attitudes, goals, and necessities) and law. The latter emerges from the existence and character of the society, *ubi societas ibi jus.* The political doctrine put

---

[15] Hans Kelsen, *General Theory of Law and State* (Cambridge, Mass.: Harvard University Press, 1945) ; see also Hans Kelsen, *Principles of International Law* (New York: Rinehart & Co., Inc. 1952) , pp. 403–47 *et passim,* 2d ed. by Robert W. Tucker (New York: Holt, Rinehart & Winston, Inc., 1966) , pp. 553–88, *et passim.*

[16] See Walter E. Sandelius, "The Question of Sovereignty and Recent Trends in Juristic Thought," J. S. Roucek (ed.) , *Twentieth Century Political Thought* (New York: Philosophical Library, 1946) , pp. 159–68.

[17] See Hugo Krabbe, *The Modern Idea of the State* (New York: D. Appleton & Co., 1922) , pp. 83–90, 236; Leon Duguit, "Objective Law," trans. Margaret Grandgent and Ralph W. Gifford, *Columbia Law Review,* Vol. XX (December, 1920) , pp. 817–31; Vol. XXI (January, 1921) , pp. 17–34; Vol. XXI (February, 1921) , pp. 126–43; Vol. XXI (March, 1921) , pp. 242–56; Jean Spiropoulos, *Théorie générale du droit international* (Paris: Librairie général de droit et de jurisprudence, 1930) , pp. 17–24 *et passim;* George Scelle, *Précis de droit des gens principes et systématique* (Paris: Librairie du recueil Sirey, 1932) , pp. 1–69 *et passim.*

forth in this volume owes much to these varied sociological theorists.

Specialized National Schools of International Law

It is hard to disagree with Professor St. Korowicz' implication that designations of national schools of international law are of dubious value. He emphasizes correctly that theories of law do not coincide with national borders.[18] Nevertheless, there have been a number of specialized national and regional interpretations of international law which have been reviewed more or less systematically in the general literature on international law. In the interest of comprehensiveness brief note will be taken here of the Italian, German, and Soviet schools of international law. In addition the regional American School will be mentioned.

Italian School. The Italian school of international law began in the era of the 19th century Italian nationalism and is in keeping with the Italian revolutionary attitudes.[19] It will be recalled that Mazzini's justification of the nation state centered upon its being the medium through which the individual could best contribute to the stature of mankind in general. The Italian school, within this tradition, stressed the right of each nationality to organize as a state and as such it is remarkably like the Wilsonian principle of self-determination. The political impact of this concept is of course evident in the continued existence of states—not all being *nation* states however—as a foundation of international law. The impact of the Italian school has been greatest in the field of private international law which is concerned with those legal relationships of persons which extend across national boundaries. Because of the prestige of its chief spokesman, P. S. Mancini, the Italian Civil Code and in time many other codes came to recognize the law of one's nationality (rather than his domicile) as governing or

---

[18] Marek St. Korowicz, *Introduction to International Law* (The Hague: Martinus Nijhoff, 1959), pp. 108–09.

[19] See Angelo Piero Sereni, *The Italian Conception of International Law* (New York: Columbia University Press, 1943).

at least influencing certain legal relationships such as marriage, divorce, and contracts.

It should be stressed that this school is essentially a tangent in the theory of international law. Italian writers particularly in recent decades have not been primarily concerned with it. However, the importance of this overall position in the area of jurisdiction over persons will be noted in a later chapter.[20]

German School. Like the Italian school, a German conception of international law has not been entirely Germanic by any means, yet the most lucid spokesmen for the view have been Germans.

There is a long thread of nationalistic sentiment running through modern German legal thought. Much of its philosophical stature comes from the Hegelian idealization of the state as being ultimately above the law, and the position is epitomized by Treitschke's quotation of Gustavus Adolphus' statement: "I recognize no power over me but God and the conqueror's sword."[21] Later and more moderate statements emphasize that all international law is based on the consent of states through agreements which each state is legally entitled to cancel. This is known as the principle of autolimitation.[22]

During the Nazi era other utterly opportunistic facets emerged which need not be reviewed here,[23] except to point out again that these views combine with others to make up a composite worldwide sentiment on international law and therefore must be weighed in terms of their political impact.

Soviet School. A specialized Soviet conception of international law has also emerged, waned, and changed.[24] While it

---

[20] See Chapter Five.

[21] Heinrich von Treitschke, "Politics" in *Introduction to Contemporary Civilizations in the West* (New York: Columbia University Press, 1946), Vol. II, p. 769; see T. M. Knox (trans.), *Hegel's Philosophy of Right* (Oxford: The Clarendon Press, 1942), pp. 212–16.

[22] For comment and some references, see Jacobini, *op. cit.*, pp. 21–23.

[23] See Joseph Florin and John H. Herz, "Bolshevist and National Socialist Doctrines of International Law," *Social Research*, Vol. 7 (February, 1940), pp. 1–31; John H. Herz, "The National Socialist Doctrine of International Law and the Problems of International Organization," *Political Science Quarterly*, Vol. LIV (December, 1939), pp. 536–54; Nussbaum, *op. cit.*, pp. 283–84.

[24] See T. A. Taracouzio, *The Soviet Union and International Law* (New York: The Macmillan Co., 1935), *passim;* Hans Kelsen, *The Communist Theory of Law*

has often seemed merely to be an excessively opportunistic adjunct to Russian foreign policy, this is in itself too simplified an explanation. At times the Soviet impact has been so inimical to the legal positions of much of the rest of the world that the resulting relationship between Soviet and non-Soviet international law has approached the vanishing point. Because of this political fact, and its fundamental significance for jurisprudence as suggested earlier, the resulting functional international law which embraces the whole world has undergone significant restrictions compared with the scope of international law embracing only the non-Soviet powers.

Soviet international law has gone through several stages, however, and Soviet writers—once in vogue—often have been discredited when their juridical views came to be considered at variance with official doctrine. Early in the history of the U.S.S.R., a repudiation of treaties and other acts seemed to presage a complete break with all international law. Even then, however, there was enough variation—e.g., adherence to certain treaties by other powers was insisted upon—that there was ambiguity regarding the completeness of the break. The need for foreign-trade arrangements and for some other treaties seems to have inspired a realization that more permanent connections were essential. After a time it was stressed that a number of rules of international law did in fact apply both to Communist and to bourgeois states as sort of temporary devices to tide over during a transitional era at the end of which, presumably, the proletarian millennium would have begun. Accordingly, many rules of traditional international law were considered to apply to the mutual relations of Communist and bourgeois states.

(New York: Frederick A. Praeger, Inc., 1955), pp. 148–92; Nussbaum, *op. cit.*, pp. 285–90; Grigory I. Tunkin, "Co-existence and International Law," *Recueil des cours* (1958), Vol. III, pp. 1–78; Bernard A. Ramundo and Armins Rusis, *The Socialist Theory of International Law* (Washington, D.C.: Institute of Sino-Soviet Studies Series No. 1, George Washington University, 1964); Marek St. Korowicz, *op. cit.*, pp. 108–56; Edward McWhinney, "Peaceful Coexistence and Soviet-Western International Law," *American Journal of International Law*, Vol. LVI, No. 4 (October, 1962), pp. 951–70; Oliver J. Lissitzyn, "International Law in a Divided World," *International Conciliation*, No. 542 (March, 1963); Jan F. Triska and Robert M. Slusser, *The Theory Law and Policy of Soviet Treaties* (Stanford, Calif.: Stanford University Press, 1962).

In time the transitional era dragged out and with its lengthiness new accommodations emerged. The Soviet conception of international law has come to look increasingly like its Western counterpart. An interesting feature of the Soviet position is the intense adherence to the principles of national sovereignty and the sanctity of domestic jurisdiction. If, as is indeed the case, these principles are important to the non-Soviet views, the position of the U.S.S.R. is doubly interesting. This emerges because, while the principles are roughly parallel to non-Soviet attitudes, the U.S.S.R. has tended to stress them even more forcefully than do the principal Western states.[25]

Emphasis upon the primary importance of treaties and the underlying norm, *pacta sunt servanda,* and growing concern with coexistence in the structure of contemporary international law further underscore the rapproachement of Soviet and non-Soviet attitudes.[26] Some recent studies have suggested a less than religious adherence to treaties as the rule by the U.S.S.R.[27] Nevertheless they do not indicate that the Soviet Union is utterly and consistently unreliable in this matter as is sometimes popularly believed.[28]

While the Soviet conception of international law has important pecularities when contrasted with Western attitudes, it is becoming evident that the differences may not be as important as the similarities.

American International Law. Several American theorists principally Latin Americans, have seen in the substance of inter-American agreements, organization, and cooperation, a typical American international law.[29] Whether or not the degree of particularity justifies the denomination "American international law" has been the source of much dispute, but it must be acknowledged that some elements of particularity do

[25] See *Soviet Textbook,* p. 97.

[26] *Ibid.,* pp. 12, 15–18, 247–48 f; Ramundo and Rusis, *op. cit.,* pp. 25–31.

[27] U.S. Senate, Committee on the Judiciary, *Soviet Political Agreements and Results,* 84th Cong., 2nd sess., Sen. Doc. No. 125 (1956) .

[28] Triska and Slusser, *op. cit., passim,* especially pp. 389–406; see also "Western and Soviet Perspectives on International Law—A Comparison," O. J. Lissitzyn, *Proceedings of American Society of International Law* (1959) , pp. 21–30.

[29] See particularly Alejandro Alvarez, *Le droit international Américain son fondement-sa nature* (Paris: A. Pedone, 1910) .

obtain.[30] Among these are the traditional inter-American emphasis on arbitration and pacific settlement of disputes, but more recently the closer ties through the Organization of American States and the Rio Pact tend to create a more cohesive sense of community.

A Useful Synthesis: A Political Conception of Law

The rich variety of viewpoints reviewed above is not indicative of ideological anarchy, but rather of emphasis on specialized aspects of the law of nations. Yet of all these particularities, not one alone adequately explains the basis of international law.

It was noted in the first chapter that the sources of international law are custom, principles, treaties, writings, and court decisions. Yet these sources do not themselves explain why they have power or validity. Some students, it has been seen, have emphasized the powers of sovereignty; some have stressed the importance of customs widely adhered to; others have noted the importance of social solidarity; and still others have felt the need for law to conform to principles of right. Perhaps some meaning may be drawn from a synthesis which suggests essentially a political interpretation of international law.

In all of these instances it is submitted that there are present powerful pressures, beliefs, ideologies, or other aggregates of force. It is further submitted, moreover, that any law must have strong support before it becomes a legal reality. This support may be direct or tacit, but in any event it must exist.

It is not important, therefore, at least from a legal and constitutional standpoint, whether valid metaphysical principles underlie a particular rule or whether it emerges from the dictate of a sovereign in the Austinian sense. On the other hand, importance does repose in consideration of whether there is sufficient support, for example, to sustain the maxim that prisoners of war must be adequately treated, or the principle that diplomats may not be molested. This support is evidenced in a highly complex way embracing considerations as to

---

[30] See survey in Jacobini, *op. cit.,* pp. 121–36.

whether force will be used to rectify irregularities, what the effect will be on political or military neutrals and allies, what direct retorsions or reprisals may be taken, how the people of one's own nation will respond to a particular course of action, reciprocity, the basic question of morality and right, and in general how public opinion would be affected.

This is not to say that these considerations are always carefully weighed, but rather to suggest that in the growth of international law as in municipal law, the pull and tug of political considerations are felt all along the line.[31] It is therefore the thesis of this survey that for the political scientist law must be viewed as a political phenomenon, that international law has an even more obvious political orientation than municipal law, and that it must be considered in that light in order to be fully understood. Alejandro Alvarez has stated this most emphatically when in speaking of the impact of politics and the psychology of peoples he says:

National law, especially social legislation, *is inspired by or takes into account* these factors, but they do not by themselves form this legislation.

In international law the said elements incorporate themselves into it, they are what constitute it; one does not treat then of a legislator who takes them into account. The best proof of my affirmation is that, if these factors are modified, by that circumstance alone the law appears antiquated in this connection or in the matter expressly affected by the change, and it is not respected.[32]

International Law Viewed in Two Segments: Political and Technical. The above comments must not be allowed to obscure the fact that within a given political setting there is room for much in the way of technical law. An understanding of this dichotomy of the political and technical aspects of international law, as in municipal law, seems difficult to grasp, yet without it a realistic appraisal of international law cannot be made.

A wholly technical appraisal of international law wrecks itself by trying to put all international law into a technical

---

[31] See Spiropoulos, *op. cit., passim*, where the effect of opinion is stressed.

[32] Alejandro Alvarez, *Despues de la guerra* (Buenos Aires: Imprenta de la Universidad, 1943), p. 288; passage translated in Jacobini, *op. cit.*, p. 107.

legal pattern governed by rules, precedents and past decisions with the result that the world is either damned for not adhering to the law, or the opposite extreme is expressed—that there is no law.[33]

The wholly political appraisal loses sight of the fact that once a political concord prevails there is ample room for the extension of technical rules. That a political consensus must exist ought not obscure the fact that such a consensus does exist in many areas and that technical rules within those areas not only *exist,* but continue to grow in strength.[34]

It is useful therefore to think of two major subdivisions of international law: (1) international constitutional law on the one hand which is essentially political in character, and (2) international administrative law on the other hand, which is concerned with technical rules.

The former is the result of a balance of power relationship often formalized by treaty. The Treaty of Versailles, the United Nations, and the post-World War II East-West relationship are indicative of both formal and of informal arrangements of constitutional scope.

The latter variety of law results, as noted earlier, from treaties, customs, principles, writings, and court decisions. Examples are seen in extradition treaties, trade agreements, and the immunities of diplomats.

THE RELATIONSHIP OF INTERNATIONAL LAW AND MUNICIPAL LAW

Once the nature of international law is grasped, it is necessary to inquire into the relationship which it bears to municipal law, that is, to national law.

The Problem. The problem is initially seen, however, if one considers an issue involving a rule of international law which is not recognized in the national law of state A. The citizen of state A who violates the rule cannot be prosecuted in

---

[33] See comments in J. L. Brierly, *The Law of Nations* (5th ed.; Oxford: The Clarendon Press, 1955), preface.

[34] The student is invited to look at copies of the *United Nations Treaty Series* (published since 1946–47) where treaties of all sorts are registered.

state A, yet state A is obliged to rectify the damage done to state B. The relationship is awkward and cumbersome, yet it frequently exists.[35]

The Explanatory Theories

There are several theories which attempt to explain the relationship between the law of nations and domestic law. They run the gamut from an assertion of the superiority of the former over the latter to its complete reverse.

Austinianism. As has been noted earlier, John Austin held that international law does not emanate from a sovereign and hence is not law, but rather "positive morality." For Austin and those few moderns who adhere strictly to his view, the juridical superiority of domestic law follows obviously and logically, for whatever international obligations there may be, exist on a moral rather than a legal plane and are therefore juridically inferior.[36]

Autolimitation. A similar theory known as the doctrine of autolimitation has also sought to answer the dilemma by pushing international rules into the background. This school has held that all rules of international law are based on treaties or customs (viewed as tacit treaties) and that they may be unilaterally terminated under the doctrine of *rebus sic stantibus.*[37]

The Monists. At the other end of the scale are a group of modern writers who have argued that all law constitutes a seamless web and that there is no real difference between international and domestic law except that the former is less particularistic. For differing reasons these observers are of the opinion that the international norms take precedence over the more parochial municipal rules and therefore that the law of nations is juridically superior to national law. Among the more impor-

---

[35] See comments in Herbert W. Briggs, *The Law of Nations* (2d ed.; New York: Appleton-Century-Crofts, Inc., 1952), pp. 60–65; see also comments in Green Haywood Hackworth, *Digest* I, pp. 24–39, particularly pp. 38–39; also Marjorie M. Whiteman, *Digest* I, pp. 103–116; see *Case Concerning Certain German Interests in Upper Silesia,* P.C.I.J. Judgments, Series A, No. 7 (1926).

[36] See Austin, *op. cit.*

[37] See comment in Charles G. Fenwick, *International Law* (3d ed.; New York: Appleton-Century-Crofts, Inc., 1948), p. 59.

tant of these positions are those of Hans Kelsen, and Hugo Krabbe.[38] Kelsen is of the persuasion that domestic law derives its validity from international recognition of the national constitution, and hence from international law, consequently the unity of municipal and international law follows. Krabbe on the other hand held that international law was superior to municipal law because of its wider scope, yet both were part of the same entity.

Dualists. Less extreme views which have the virtue of falling within prevailing practice are the dualist approach and the doctrine of incorporation. The dualists, especially Heinrich Triepel and Dionisio Anzilotti, have held the opinion that international law and domestic law constitute two entirely separate systems, each sovereign in its own sphere and each based on its own premises.[39]

The dualists observed that a rule of international law has to be enacted or absorbed into municipal law before it is a valid precept of domestic law, and that a rule of domestic law has to be enacted or absorbed into international law before it becomes a rule of the law of nations.

Doctrine of Incorporation. The closely related incorporational view has been held by such American and British scholars as W. W. Willoughby, James L. Brierly, James W. Garner, and Charles G. Fenwick. It stresses the empirical fact that in the last analysis from the standpoint of judicial action within states themselves, the courts can enforce only those international rules which have been "incorporated" into municipal law. From this standpoint municipal law appears as the superior juridical norm, but it is in reality only half of the dualist approach for these writers emphasize the point that while this is the only course open to national courts, it in no way relieves states of their international obligations.[40]

Illustrative of the problem is the important case of *Morten-*

---

[38] See references this chapter, fns. 15, 17.

[39] Heinrich Triepel, *Droit international et droit interne* (Paris: A Pedone, 1920); Dionisio Anzilotti, *Cours de droit international* (Paris: Recueil Sirey, 1929).

[40] See, e.g., in James W. Garner, *Recent Developments in International Law* (Calcutta: University of Calcutta, 1925), pp. 11–12.

sen v. *Peters,*[41] in which a Scottish court acting under an act of Parliament which restricted fishing in an area beyond the 3-mile limit, convicted a Norwegian with these words: "For us an Act of Parliament duly passed by Lords and Commons and assented to by the King, is supreme, and we are bound to give effect to its terms."

This case has an especially interesting conclusion, however, for although the court reflected only the national law, the decision was for all practical purposes set aside by the executive who remitted the fine in order to keep England's action in conformity with its international obligations.[42]

On another level the related question has arisen as to whether a treaty takes precedence over a regularly enacted law. In the United States, while treaties are a part of the law of the land,[43] the principle is essentially that of *lex posterior*, that is, a treaty enacted after a law takes precedence over the law and vice versa.[44] In some other national jurisdictions, however, the pattern is considerably different in that treaties are given a judicial status superior to that of regularly enacted laws. Elsewhere, e.g., in Great Britain, many treaties apply internally only after implementing legislation has been enacted.[45]

Analysis. It should be apparent from the foregoing that there are essentially three theories of the relationship of municipal and international law to each other. First, that international law is really not binding and that municipal law is therefore the superior set of legal norms. Second, that all law is a seamless web but that the international norms are superior because of their wider scope. Third, that international and

---

[41] 14 Scots L.T.R. 227 (1906).

[42] Hackworth, *Digest* I, p. 712.

[43] U.S., *Constitution*, Art. 4.

[44] *Head Money Cases*, 112 U.S. 580 (1884); *Whitney* v. *Robertson*, 124 U.S. 190 (1888).

[45] Louis C. Bial, "Some Recent French Decisions on the Relationship between Treaties and Municipal Law," *American Journal of International Law*, Vol. XLIX (July, 1955), pp. 347–48 ff.; L. Preuss, "The Relation of International Law to Internal Law in the French Constitutional System," *American Journal of International Law*, Vol. XLIV (October, 1950), pp. 141–669; W. L. Gould, *An Introduction to International Law* (New York: Harper & Bros., 1957), p. 330, fn. 49 for useful reference; L. Oppenheim, *International Law, a Treatise* (2 vols.; 8th ed. by H. Lauterpacht; London: Longman's, Green & Co., Inc., 1955), Vol. I, pp. 35–47; Whiteman, *Digest* I, pp. 111–14.

municipal law constitute two separate sets of norms which are equal in status and each of which is superior in its own realm. It further states that international law must be incorporated into municipal law before having validity there, and vice versa.

It is impossible to discuss these problems meaningfully without paying close attention to the pattern of prevailing international practice. It must be remembered that prevailing practice is one of the important criteria of political preference and hence of political power, and it is in this context that it acts to support or reject rules of law.

In the United States it is clearly recognized, as noted above, that treaties are a part of the law of the land, and, more broadly, that international law is a part of American law. This practice of recognizing the law of nations as a part of national law is not restricted only to common law countries, for many modern constitutions specifically or inferentially state that international law is a part of the municipal law.[46]

Incorporation Is Prevailing Practice. What has happened in these instances is, however, quite obvious. By municipal fiat either in the form of court decisions or of specific constitutional statement, the law of nations or certain phases of it have been decreed to be a part of the national legal system. On the other hand failure of a state to follow the prevailing pattern is an entirely possible procedure. This is the essence of the doctrine of incorporation.

It must be remembered that the only question involved here centers upon whether and under what circumstances national courts will apply international law as national law. Where there is clear-cut conflict between rules of international law and national law a frequent solution may be that of applying domestic law by the courts while rectifying the matter otherwise in the international arena. This can be seen rather clearly in *Mortensen* v. *Peters,* the pertinent aspects of which have already been discussed. It should perhaps be noted that courts have often tried to minimize the basic problem here by stressing the obligation to interpret laws, wherever it is possible, so

---

[46] See e.g., U.S., *Constitution*, Art. 2, Sec. 3; Italy, *Constitution*, Art. 10; France, *Constitution* (1946) , preamble; the Constitution of the Fifth Republic is much more restrained, however. See, e.g., Title VI.

that they do not contravene the law of nations,[47] or, as noted in the previously cited case of *Whitney* v. *Robertson*, to interpret laws in such a way that they will not be held to violate treaties already in force; yet where such laws and treaties are clearly incompatible, the more recent document is authoritative.[48]

A special facet of this matter applicable in the United States is seen in the *Migratory Bird* case which reflects a problem of American federalism. The Supreme Court found that a treaty protecting migratory birds and a congressional act passed to enforce it were constitutional despite an earlier finding that an act of Congress attempting to accomplish this same purpose alone was a contravention of the 10th Amendment.[49]

It must be emphasized, however, that regardless of the internal action taken, the state retains its international obligations under international law.

SUMMARY

All law is in a sense the product of political pressures and even the most highly technical phases of law can retain their validity only in a sympathetic political environment. International law presents no exception to this pattern, except perhaps that its political aspects are more obvious. It is instructive and useful, however, to visualize international law—and in fact all law—in two major categories: (1) the broadly political constitutional phases of law, and (2) the less obviously political or the technical and administrative aspects of law. An example of the former in international law is a peace treaty or an alliance, while an example of the latter may be seen in an agreement for the exchange of prisoners or a commercial treaty.

International law and municipal law bear a relationship to each other which is interesting to observe. There are several theories which seek to explain it, but the most accurate is the dualist-incorporational theory which notes that the law of na-

---

[47] *Murray* v. *The Charming Betsey*, 2 Cranch 64 (1804).

[48] See remarks in Walter Sandelius, "National Sovereignty versus the Rule of Law," *American Political Science Review*, Vol. XXV (February, 1931), pp. 12–13.

[49] *Missouri* v. *Holland*, 252 U.S. 416 (1920).

tions becomes domestic law only by being incorporated into national law, and vice versa.

Incorporation has progressed quite far, however, for either through court decisions or through specific constitutional stipulations many states provide that treaties are equal or superior to national law and that international law is a part of the law of the land.

Finally, the relationship of the law of nations to municipal law is also concerned with how national courts will act in regard to them. This is determined by national law, but the course of action followed by the national courts cannot absolve the state of its responsibilities to other states under international law.

CHAPTER 3

International Community, Personality, Recognition, and Succession

THE PROBLEM OF what entities are subject to international law is an interesting one. For the most part these are sovereign states or near sovereign states, but that is not the whole of the matter, for international organizations, the Vatican, and sometimes even individuals are accorded international legal status. States, however, are the basic units of world society and these states taken collectively constitute the community or family of nations. Finally the matter of how states and governments are accorded recognition and how they become extinct should be noted and some of the consequences of these considered.

THE INTERNATIONAL COMMUNITY

The international community is the society of international entities, mostly sovereign states, upon which international law is binding. It has its origin in the remnants of universalism which Stoic philosophy, the Roman Empire, the concept of a universal church, the Holy Roman Empire, and Western civilization in general have bequeathed to the modern world. It is felt by some writers that the community of nations is the mother earth from which the plant of international law has sprung, *ubi societas, ibi jus*,[1] but whether or not this particular relationship is valid, the society in which this legal system operates has great significance.

Emergence

The international community emerged with the rise of the independent state system in the period around 1648, and it consisted originally of the parties signatory to the Peace of Westphalia. It was enlarged from time to time by the recognition of other states such as Russia in 1721, the United States in 1783, and the Ottoman Empire in 1856, the last of which was its first predominantly non-Christian member. Now it embraces virtually the entire world,[2] yet in broadening its scope it may well have weakened its superstructure at least along historical-philosophical lines.

Perhaps the idea of a community of nations can best be understood if international society is likened to a state. The law of a state applies to citizens, subjects, nationals, and resident and visiting aliens only. It does not ordinarily bear upon the actions of aliens in a foreign land. Similarly, international law applies only to entities which form a part of the system in which it operates. Thus, semiautonomous entities such as the American Indian tribes are not considered to form a part of the community of nations, nor are constituent members of federations as a rule.[3] But as new nations emerged or old ones exhibited their ability to withstand European pressures, these entities came to be recognized as participants in the international community.

Traditionally the members of the community of nations have been states. Other entities such as international organizations, the Vatican, and individual human beings have also attained varying status as participants in the privileges and duties of international law. Yet it can be said by way of defini-

---

[1] D. Simon Planas Suarez, *Tratado de derecho internacional publico*, Vol. I (Madrid: Hijos de Reus, 1916) , pp. 5–6.

[2] See John Bassett Moore, *Digest* I, pp. 72–119; Green Haywood Hackworth, *Digest* I, pp. 195–222; Marjorie M. Whiteman, *Digest* II, pp. 133–242.

[3] See Moore, *Digest* I, pp. 30–35, 23–25, *et passim*.

tion that the community of nations consists of that body of political sovereignties which maintain relationships with each other through diplomatic and consular establishments and through international organizations. To be sure, not all members maintain universal representation, but these states for the most part mutually recognize each other.

Machinery

If again for purposes of comparison and explanation the international community may be likened in a very broad way to a state, the machinery of government for that community which would correspond to the government of a state would be seen through the years as being not at all uniform or cohesive. The diplomatic and consular services have constituted the only consistent and constantly operating machinery. Though highly decentralized, these devices remain at the heart of contemporary international intercourse. Beyond these, however, there are other important considerations. Until the establishment of the League of Nations, great international conferences like the Congress of Vienna and the Hague Conferences were the only other mechanisms remotely resembling governmental machinery. Following the Versailles treaty, however, the League of Nations became in a way the central machinery of the community. With its demise and the subsequent development of the United Nations, the latter took over the functions of the former. It should be remembered, however, that neither the earlier conferences and congresses nor the more recent League of Nations nor the contemporary United Nations has represented *all* of the members of the community of nations.

It has been observed that the community of nations is that group of political sovereignties the members of which in an overlapping and nonuniversal way recognize the legal status of one another, and, again without unanimity, maintain diplomatic relations with each other. It cannot be held, therefore, that the United Nations, which is not coextensive with the international community, is its sole governmental mechanism. Thus the governmental apparatus of the community of nations includes near universal organizations like the United Nations;

other associated or nonassociated international agencies such as the International Labor Organization, the Food and Agriculture Organization, the Universal Postal Union, and the Organization of American States; the regular diplomatic and consular apparatus; and special official conferences and congresses ranging from technical meetings to summit conferences.

INTERNATIONAL PERSONALITY

The question now arises as to what entities enjoy personality within international society. It has already been observed that states are the entities around which this society is constructed, and out of which it has developed. Furthermore, it is substantially correct to observe that, for the most part, sovereign states are the "persons" of the community of nations.[4] Yet there are at least two complicating factors. In the first place the sovereign quality of statehood fades out into a twilight zone where states not entirely sovereign in a technical sense seem, nevertheless, to possess some international legal status. Secondly, there is much evidence to sustain the view that in addition to states there are other entities which partake also of a degree of international personality.[5]

Customarily, legal personality and subjects of law are used more or less interchangeably. If these terms are defined as the quality of having legal rights and duties,[6] the problem more readily comes into perspective. One may then attempt to analyze each pertinent entity in terms of the extent to which it partakes of this quality. With this as the principal guideline it is not difficult to see that states have a full measure of rights and duties while, e.g., man as an individual only occasionally comes into this focus. It is in this relative sense then that some entities

---

4 See discussion in L. Oppenheim, *International Law, a Treatise* (2 vols.; 8th ed. by H. Lauterpacht; London: Longman's, Green & Co., Inc., 1955), Vol. I, pp. 117–262 *et passim* (hereafter cited as Oppenheim-Lauterpacht, *Treatise* I) Charles G. Fenwick, *International Law* (4th ed.; New York: Appleton-Century-Crofts, 1965), p. 148.

5 See this chapter, below, "Borderline Cases."

6 See, e.g., in *Blacks Law Dictionary* (3rd ed.; St. Paul, Minn.: West Publishing Co., 1933), pp. 1355–56, 1668; see also *Reparation for Injuries Suffered in the Service of the United Nations* (1949), I.C.J. Reports, 174.

are said to have full personality while others enjoy only a degree of international personality.

State Definition

A state for political-legal purposes may be defined as an internationally recognized, politically organized, populated, geographical area which possesses sovereignty.[7] Sovereignty, the only quality enumerated which may need explanation at this point, can be defined in the words of Grotius who observed, "That power is called sovereign whose actions are not subject to the legal control of another, so that they cannot be rendered void by the operation of another human will."[8] There is some dispute as to whether the term "sovereignty" ought to be used in the sense of ability to carry out the foreign relations of a country as well as to include nearly absolute internal control. For purposes here, however, it can be assumed that the term sovereignty embraces both elements as it appears unrealistic to differentiate markedly in this regard. It should also be mentioned in passing, however, that in the strict sense of having supreme political power in the international realm, no state is entirely sovereign except in the sense that it may make the decision to do anything, as contrasted with its lack of ability to in fact accomplish its objectives. Thus Belgium in the exercise of its sovereignty might elect to invade France (though legally it would now seem bound not to under the United Nations Charter),[9] but for it to do so unaided would certainly be the height of chauvinistic folly. Similarly, though less extremely posited, a decision of the U.S.S.R. to overrun Europe might logically stem from its sovereign status, yet to accomplish the fruits of such an expedition would be another matter.

Despite some of these aspects, the interesting and important

---

[7] See Oppenheim-Lauterpacht, *Treatise* I, pp. 118–19 and other standard treatises. The term "internationally recognized" used in the above definition refers to the quality of receiving recognition by other members of the international community.

[8] Hugo Grotius, *De jure belli ac pacis libri tres,* 1645 edition (*The Classics of International Law,* trans. F. W. Kelsey; 2 vols.; Oxford: The Clarendon Press, 1925) , Vol. II, p. 102.

[9] U.N., *Charter,* Art. 2 (3, 4) .

matter of the political quality of international personality of
the state should not be lost sight of, however, for recognition as
a state embraces more than the acknowledged existence of a
mere geographical and historical phenomenon. These are entities which by force or diplomacy or the exercise of other sustaining qualities have been able to exist in the family of nations as units in themselves. They were not vanquished and
absorbed like the American Indian tribes or Westphalia or
Venice or the American Confederacy. Even though these enumerated entities may retain a cultural vitality of other than
sovereign status, it is thus important to note the political quality of the units which have retained sovereignty and which are
at the very base of the law of nations.

Borderline Cases

In addition to sovereign states such as the United States,
Belgium, Mexico, Great Britain, the Philippines, and the
U.S.S.R., there are other polities which for one reason or another seem to have a status sufficiently independent to enjoy a
degree of international personality, yet not essentially sovereign
statehood.

It is quite apparent that neutralized states[10] like Switzerland
enjoy virtually the same standing as states not bound by neutralization, and that tiny states such as Liechtenstein, Monaco,
and San Marino, and a vassal state like Andorra do enjoy a
considerable degree of international personality. But it is also
apparent that international recognition would stop short of the
American Indian tribes or of a member of a federation such as
Alabama, Kansas, Ontario, Sonora, Minas Gerais, or the Soviet
Republic of Georgia.[11] On the other hand the Soviet republics
of the Ukraine and Byelorussia possibly enjoy a modicum of
personality by virtue of their anomalous status within the
United Nations and under the Soviet constitution.[12]

---

[10] See below, Chapter Ten.

[11] Hackworth, *Digest* I, pp. 74–97; William Edward Hall, *A Treatise on
International Law* (5th ed. edited by J. B. Atlay; Oxford: The Clarendon Press,
1904), pp. 23–40; see also W. S. G. Kohn, "The Sovereignty of Liechtenstein,"
Vol. LXI, *American Journal of International Law*, pp. 547–57.

[12] For initial agreement, see *Protocol of the Proceedings of the Crimea*

Belligerent Communities: Belligerency and Insurgency

Closely related to the concept of the state is that of the belligerent community. Thus when within a state there is a civil uprising bent upon setting up a new state or capturing control of the whole of the existent state itself, a condition of civil war exists. At precisely what point a rebellion becomes extensive enough to warrant recognition of the antigovernment combatants as belligerents is essentially a political question, but it should be noted that recognition at too early a moment may be viewed as an unfriendly act by the parent state.[13] In any event when the parent state or foreign states recognize the existence of a state of belligerency, certain rights and duties flow from such recognition. For example, the rights and duties of belligerents in warfare apply vis-à-vis the recognizing parent state or vis-à-vis the recognizing foreign state.[14] When the combatants are recognized merely as insurgents, however, a somewhat more restricted status is involved. It amounts to little more than an acknowledgment of the right of the insurgents to govern those areas under their *de facto* control, and it does not recognize belligerent rights regarding foreigners.[15]

Conference, Vol. I (2) (b) , in *Foreign Relations of the United States Diplomatic Papers. The Conferences at Malta and Yalta 1945* (Washington, D.C.: U.S. Government Printing Office, 1955) , pp. 975–76. See also this chapter, below, "State Recognition." Also, U.S.S.R, *Constitution,* Art. 17. The status of these constituent republics is not easily determined. At most their international personality must be considered minimal, but to deny any at all is difficult. Authorities are not completely clear as to whether admission to the United Nations conveys some measure of personality. If there is a negative inclination it is not without inconsistencies and qualifications. On another tack, the U.S.S.R. apparently maintains that these republics are international persons. Query: How many states must recognize an entity before it enjoys a measure of personality? See Edward Dolan "The Member Republics of the U.S.S.R. as Subjects of the Law of Nations," *International and Comparative Law Quarterly,* Vol. IV (October, 1955) , pp. 629–36; Hans Aufricht, "Principles and Practices of Recognition by International Organizations," *American Journal of International Law,* Vol. XLIII (October, 1949), pp. 679–704; *Soviet Textbook,* pp. 91–2; Whiteman, *Digest* I, pp. 406–13.

[13] *The Three Friends,* 166 U.S. 1 (1897) . Moore, *Digest* I, pp. 164–68 ff. Hackworth, *Digest* I, p. 318 *et passim.*

[14] Hackworth, *Digest* I, pp. 318–27.

[15] *The Three Friends, op. cit.,* George Grafton Wilson, "Insurgency and International Maritime Law," *American Journal of International Law,* Vol. I (1907) , pp. 46–60; Whiteman, *Digest* I, pp. 930–46. See account in Kurt von

Vatican

Though primarily a religious authority, the papal holdings of about 100 acres in the center of Rome are also considered by many authorities to constitute an international person, and even during the period from 1870 to 1929 when the Vatican possessed no territorial sovereignty, it continued to be recognized by many states.[16] On the basis of historical precedent and contemporary recognition there is reason to sustain its claim to at least some international status. It should be asserted that this is in no sense a recognition of spiritual primacy as most religious societies reject such international political-legal status for themselves. It does point, however, to the essentially political quality of international personality as being the result of pronounced political power coupled with historical precedent.

International Organizations

Another type of entity which enjoys a degree of international personality is the international organization. These agencies must for various reasons be considered to have such personality and in fact there appears to be little controversy about the matter. Their corporate character, itself suggestive of such personality, is derived from multilateral agreements and is augmented ordinarily by explicit recognition of various rights which appertain to them. Thus the Charter of the United Nations specifies that:

The Organization shall enjoy in the territory of each of its Members such legal capacity as may be necessary for the exercise of its functions and the fulfillment of its purposes.[17]

The Charter also states that:

The Organization shall enjoy in the territory of each of its

Schuschnigg, *International Law: An Introduction to the Law of Peace* (Milwaukee, Wis.: The Bruce Publishing Co., 1959), pp. 92–93; Herbert W. Briggs, *The Law of Nations* (2d ed.; New York: Appleton-Century-Crofts, Inc., 1952), pp. 998–1004.

[16] See discussion in Oppenheim-Lauterpacht, *Treatise* I, pp. 250–55.

[17] U.N., *Charter*, Art. 104.

Members such privileges and immunities as are necessary for the fulfillment of its purposes.[18]

The Charter further specifies that the General Assembly and Security Council and under some circumstances other organs of the United Nations may obtain advisory opinions from the International Court of Justice.[19] In its relationship with member states this status has been even more clearly spelled out in an agreement on United Nations privileges and immunities.[20] This has been further amplified by an advisory opinion of the International Court of Justice in which it was held that the United Nations is an international person and can bring a legal claim on the international level regardless of whether the defendant is a member of the United Nations.[21] Finally, certain privileges and immunities ordinarily appertain to the personnel of such international organizations.[22]

Related yet differing in some respects are the International Red Cross and the Sovereign Order of Malta (Order of St. John). The former, while not a public international agency, has been acknowledged in function and status by international accord and by general usage. The latter enjoys a long-standing international role including continuing diplomatic recognition by states. Both appear to enjoy a degree of international personality.[23]

---

[18] *Ibid.*, Art. 105 (L).

[19] *Ibid.*, Art. 96.

[20] *Convention on the Privileges and Immunities of the United Nations,* Vol. I, *U.N.T.S.,* pp. 15–33.

[21] See *Reparation for Injuries Suffered in the Service of the United Nations,* I.C.J. Reports, 1949, p. 174. For a dissenting Soviet view, see, however, *Soviet Textbook,* pp. 89–90.

[22] See e.g., U.N., *Charter,* Art. 105 (1, 2); *General Convention on the Privileges and Immunities of the United Nations,* Art. 4; *Statute of the International Court of Justice,* Art. 19.

[23] See A. C. Breycha-Vauthier and M. Potulicki, "The Order of St. John in International Law: A Forerunner of the Red Cross," *American Journal of International Law,* Vol. XLVIII (October, 1954), pp. 554–63; C. d'Olivier Farran, "The Sovereign Order of Malta in International Law," *International and Comparative Law Quarterly,* Vol. III (January, 1954), pp. 217–34; C. d'Olivier Farran, "The Sovereign Order of Malta: A Supplementary Note," *International and Comparative Law Quarterly,* Vol. IV (April, 1955), pp. 808–09. See *Geneva Convention Relative to the Treatment of Prisoners of War* (August 12, 1949) (Department of the Army Pamphlet No. 20–150 [Washington, D.C.: U.S. Government Printing Office, 1950]), Art. 125. See account in Schuschnigg, *op. cit.,* pp.

International Areas

Some areas which for one reason or another have been the subject of action by an important segment of the international community may be held to possess a degree of status in the society of nations, although such status cannot by any objective standard be ordinarily considered as advanced. Trusteeship territories are perhaps the most important areas in this category, their collective claim to some status being specified in the United Nations Charter.[24]

Still another example of an international territory may be seen in the various attempts to set up "free cities" under the supervision of international agencies or under some other sort

90–91. See also P. Ruegger, "The Juridical Aspects of the Organization of the International Red Cross," 82 *Recueil des cours*, I (1953), pp. 483–584.

Mention should perhaps be made of a number of terms which often appear in works on the law of nations and which sometimes imply or seem to imply varying degrees of international personality. Protectorate, colony, commonwealth, British Commonwealth, condominium, union, personal union, real union, confederation and federation are among the most common. Of these only the last named is normally a fully endowed international person. The British Commonwealth, which rather defies classification, certainly enjoys a degree of international personality if in no other sense than as an international organization. A protectorate occasionally figures peripherally in that the internal arrangement governing its relationship with the sovereign authority may recognize a measure of autonomy in the protectorate and the local "sovereign" is sometimes accorded some of the privileges due a chief of state. This appears, however, to be a measure of municipal rather than of international law. A personal union such as Great Britain and Hanover, 1714–1834, is one in which two fully sovereign states are connected by virtue of having the same individual sovereign, while a real union such as Austria-Hungary represented the connection by treaty of two such states under circumstances where the union formed a composite international personality. The former is not an international person while the latter obviously is. A condominium is the joint exercise by several states of sovereignty over a territory. The British-American condominium over Canton and Endenbury is one of the few examples. A condominium as such has no international personality. Colonies, confederations, provinces, commonwealths (e.g., Puerto Rico), unions (e.g., the abortive Netherlands-Indonesian Union) are probably not endowed with international personality as such. Nevertheless the precise character of an entity together with the recognition it has received in the international community determines status rather than some quality inherent in an organizational pattern. On these and related matters, see Oppenheim-Lauterpacht, *Treatise* I, pp. 169–88, 453–60. J. E. S. Fawcett, *The British Commonwealth in International Law* (London: Stevens & Sons, 1963). *Stratham* v. *Stratham and Gaekwar of Baroda*, Great Britain, Probate, Divorce and Admiralty Division, 1911, Probate 92. M. Ydit, *Internationalised Territories* (Leyden; A. W. Sythoff, 1961). Whiteman, *Digest* I, chap. II.

[24] U.N., *Charter*, Chaps. 11, 12, 13.

of international control. Historical examples which may be cited are those of Danzig, Trieste, and Tangiers, there being apparently no contemporary specimen extant.[25]

Man as a Subject of International Law

Finally it must be noted that there are many writers and authorities who consider men as individuals to be possessed of a certain international personality. The personal rights of a head of state, and of diplomats and their families as well as the status of military men in relation to the laws of war, or the status of an individual who has committed piracy are traditional examples of this matter. More recently the litigation before the Polish-German claims tribunals and the now defunct Central American Court of Justice, and the still more recent Nüremberg and other war crimes trials have pointed up this matter further, as has the development of the international bill of rights.

Such claims for the individual appear to be based in small part at least upon fairly sound ground, but on the other hand they seem to be partially—perhaps largely—the result of wishful thinking. The fact that international rules have been established which serve to benefit the individual, frequently establish him merely as an "object" of international law, that is, the thing about which international law expresses concern. That does not mean necessarily that it transforms him into a "subject" of the law of nations, that is, an entity endowed with international personality and possessed of personal rights and duties. Similarly, special status for the person of a head of state or for a diplomat may seem more to reflect the quality of an extension of the state rather than of an individual right. Nevertheless, the position of a war criminal, a spy, a pirate, and a soldier as such do seem to partake fairly clearly of international personality, for such persons appear to be endowed with both rights and duties and they lack only the personal right to sue in international courts, a right which for states is nugatory if the party being sued does not grant its consent. Even the head of

---

[25] Hackworth, *Digest* I, pp. 92–97. On this matter generally, see Ydit, *op. cit., passim.*

the state and the diplomat, while clearly extensions of the state,
are protected individuals and may seem to enjoy special personality. Finally, international legislation which confers rights of
litigation upon certain individuals, and such documents as the
Genocide Convention seem further to point to at least a degree
of international personality. In the last analysis, however, this
appears to be a matter in transition, which, while at present not
of much practical importance, may very well be pointing the
way to significant developments in the future.[26]

Political Significance

International personality is an interesting concept with
far-reaching significance. Yet it cannot be viewed as a legal
concept in the narrow sense only. Personality is largely the
result of political fact and is in substance directly related to
political phenomena. Thus, as noted above, those states and
belligerent communities together with the Vatican and a number of tiny states which through force, alliance, diplomacy, or
chance have maintained their independence as such are the
chief subjects of the law of nations. Secondly, international
organizations which for one reason or another have been expressly created and clearly endowed with international personality are subjects of the international legal regime. Finally,
although the matter is somewhat obscure, it must be recognized
that man as an individual enjoys at least minimal personality
under international law.

------

[26] There has been a good deal written on this matter. See George Manner,
"The Object Theory of the Individual in International Law," *American Journal
of International Law,* Vol. XLVI (July, 1952), pp. 428–49; W. B. Cowles, "The
Impact of International Law on the Individual," *Proceedings of the American
Society of International Law* (1952), pp. 71–85; Phillip C. Jessup, *A Modern Law
of Nations* (New York: The Macmillan Co., 1948); H. Lauterpacht, *International
Law and Human Rights* (New York: Frederick A. Praeger, Inc., 1950). Briggs,
op. cit., pp. 93–98. Peter P. Remec, *The Position of the Individual in International Law according to Grotius and Vattel* (The Hague: Martinus Nijhoff,
1960). See also Clyde Eagleton, "The Individual and International Law," *Proceedings of the American Society of International Law* (1946), pp. 22–29; also
H. B. Jacobini, *A Study of the Philosophy of International Law as Seen in Works
of Latin American Writers* (The Hague: Martinus Nijhoff, 1954). For the negative
view of the U.S.S.R., see *Soviet Textbook,* pp. 89–90.

RECOGNITION AND SUCCESSION

The question arises at this point as to the process by which a state which aspires to international status becomes a member of the international community, and, where applicable, loses international status. A related matter concerns the recognition of governments as contrasted with the recognition of states. The political factors in these processes have already been suggested, but some other matters need to be considered as well.

State Recognition

It is suggested by most authorities that a state must meet certain basic requirements before it may be accorded recognition. As suggested above, it is to have territory, people, a government, and possess sovereignty in order to be a normal candidate for recognition.[27] Yet it would appear that the legally important crux of the matter centers upon the political act of recognition itself. Thus Luxembourg with a few square miles and a handful of people is a state by virtue of recognition as such, while the Cherokee Nation is not considered to be a state. Furthermore Poland between 1795 and 1918 may have existed in the hearts and minds of the Polish people, but it was not legally recognized and did not have international status. Yet after 1918 it was recognized as a state, and, particularly to the point, it continues in that capacity even though its relationship to the U.S.S.R. has often seemed to cast significant doubt upon the degree of sovereignty which it enjoys. Representing even greater disparity, is the contrast between a constituent state of the United States such as Kansas, Alabama, or Illinois, none of which enjoys any degree of international personality or recognition, and, on the other hand, two of the states of the U.S.S.R.— Ukraine, and Byelorussia. These two states, by virtue of a political decision made prior to creation of the United Nations Charter, are member states of the United Nations even though

---

[27] See this chapter, above, "State Definition."

their primary claim to independence is the dubious clause in the Soviet constitution which theoretically allows the member republics to have separate status.[28] This is rendered even more awkward by virtue of the fact that the other constituent republics enjoy no such status in the United Nations.[29]

Whether recognition is *constitutive* of the state or whether it is merely *declarative* of existing fact is a matter of some theoretical interest.[30] Thus it may be asked whether the recognition of statehood has the effect of constituting or creating a new legal entity and whether it is therefore the supreme act of creation, or conversely, whether recognition merely declares or acknowledges the fact that a state does in reality exist?

As is often true of rigid theoretical frameworks, neither position is entirely satisfactory if pushed to its logical conclusion. Yet each position is significant in certain aspects of international affairs. Thus while actual existence *demands* acknowledgment, legal status may at the same time *depend* upon the formality of recognition. It may be useful to point out that if recognition were declarative in an absolute sense, a nascent state, still unrecognized, would seem to be devoid of all rights. As a practical matter this appears to be excessive for international law acknowledges that such an entity has both certain obligations of behavior and, at least in combat, certain rights. On the other hand, in the unlikely event that a political entity had all the properties of statehood except that it were not

---

[28] U.S.S.R., *Constitution*, Art. 17.

[29] For references and brief discussion of these problems, see this chapter, above, fn. 12.

[30] See analysis in H. Lauterpacht, *Recognition in International Law* (Cambridge, Mass.: Harvard University Press, 1948), pp. 38–66; for a good brief discussion of this matter see W. L. Gould, *An Introduction to International Law* (New York: Harper & Bros., 1957), pp. 213–40. In a recent study of the Philippines, after citing commentary to the effect that a state may exist apart from recognition, the author makes the following significant observation about events at the turn of the century:

"Be that as it may, the very lack of recognition by foreign governments was fatal to the life of the young Philippine Republic. Despite the efforts of Felipe Agoncillo and other Filipino 'Diplomatic agents' in several state capitals, no foreign state accorded the Philippine Republic diplomatic recognition." Alejandro M. Fernandez, "International Law in Philippine Relations, 1898–1946" (unpublished Ph.D. dissertation, Department of Political Science, Duke University, 1966), p. 48.

recognized by any other state, it is difficult to imagine that it could be considered to have significant international personality. In this extreme sense the constitutive position seems valid.

It may be useful however to conjecture that as a practical matter recognition is *both* declarative and constitutive. The political fact of existence demands recognition in order for the legal regime to remain in touch with political reality. Yet the act of recognition is constitutive in the ultimate sense of endowing the entity with the legal status and competence of statehood. Hence to deal with this matter on the two levels of (*a*) the essentially political and (*b*) the purely legal has some narrow theoretical utility. In the final analysis, however, it should be apparent that the act of recognition—while itself significantly political—is of primary legalistic consequence, hence a juridical primacy must ultimately be assigned to the constitutive position.

Loss of International Personality

Once a state is recognized, it is then assumed that only by extinction of the state itself through fragmentalization, merger, or conquest does it cease to have international status. Thus Poland was split in 1795 among Russia, Austria-Hungary, and Prussia and as a consequence lost its international personality; Texas became merged voluntarily with the United States in 1845 and lost its international status. Similarly, Austria-Hungary ceased to exist as such in 1918, though a degree of its personality threaded into the successor states of Austria and Hungary.[31]

State Succession

It remains to be noted that when a state ceases to exist or when it is decimated, there may be problems concerning debts or obligations of the old extinct state. It appears that there is no

---

[31] Hackworth, *Digest* I, pp. 192–222. For an interesting discussion of the pertinent problems resulting from the Austrian-German *anschluss,* see Robert E. Clute, *The International Legal Status of Austria 1938–1955* (The Hague: Martinus Nijhoff, 1962) .

general duty for successor states to assume these obligations,[32] but as a matter of practice such obligations are often assumed. Thus, for example, the Treaty of St. Germain provided that each of the successor states of the Austro-Hungarian Empire should assume a proportion of the debt of the old empire.[33]

The matter is further complicated by the procedure of splitting states such as Germany, Korea, and Vietnam. The emergence of mainland China and Formosan China though stemming from different sources represents a related problem. Whatever may be said about the obligation to recognize a *de facto* state as a state, what is to be done when that entity obviously exists in two separate mutually hostile segments neither of which can control the other and neither of which acquiesces in the recognition of the other by foreign powers? Accordingly, is Germany one state or two? What about Korea, Vietnam, and China? Is resolution of this problem brought about by the pattern of recognition which already established states follow, or by what might be called *de facto* reality, or does some other principle govern?[34]

Recognition of Governments

A related but basically different matter is that of recognition of governments.[35] Once the existence of a state is recognized, it remains as an international entity regardless of whether or not its government has been acknowledged. When a government changes by constitutional process there is ordinarily no problem relative to recognition of the new government, but when a government changes by other means such as through force or

---

[32] See discussion in Fenwick, *op. cit.*, pp. 172–78; for a somewhat different view, see Oscar Svarlien, *An Introduction to the Law of Nations* (New York: McGraw-Hill Book Co., Inc., 1955), pp. 110–21. See materials in Whiteman, *Digest* II, pp. 754–1027.

[33] *Treaty of Peace between the Allied and Associated Powers and Austria* (Treaty of St. Germain), September 10, 1919, Art. 203; see conveniently in Naval War College, *International Law Documents 1920* (Washington, D.C.: U.S. Government Printing Office, 1922). See *Case Concerning Certain German Interests in Upper Silesia*, P.C.I.J. Judgments, Series A, No. 7 (1926).

[34] See discussion and citation of some of the literature on this matter in Whiteman, *Digest* II, pp. 787–99; also *Digest* I, pp. 320–38.

[35] Hackworth, *Digest* I, pp. 222–318. Also Whiteman, *Digest* II, pp. 242–67.

conspiracy, such a question does arise. This becomes particularly acute when there are two different governments contending for control of the state as in Spain during the 1936 revolution or as in revolutions in Latin America. Under these circumstances recognition of a new government often merges into the question of recognition of belligerency. In fact these two concepts are often closely related.[36]

There is also the matter of moral or political factors as they bear on the subject of recognition. During the early history of the United States and up until the early 20th century, this country followed what has been called the Jeffersonian view, that is, that a *de facto* government should be recognized as the legal government of the state. During the present century, however, subjective considerations have played a significant role in determining whether or not recognition should be accorded. Thus, it is relatively common for a state to recognize the deposed government of another state as its *de jure* government despite the fact that there is another *de facto* government in actual control of the country.[37] Factors which influence recognition and nonrecognition in such instances are of various sorts. For example, the United States during the Wilson administration refused to recognize the Huerta government in Mexico substantially because Huerta's record had been vicious and unscrupulous to a degree which seemed extreme. Similarly, the United States withheld recognition of the Communist government in Russia until 1933, and at the present writing (1967) the Communist government in China is still unrecognized by the United States.

As might be inferred from the above paragraph, there is some controversy regarding the principle which *should* govern recognition, a fact which points up the potentially political emphasis inherent in the process. On the one hand, following the Jeffersonian approach, it is believed that *de facto* control should be the criterion of recognition. On the other hand, following the Wilsonian tack, it is held that subjective elements should be allowed to enter into the picture. Thus, under the former ap-

---

[36] See comment this chapter, below, "Recognition of Belligerency."

[37] Moore, *Digest* I, pp. 119–20 *et passim;* Briggs, *op. cit.,* pp. 125–32; Hackworth, *Digest* I, pp. 180–92, 127–28 f.

proach the only valid question is whether or not the government to be recognized does in fact have control over the state, while under the latter approach questions are considered as to whether the government under consideration *will* as well as *can* assume its proper obligations under international law, and even whether it came to power properly.[38] That the problem involved is a broad one may be seen more clearly perhaps if it is realized that Latin-American countries, which probably have been more concerned with the problems of recognition than countries of any other area, also are divided on the matter. One view, called the **Tobar Doctrine** stresses that governments which come to power by nonconstitutional means should not be accorded recognition; while another view, called the **Estrada Doctrine,** and which is probably more in accord with Latin-American preferences, seeks to see the Tobar Doctrine and all other subjective considerations regarding recognition repudiated.[39]

Finally it should be noted that there are different degrees of what might be called official recognition. These are of two basic sorts and they are designated as **de facto** and **de jure** recognition. Under the former variety a government officially recognizes another government as the *de facto* government of the state, which is as much as to say that we recognize you as the government in power and will do business with you but we will wait and see how you pan out and how you behave before we fully recognize you. At a later date the recognizing government may extend *de jure* recognition which in turn suggests that the probationary period is over.[40]

It should be noted that recognition of a government is called formal if it is the result of explicit recognition, or tacit if it is an

---

[38] Hackworth, *Digest* I, pp. 161–95 and pp. 222–327.

[39] On the matter see rather full discussion in Fenwick, *op. cit.*, pp. 168–73. The dilemma persists in regard to Latin America. Attempts by the Kennedy administration to discourage military dictatorships by delayed recognition appear to have been neither consistent nor particularly successful. This Wilsonian procedure has been largely replaced by a reversion to the Jeffersonian approach by the Johnson administration. See discussion in Edwin Lieuwen, *Generals Vs. Presidents Neomilitarism in Latin America* (New York: Frederick A. Praeger, Inc., 1964), pp. 3–9, 114–29, 142–50 *et passim*.

[40] See data compiled conveniently in Briggs, *op. cit.*, pp. 124–25.

implication of some act, but in either case it is the act required to achieve legal personality.[41]

Effects of Recognition

It has already been suggested that recognition clearly has an essential generative quality in that it conveys a significant measure of international personality. This, of course, is the first effect of recognition and has bearing on all three of its aspects: recognition of states, of governments, and of belligerency.

This is not to say, however, that an unrecognized entity has no rights or duties and therefore, *absolutely* no personality. Some evidences of this minimal status can be seen in the requirement that even unrecognized insurgent captives are to be treated as prisoners of war.[42] Moreover, even the actions of an unrecognized government in its own territory are not very likely to be successfully contested in foreign courts.[43] Nevertheless, the degree of personality residing in mere existence is minimal, and elevation to full international personality is a product of recognition.

A second effect of recognition, in many ways closely related to the one just considered, is that mere continued recognition sustains the jural quality of an entity which has lost its physical base and which exists merely as a government (or state) in exile.[44]

This is particularly instructive because it illustrates with some force the constitutive character of recognition.

A third effect of recognition is the right—or at least the privilege—of bringing litigation in the courts of the recogniz-

[41] See *Republic of China* v. *Merchants' Fire Assurance Corporation of New York,* U.S. Circuit Ct. of Appeals, 30 F. 2nd 278 (1929). Whiteman, *Digest* II, pp. 51–9 *et passim.*

[42] See *Geneva Convention Relative to the Treatment of Prisoners of War, op. cit.,* Art. 3. Query: Is this an incidence of significant personality attaching to the insurgent entity or to the prisoner of war as an individual?

[43] This doctrine, known as the Act of State Doctrine, will be considered in this work, below, Chapter Four. See *Underhill* v. *Hernandez,* 168 U.S. 250 (1897). Also *Banco Nacional de Cuba* v. *Sabbatino,* 376 U.S. 398 (1964).

[44] See *Latvian State Cargo & Passenger S.S. Line* v. *McGrath,* U.S. Ct. of App., D.C., 188 F.2 1000 (1951). See also Whiteman, *Digest* II, pp. 656, 467–86.

ing state. This is normally denied to nonrecognized entities, but once recognition has been tendered, this right or privilege normally follows. In a leading American case on this matter the Court said:

. . . a foreign power brings an action in our courts not as a matter of right. Its power to do so is the creature of comity. Until such government is recognized by the United States no such comity exists.[45]

It should be added, however, that this does not imply that unrecognized governments are to be treated by the courts as though they did not exist. American courts have held that decrees of unrecognized governments purporting to have certain kinds of extraterritorial effect will not be enforced or recognized in this country; e.g., the court refused to recognize the validity of acts of the not yet recognized Soviet government in claiming the assets of a branch bank in the United States. The court said:

We do not recognize the decrees of Soviet Russia as competent to divest the plaintiff of the title to any assets that would otherwise have the protection of our law. At least this must be so where the title thus divested is transferred to the very government not recognized as existent. For the same reason we do not admit their competence in aid of a like purpose to pass sentence of death on the expropriated owner.[46]

Nevertheless, the courts did not question decrees of such governments which concerned commodities physically within their domain at the time the decree was promulgated, even though the same commodities were physically within the domain of the United States at the time the legal action was brought.[47]

A fourth effect of recognition is that once proffered, it tends to be retroactive back to the time when the government came

---

[45] *Russian Socialist Federated Soviet Republic* v. *Cibrario*, 235 N.Y. 255 (1923).

[46] *Petrogradsky Mejdunarodny Kommerchesky Bank* v. *National City Bank of New York*, 253 N.Y. 23 (1930).

[47] *Salimoff & Co.* v. *Standard Oil of New York*, 262 N.Y. 220 (1933).

into actual existence.[48] This does not appear to be an absolute but it is nevertheless a matter of importance.

A fifth effect of recognition, particularly of belligerency, is that once recognized, a base is created for proclamations of neutrality. Moreover, the mother country may employ it as a base from which the normal legal prosecution of the war may take place.[49]

A sixth general effect of recognition, particularly of governments, is that reciprocal recognition becomes a base upon which exchange of diplomatic representatives can normally take place. From this fact all sorts of advantages flow not the least of which is the setting up of the machinery, functioning diplomacy, through which most international claims and problems are ultimately resolved.[50]

Against the background of the above discussion, together with earlier commentary to the effect that admission to an international organization does not confer recognition upon the admitted state as far as the other members of the international organization are concerned, the student may find it instructive to consider the various possibilities open to the United States in its relations with China, and to consider the effects of each.

Recognition of Belligerency

Recognition of a state of belligerency may well presage the emergence of a new state or a new government. On the other hand it may be no more than recognition of a state of war in which the belligerent community ultimately fails to win. It may be a device the chief function of which is to render legitimate and well founded a state of neutrality for a disinterested power. Belligerency comes into existence by action, tacit or formal, either by the parent state or government or by a foreign state.

It is here, however, that the matter of premature recognition

---

[48] *Oetjen* v. *Central Leather Co.*, 246 U.S. 297 (1918).

[49] Hans Kelsen, *Principles of International Law* (2d ed. by Robert W. Tucker; New York: Holt, Rinehart & Winston, Inc., 1966), pp. 412–14. Whiteman, *Digest* II, pp. 486–523.

[50] See, e.g., comment in Whiteman, *Digest* II, pp. 655–56. See also discussion in this work, below, Chapters Seven and Eight.

is most likely to become a problem. Premature recognition may give offense to the *de jure* government, and excessively delayed recognition may be thought to be a slighting gesture directed against the new regime.[51]

Continuity of State Personality

Since a state continues as the same international entity regardless of which government is recognized and even regardless of whether any government is recognized at a given moment, the principle has arisen that governments may come and go but the continuity of personality of the state is unimpaired. This principle was clearly recognized in the case of *The Sapphire* which was begun by the French government under Napoleon III. The fact that the emperor was deposed did not alter the right of the successor government, once it was recognized by the United States, to continue the suit in the name of the French government.[52]

SUMMARY

It has been observed that the world stage is inhabited by states which compose the international community. This community of states is the society in which international law functions.

The question of exactly what entities are acknowledged to have the status of subjects or persons under international law can be resolved specifically only up to a point. Beyond that a certain vagueness obtains. These subjects clearly include states and certain public international organizations and the Vatican. In addition there are a number of borderline entities such as two of the constituent states of the U.S.S.R., vassal states, belligerent communities, insurgents, and in some instances man as an indi-

---

[51] See Hackworth, *Digest* I, pp. 318–27; Whiteman, *Digest* II, pp. 486–523; see also this chapter, above, "Belligerent Communities: Belligerency and Insurgency." *The Arantzazu Mendi*, Great Britain, House of Lords, 1939, A.C. 256.

[52] *The Sapphire,* 11 Wallace 164 (1871). See also Krystyna Marek, *Identity and Continuity of States in Public International Law* (Geneva: Librairie E. Droz, 1954) ; also D. P. O'Connell, *The Law of State Succession* (Cambridge: University Press, 1956) .

vidual, all of which to a greater or lesser degree also have qualities of international personality.

The normal process by which new states and new governments as well as other international entities attain international status is through recognition. By this process a state or states acknowledge the existence of the new entity by treaty or by some tacit act. The acknowledgment may be provisional as in *de facto* recognition, or more permanent and binding as in *de jure* recognition. Also, the process may result from a realization that the government being recognized is the actual government in power, or it may be attendant upon subjective matters as to whether or not it will or can assume the obligations of a government or upon some other considerations. Also, it is probably true that even though unrecognized, an entity which satisfies all other requirements for statehood (or for being a government or a belligerent community) possesses some sort of minimal international personality.

Finally, a state once recognized continues to have international personality while it continues to exist, whereas its governments may come and go.

CHAPTER 4

The Rights and Obligations of States

THE EXISTENCE of a system of international law—indeed of any system of law—implies certain basic relationships. Among these are a number which are necessary if a pacific legal pattern is to continue. On the other hand, it is difficult to discuss in terms of strict law some of the materials often surveyed under the heading of "rights and obligations." Some of them are *sine qua non* of legal existence, but are themselves so highly political in character that their quality as legal rights is open to question. In this category particularly is the basic and traditional—as contrasted with the contractual—right of existence.

RIGHTS OF STATES

Rights of Existence, Independence, and Sovereignty

The so-called right of existence allegedly appertaining to states is a matter which needs to be approached with great care. Authors in the past frequently have based the science of international law upon the supposition that states enjoyed a legal right to exist. It is, however, highly questionable whether a good case can be made for the operation of such a right—at least on a legal basis.

Excepting where a right of existence is a political reality and is written into treaties, this right, as the term is usually employed, means only that a state is entitled to protect itself and

68

may attempt to maintain its independence. There is little evidence that it ever meant more than this in practical application, though theoretical claims to the contrary have not been uncommon.[1]

The "right of independence" is virtually identical to the concept of the right of existence, but it is often discussed separately. According to Fenwick this is out of convenience rather than logic.[2] It follows, therefore, that no important legal right of independence as such exists, except where realistically guaranteed by the political *status quo,* often to be ascertained by the existence of treaties.

The term "independence" in its more proper usage refers to two closely related concepts. It includes both (1) the right of a state to manage its own domestic affairs, and (2) the right to conduct its own relations with other states.[3] These are sometimes called "internal independence" and "external independence" respectively. In addition, it should be mentioned that the term "sovereignty" is used to signify substantially the same thing as "independence" and "state existence" in the sense in which those terms are usually understood.[4]

Political Foundations of State Existence. It is evident, of course, that customarily a right of existence and independence is acquiesced in and often maintained by the force of the nation itself, or by its allies. Insofar as this is true, a right may be said

---

[1] See, e.g., comments in Robert Phillimore, *Commentaries upon International Law* (Philadelphia: T. and J. W. Johnson, 1854), Vol. I, pp. 91–92, 149–50; Edward M. Gallaudet, *A Manual of International Law* (New York: Henry Holt & Co., 1893), p. 80; see comment in Oppenheim-Lauterpacht, *Treatise* I, pp. 250–61; James Brown Scott, "Declaration of the Rights and Duties of Nations Adopted by the American Institute of International Law at Its First Session in the City of Washington, January 6, 1916," *American Journal of International Law,* Vol. X (January, 1916), pp. 124–26.

[2] Charles G. Fenwick, *International Law* (3d ed.; New York: Appleton-Century-Crofts, Inc., 1948), p. 249; 4th ed. (1966), p. 296.

[3] Moore, *Digest* I, pp. 18–20; see also International Law Commission, "Draft Declaration on Rights and Duties of States," *American Journal of International Law,* Vol. XLIV (January, 1950), pp. 16–18 (document's section), see Art. I (hereafter cited as *U.N. Draft*); also International Law Commission, *Preparatory Study Concerning a Draft Declaration on the Rights and Duties of States* (U.N. Document A/CN.4/2: 15 December, 1948), Arts. I, II, III, IV, and commentary, pp. 49–62 (hereafter cited as *1948 Draft*); still another draft and commentary is available in *Yearbook of the International Law Commission* 1949 (U.N., 1956), pp. 134–77.

[4] Moore, *Digest* I, pp. 18–20.

to obtain in fact, but it should be realized that often this
"right" is violated, and that the violation is subsequently
made good with the ultimate acquiescence of the international
community as a whole. In these latter cases it is evident that no
effective legal right of existence or independence really obtains,
and it only gives a sense of false security to maintain that there
is such a right.[5]

Self-Defense and Intervention. Closely connected with
what has been discussed above are the rights of self-defense and
of intervention. The first of these is the obvious concommitant
of the right of existence either as a political or as a legal
concept. The right of intervention, on the other hand, is from a
legal standpoint merely an extension of the right of self-
defense.

The right of self-defense is a naturalistic concept, the character of which is more or less obvious. It has long enjoyed legal
status and is now recognized in the United Nations Charter.[6] As
this concept has operated within the framework of general
international law it is, however, only the assurance that a state
may properly and legally defend its existence by force. By
extension this right becomes subject to abuse when, for example, it is used by state A as an excuse for attacking state B on
the grounds that state B was planning to attack but that state A
just "beat it to the draw."[7] If state A's claim in this regard were
substantively valid, the attack would, of course, have a certain
justification under general international law which it would
lack were the attack merely an excuse for aggression and conquest.

Whether "anticipatory self-defense" is still legally viable,
however, is now a matter of some dispute.[8] Restrictive interpretations of Article 51 of the United Nations Charter emphasize
the requirement that self-defense is appropriate only "if armed

---

[5] See H. B. Jacobini, "The Right of State Existence in International Law,"
Southwestern Social Science Quarterly, Vol. XXX (March, 1950) , pp. 277–81.

[6] U.N., *Charter,* Art. 51; see also *U.N. Draft,* Art. 12; also *1948 Draft,* Art. 17
and commentary, pp. 107–10.

[7] See justification for German attack on Poland, September 1, 1939 as reported
in *New York Times,* September 1, 1939, pp. 1, 3.

[8] For a convenient review of materials on both sides of this controversy, see
Whiteman, *Digest* V, pp. 971–1048 *et passim.*

attack occurs." They argue that this means only *after* the attack takes place.[9] Other commentaries suggest that a less-restrictive reading of Article 51 is indicated. These latter arguments which are embraced in one way or another by "the vast majority of scholars"[10] point, *inter alia,* to the exigencies of modern war, the unanticipated weaknesses of the United Nations in this area, the inept drawing of Article 51, the moderating effects of other clauses in the Charter, the differing meaning of the French text of Article 51, and the decision of the International Court of Justice in the *Corfu Channel* case.[11] To these arguments must be added the politico-legal view that as long as primary responsibility for defense and security rests with the state, emergency circumstances of the sort outlined in Mr. Webster's classic analysis (to be discussed below) will, it is submitted, underscore and reinforce the more liberal interpretation.

Although the right of intervention will be discussed in another connection, it should be noted here too that under some circumstances a state is justified in interfering with the affairs

[9] See Louis Henkin, "Force, Intervention, and Neutrality in Contemporary International Law," *Proceedings of the American Society of International Law,* 1963, pp. 147–62. Also Josef L. Kunz, "Individual and Collective Self-Defense in Article 51 of the Charter of the United Nations," *American Journal of International Law,* Vol. XLI (October, 1947), pp. 872–79; also Hans Kelsen, *The Law of the United Nations* (New York: Frederick A. Praeger, Inc., 1951), pp. 797–800. For a review of the various positions pro and con see Hans Kelsen, *Principles of International Law* (2d ed. by Robert W. Tucker; New York: Holt, Rinehart & Winston, Inc., 1966), pp. 58–87.

[10] Rosalyn Higgins, *The Development of International Law through the Political Organs of the United Nations* (New York: Oxford University Press, 1963), p. 200, fn. 49.

[11] Myres S. McDougal and Florentino P. Feliciano, *Law and Minimum World Public Order* (New Haven, Conn.: Yale University Press, 1961), pp. 232–41 *et passim;* H. Waldock, "The Regulation of the Use of Force by Individual States in International Law," 81 *Recueil des cours,* Vol. II (1952), pp. 455–514; D. W. Bowett, *Self-Defence in International Law* (New York: Frederick A. Praeger, Inc., 1958), pp. 184–93; J. L. Brierly, *The Law of Nations* (6th ed. by Sir Humphrey Waldock; New York: Oxford University Press, Inc., 1963), pp. 413–32. Ann Van Wynen Thomas and A. J. Thomas, Jr., *Non-Intervention, the Law and Its Import in the Americas* (Dallas, Tex.: Southern Methodist University Press, 1956), pp. 123–28. Philip C. Jessup, *A Modern Law of Nations* (New York: The Macmillan Co., 1948), pp. 163–69. *The Corfu Channel* case (Merits), I.C.J. Reports (1949), pp. 29–32. Rosalyn Higgins, "The Legal Limits to the Use of Force by Sovereign States, United Nations Practice," *The British Yearbook of International Law 1961,* Vol. XXXVII, pp. 269–319, especially pp. 301–02. Cf., however, Ian Brownlie, "The Use of Force in Self-Defence," *The British Yearbook of International Law 1961,* Vol. XXXVII, pp. 183–268.

of another state. For example, the intervention of the United States in Mexico in 1917 following the Villa raids on U.S. territory was generally considered to be appropriate—though highly impolitic internationally—in view of the inability of the existing Mexican government to exert effective control in northern Mexico.[12]

Another classic case in point is that of the *Caroline,* a private American vessel which was destroyed in American waters by a British contingent to prevent action in support of the Canadian rebellion of 1837. While the matter was resolved without clear acknowledgement of the appropriateness of the action, Secretary of State Webster stated the general rule pertinent to intervention:

Undoubtedly it is just, that, while it is admitted that exceptions growing out of the great law of self-defence do exist, those exceptions should be confined to cases in which the "necessity of that self-defence is instant, overwhelming, and leaving no choice of means, and no moment for deliberation."[13]

This sort of action is to be justified, however, only as an extension of the right of self-defense. It must be realized, moreover, that this position is open to all kinds of abuse as was noted in the hypothetical example given above.

From another standpoint it may be suggested that there are two varieties of the obligation not to interfere in the affairs of other nations. These are (1) moral, and (2) legal. On the moral level it is widely proclaimed and argued in naturalistic as well as political terms that an obligation prevails under which a state ought not to interfere in the affairs of another state except for reasons having to do with its own security. Though probably not widely violated, obedient adherence to morality has been assured only where political-military considerations made it practical.

On the legal level, many states have bound themselves by solemn treaty not to interfere in the internal affairs of other states. Thus many of the American nations have agreed that

---

[12] See explanation in Green Haywood Hackworth, *Digest* II, pp. 291–301, and particularly communication of U.S. Secretary of State, p. 300; see also Amos S. Hershey, "Incursions into Mexico and the Doctrine of Hot Pursuit," *American Journal of International Law,* Vol. XIII (July, 1919) , pp. 557–69.

[13] Moore, *Digest* II, pp. 409–14; quotation at p. 412.

"No state has the right to intervene in the internal or external affairs of another.[14] On a broader basis the members of the United Nations have agreed that they

. . . shall refrain in their international relations from the threat or use of force against the territorial integrity or political independence of any state, or in any other manner inconsistent with the Purpose of the United Nations.[15]

This is a clear and rather comprehensive legal obligation, but in the absence of sufficient political power it can be a dead letter as the activities of the U.S.S.R. in Hungary during October and November of 1956 would seem to attest.[16]

New Basis of the Right of Existence. On the basis of what has just been said, a modern reassessment of the matter of the right of state existence must be attempted. If, as has been asserted, the rights of existence and independence together with the status of intervention mean that a state has every right to defend its existence, this whole matter can scarcely be discussed intelligently on a legalistic level. Nevertheless, the world is now blanketed with a network of overlapping and counterpoised treaties under which the existence and independence of a great many nations are guaranteed at least to some extent, and still others derive some protection of their "right to exist" from the existing complex of world politics. This is to some extent very real, but the partial reality must not blind one to the partial spuriousness of these guarantees.

Thus, under the terms of the North Atlantic Treaty and the Rio Treaty, the participating nations are assured that an attack upon them will bring retaliation from the allies of the injured state.[17] Similarly, the Warsaw Pact and the Sino-Russian alli-

---

[14] *Convention on Rights and Duties of States,* Montevideo, 1933, 49 *U.S. Statutes at Large,* p. 3097, Art. 8.

[15] U.N., *Charter,* Art. 2 (4) ; see also *U.N. Draft,* Arts. 3, 4, 8, 9; also *1948 Draft,* Arts. 5, 8 and commentary, pp. 62–65, 74–78; also *Convention on Duties and Rights of States in the Event of Civil Strife,* Habana, 1928; *U.S.T.S.* No. 814; see conveniently in L. Pfankuchen, *A Documentary Textbook in International Law* (New York: Farrar and Rinehart, Inc., 1940) , pp. 954–55 (hereafter cited as *Convention on Civil Strife*) .

[16] See in *New York Times,* issues in October, November, and December, 1956; see particularly issues of October 25 and November 4, 1956.

[17] *North Atlantic Treaty Pact,* Department of State Publication 3464, Art. V; *The Rio Pact,* State Department Publication 3016, Art. III.

ance point toward what, in some respects at least, is a similar arrangement.[18] Finally, the United Nations Charter provides, as noted above, that no member may use force against a fellow member. From the foregoing remarks it should not be concluded that a solid body of protective law exists, for the whole picture is spotty. For example, it must be recognized that these treaties (excluding the U.N. Charter) are first and foremost political-military alliances which are designed to protect certain areas and states from certain other states. They do not, from a practical political standpoint at least, present barriers of general scope. Thus, the Warsaw Pact would appear to protect the Hungarians against the United States, but of more serious moment, it presents no security against the Russians either legally or practically. Moreover while the restraints of the U.N. Charter cannot be written off, yet in certain political contexts they can be almost meaningless.[19]

In assessing the present status of the right of existence, consideration must be given to this network of treaties and defense agreements which has developed in recent years by which almost every state is guaranteed against the encroachments of other states. While this is far from foolproof, it represents a movement in the direction of a meaningful but highly political—yet legal—right of existence under which the community of nations may eventually undertake to protect its inherent parts in their exercise of this right.

States: Equal or Unequal. A concept of some importance, also related to the right of existence, is the view that all states

---

[18] *Treaty of Friendship, Cooperation and Mutual Assistance*, May 14, 1955 (The Warsaw Pact) , Art. 4, see in *American Journal of International Law*, Vol. XLIX (October, 1955) , pp. 194–98 (documents section) ; *Treaty of Friendship, Alliance, and Mutual Assistance*, February 14, 1950 (The Sino-Russian Alliance) , Art. 1, see in *American Journal of International Law*, Vol. XLIV (July, 1950) , pp. 84–86 (documents section). At the moment of writing (1967) the utility of the Sino-Soviet pact is, of course, a matter of some doubt. Also, there have been evidences of strain in the NATO alliance. These stresses illustrate the intensely political character of the fabric of international constitutional law. See reference above, *North Atlantic Treaty Pact*, pp. 29–30.

[19] On November 4, 9, 1956, the U.N. General Assembly requested that the Russian troops leave Hungary, and on November 7, Britain, France and Israel were similarly requested to withdraw from Egypt. The former rejected while the latter agreed. See *New York Times*, November 5, 8, 9, 10, 11, 12, 13, 1956; also Keesing's *Contemporary Archives*, November 17–24, 1956, pp. 15221–24, 15201–7.

are equal, sometimes called the "right of equality." This is a concept of long standing in international law, stemming from a segment of natural law philosophy.[20] Despite its acceptance by most publicists.[21] and regardless of its acceptance in leading court decisions,[22] many modern publicists have expressed reservations about it.[23]

In the leading work on the subject, the view is expressed that this principle involves two aspects: (1) equality before the law, and (2) equality of rights or equal capacity for rights. Of these two, Dickinson feels that the former is "essential to a stable society of nations" while the latter is not essential and "has never been anything more than an ideal in any system of law."[24]

It must be suggested, however, that at best states enjoy only the barest rudiments of equality. They are unequal in size, power, and political stature; they are often unequal regarding externally imposed, internally imposed, or geographically imposed rights. Thus, a neutralized state, a state laboring under capitulations, or a state to which the principle of diplomatic asylum applies are not equal in these respects to states not so encumbered. In international organizations, moreover, very real inequalities exist. For example, the unanimity principle enjoyed in the United Nations by the "Big Five" gives them distinct superiority over the other member states. Finally, in international conferences, inequality seems to be the rule.

On the other hand, the Charter of the United Nations avowedly rests upon the basis of "the principle of the sovereign equality of all its members" and it would seem that within the limitation of the optional jurisdiction arrangements, all states—on an equal basis—may sue and be sued in the International Court of Justice. Furthermore, all have equal representa-

---

[20] Edwin D. Dickinson, *The Equality of States in International Law* (Cambridge, Mass.: Harvard University Press, 1920), pp. 68–99, 334.

[21] See references in Moore, *Digest* I, pp. 62–63; see also *U.N. Draft,* Art. 5; also *1948 Draft,* Art. 6 and commentary, pp. 66–70.

[22] See, e.g., *The Schooner Exchange* v. *McFaddon,* 7 Cranch, 116 (1812).

[23] See, e.g., Fenwick, *op. cit.,* (3d ed.), pp. 218–27; Oscar Svarlien, *An Introduction to the Law of Nations* (New York: McGraw-Hill Book Co., Inc., 1955), pp. 127–29.

[24] Dickinson, *op. cit.,* pp. 334–35, quotation on p. 335.

tion in the General Assembly of the United Nations.[25] Finally, it would appear that they have substantially equal rights of contract. It is doubtful, however, despite these shells of equality, whether all can be held equally responsible for the maintenance of world peace or for upholding a multilateral treaty.[26]

Now where does this leave the matter? Perhaps, for the American student it may be useful to say that states in the international community approach having ideally the same status vis-à-vis each other that constituent states within the American union have in relation to each other. While one does not have to look very far to see serious fallacies in this analogy, the legal equality contrasted with political inequality may help to simplify the concept.

If equality before the law is a characteristic of the American relationship for constituent states and an ideal for the international community, it should be realized, nevertheless, that in the international community political and military pressures can make this concept meaningless for the smaller states, particularly for those outside the United Nations. Still another statement regarding this matter suggests that states do not have equal rights, but rather equal right to the enforcement of whatever rights each may have.[27] This seems to be a *reductio ad absurdum* in defense of equality, for it is almost equivalent to saying "that which is is," but nevertheless it is perhaps a reasonable expression of the actual facts of the matter.

Thus, by way of summary, the best that can be said is that equality before the law is a noble ideal and a partial fact. To go beyond that would be to fly in the face of political reality.

OBLIGATIONS OF STATES

In the previous paragraphs doubt was suggested concerning the traditional position that an a priori legal right of state

---

[25] U.N. *Charter,* Arts. 2 (1), 18; *Statute of the International Court of Justice,* Art. 35.

[26] For an extreme example see case of Liechtenstein's attempt to gain admission to the League of Nations cited in Hackworth, *Digest* I, pp. 48–49.

[27] J. L. Brierly, *The Law of Nations* (5th ed.; Oxford: The Clarendon Press, 1955), pp. 124–25 (see also 6th ed., pp. 130–33).

existence obtains, and also regarding the reality of the concept
of state equality. Yet, if peaceful relations are to obtain among
states, a degree of mutual respect must exist, and in this connection a number of principles have come forth which if not
always equal in application, are nevertheless generally respected. It must be realized, of course, that where an obligation
exists, a right may also be held to exist in that other states have
a right to expect that an obligation will be honored.

World juridical opinion and pragmatic practice have marked
out certain guideposts in these matters, but it must be noted
that the legal remedies are not always the same for all states.
Among certain states, for example, the obligation to arbitrate
or adjudicate is recognized, while among other states no such
obligation exists, and other media or remedies obtain. In some
instances, moreover, there is little practical remedy save the
reaction of anguish and despair.

Good Faith

Of first importance in any survey of the obligations of states
is the recognition that if there is to be any degree of harmony
among nations, the sanctity of treaty obligations must be recognized. Applied to pacts this is referred to as the principle
pacta sunt servanda, meaning that agreements are to be upheld and honored, or more simply, that treaties are binding.
This is, of course, the basic assumption upon which all treaty
law rests.[28] The principle itself, as noted in the first chapter, is
based upon different justifications, but whether it is best characterized as a rule of customary origin, a basic natural law
principle, or an elementary rule of order is not a matter
which need be resolved here. The important issue is the fact
that good faith in treaties is a basic and necessary assumption.
Consequently, in a case decided by the World Court in 1927,
the view was judicially expressed that "the breach of an engage-

---

[28] See brief comments in Oppenheim-Lauterpacht, *Treatise* I, pp. 880–81; also
in Hackworth, *Digest* V, pp. 164–65; also *U.N. Draft,* Art. 13; also *1948 Draft,*
Arts. 11, 12, and commentary, pp. 82–87; Whiteman, *Digest* V, pp. 221–23. See
also comment in Kelsen, *op. cit.* (2d ed.) , p. 456 *et passim;* also *Soviet Textbook,*
pp. 248–49.

ment involves an obligation to make reparation."[29] To enforce
this rule may, however, involve great difficulties on occasion,
yet the rule is clearly recognized, and pressure to maintain its
status may derive from world public opinion or from external
force. The political character of the remedy should, however,
be apparent.

Beyond the status of good faith in relation to treaties, there is
the broader recognition that good faith with other nations in
general is a requisite of amicable relationships. Its importance
on that level cannot be overstated for, as in virtually all human
relations, integrity is highly valued.

Rebus sic stantibus. It should be noted here, though more
detailed comment will be made in a later chapter,[30] that it is
sometimes impossible for a state to abide by its commitments.
In the face of impossibility of performance, or of a fundamental change of circumstances a state is generally absolved of its
treaty responsibilities. This absolvement, particularly in regard
to change of circumstances (including particularly those
material circumstances leading a party to enter into an agreement) but also loosely (and perhaps somewhat improperly) in
reference to impossibility of performance, is known as the *clausula rebus sic stantibus.*[31]

Territory as Source of Danger or Nuisance

The concept of the state as a sovereign entity which is not
subject to supervision from without implies that the state itself
must then maintain a degree of decorum on its borders both
from the standpoint of military threat to other powers and
from the standpoint of other aspects which may be classed as
nuisances.

Use of Territory for Attack. Of first importance in this regard is the requirement that a state must not let its territory

---

[29] *Chorzow Factory* case, P.C.I.J., Judgment, Series A, No. 9 (1927), p. 21; see
also Hackworth, *Digest* V, p. 165.

[30] See Chapter Six.

[31] See comments in Moore, *Digest* V, pp. 221, 335–41; Chesney Hill, *The
Doctrine of Rebus Sic Stantibus* (Columbia, Mo.: University of Missouri Press,
1934), pp. 79–83 *et passim.*

become a base for attack upon some other power. This applies both to harrassing operations by more or less irresponsible bands as well as to serious invasion attempts and to the outfitting of military and naval units.[32]

The key concept here is that of "due diligence" which, as established in the *Alabama Claims* case, represents the attention which a government is obliged to devote to making sure that its territory has not been used for offensive purposes.[33] Illustrative of the obligation are a number of instances in which the United States exerted considerable effort to discourage Mexican insurrectionists from preparing on American soil for attacks against Mexico.[34]

Duty to Discourage Small Raiding Parties. The concept of obligation also extends to lesser operations such, for example, as discouraging the activities of small raiding parties from raiding across an international boundary. An illustration of this matter also appears in the relationship between the United States and Mexico resulting from the raids in 1916 by the Mexican bandit-patriot, Francisco Villa, upon two American towns, one in New Mexico and the other in Texas. It is interesting to note that the Mexican ambassador acknowledged an obligation on the part of Mexico to discourage such raids, but felt that U.S. pursuit of the raiders into Mexico was inappropriate.[35]

In a more recent context, it is most difficult to view the Bay of Pigs incident of early 1961 as conforming to the principle under discussion. United States encouragement of these Cuban refugee raiders, unless justifiable as a form of reprisal, (which is doubtful), appears to be a violation.[36]

---

[32] See in Hackworth, *Digest* II, pp. 336–42; Moore, *Digest* VII, pp. 906–16.

[33] See Hackworth, *Digest* VII, pp. 383–87; also John H. Wigmore, *A Guide to American International Law and Practice* (Albany, N.Y.: Matthew Bender & Co., 1943), pp. 335–99; John Bassett Moore, *History and Digest of the International Arbitrations to Which the United States Has Been a Party* (6 vols.; Washington, D.C.: U.S. Government Printing Office, 1898), Vol. I, pp. 495–682, see especially discussion at pp. 653–59; see also *Convention on Civil Strife.*

[34] Hackworth, *Digest* II, pp. 336–42.

[35] *Ibid.*, pp. 291–301; see also, however, *U.N. Draft*, Arts. 3, 8, 9; also *1948 Draft*, Art. 22 and commentary, pp. 123–24.

[36] R. A. Falk, "American Intervention in Cuba and the Rule of Law," *Ohio Law Journal*, Vol. XXII (Summer, 1961), pp. 546–85. For discussion of reprisals see this work, below, Chapter Eight.

Nuisance Damage. Beyond the scope of armed invasion or raider bands, activities within the confines of one country may have deleterious effects in other nations. Examples would seem to include instances where sewage, gas fumes, oil, and other substances are discharged on one side of a boundary or in boundary or coastal waters under circumstances which are injurious to a neighbor state. It appears that such activities are improper and the rightful subject of protest.[37]

Illustrative of the matter is the *Trail Smelter* case which, however, was decided under the terms of a British–U.S. treaty prohibiting pollution. Under this arbitral decision damages were awarded to the United States for injuries resulting from fumes coming across the Canadian boundary from a smelter in British Columbia. Although the arbitral commission was concerned only with the terms of the convention and not with general international law, the issue is illustrative of the nuisance type of international problem and it may be conjectured that the treaty is expressive of international obligations.[38]

Counterfeiting. Another area in which there appears to be a mutual obligation among states is that of counterfeiting,[39] and many nations have agreed to aid each other in the supression of these fraudulent processes.[40] The United States, though not a party to the international convention which prohibits counterfeiting has long utilized domestic legislation to help curb this sort of activity.[41]

Other Injuries. It should not be assumed that the offenses enumerated above exhaust the possibilities. They are merely the most common sources of friction. As Mr. Chief Justice Waite observed in the *Arjona* case:

The law of nations requires every national government to use "due diligence" to prevent a wrong being done within its own dominion to another nation with which it is at peace, or to the people thereof. . . .[42]

---

[37] Hackworth, *Digest* II, pp. 342–46. Also Whiteman, *Digest* III, pp. 1040–50.

[38] Hackworth, *Digest* II, pp. 344–46.

[39] *Ibid.*, pp. 350–54.

[40] *Convention on the Suppression of Counterfeiting Currency,* 1929, in Hudson, *International Legislation,* Vol. IV, p. 2692.

[41] *U.S.* v. *Arjona,* 120 U.S. 479 (1887).

[42] *Ibid.;* see also *1948 Draft,* Art. 13 and commentary, pp. 88–90.

Thus a rather wide variety of acts are embraced within this scope, including such matters as hygienic situations, certain offensive business procedures, and slander.[43]

Injuries from State Action and State Agents

Along this same line, the state itself, as contrasted with its subjects or other persons using its territory, may be the offender. When such is the case, protest is also in order as may be seen in the example of the *Corfu Channel* case. In this instance the World Court held Albania responsible for damage done by mines in its territorial waters to two British ships.[44] In a somewhat similar vein the United States took action against one of its Marine generals because of slanderous remarks made against the Italian Premier, Benito Mussolini, and proffered an apology to the Italian government. This is an instance of assuming a degree of responsibility for the utterances of a governmental agent. Similar remarks by the mayor of New York were beyond the authority of the national government, but also gave rise to an explanation to the German government that the national government could not be held responsible.[45] It might be conjectured that sensibilities along these lines have waned during the U.S.–Russian post-World War II difficulties.

Immunities

States are obliged to recognize the immunity of foreign states[46] and of certain foreign persons[47] from suit. These immunities have the effect of protecting the foreign state and its agents against unreasonable restraints and against certain types of effrontery to their sovereignty. In other instances these immunities serve merely to oil the cogs of friendly relationships.

---

[43] Hackworth, *Digest* II, pp. 347–50, 145–46, *et passim*.

[44] *The Corfu Channel* case I.C.J. Reports, 1949, p. 4.

[45] See Fenwick, *op. cit.* (3d ed.), pp. 305–6; Hackworth, *Digest* II, pp. 145–46; for a good brief account see Ellery C. Stowell, "The General Smedley D. Butler Incident," *American Journal of International Law*, Vol. XXV (April, 1931), pp. 321–24.

[46] *Hassard* v. *U.S. of Mexico*, Supreme Court of New York, 29 Misc. Rep. 511 (1899).

[47] See e.g., *Carrera* v. *Carrera*, U.S. Court of Appeals, D.C., 174 F. 2d 496 (1949); also Chapter Seven of this book.

Property. The property of one state within the confines of another state is ordinarily held to fall within this category. Thus, a British court held that certain property of the Japanese government could not be attached for damages by a person claiming to be injured by an infringement of patent rights. The matter could be taken cognizance of by the local court, however, in order to determine ownership.[48]

Sovereigns, Diplomats, and Public Ships. Although a matter to be noted in some detail at a later point,[49] it should be observed that the heads of states, diplomats, and public ships are also immune from suit.

Obligation to Allow Foreign States to Bring Suit in Courts. Although a state may not be sued without its consent in the courts of another state or in international courts, it is ordinarily entitled to bring suit in those courts. Thus, in *The Sapphire* Mr. Justice Bradley stated that "A foreign sovereign as well as any other foreign person, who has a demand of a civil nature against any person here, may prosecute it in our courts. To deny him this privilege would manifest a want of comity and friendly feeling."[50] It appears, however, that such suit is more a matter of comity than strict right,[51] but for practical purposes this may make little real difference. It should be added, however, that although a state may not be sued without its consent, once it has instituted a suit it may be subjected to counterclaims.[52]

Acts of State. Not all foreign legal actions are immune from the jurisdiction of foreign states,[53] but in practice a great many

---

[48] *Vavasseur* v. *Krupp,* Gr. Brit., Court of Appeals, L.R. 9 Ch. D. 351 [1878].

[49] Chapters Five, Seven.

[50] *The Sapphire,* 11 Wallace 164 (1871).

[51] Hackworth, *Digest* II, pp. 82–83. Comity is an interesting term, but it has a certain ambiguity about it. It suggests something which is somewhat less binding than a legal obligation, yet more legally constraining than mere courtesy. In *Hilton* v. *Guyot,* 158 U.S. 113 (1895), the U.S. Supreme Court said

" 'Comity,' " in the legal sense, is neither a matter of absolute obligation, on the one hand, nor of mere courtesy and good will, upon the other. But it is the recognition which one nation allows within its territory to the legislative, executive or judicial acts of another nation, having due regard both to international duty and convenience, and to the rights of its own citizens or of other persons who are under the protection of its laws."

[52] *Kingdom of Norway* v. *Federal Sugar Refining Co.,* U.S. District Court, Southern District of N.Y., 286 Fed. 188 (1923).

[53] See e.g., *Petrogradsky Mejdunarodny Kommerchesky Bank* v. *National City*

are. In general those actions which take place wholly within the physical domains of a state are not questioned by foreign courts whether the government be *de jure* or *de facto*. This is known as the act of state doctrine. In the leading American case the U.S. Supreme Court said:

> Every sovereign state is bound to respect the independence of every other sovereign state, and the courts of one country will not sit in judgment on the acts of the government of another, done within its own territory. Redress of grievances by reason of such acts must be obtained through the means open to be availed of by sovereign powers as between themselves.
>
> Nor can the principle be confined to lawful or recognized governments, or to cases where redress can manifestly be had through public channels.[54]

In later litigation the same Court observed that this general position stands

> upon the highest considerations of international comity and expediency. To permit the validity of the acts of one sovereign State to be reexamined and perhaps condemned by the courts of another would very certainly "imperil the amicable relations between governments and vex the peace of nations."[55]

More recently there has been much dispute about this view. After Iran had nationalized the Anglo-Iranian Oil Company, cases arose in Aden, Italy, and Japan in which the act of nationalization was questioned. The Supreme Court of Aden found the nationalization decrees to be illegal, while the Italian and Japanese courts found otherwise.[56]

Bank of New York, New York Court of Appeals, 253 N.Y. 23 (1930). *Bernstein v. N.V. Nederlandsche-Amerikaansche Stoomvart-Maatschappij*, 210 F. 2d 375 (1954).

[54] *Underhill v. Hernandez*, 168 U.S. 250 (1897). Also see *Salimoff & Co. v. Standard Oil Co. of New York*, New York Court of Appeals, 262 N.Y. 220 (1933).

[55] *Oetjen v. Central Leather Co.*, 246 U.S. 297 (1918).

[56] *Anglo-Iranian Oil Co. v. Jaffrate et al.*, Supreme Court of Aden, *American Journal of International Law*, Vol. XLVII (July, 1953), p. 325. *Anglo-Iranian Oil Co. v. Societa Unione Petrolifera Orientale*, Civil Tribunal of Venice, *American Journal of International Law*, Vol. XLVII (July, 1953), p. 509. *Anglo-Iranian Oil Co. v. Idemitsu Kosan Kabushiki Kaisha*, *International Law Reports*, 1953, p. 305.

In the United States the *Sabbatino* case turned on related issues. The district and circuit courts accepted doctrine which was at variance with the ruling in *Underhill* v. *Hernandez*. The Supreme Court, however, returned the law to the more established doctrine, but in doing so, it did not hold that international law required this.[57] If the act of state doctrine rests, therefore, upon a jural foundation somewhat less sturdy than law, possibly upon comity, it remains nevertheless a persistent and generally prevailing norm of international intercourse.

Status of Aliens. It must be acknowledged from the beginning that the exact status of aliens is often very difficult to determine. States have complete legal control over immigration. Thus while it may be poor policy to exclude aliens altogether or special categories of aliens, it seems that a state enjoys a sovereign right to do so. Attempts by oriental nations to exclude all foreigners were nullified by external force. On the other hand, Mr. Justice Field ruled for the U.S. Supreme Court in 1889 that the "exclusion of foreigners . . . [is] an incident of sovereignty."[58] More generally this principle has been written into multilateral conventions. Thus the Inter-American Convention on the Status of Aliens specifies that "States have the right to establish by means of laws the conditions under which foreigners may enter and reside in their territory."[59]

Once aliens are admitted, however, prevailing authority suggests that the host state owes certain obligations to them. While aliens are required to obey the law of the host state and gener-

---

[57] *Banco Nacional de Cuba* v. *Sabbatino et al.*, 376 U.S. 398 (1964), District and Circuit Court decisions reported in 193 F. Supp. 375 (Southern District, N.Y.) (1961). For some of the pertinent literature both on Sabbatino and on the act of state doctrine in general and for references to other materials, see James N. Hyde, "The Act of State Doctrine and the Rule of Law," *American Journal of International Law*, Vol. LIII (July, 1959), pp. 635–38; William Harvey Reeves, "Act of State Doctrine and the Rule of Law—A Reply," *American Journal of International Law*, Vol. LIV (January, 1960), pp. 141–56; Richard A. Falk, "The Complexity of Sabbatino," *American Journal of International Law*, Vol. LVIII (October, 1964), pp. 935–51; Richard A. Falk *et al.*, *The Aftermath of Sabbatino* (Dobbs Ferry, N.Y.: Oceana Publications, Inc., 1965). See also brief comment in Oppenheim-Lauterpacht, *Treatise* I, pp. 267–70.

[58] *Chae Chan Ping* v. *U.S.*, 130 U.S. 581 (1889). On the subject of the treatment of foreigners see John Ward Cutter "The Treatment of Foreigners," *American Journal of International Law*, Vol. XXVII (April, 1933), pp. 225–46.

[59] Cited in Hackworth, *Digest* III, p. 549.

ally must refrain from political activity, the state itself is obliged to treat them with a certain degree of rectitude. Thus, such persons ordinarily enjoy at least certain basic civil rights; they are to be protected up to the extent specified by the term "due diligence," and they ordinarily have access to the courts.[60] These matters together with provisions for taxation and labor rights are frequently the subject of treaty stipulations.

Normally it is presumed that aliens should enjoy the same rights as citizens in regard to seeking redress for wrongs committed against them. This may be meaningless, however, in those places where the citizens themselves enjoy virtually no such legal rights. As a counterpoise to this type of situation where aliens and citizens alike are powerless, the view has been advanced that the minimum level of an international standard of justice must be maintained in the treatment of aliens. In this connection Hackworth states:

Aliens within the jurisdiction of a state are entitled, generally speaking, to the protection of person and property assured by local law to nationals of this country. Equal protection of the law in this sense presupposes the maintenance by the state of a standard of law and order conformable to the requirements of international law, i.e., to the standard generally observed by well-organized and administered states and governments.[61]

In regard to the rights of aliens, states are often in the position of acting to protect their citizens living abroad. It should be noted, however, that when an alien feels he has been wronged, he is usually obliged to exhaust the local judicial remedies before making an attempt to secure aid from his home country. This principle is known as the *Calvo Doctrine.* When it is written into contracts with foreigners, as is often the practice, it is called the *Calvo Clause.*[62] The ruling case on this subject suggests, however, that a state's right to protect its citizens abroad is not altered by the existence of such a clause. At the same time, it upholds the principle of exhausting local

---

60 *Ibid.,* pp. 552–74.

61 *Ibid.,* p. 630.

62 Hackworth, *Digest* V, pp. 635–54; for a detailed study, see D. R. Shea, *The Calvo Clause* (Minneapolis, Minn., University of Minnesota Press, 1955).

judicial remedies when specified by contract before other action such as diplomatic intervention appears proper.[63]

One area in which the rights of aliens become particularly important is that of the expropriation of private property. Aspects of this matter have been much debated, but it appears clear that nationalization of private property owned by aliens is not in itself an illegal act unless, of course, such action is barred by treaty, and unless the necessary accompanying actions are not provided for. The most important of these actions centers upon compensation which must be fair and prompt. Nationalization should be for some public purpose and should not be discriminatory. A pertinent General Assembly resolution is reasonably descriptive.

Nationalization, expropriation or requisitioning shall be based on grounds or reasons of public utility, security or the national interest which are recognized as overriding purely individual or private interests, both domestic and foreign. In such cases the owner shall be paid appropriate compensation, in accordance with the rules in force in the State taking such measures in the exercise of its sovereignty and in accordance with international law. In any case where the question of compensation gives rise to a controversy, the national jurisdiction of the State taking such measures shall be exhausted.[64]

What has been said thus far in regard to aliens represents substantially a traditional view. It must be conjectured, however, that the "international standard of justice" is a highly flexible concept at best. Like the matter of exclusion of aliens it is probably demonstrable that such an international standard is

---

[63] *United States of America on Behalf of North American Dredging Company of Texas, Claimant* v. *The United Mexican States* (*North American Dredging Company* case), General Claims Commission, 1926; see Shea, *op. cit.*, pp. 121–257 for analysis of cases.

[64] Res. 1803 (XVII), U.N. General Assembly, 17th sess., *Official Records*, Supp. No. 17 (A/5217), p. 15. For a discussion of the whole problem of nationalization, see Martin Domke, "Foreign Nationalizations: Some Aspects of Contemporary International Law," *American Journal of International Law*, Vol. LV (July, 1961), pp. 585–616. Also Louis B. Sohn and R. R. Baxter, "Responsibility of States for Injuries to the Economic Interests of Aliens" (including 1961 Harvard "Draft Convention on the International Responsibility of States for Injuries to Aliens"), *American Journal of International Law*, Vol. LV (July, 1961), pp. 545–84.

closely tied to political forces and at times to military considerations.

ENFORCEMENT PROCEDURES

Questions now arise, first as to the exact determination of these obligations, and second as to their enforcement. These are matters which will be considered more fully in a later chapter[65] but to which a few comments should be devoted at this point.

In the first place it must be candidly admitted that under some circumstances it is impossible to achieve either of these goals. On the other hand *where there is a desire for amicable relations* a suitable determination is often possible. This, it may be conjectured, is more often than not the case. The conventional remedies include direct diplomatic representation and protest, diplomatic pressure to submit the case to arbitration or adjudication, and bringing the case to the World Court as a matter of right where the optional jurisdiction clause of the World Court has been adhered to. Other procedures include airing the matter before the United Nations or otherwise bringing it to general attention throughout the world, the use of forceful pressures including retaliation and direct intervention, and ultimately, war.[66] Where treaties operate to describe procedures, however a greater measure of precision obtains. A treaty standard is a more accurate device than its counterpart in general international law.[67]

Perhaps an unusual incident can be used to illustrate the problem.[68] A number of years ago an American citizen, Robert Vogeler, was arrested by the Russian-dominated Hungarian government. He was subsequently released, but the treatment given him seems to have been such that it makes a mockery of

---

[65] See Chapter Eight.

[66] Mention of war in this context is designed to indicate what is in fact a final arbiter. It does not imply the legality of war as a device of self-help in any categorical sense. This question will be discussed below, Chapters Eight and Nine.

[67] Robert R. Wilson, *The International Law Standard in Treaties of the United States* (Cambridge, Mass: Harvard University Press, 1953), *passim*.

[68] See account in *New York Times*, April 29, 1951, pp. 1, 49.

the concept of an international standard of justice. It further illustrates the American government's inability—at least for a time—to secure justice for such a person short of war. On the other hand, it illustrates too, that an assortment of pressures and concessions finally can secure release. Thus, from one standpoint it may be said that a degree of justice ultimately did obtain; yet such a view seems to torture reality. From another standpoint, it may be suggested that this Soviet-Hungarian action can be viewed merely as a violation of law which, nevertheless, lacked prompt remedy. Whichever view one takes may be of relatively little importance, however, so long as the process is viewed in realistic political perspective. If there is reason and desire for amicable relations between states most of the rules are generally followed. If such reason and desire is lacking, however, there may be no remedy short of war; and if war is too great a price to pay, there may be then no effective remedy. Finally, in instances of this last sort, it may be possible on a political basis to reach negotiated agreement as a *modus vivendi*. In all events the flexible and political character of the matter should never be lost sight of.

SUMMARY

A system of international law implies a certain propriety in interstate relationships. On a very primary level this includes the right of states to exist and the right of self-defense. These have been largely meaningless—as highly refined a priori legalistic rights—in that they recognized only the right of states to act to secure independence. More recently the world has become blanketed with treaties which attempt to put the matter of state security on a basis whereby the community of nations or sizable groups of states attempt to guarantee their mutual security.

Similarly the right of state equality has been the subject of much loose conjecture. In reality it seems to mean that states have an equal right before the law to have their rights enforced, and that this is at least partially effected in reality.

Beyond these matters which are none too secure, there are a number of rather basic mutual obligations of states. These include the requirement of good faith, the obligation to attempt to settle disputes peacefully, the duty of a state to keep its territory from being used as a base of attack against another state, and the obligation to keep nuisances such as polution and counterfeiting from being committed. A further state duty exists to recognize the immunity of property owned by other states and the immunity of certain foreign personages. Also the right of foreign states to bring suit is usually recognized as a matter of comity. Lastly, the obligation to afford reasonable protection to aliens is recognized.

Finally, it was observed that several modes of enforcement are usually available among states desiring to maintain amicable relations, and that these include diplomatic representation and negotiation, arbitration, adjudication, and placing the matter before the political organs of the United Nations. Where no such desire exists, other pressures, negotiation, retaliation, and even war may be necessary. Finally it was observed that under some circumstances effective enforcement may be essentially impossible. Throughout the whole discussion of enforcement, the matter of the desire for amicable relationships is a key factor which emphasizes the political character of the problem.

CHAPTER 5

Jurisdiction and Boundaries

Put very simply the basic question of jurisdiction centers upon which state has sovereignty or legal control over land, persons, and ships at sea in various situations. Such matters as how territorial sovereignty is obtained, what principles of control exist on the high seas and in the airspace, the problem of exceptions to ordinary jursidiction as seen in servitudes, extradition of criminals, nationality of persons, and control in borderline areas are all of concern to this general topic.

A survey of the scope of jurisdiction falls more or less naturally into four main divisions. In this chapter the first of these will concern territory and its appurtenances; the second will center upon maritime jurisdiction; the third will deal with international servitudes; and the fourth will have to do with matters of nationality and jurisdiction over persons. Jurisdictional practices are often routine in nature and hence accorded general support. In some circumstances, however, highly political considerations arise. The political processes by which rules are formed are readily seen in certain instances but are more obscure in others. Where instructive, these political pressures will occasionally be noted, but in this chapter emphasis will center largely upon a mere detailing of the principal legal rules and practices.

JURISDICTION OVER TERRITORY AND ITS APPURTENANCES

It should be noted initially that the "jurisdiction of a state extends over not only the land within the territorial limits and the marginal sea or territorial waters, as well as the airspace above them, but also over all persons and things within such territory, with certain exceptions."[1] Jurisdiction extends beyond the territorial sea, however, to ships at sea and even to foreign countries, for example, to nationals living abroad under certain circumstances.

It must also be realized that national jurisdiction is not quite the same thing as a property right. It is, for example, quite possible for a government to own pieces of property within the confines of a foreign nation or even to own foreign government bonds without, of course, enjoying the attributes of sovereignty in regard to them. This is the distinction between *imperium* on the one hand and *dominium* on the other.[2] In speaking of the former, Oppenheim states that "The importance of State territory lies in the fact that it is the space within which the State exercises its supreme authority."[3]

Acquisition of Territory

In regard to territory it should be noted first that a state may obtain sovereignty in five basic ways: (1) by discovery followed by occupation, (2) by prescription, that is, by remaining in occupation for a protracted period following abandonment by another power, (3) by conquest (except presumably that this procedure is now legally dubious), (4) by treaty signifying sale, exchange, gift, and the like, and (5) by accretion, that is, by the gradual building up of territory as in the case of silt being deposited in a delta and the consequent growth of an island,

---

[1] Green Haywood Hackworth, *Digest* II, p. 1.

[2] See definitions in *Black's Law Dictionary* (3d ed.; St. Paul, Minn.: West Publishing Co., 1933), pp. 610, 923.

[3] Oppenheim-Lauterpacht, *Treatise* I, p. 452.

or as in the case of a river boundary's moving slowly one way
or the other.[4]

Discovery Followed by Occupation. In the first of these,
discovery followed by occupation, it is important to note that
discovery alone does not convey title, though it is recognized as
giving "inchoate title," a sort of right to occupy within a reasonable time, but nothing more. Though early practice in this
matter may have been somewhat different, the process of real
importance involves occupation to an extent sufficient to exercise at least a degree of control. This is apparently satisfied in
some instances by periodic displays of sovereignty.[5]

Prescription. The second method, prescription, involves a
situation in which an area formerly discovered and even occupied by one state, has been subsequently abandoned—or the
discovery was not suitably followed by occupation—and another state has undisputedly occupied it for a long period of
time. Under these circumstances the occupying state may be
said to have acquired title by prescription.[6]

Conquest. There can be little doubt that conquest conveys
title to territory. This by all accounts has been true in times
past.[7] It is well known, of course, that most nations are signatories of the Paris Peace Pact[8] which outlaws war, and it might
appear to follow logically that the fruits of war are therefore
illegal. Also some doctrines, such as the Stimson Doctrine, attempted to support the view that conquest should not be recognized.[9] Yet a realistic appraisal of the matter suggests that
however meritorious such positions may be from the standpoint
of abstract justice, prevailing international practice seems to
support the contrary view. The Italian conquest of Ethiopia
and, since World War II, the boundary arrangements estab-

---

[4] Hackworth, *Digest* I, pp. 393–449; Whiteman, *Digest* II, pp. 1028–1173.

[5] Hackworth, *Digest* I, pp. 398–409; Legal Status of Eastern Greenland,
P.C.I.J. Judgments, Orders and Advisory Opinions, 1933, Series A/B, No. 53; also
discussion in *Island of Palmas* case, Tribunal of the Permanent Court of
Arbitration, 1928, U.N., *Reports of International Arbitral Awards* II, 829.

[6] *Island of Palmas Arbitration* case.

[7] *Fleming* v. *Page,* 9 Howard 614 (1850).

[8] *General Treaty for the Renunciation of War* (Kellog-Briand Pact), 1928,
U.S.T.S., No. 796.

[9] See reference in Hackworth, *Digest* I, pp. 334–35.

lished for the U.S.S.R., Poland, and East Germany point in that direction. Professor Brierly, in the opinion of the present writer, put the matter in a realistic political context when he wrote that "international law can no more refuse to recognize that a finally successful conquest does change the title to territory than municipal law can a change of regime brought about by a successful revolution."[10]

Treaty or Cession.   The fourth method, by treaty, is so obvious that it should need little amplification. Much of the territory of the United States has been acquired by treaty and ordinarily there can be no question whatever about the validity of such title. It may indicate sale, trade, or conquest, but formalization is by treaty.[11]

It is perhaps useful to differentiate here between treaties which in fact represent essentially permanent transfers of territory and those which merely formalize transfers which are not fundamentally of lasting quality. A treaty such as that solemnizing the Gadsden Purchase is illustrative of the former while the Treaty of Frankfort ending the Franco-Prussian War and especially its clauses conveying Alsace and Lorraine to Germany was of the latter sort. The real differences, it is important to note, are not in form or word, but rather they pertain to the political essentials. Only transfers by treaty which prove permanent in character are not at variance with the political facts. The momentary aspects of jurisdiction moreover, do not differ between these categories of treaties, but stability does. The former is law in relatively stable form, the latter is law on the raw edge of politics.

Somewhat related to the matter of acquisition by treaty consumating sale is the acquisition of control through lease. In strict law a lease is not a device for acquisition of territory in international law, and in many instances there is little or no resemblance. On the other hand, leases such as those concerning the Panama Canal Zone and the Guantanamo Base have

---

[10] J. L. Brierly, *The Law of Nations* (5th ed.; Oxford: The Clarendon Press, 1955) ; pp. 156–57, see also J. L. Brierly, *The Law of Nations* (6th ed. by Sir Humphrey Waldock; New York: Oxford University Press, Inc., 1963) , pp. 172–73.

[11] *Island of Palmas Arbitration* case. See discussion of treaties, below, Chapter Six.

much in common with acquisition of territory. Bearing in mind that ultimate sovereignty is not transferred by lease, sometimes nevertheless, virtually complete control is vested in the lessee.[12]

Accretion.   Finally the acquisition or loss of territory by accretion remains to be mentioned. The problem here involves the gradual increase of territory through erosive processes. Thus islets formed at the mouth of the Mississsippi River by the process of that river's depositing silt are considered to be a part of the territory of the United States.[13] Also, where a boundary river gradually moves its channel by a slow erosive process, the boundary changes with the river with consequent loss of territory on one side and gain on the other. Should the river move violently, however, as in flood time, and jump into a new channel, the change is called *avulsion* and the boundary remains in the old channel.[14]

Once title is established, the general rule follows that a state has jurisdiction or control over all persons and events within that territory. This includes the subsoil beneath it, the airspace above it, and the marginal sea around it. There are, however, a few exceptions which will be considered subsequently.

BOUNDARIES AND RELATED MATTERS PERTAINING TO JURISDICTION

Since the area within a state's territory is almost wholly subject to its jurisdiction, the crucial issue may often be in terms of fixing the exact location of the boundary. The ques-

---

[12] *United States* v. *Spelar,* 338 U.S. 217 (1949). Whiteman, *Digest* II, p. 1216 ff. The recent North Borneo question involving the Philippines and Malaysia is an interesting controversy in which the character of a lease is a significant factor. See H. B. Jacobini, "Fundamentals of Philippine Policy toward Malaysia," *Asian Survey,* Vol. IV (November, 1964), pp. 1144–51; also Pacifico A. Ortiz, "Legal Aspects of the North Borneo Question," *Philippine Studies,* Vol. XI (January, 1963), pp. 18–64 (This article together with some documentary correspondence appears as a Philippine government "white paper.") ; Pacifico A. Ortiz, *Legal Aspects of the North Borneo Question* (Manila: Bureau of Printing, 1963) ; also Martin Meadows, "The Philippine Claim to North Borneo," *Political Science Quarterly,* Vol. LXXVII (September, 1962), pp. 321–35.

[13] *The Anna,* G. B., High Court of Admiralty, 5 C. Rob. 373 (1805).

[14] *Kansas* v. *Missouri,* 322 U.S. 213 (1944).

tion here is where does the jurisdiction of one state stop and that of another begin? In the words of one publicist, "Boundaries of State territory are the imaginary lines on the surface of the earth which separate the territory of one State from that of another, or from unappropriated territory, or from open sea."[15] It should be noted that some related topics will also be taken up here. These have to do with jurisdictional problems but are not altogether boundary matters.

Land Boundaries

Border lines on land between states fall into a number of categories. Often, however, they are truly imaginary lines which, because of the territory through which they run, may merely separate one unknown border region from another of like character. When such regions become important, problems of jurisdiction often arise. It is well to realize that these disputes like any others are subject to various kinds of settlement. Arbitration, adjudication, negotiated agreement, and the use of force have all been employed.

Maps and Reference Points. Often maps are used to designate boundaries but, of course, if the maps are not accurate obvious difficulties can arise.[16] Similarly, treaties frequently locate borders in terms of certain known or allegedly known locations. When these reference points prove to be inaccurate, obscure, or nonexistent, further complications result. Thus, in a classic case concerning the U.S.–Canadian boundary, a St. Croix River is mentioned which did not exist in that region.[17] Under circumstances where geographic designations and maps are clear, and particularly where treaty designations and pertinent maps clearly corroborate each other, these imaginary lines can be quite adequate. Where inaccuracies and divergencies occur, however, great confusion and difficulty may result. In

---

[15] Oppenheim-Lauterpacht, *Treatise* I, p. 531.

[16] Charles Cheney Hyde, *International Law Chiefly as Interpreted and Applied by the United States* (2d ed.; Boston: Little, Brown & Co., 1945), Vol. I, pp. 492–97. On boundaries generally, see also Whiteman, *Digest* II, *passim.*

[17] Hyde, *op. cit.*, p. 493, fn. 2; John Bassett Moore (ed.), *International Adjudications* (6 vols.; New York: Oxford University Press, Inc., 1929–33), Vols. I, II, decision in Vol. II, p. 373.

times past maps were ordinarily of only secondary importance, but it now appears that their significance has increased.

In the recent *Preah Vihear Temple* case the International Court of Justice relied very heavily upon map evidence in determining a particular segment of the Thai-Cambodian border. The dissenting judges, on the other hand, felt that the maps were given greater significance than was warranted.[18]

Uti Possidetis Juris. In areas which formerly had colonial status, a boundary between sovereign states which were formerly colonies may sometimes be determined by reference to the former colonial boundaries. This has been particularly important in Latin America, and the principle is termed *uti possidetis juris.* Thus, the border between adjacent states can be determined by merely using the old colonial boundary lines. Needless to say, where these lines were themselves obscure, or where differences have arisen as to whether a particular colonial boundary was *de facto* or *de jure,* problems obtain.[19]

Uti Possidetis. In some instances use has been made of the concept of *uti possidetis,* as contrasted with *uti possidetis juris,* to designate a boundary at that point where a *de facto* colonial boundary line existed in terms of effective control. This too is particularly a Latin-American usage.[20]

Natural Boundaries

It is often a much more simple matter if a given boundary is determined with reference to natural barriers. Thus, a range of mountains or hills, a river, a strait, or some other natural line

---

[18] *Case Concerning the Temple of Preah Vihear (Cambodia v. Thailand),* Merits, I.C.J. Reports (1962), p. 6; see also in *American Journal of International Law,* Vol. LVI (October, 1962), p. 1033. For an excellent discussion of the role of maps and the difficulties attending their use, see Guenter Weissberg, "Maps as Evidence in International Boundary Disputes: A Reappraisal," *American Journal of International Law,* Vol. LVII (October, 1963), pp. 781–803. See also *Minquiers and Ecrehos* case *(France v. United Kingdom),* I.C.J. Reports (1953), p. 47, digested in *American Journal of International Law,* Vol. XLVIII (April, 1954), p. 316. Also *Case Concerning Sovereignty over Certain Frontier Lands (Belgium v. Netherlands),* I.C.J. Reports (1959), p. 209, digested in *American Journal of International Law,* Vol. LIII (October, 1959), p. 937.

[19] Hyde, *op. cit.,* pp. 498–510; Hackworth, *Digest* I, pp. 733–45.

[20] Hackworth, *Digest* I, pp. 739–45.

may be relatively free from ambiguity. Yet here too there are difficulties.

Mountains. Mountains or hills sometimes form boundaries between nations. The correct rule seems to be that "where a boundary follows mountains or hills, the water divide constitutes the frontier."[21] It should be noted, however, that exceptions may be specified by treaty and that "it is quite possible for boundary mountains to belong wholly to one of the States which they separate."[22]

Rivers. Where the boundary line is formed by a river, the basic principle is that of the *thalweg* which, simply stated, means that the center of the main channel is the boundary. As noted above, insofar as the center of the main channel may move slowly and gradually (called accretion) the boundary changes with it, but a radical jump of the river from one channel into a new river bed (called avulsion) leaves the boundary where it was.[23]

Aside from simple boundary questions, other related jurisdictional problems may arise regarding rivers. In general these apply to the questions of whether or not a river is open to navigation by foreign states. The general rule which applies, however, is that in the absence of conventional law to the contrary, all rivers are completely subject to the jurisdiction of the riparian state. Thus, rivers wholly within one state, such as the Mississippi, called *national rivers,* are completely under the jurisdiction of the state in which they are located and there is no obligation to open them up to other states. Rivers which form boundaries, called *boundary rivers,* are jointly owned by the two riparian states—each state possessing that portion on its side of the boundary line. Where a river runs through two or more states, called *not-national* or *multinational rivers* by Oppenheim, the same principle usually applies, though this has not always been the case. Thus, if a river passes through two states, each ordinarily has complete control over that portion within its own boundaries. There are, however, a great many

---

[21] Moore, *Digest* I, p. 616.

[22] Oppenheim-Lauterpacht, *Treatise* I, p. 534.

[23] *Kansas* v. *Missouri.*

rivers which have been internationalized by treaty. These obviously present exceptions and are called *international rivers*.[24]

There is evidence that international attitudes regarding rivers are undergoing changes and they are being considered for some purposes as international river systems. Whether this has effected any meaningful changes in the law regarding navigation as of this writing (1967) is doubtful.[25] It is probably still correct as Professor de Visscher notes, that "international river law remained very largely a particular law,"[26] *i.e.,* insofar as treaty law differs from the discription above, it is on the basis of each river's special regime.

Beyond the questions of boundaries and navigation there are still other fluvial aspects which have legal ramifications. The increasingly pressing problem of division of water use is one such aspect which, however, is illustrative of a general problem area. It appears correct to say that where rivers or other bodies of water have a natural flow through two or more states, each has both a right to certain use of the water and a duty to refrain from use to the material detriment of the other riparians.[27]

Bridges. A boundary problem which is closely related to

---

[24] Oppenheim-Lauterpacht, *Treatise* I, pp. 463–76; *The Faber* case, in German-Venezuelan Mixed Claims Commission, 1903, J. R. Ralston and W. T. S. Doyle, *Venezulan Arbitrations of 1903*, Senate Doc. 316, 58th Cong., 2d sess. (Washington, D.C.: U.S. Government Printing Office, 1904), pp. 600–630. C. J. Colombos, *The International Law of the Sea* (4th rev, ed.; London: Longmans, Green, & Co., Inc., 1959), pp. 193–220.

[25] Whiteman, *Digest* III, pp. 872–929. International Law Association, *Report of the Fiftieth Conference* (Brussels, 1962), p. 451. F. J. Berber, *Rivers in International Law* (London: Stevens & Sons, Ltd., 1959), pp. V–VI, *passim*.

[26] Charles de Visscher, *Theory and Reality in Public International Law,* trans. P. E. Corbett (Princeton, N.J.: Princeton University Press, 1957), pp. 207–10, quotation on p. 207.

[27] See discussion and examples in Whiteman, *Digest* III, pp. 919–1075. *Lake Lanoux* case *(France* v. *Spain)*, Arbitral Tribunal (1957), digested in *American Journal of International Law*, Vol. LIII (January, 1959), p. 156. *Nebraska* v. *Wyoming*, 325 U.S. 589 (1945). See also Berber, *op. cit.;* William L. Griffin, "The Use of Waters of International Drainage Basins under Customary International Law," *American Journal of International Law,* Vol. LIII (January, 1959), pp. 50–80; John G. Laylin and Rinalde L. Bianchi, "The Role of Adjudication in International River Disputes," *American Journal of International Law,* Vol. LIII (January, 1959), pp. 30–49; also A. P. Lester, "River Polution in International Law," *American Journal of International Law,* Vol. LVII (October, 1963), pp. 828–53. For discussion of the rights and duties of states, see above, Chapter Four; for discussion of remedies, see below, Chapter Eight.

that of rivers concerns international bridges. Strict logic would seem to decree that gradual changes in the boundary due to accretion would be reflected in the boundary line on the bridge above the river, yet the practical disadvantages of such a situation are manifest. General practice seems to suggest that the boundary is usually located by treaty at the middle of the bridge,[28] and one publicist categorically states that the middle line is the boundary on international bridges.[29] By contrast, however, there are a number of instances where the boundary on a bridge was located above the center of the channel, but that once fixed, it is not to be affected by changes in the river. An example of this is seen in the boundary arrangement between the United States and Mexico.[30]

Lakes. Another closely related matter concerns the status of lakes or inland seas which are located on an international boundary. Lakes or inland seas wholly within the borders of a single state present no problem, of course, for they are obviously a part of the national territory. Thus, the Great Salt Lake in the United States, Lake Como in Italy, and Lake Taal in the Philippines are wholly under the sovereignty of their respective states. Lakes which form international boundaries, however, such as Lake Constance between Switzerland, Austria and Germany and several of the Great Lakes between the United States and Canada present a very different problem. It appears, however, that despite a few notes of dissent, prevailing practice which is generally written into treaties, places the boundary in the middle of the body of water, or splits jurisdiction according to some other more or less equitable pattern.[31]

While in most instances inland seas which have navigable access to the high seas are open to international traffic, it appears that this is entirely a matter of treaty concession wherever it exists. One exception to the rule of riparian sovereignty,

---

[28] Hyde, *op. cit.*, p. 450; Charles G. Fenwick, *International Law* (3d ed.; New York: Appleton-Century-Crofts, Inc., 1948), p. 374.

[29] Daniel Antokoletz, *Derecho international publico* (Buenos Aires: Bernabe y Cia, 1944), Vol. II, p. 538.

[30] Hyde, *op. cit.*, p. 450; Fenwick, *op. cit.*, p. 374.

[31] Oppenheim-Lauterpacht, *Treatise* I, pp. 476–79.

however, is the case of the Black Sea which is considered to be a part of the high seas.[32]

Territorial Sea. Every state which borders on an open sea or ocean, that is, one to which the principle of freedom of the seas applies, has a contiguous strip of that marine body over which it exercises sovereignty. This strip of water is known as the territorial sea, the maritime boundary, or the marginal sea. The extent or width of this strip of ocean is not altogether clear, but it may be said that 3 nautical miles has been quite widely applied. There are major exceptions, however, a 4-mile limit being recognized in Scandinavia, and other claims by some countries to 6-, 9-, 12-, and even 18-mile limits are of fairly long standing.[33] There has never been a clear consensus, but there are more states which adhere to the principle of the 3-mile limit than adhere to any other proposed limit though the 3-mile adherents represent less than half of the nations of the world. Nevertheless, the U.N. International Law Commission in 1956 could agree on only the very indefinitive statement which follows:

1. The Commission recognizes that international practice is not uniform as regards the delimitation of the territorial sea.

2. The Commission considers that international law does not permit an extension of the territorial sea beyond twelve miles.

3. The Commission, without taking any decision as to the breadth of the territorial sea within that limit notes, on the one hand, that many States have fixed a breadth greater than three miles, and on the other hand, that many States do not recognize such a breadth when that of their own territorial sea is less.

4. The Commission considers that the breadth of the territorial sea should be fixed by an international conference.[34]

Moreover, the Geneva Convention on the Territorial Sea and The Contiguous Zone[35] avoids any specific designation of the extent of the territorial sea.

---

[32] *Ibid.;* Hyde, *op. cit.,* pp. 482–84.

[33] See Hackworth, *Digest* I, pp. 628–29 *et passim;* B. A. Brittin, "Article 3, Regime of the Territorial Sea," *American Journal of International Law,* Vol. L (October, 1956) , pp. 934–41. See Whiteman, *Digest* IV, pp. 1–207.

[34] Brittin, *op. cit.,* pp. 939–40.

[35] See text in *American Journal of International Law,* Vol. LII (October,

Whatever may be the extent of the territorial sea, the coastal state is entitled to exercise jurisdiction in that area subject only to a number of servitudes, *i.e.,* limitations on sovereignty in favor of other states, which will be discussed later in this chapter. It should be noted that there is some dispute as to whether a state exercises sovereignty in its territorial waters subject to certain servitudes such as the right of innocent passage by merchant ships, or, on the other hand, whether the state's jurisdiction represents an aggregate of rights and influences entailing control of somewhat less-comprehensive scope than is embraced in the concept of sovereignty. Leading authorities would seem to support the former view; moreover the pertinent 1958 Geneva agreement uses the term "sovereignty."[36] It should also be noted, perhaps, that a distinction is sometimes made between territorial waters and national waters. What this means is not exactly certain except that the latter are even more closely approximated to the territory of the state than are the former, and that while a right of innocent passage pertains to the territorial waters, no such right applies to national waters. Thus, the inland waterways of the United States and the ports themselves would ordinarily be considered as national waters.[37]

The factors which have influenced the various claims to territorial seas in recent times are geared fairly closely to the security and economic interests of the riparian states.[38] There is steady and apparently increasing pressure to extend the territorial sea to 12 miles, but at the present writing the matter remains unresolved. It may be pointed out, however, that a concensus of important states can, for reasons outlined at var-

1958), pp. 834–42 Official Documents (hereafter cited as *Geneva Terr. Sea Accord*). For commentary on the conference see A. H. Dean, "The Geneva Conference on the Law of the Sea; What Was Accomplished," *American Journal of International Law,* Vol. LII (October, 1958), pp. 607–28.

[36] Hyde, *op. cit.,* pp. 515–19; Oppenheim-Lauterpacht, *Treatise* I, pp. 493–95; Colombos, *op. cit.,* p. 74, Fenwick, *op. cit.,* p. 376; *Geneva Terr. Sea Accord,* Art. I. Whiteman, *Digest* IV, pp. 1–13.

[37] Colombos, *op. cit.,* pp. 74–75, *Geneva Terr. Sea Accord,* Art. 5.

[38] A. P. Daggett, "The Regulation of Maritime Fisheries by Treaty," *American Journal of International Law,* Vol. XXVIII (October, 1934), pp. 693–717. For brief reference to pending fishing agreements involving the United States, the U.S.S.R., and other states, see "Contemporary Practice of the United States Relating to International Law," *American Journal of International Law,* Vol. LXI (April, 1967), pp. 796–98.

ious places in this volume, influence the ultimate pattern of usage and law.

Extensions beyond the Territorial Sea

Closely related, yet in many respects different from the question of the territorial sea are a number of matters having to do with extensions of sovereignty, jurisdiction, or a lesser extent of control of maritime areas heretofore outside the territorial bailiwick. At various times nations have for one reason or another attempted to extend their jurisdiction to what may be termed "other extended coastal areas." Some of these extensions have been accorded a degree of recognition while others seem to have been rather completely discouraged.

Subsoil Adjacent to the Coast. There seems to be no doubt that nations may extend sovereignty to land areas appurtenant to their coasts. Thus, if a mine tunnel should extend for several miles beyond the coastal waters, there is every reason to believe that it would involve an entirely proper extension of national jurisdiction.[39]

Customs Jurisdiction Areas and Related Matters: "The Contiguous Zone." At various times nations have extended their police jurisdiction beyond the scope of the territorial sea. The United States attempted to do so during the prohibition era in order to enforce the prohibition laws. Somewhat similar attempts were made to neutralize the western hemisphere during the early part of World War II. Such attempted extensions have almost always been opposed as unwarranted interferences with the principle of freedom of the seas. Nevertheless, some of these have been agreed upon on a bilateral treaty basis as in the U.S.-British agreement that British ships could be investigated if within 1 hour's distance of the coast.[40] On the other hand the

---

[39] Colombos, *op. cit.,* p. 75; Oppenheim-Lauterpacht, *Treatise* I, pp. 629–31; see also *Convention on the Continental Shelf,* Art. 7 in *American Journal of International Law,* Vol. LII (October, 1958), p. 860. Whiteman, *Digest* IV, pp. 918–20.

[40] Hyde, *op. cit.,* pp. 461–63; Hackworth, *Digest* I, pp. 663–90; Whiteman, *Digest* IV, pp. 480–98.

19th-century Russian claims to "100 Italian miles" of territorial sea were never recognized.[41]

In the 1958 territorial sea convention a contiguous zone was formally provided for. The total extent of territorial sea and contiguous zone was specified as being not more than 12 miles.[42] In the contiguous zone the coastal state is allowed to "exercise the control necessary to":

a) Prevent infringement of its customs, fiscal, immigration or sanitary regulations within its territory or territorial sea;
b) Punish infringement of the above regulations committed within its territory or territorial sea.[43]

Continental Shelf and Coastal Fisheries. In a somewhat different vein claims have been made, beginning for most practical purposes,[44] with those of the United States in 1945, to what is known as the continental shelf. These claims state in substance that the land under the sea which extends out as a natural appurtenance of the land is under national jurisdiction for purposes of mineral and other exploitation. As this concept is usually conceived, it does not lay claim to sovereignty over the sea or airspace above the continental shelf, and there is the frequent stipulation that when the shelf is more than 200 meters (600 feet) below the surface of the ocean, it ceases to be claimed. Since there has been no dispute about the reasonableness of these claims, it may be said that if a rule of law has not yet been crystallized, it is, *de lege ferende,* in the process of being formed. Moreover, the continental shelf has recently become the subject of an international accord. That agreement recognizes exclusive sovereign rights to a continental shelf to a depth of 200 meters and possibly even more.[45] At the same time

---

[41] Hyde, *op. cit.,* p. 456.

[42] *Geneva Terr. Sea Accord,* Art. 24 (2) .

[43] *Ibid.,* Art. 24 (1) .

[44] Claims of this sort appear to have actually begun with a Portuguese decree in 1910; see M. Mouton, *The Continental Shelf* (The Hague: Martinus Nijhoff, 1952) , p. 61.

[45] *Convention on the Continental Shelf,* Art. 12; see also M. M. Whiteman, "Conference on the Law of the Sea: Convention on the Continental Shelf," *American Journal of International Law,* Vol. LII (October, 1958) , pp. 629–59. On the general topic see also Whiteman, *Digest* IV, pp. 740–931. Mouton, *op. cit.;*

it is specified that the coastal state does not possess sovereignty over the superjacent seas and airspace, that it cannot impede navigation or cable laying and use, except for 500 meter areas around installations.[46] Finally, it specifies that where a "shelf is adjacent to the territory of two or more states," the boundary is to be established by agreement or by a line equidistant from each state.[47]

At the same time that the United States put forth its view on the continental shelf, it also claimed the right to set up conservation zones for protection of fisheries used solely by the United States or to enter into conservation agreements with nations with which it shared fishing activities in other areas. This, like the shelf proclamation, seems to have elicited no opposition.

In 1958, the Geneva Conference on the Law of the Sea adopted a fishing and conservation convention which attempts to provide for the interests of all fishing states concerned. It provides that subject to certain other restrictions all states have fishing rights on the high seas, but at the same time they have the obligation to cooperate in conservation measures.[48] Where nationals of two or more states have conflicting interests they are to cooperate in conservation measures, but if no agreements are forthcoming, the convention provides for obligatory settlement.[49] The interests of coastal states are given a degree of primacy, however, and pending settlement of disputes, they may make unilateral conservation measures about which, however, the following requirements exist:

    a) That there is a need for urgent application of conservation measures in the light of the existing knowledge of the fishery;

    b) That the measures adopted are based on appropriate scientific findings;

---

for a discussion of this matter in relation to sources of oil, see Richard Young, "Offshore Claims and Problems in the North Sea," *American Journal of International Law*, Vol. LIX (July, 1965), pp. 505–22.

[46] *Convention on the Continental Shelf*, Arts. 3, 4, 5.

[47] *Ibid.*, Art. 6.

[48] *Convention on Fishing and Conservation of the Living Resources of the High Seas*, Art. 1; *American Journal of International Law*, Vol. LII (October, 1958), pp. 851–58 (documents section) (hereafter cited as *Fisheries and Conservation Accord*).

[49] *Ibid.*, Arts. 3, 4, 5, 9, 10, 11, 12.

  c) That such measures do not discriminate in form or in fact against foreign fisherman.[50]

Such measures are subject to obligatory settlement, but may be temporarily instituted.[51] It may be mentioned, finally, that fisheries where equipment is embedded in the sea floor are to be open to nationals or nonnationals of the state having such equipment except where there may be exclusive prescriptive rights.[52]

  Closely related to what is properly the shelf theory and to the U.S. coastal fisheries proclamation are a number of claims which go well beyond those described above. Several states have laid claim to sovereignty over expanses not only of the bed of the sea, subsoil adjacent to the coasts and to national fisheries, but to the sea itself and to the airspace over it for distances ranging up to 200 miles from the coast. These claims have been disputed on various grounds, and the United States itself has protested that they are very different from its own continental shelf and fisheries position. It is also argued that on the theoretical level the sea is *res communis* rather than *res nullius* and therefore not subject to appropriation to an extent which would interfere with the principle of freedom of the seas.[53] It is of course a matter of some dispute as to which of these two concepts most correctly describes the status of the high seas, but it is consistent with principles described elsewhere in this volume to suggest that regardless of the solution of that matter, a sufficient support for the extreme views would eventually validate them while sufficient opposition would push them back within a consensus of acceptability.[54] The student is invited to watch these developments from the standpoint of the political

---

[50] *Ibid.*, Arts. 7, 8; [quotation Art. 7 (2)].

[51] *Ibid.*, Arts. 7 (3, 4) , 9.

[52] *Ibid.*, Art. 13.

[53] See discussions in *Proceedings of the American Society of International Law* (1956) , pp. 116–54; Josef L. Kunz, "Continental Shelf and International Law: Confusion and Abuse," *American Journal of International Law*, Vol. L (October, 1956) , pp. 828–53.

[54] See comment, this chapter, fn. 90 regarding the status of the high seas; see comment in *New York Times*, July 29, 1956, p. 22, where it is reported that Peru plans to modify its claim which originally called for a 200-mile belt of marginal sea.

processes which go into the development of a rule. The two
Geneva accords cited above point toward final developments in
these areas.

Bays and Gulfs. Boundary lines are often simple enough to
define when they are clearly established natural limits, yet even
under these circumstances difficulties sometimes arise. There
are many instances in which there is considerable difficulty in
specifying when and under what circumstances certain partially inclosed bodies of water can justifiably be considered as
territorial or national in character. A related issue has to do
with the method of measuring the territorial sea from the
mouth of a bay or gulf. Traditionally there has been perhaps
only one rule that could be called an absolute in this matter
and that was that if the distance between the headlands of a
bay or gulf which is otherwise flanked on all sides by the same
state is no greater than 6 miles, the whole bay might be confi-
dently classed as national or territorial. Beyond that there have
been several partially applicable guides. It has been fairly
widely recognized—usually by treaty—that the distance of 10
miles rather than 6 was adequate to justify the claim of territoriality for a body of water. This view was recommended by the
arbitral tribunal in the *North Atlantic Fisheries* case.[55] The
1958 Geneva Accord on the Territorial Sea has changed this
uncertainty for those states which may accede to its terms. In
this connection it specifies:

> If the distance between the low-water marks of the natural
> entrance points of a bay does not exceed twenty-four miles, a closing
> line may be drawn between these two low-water marks, and the
> waters enclosed thereby shall be considered as internal waters.[56]

Also, there are a number of inlets of this sort, the so-called
historic bays, where it appears to be proper to hold that a
prescriptive right obtains by which such bays or gulfs with
mouths of 10 miles or more are to be classed as territorial.[57]
Examples of this have traditionally included Delaware and

---

[55] *North Atlantic Coast Fisheries* case, *Permanent Court of Arbitration,* 1910;
Scott, *The Hague Court Reports,* p. 146.

[56] *Geneva Terr. Sea Accord,* Art. 7 (4).

[57] *Fisheries* case, *(United Kingdom* v. *Norway)* I.C.J. Reports, (1951), p. 116.
See in *American Journal of International Law,* Vol. LII (October, 1958), p. 348.

Chesapeake bays in the United States with headland distances of 10 and 12 miles respectively, and Varanger Fjord in Norway with a headland to headland distance of over 30 miles.[58] This seems to leave the matter largely to whatever claims a state can make good from the standpoints of rational and prescriptive arguments.

Where bays are classed as national or territorial, the extent of the territorial sea is to be figured by drawing a line from headland to headland at an appropriate point—frequently where the distance is 10 miles—and the extent of the sea is to be considered as being 3 miles (where that distance is proper) seaward from that point.

One additional point remains to be mentioned, that being the determination of the boundary in a bay when it forms a division between two states. In such instances the principle of the *thalweg* ordinarily applies and as a consequence the boundary is usually the center of the main channel.[59]

Straits. A strait is a narrow natural passageway connecting two bodies of water and, in the words of one commentator, " (t) here are straits and straits."[60] Where they form the entrance to bays or gulfs properly within the exclusive jurisdiction of one state, the headland theory detailed above is obviously applicable. Similarly, where a strait forms the entrance to a gulf which is bordered by two states and where the passageway cannot be said to form an important avenue of commerce, it may sometimes be claimed as territorial, with the boundary—where that is appropriate—being determined by the *thalweg* principle.[61]

---

[58] Colombos, *op. cit.* pp. 152–64; *Varanger Fjord* case, Norwegian Supreme Court, 1934, reported in Lauterpacht's *Annual Digest and Reports of Public International Law Cases,* 1933–1934, Case No. 51; see also *Geneva Terr. Sea Accord,* Art. 7 (6) .

[59] Hackworth, *Digest* I, pp. 697–98.

[60] Hyde, *op. cit.,* p. 487.

[61] *Ibid.,* p. 489. It should be noted, however, that Art. 12 of the *Geneva Terr. Sea Accord* specifies that "Where the coasts of two states are opposite or adjacent to each other, neither of the two states is entitled, failing agreement between them to the contrary, to extend its territorial sea beyond the median line every point of which is equidistant from the nearest points on the base-lines from which the breadth of the territorial seas of each of the two states is measured. The provisions of this paragraph shall not apply, however, where it is necessary by reason of historic title or other special circumstances to delimit the territorial seas of the two states in a way which is at variance with this provision.

The line of delimitation between the territorial seas of two states lying

A problem of very different character exists when the strait forms an important avenue of commerce and connects important bodies of water. Although it may often be considered as part of the territorial waters of the riparian state if it is only about 6 miles in width, nevertheless a clear right of passage is ordinarily recognized. The committee report on territorial waters of the Hague Conference on the Codification of International Law (1930), though never incorporated into a treaty, is often quoted as expressive of prevailing practice. It states:

> In straits which form a passage between two parts of the high sea, the limits of the territorial sea shall be ascertained in the same manner as on other parts of the coast, even if the same State is the Coastal State of both shores.
> When the width of the straits exceeds the breadth of the two belts of territorial sea, the waters between those two belts form part of the high sea. If the result of this delimitation is to leave an area of high sea not exceeding two miles in breadth surrounded by territorial sea, this area may be assimilated to territorial sea.
>
> .   .   .   .
>
> Under no pretext whatever may the passage even of warships through straits used for international navigation between two parts of the high sea be interfered with.[62]

In conformity with this view it appears that the Straits of Magellan are within Chilean territorial waters yet clearly open to world commerce.[63] In 1949, the International Court of Justice held:

> The North Corfu Channel should be considered as belonging to

---

opposite to each other or adjacent to each other shall be marked on large-scale charts officially recognized by the coastal states."

Recent controversy regarding passage through the Straits of Tiran and the Gulf of Aqaba highlights the problem of determining whether a gulf is territorial in character or essentially a segment of the high seas. For excellent commentary, see Leo Gross, "The Geneva Conference on the Law of the Sea and the Right of Innocent Passage through the Gulf of Aqaba," *American Journal of International Law,* Vol. LIII (January, 1959), pp. 564–94; Charles B. Selak, Jr., "A Consideration of the Legal Status of the Gulf of Aqaba," *American Journal of International Law,* Vol. LII (October, 1958), pp. 660–98.

[62] Quoted in Hackworth, *Digest* I, p. 611.

[63] *Ibid.,* p. 612.

the class of international highways through which passage cannot be prohibited by a coastal State in time of peace.[64]

Finally, the 1958 Geneva Accord on the Territorial Sea specifies:

There shall be no suspension of the innocent passage of foreign ships through straits which are used for international navigation between part of the high seas and another part of the high seas or the territorial sea of a foreign state.[65]

The Bosporus and Dardanelles constitute somewhat of an exception to the general rule. They were originally closed to warships but have gradually undergone transformation. Now they remain the territorial waters of Turkey, but are open to both merchantmen and warships, with the exception that Turkey can make certain regulations and close them entirely to warships if it is a belligerent.[66]

Where a strait is the border between two nations and is wholly within their territorial waters, it appears that the boundary "is governed by substantially the same principles as that of the limits of territorial jurisdiction in and over rivers."[67]

Canals. Canals like straits connect bodies of water. They are considered to be under the complete jurisdiction of the state within whose borders they are located except where treaty arrangements provide otherwise. It appears that the main international canals are the Kiel, Corinth, Suez, and Panama canals, and the St. Lawrence Seaway System. In general all appear to be open to the ships of all nations, but the basis for international transit is somewhat different among them.

The *Kiel Canal* was opened by the terms of the Versailles Treaty to the use of all ships except those of states at war with Germany, and the Permanent Court of International Justice upheld this in 1923.[68] In 1936, however, Germany denounced

---

[64] *The Corfu Channel* case, I.C.J. Reports (1949).

[65] *Geneva Terr. Sea Accord*, Art. 26 (4).

[66] *Convention Regarding the Regime of the Straits*, Montreux, 1936, 173 L.N.T.S. 213.

[67] Moore, *Digest* I, p. 658; see also Hyde, *op. cit.*, p. 489; and Colombos; *op. cit.*, p. 169.

[68] Great Britain *et al.* and Germany: *Case of the S.S. Wimbledon*, P.C.I.J. Reports, Series A, No. 1. (1923). The pertinent articles of the Treaty of

the pertinent section of the treaty with no protest from interested powers. Nevertheless, Germany apparently maintained freedom of transit through the canal, subject to appropriate reciprocity, until World War II began. Since the war, the canal has been open. Accordingly, there has been some doubt about the international legal status of the canal. This uncertainty has not yet been entirely dispelled, and ambiguities remain. On the theory that in wartime treaty rights of this sort are merely suspended, not terminated, there has been a considerable presumption that the obligatory opening of the canal would obtain.[69]

The *Corinth Canal* has always been wholly within Greek control, but it has been opened by municipal fiat to the use of all nations.[70]

The *Suez Canal* is wholly within Egyptian territory, yet in 1888 it was neutralized by treaty which together with prescriptive considerations would seem to make it obligatory that it be kept open to the use of all nations. Egypt has indicated, moreover, that it will conform to that convention. The use of the Suez Canal by a state which is at war with Egypt is somewhat obscure, however, not only because of Egypt's attitude toward Israeli shipping, but also because of the historical fact that practice in the past seems to have been somewhat at variance with the stipulations of the 1888 convention that the canal would be open to warships of all nations regardless of a state of war.[71]

Versailles are on pp. 380–386. See generally Oppenheim-Lauterpacht, *Treatise I*, pp. 482–83; also pp. 470–71. Whiteman, *Digest* III, pp. 1256–61. Brierly, *op. cit.* (6th ed.) , p. 236.

[69] Whiteman, *Digest* III, pp. 1256–61. *Kiel Canal Collision* case, Germany (British Zone) , Supreme Court, 1950. I.L. Reports, 1950, pp. 133–35. In this rather ambiguous case, the Court stated in *dicta* that it "seems doubtful" that the Canal is still internationalized. Nevertheless, it went on to discuss jurisdiction, rates and related matters in the light of the Versailles articles.

[70] Colombos, *op. cit.*, p. 192.

[71] *Constantinople Convention*, October 29, 1888, Art. 4; also *Anglo-Egyptian Agreement Suez Canal Base*, October 19, 1954 [these may be seen conveniently in the *Suez Canal Problem* (1956) U.S. Department of State Publication 6392, pp. 16–23]; see H. J. Schonfield, *The Suez Canal in World Affairs* (New York: Philosophical Library, 1953) , pp. 110–11 *et passim;* see Egypt's *Declaration on the Suez Canal*, April 24, 1957 reprinted in *American Journal of International Law*, Vol. LI (July, 1957) , pp. 673–75.

The *Panama Canal* is located on a strip of territory which the United States controls under the terms of a perpetual lease from Panama. Panama appears to retain sovereignty, though the United States is to exercise the powers that it would exercise "if it were the sovereign"; and the ships of all nations are free on an equal basis to use the waterway except that in time of war the United States may provide for its defense. This last guarantee is based on the provisions of a treaty with Great Britain.[72]

The *St. Lawrence Seaway,* which runs over 2,300 miles from the Gulf of St. Lawrence through the Great Lakes, is one of the world's greatest inland waterways systems. It is operated under a cooperative regime between the United States and Canada which allows ships of other nations to navigate its waters. Such navigation operates as a matter of privilege, however, and not as an international obligation.[73]

Subsoil, Superjacent Areas, and the Poles

In considering the matter of territorial boundaries and jurisdiction notice must also be taken of third dimensional factors. Thus jurisdiction does not function only on a plane, but also beneath the surface of land and in areas superjacent to the land. The ancient principle of private property ownership, *cuius est solum ejus est usque ad coelum et ad inferos,* expresses this principle fairly well except, of course, that it is excessive. That jurisdiction extends beneath the surface does not automatically mean that it extends to any definitely prescribed point, nor can it be held that superjacent areas are held "up to the heavens." Jurisdiction in these areas or elsewhere is related to effective control. There has never been any doubt, however,

---

[72] *Hay-Pauncefote Treaty, U.S. Statutes at Large,* 57th Cong., Vol. 32, Part II, pp. 1903–5; *Hay-Varilla Treaty, U.S. Statutes at Large,* 58th Cong., Vol. 33, Part II, pp. 2234–41; (U.S.T.S. No. 431).

At the time of the revision of this text (1967), it is reported that agreement affecting the Panama Canal has been reached by the United States and Panama. A new treaty not yet in force, appears to recognize Panamanian sovereignity somewhat more effectively than have past arrangements, and it provides for joint control of the Canal itself. See John W. Fenney, "U.S. and Panama Agree on New Canal Treaty," *New York Times,* June 27, 1967, pp. 1, 2.

[73] Whiteman, *Digest* III, pp. 909–18.

that states have, as a practical matter, complete and exclusive sovereignty over their subsoil.[74] Also, as noted above, these subsoil rights may extend beyond the limits of the territorial sea.

Airspace. In the other direction it is a clear and universally accepted maxim of international law that "every Power has complete and exclusive sovereignty over the airspace above its territory."[75] Unlike the question of sovereignty over the subsoil which is so obvious that it scarcely merits mention, the question of whether a state has sovereignty over its airspace was of little practical concern until the present century, but it was in fact much debated by scholars until about the time of World War I. Just before and during that war nations laid claim to their superjacent airspace and attempted to secure it by force where necessary. After the war the principle was written into a number of treaties and is now a firmly accepted rule.[76] It may be noted also that this is one of the best examples of the process by which political forces and eventually custom participate in the formulation of a rule with ultimate culmination in treaty form. Although the principle of airspace sovereignty includes the right to prevent passage of aircraft and presumably even radio waves through the superjacent airspace, treaties have been drawn up among the nations of the world which regulate the circumstances of air traffic and radio.

The two principal air navigation agreements following World War I were the Paris Agreement of 1919 and the Habana Agreement of 1928.[77] In 1944 these were abandoned in

---

[74] Hyde, *op. cit.*, p. 439; *Geneva Terr. Sea Accord*, Art. 2.

[75] *Convention on International Civil Aviation*, Chicago, 1944, U.S. Department of State, Conference Series 64 (Washington, D.C.: U.S. Government Printing Office, 1944), Art. I. It should be added that this includes the airspace over the territorial sea: *Geneva Terr. Sea Accord*, Art. 2.

[76] See Hackworth, *Digest* IV, pp. 357–69; C. Q. Christol, Jr., "Transit by Air in International Law" (unpublished thesis, University of Chicago, 1941); J. M. Spaight, *Air Power and War Rights* (3d ed.; London: Longmans, Green & Co., Inc., 1947), pp. 420–23 *et passim;* H. B. Jacobini, "International Aviation Law, A Theoretical and Historical Survey," *Journal of Public Law*, Vol. 2 (Fall, 1953), pp. 314–32. Whiteman, *Digest* II, pp. 1270–85.

[77] *International Convention Relating to the Regulation of Aerial Navigation*, October, 1919; Convention on Commercial Aviation, Habana, 1928, U.S. Treaty Series No. 840.

favor of the Chicago Convention,[78] and under its auspices a number of technical matters have been advanced, particularly through the International Civil Aviation Organization. The Convention of 1944 provides for the national sovereignty theory but allows nonscheduled aircraft to cross the borders and provides machinery for facilitating scheduled air traffic and for protecting certain interests of the states through which the aircraft are flying. Provision is made for such matters as aircraft nationality and registration, use of aircraft papers, documents, and safety devices. A special arrangement called the Air Services Transit Agreement, adhered to by most states, allows scheduled craft to fly across the territory of all of the signatories without landing and grants the privilege to land for nontraffic purposes. Additional bilateral agreements provide broadly that scheduled craft may discharge and take on passengers and cargo.[79]

Finally, it should be mentioned that the Chicago Convention provides for creation of the International Civil Aviation Organization (ICAO) now a technical organization under the United Nations, which is designed to facilitate the development of civil aviation in a variety of ways.[80]

This organization and the law that surrounds it are moderately good examples of the concept of "administrative or technical international law." They are concerned with structuring international flying regulations which are in line with modern technology and the focus is essentially nonpolitical. While Western states see it in that context, the U.S.S.R. has never become affiliated which in itself suggests the relative character of the concept of the nonpolitical.

While the national sovereignty principle applied to airspace pertains to the passage of radio waves as much as to aircraft transit, less of a practical threat to sovereignty is involved and a greater problem of control exists. The chief practical problems center upon allocation of frequencies and the use of radio and telegraphic facilities for humanitarian purposes in time of

---

[78] *Convention on International Civil Aviation*, Chicago, 1944, *op. cit,*

[79] Jacobini, *op. cit.*, pp. 326–27.

[80] *Convention on International Civil Aviation*, Part II.

emergency. These matters have been provided for in a number of multilateral treaties, and by an international organization now within the United Nations, the Universal Telecommunications Union (ITU).[81]

Space. Closely related to the matter of airspace jurisdiction, is the question of jurisdiction over those areas of space beyond airspace. This is an issue which has arisen only since World War II and which remains the subject of some academic dispute. A number of writers have made suggestions that national jurisdiction be limited at varying distances from the earth. These include 40 to 60 miles up, about 135 to 190 miles up, 300 miles up, and the highest point where the strongest states can control their superjacent space. All are agreed, however, that some formal limit must eventually be established.[82]

It is, of course, possible to limit jurisdiction by treaty at any point which seems suitable to the contracting states, and this will undoubtedly come about eventually. It may be conjectured that the line will ultimately be drawn with security considerations foremost in mind. If this is a sound assumption, it is likely that the space boundary can be established specifically at a place short of the farthest point of effective control only to the extent deemed consistent with national security.[83] The consistency of this view with a political conception of law should be apparent.

While it is clear that a considerable ferment has taken place

---

[81] See survey in Hackworth, *Digest* IV, pp. 274–323; *International Telecommunications Convention*, Atlantic City, 1947, 63 U.S., *Statutes at Large*, Part II, 1399 (Series, 1901) ; the *International Telecommunications Convention*, Buenos Aires, 1952, 6 *U.S.T.S.*, 1213.

[82] See H. B. Jacobini, "Problems of High Altitude or Space Jurisdiction," *The Western Political Quarterly*, Vol. 4 (December, 1953) , pp. 680–88; see papers in *Proceedings of the American Society of International Law* (1956) , pp. 84–115. A number of detailed studies of the problems of space jurisdiction have been published. Among these are M. S. McDougal, H. D. Lasswell, and I. A. Vlasic, *Law and Public Order in Space* (New Haven, Conn.: Yale University Press, 1963) ; C. Q. Christol, *The International Law of Outer Space* (International Law Studies 1962, Vol. LV; Washington, D.C.: U.S. Government Printing Office, 1966) ; P. C. Jessup and H. L. Taubenfeld, *Controls for Outer Space and the Antarctic Analogy* (New York: Columbia University Press, 1959) . For an interesting and useful lead to sources and topics, see also L. Lipson and N. DeB. Katzenbach (Rep.) , *Report to the National Aeronautics and Space Administration on the Law of Outer Space* (Chicago: American Bar Foundation, 1961) .

[83] See H. B. Jacobini, "Effective Control as Related to the Extension of Sovereignty in Space," *Journal of Public Law*, Vol. 7 (Spring, 1958) , pp. 97–119.

in this area, it is not apparent that many precise limitations have crystallized. It is evident—notwithstanding U.N. Committee deliberations—that the boundary between airspace and outer space remains vague.[84] On the other hand, *extra territorium* or outer space itself has become the subject of several important limitations. In 1963, the Test Ban Treaty was signed which proscribes the testing of nuclear weapons in space as well as in the atmosphere and under water.[85] Beyond this important first step, a new agreement—based upon U.N. spadework—was entered into in early 1967. This agreement, *inter alia,* limits outer space to peaceful uses, and bars national appropriation of areas in outer space including celestial bodies.[86]

Once the question of the extent of space subject to national jurisdiction has been determined, additional questions may arise—should technological advancements warrant. It may be expected that these questions will center upon the legal status of *extra territorium* space, that is, that area of space and those bodies in space beyond national jurisdiction—wherever that latter point may be established. It has been widely suggested that some application of the laws governing the high seas may very probably obtain.

Polar Areas. Polar areas present special jurisdictional problems due to the difficulty of occupation. Though there is no dearth of claims in these areas, their exact legal status remains obscure. Perhaps the most widely accepted theory for the northern areas at least is the so-called *sector theory* which specifies in substance that the north polar land areas are to be considered as a part of the countries which, so to speak, front on the north pole. Thus a sector of any country concerned would include "all of the area between a base line connecting the meridians of longitude marking the limits of its easterly and westerly frontiers and extending as far north as the final intersection of those meridians at the North Pole,"[87] presumably exclusive of such

---

[84] Whiteman, *Digest* II, pp. 1285–1321, 1281–85.

[85] U.S., T.I.A.S. 5433; Whiteman, *Digest* II, pp. 1320–21.

[86] See "Treaty on Principles Governing the Activities of States in the Exploration and Use of Outer Space, Including the Moon and Other Celestial Bodies" in *American Journal of International Law,* Vol. LXI (April, 1967), pp. 644–49.

[87] Hyde, *op. cit.,* 346.

intervening areas as may already constitute the recognized territories of other states. It appears that the U.S.S.R. and Canada
are agreeable to the sector theory but that Norway seems opposed and that the United States and other states fronting on
the arctic, Denmark and Iceland, do not appear to have become committed.[88]

In the south polar region claims are in part based on discovery or exploration, and in part on the sector theory—even
though, unlike the arctic, there is no natural tableland extension to give such claims a degree of geographic justification.
Accounts and claims are conflicting and inconclusive, but interesting—even humorous—to read.[89] Beyond these vagueries, one
additional consideration remains. In 1959 a number of states
interested in the south polar region agreed to a neutralization
of the area and to a continuation of freedom and cooperation
in scientific research. Nuclear explosions are forbidden there as
is the establishment of military bases. Moreover all areas under
the treaty are subject to inspection by all signatory states. This
is not an inconsequential accomplishment considering that it
embraces an area greater than the United States and Europe
together and numbers among its signatories both the United
States and the Soviet Union. The treaty does not prejudice
prior claims, however.[90]

JURISDICTION ON THE HIGH SEAS AND OVER SHIPS

High Seas

The term "high seas" refers to those areas of water falling
outside the limits of the national waters and the territorial or

---

[88] *Ibid.*, pp. 349–50; Hackworth, *Digest* I, pp. 463–64.

[89] Hackworth, *Digest* I, 449–62; Hyde, *op. cit.*, pp. 347–55; G. Smedal, *Acquisi-
tion of Sovereignty over Polar Areas* (Oslo: Dybwad, 1931), pp. 54–76 (see
French ed. pp. 85–115); for a recent statement and references, see R. D. Hayton,
"Polar Problems and International Law," *American Journal of International
Law*, Vol. LII (October, 1958), pp. 746–65.

[90] See *Antarctic Treaty*, Washington, D.C., 1959, text in *American Journal of
International Law*, Vol. LIV (April, 1960), pp. 476–83; see also John Hanessian,
Jr., "The Antarctic Treaty," *American Universities Field Staff Report Service*,
Polar Areas Series, Vol. I, No. 2 (July 6, 1960). Whiteman, *Digest* II, pp.
1232–70.

marginal sea. Such areas are now considered by most authorities to be the common property of all nations. Although it was once legitimate for a state to appropriate sizable segments of the high seas, these claims have long since been abandoned except for those to the marginal seas of relatively modest scope. The present political complexion of international society would seem to sustain the legal view that the seas are not subject to appropriation, yet the continental shelf and coastal fisheries developments suggest that it may be rash to consider the seas as entirely *res communis.*[91]

Police Activities and Piracy. It may be taken as a general rule that at least in time of peace each state has virtually exclusive police jurisdiction over the ships flying its flag which are properly in its registry. The question arises, however, in regard to ships which are not properly in the registry of any state and ships which may have proper papers but which are engaged in depredations upon the high seas. It appears that there are only two main categories of maritime offenses which at least in a general way can be called offenses against the law of nations. These are (1) piracy, and (2) offenses stipulated specifically by treaty.

Piracy is of two sorts, *statutory piracy* and *piracy jure gentium.* The former is piracy as it is defined in the laws of individual states, and it has only national application. The latter is piracy under international law and is the subject of concern here. *Piracy jure gentium* is not easy to define, for its meaning has undergone change over the years. It was qualifiedly defined by Oppenheim as follows:

Piracy in its original and strict meaning, is every unauthorized

---

[91] It may be suggested that the concepts of *res communis* and *res nullius* are essentially concepts of property ownership whereas the vital factor in freedom of the seas is a matter of usufruct; it may be further suggested that the history of property rights in the high seas, the recent emphasis on ownership of sea resources, the expanding territorial belts, the attitudes on artificial islands, and related matters raise questions as to whether the concept of *res communis* is as appropriately descriptive as *res nullius.* See *Convention on the High Seas,* Geneva, 1958, Arts. 1, 2, 38, *American Journal of International Law,* Vol. LII (October, 1958), pp. 842–51 (documents section) (hereafter cited as *High Seas Accord*). See generally Moore, *Digest* II, pp. 884–1123; Hackworth, *Digest* II, pp. 651–769; Whiteman, *Digest* IV, pp. 499–739.

act of violence committed by a private vessel on the open seas against another vessel with intent to plunder *(animo furandi)* .[92]

It is probably safe to say that the definition could be expanded to the following: Piracy is the act of doing or attempting to do an unauthorized act of violence by persons aboard one private ship or aircraft to persons or property aboard another ship or aircraft (or to the ship itself) on the high seas with intent of depredation; piracy also includes successful mutiny.

There is a considerable body of case law and comment which defines and limits further the meaning of piracy. Thus, for example, the term will include acts of the personnel of a ship who have revolted and taken over their vessel even though no other ship has been damaged, but it would not include an act of robbery by one passenger on an ocean liner against a fellow passenger, nor would it appear to include a ship and crew engaged in the slave trade.[93] Finally, acts of insurgency or belligerency are not piracy.

Once the concept of *piracy jure gentium* has been properly defined, those engaged in it are considered to be *hostes humani generis,* that is, enemies of all nations and of the human race. Any nation may use its public vessels to apprehend them and may convict them in its own courts and subject them to whatever punishment its laws provide. If a nation should unjustly capture and punish a ship and its personnel, it is, of course, liable for whatever damages are appropriate to the state whose registry the allegedly piratical ship carried.[94] Descriptive of

---

[92] Oppenheim-Lauterpacht, *Treatise* I, p. 608; see also text of statement by the Judicial Committee of the Privy Council, in Great Britain, 1934, generally referred to as "In Re Piracy Jure Gentium," in *American Journal of International Law,* Vol. XXIX (January, 1935) , pp. 140–50; also *High Seas Accord,* Arts. 14–18; Art. 16 identifies piracy in terms similar to those cited here but includes aircraft.

[93] *Le Louis,* Great Britain, High Court of Admiralty, 2 *Dodson* 210 (1817) .

[94] See "Case of the Virginius," in Moore, *Digest* II, pp. 895–903; see also the *Marianna Flora,* 11 *Wheaton* 1 (1826) . In the case of the *Santa Maria* Captain Galvão seized a Portuguese liner and announced it as an act of political revolt. In the process one of the ship's officers was killed. Was this action piracy or insurgency? See C. G. Fenwick, " 'Piracy' in the Carribean," *American Journal of International Law,* Vol. LV (April, 1961) , pp. 426–28; L. C. Green, "The *Santa Maria:* Rebels or Pirates," *The British Yearbook of International Law 1961,* Vol. XXXVII, pp. 496–505.

pertinent rights and procedures are the following articles from the 1958 Geneva Convention on the High Seas:

On the high seas, or in any other place outside the jurisdiction of any state, every state may seize a pirate ship or aircraft, or a ship taken by piracy and under the control of pirates, and arrest the persons and seize the property on board. The courts of the state which carried out the seizure may decide upon the penalties to be imposed, and may also determine the action to be taken with regard to the ships, aircraft or property, subject to the rights of third parties acting in good faith.

Where the seizure of a ship or aircraft on suspicion of piracy has been effected without adequate grounds, the state making the seizure shall be liable to the state the nationality of which is possessed by the ship or aircraft, for any loss or damage caused by the seizure.

A seizure on account of piracy may only be carried out by warships or military aircraft, or other ships or aircraft on government service authorized to that effect.[95]

Offenses specified by treaty represent the other area besides piracy in which foreign state jurisdiction may sometimes be exercised on the high seas. States have been reluctant to allow visit and search in peacetime for offenses other than piracy, but there are exceptions. In these instances the activities of foreign states are limited to those police functions clearly specified by treaty.[96] Thus, an arbitration tribunal found the United States in error for having exceeded the powers authorized in a seal protection treaty between Britain and the United States,[97] and in another case the court found that while the slave trade was odious, it was neither piracy nor an act sufficiently limited by treaty to warrant seizure.[98] On the other hand, a good example

---

[95] *High Seas Accord*, Arts. 19, 20, 21; for a similar statement in a League of Nations document, see Hackworth, *Digest* II, pp. 682–83.

[96] *In the Matter of the Wanderer*, Great Britain–United States, American and British Claims Arbitration Tribunal, 1921; see in *American Journal of International Law*, Vol. XVI (April, 1922), pp. 305–14; see also in U.N., *Reports of International Arbitral Awards*, Vol. VI, pp. 68–77.

[97] *Ibid.*

[98] *Le Louis, op. cit.*, It may be noted, however, that Art. 13 of the *Geneva Convention on the High Seas* of 1958 provides that: "Every state shall adopt effective measures to prevent and punish the transport of slaves in ships authorized to fly its flag, and to prevent the unlawful use of its flag for that purpose. Any slave taking refuge on board any ship, whatever its flag, shall *ipso facto* be free."

of a police agreement is the convention among several European states which prohibits the sale of liquor to fishermen in the North Sea, and which grants a right of visit and search to all signatories in order to facilitate enforcement.[99]

Navigation, Salvage, and Safety at Sea. While the high seas are common property at least for purposes of transit, a number of rules and practices have come into existence which help to regulate its use. Among these are the "rules of the road," rules governing "general average," salvage arrangements, and safety regulations.

The *Rules of the Road* are merely a set of regulations originally adopted by Great Britain in 1862 which were designed to specify how ships should signal and navigate when near other ships in order to avoid collisions. These regulations were adopted by some 30 or more states within 10 years of their formulation by the British. These rules, interestingly enough, have not been adopted by convention, but rather were enacted and are enforced by separate national action and they operate on that basis at present.[100] Whether they are properly considered as international law may be open to some debate, but they serve the same ends and therefore justify mention here.

In much the same way rules known as the *York-Antwerp Rules of General Average* have come into common use. In brief these rules establish that if goods are thrown overboard to enable a ship to withstand the elements, all shippers are to bear the burden and not merely the ones owning the jettisoned goods. These rules are based on ancient principles of maritime law and are widely used in bills of lading, although they are not incorporated into international conventions.[101] Thus, here too it may not be quite proper to consider these rules as international law.

A number of other matters are written into treaties. These include the use of signals at sea, use of lighthouses, buoys, and lightships, action regarding collisions, assistance at sea to vessels in distress, limitations on the liability of owners of ships lost at

---

99 Oppenheim-Lauterpacht, *Treatise* I, p. 620.

100 Colombos, *op. cit.,* pp. 291–93.

101 *Ibid.,* pp. 315–17.

sea, establishment of a standard bill of lading, safety rules pertaining to the building of ships, the use of radio and other safety devices, the protection of submarine telegraph cables and pipelines, freedom of access to ports, the setting of minimum age limits for maritime employees, providing medical examinations for children employed at sea, prohibition of oil or radioactive waste pollution of the high seas, and some limitations on the transportation of slaves.[102]

Altogether these rules and usages provide a network of law and practice which governs navigation, salvage, and other procedures on the high seas. They cannot all be classified strictly as public international law, but all are closely related and serve the same ends.

Jurisdiction over Private Vessels

While it may not be quite correct to liken private vessels to the territory of the state whose registry they possess, it is nevertheless a metaphor which is not too far from reality to use as a point of departure for purposes of instruction. The general rule for the regulation of private merchant ships is that the law of the state of registry applies to them under most circumstances.[103]

Nationality of Ships. Nationality or registry is granted to ships by each state according to its own rules. The qualifications in order to be allowed nationality vary considerably. Thus, while the United States requires ships in its registry to be wholly owned by citizens, Belgium requires only that part of the ownership be by nationals, and Panama appears to have no restrictions at all regarding the nationality of owners.[104] Nation-

---

[102] *Ibid.,* pp. 291–400; see *High Seas Accord,* Arts. 10, 11, 12, 13, 24, 25, 26, 27, 28, 29. Whiteman, *Digest* IV, pp. 640–48, 687–739.

[103] *High Seas Accord,* Arts. 5, 6, 22.

[104] B. A. Boczek, *Flags of Convenience* (Cambridge, Mass.: Harvard University Press, 1962), pp. 55–56 *et passim.* Colombos, *op. cit.,* pp. 252–53, 336; also *High Seas Accord,* Art. 6. For a discussion of the whole matter of "flags of convenience," i.e., the shipping device by which ships are registered in states where tax, registration, wage, and/or other advantages obtain, see Boczek, *op. cit.;* also T. J. Romans, "The American Merchant Marine—Flags of Convenience and International Law," *Virginia Journal of International Law,* Vol. III, No. 2 (1963), pp.

ality is outwardly manifested by the appropriate national flag
or national merchant flag. Inappropriate use of the flag is
usually an offense against the state whose flag has been abused,
but not against other states or the community of nations.[105]

Besides the flag, other evidences of nationality are the ship's
papers which, while there is some variation, usually include the
following: (1) certificate of registry or nationality, or if recently purchased, a bill of sale, (2) crew and passenger lists,
(3) log book, (4) bill of health, (5) clearance papers, (6)
charter party if chartered, (7) invoices or cargo manifests, and
(8) bills of lading.[106]

Jurisdiction on the High Seas. The basic rule of jurisdiction over merchant vessels on the high seas is, as noted
above, that the law of the state of registry applies to events and
persons aboard ship. Thus a crime committed aboard a U.S.
merchant ship on the high seas is governed by U.S. law and acts
having legal significance of a civil character are governed by
the pertinent national laws. For example, a ceremony of marriage performed aboard a U.S. ship has whatever validity
American laws allow to such a marriage.[107] This is not to say,
however, that the rules for national territory and for merchant
ships are necessarily the same, but only that national rules
apply. Thus, for example, children of alien parents born on an
American merchant ship on the high seas do not acquire U.S.
nationality by *jus soli;* on the other hand *jus soli* does apply to
such children born aboard British merchant ships.[108]

There are perhaps four basic types of instances in which

121–52. The most notable flag of convenience states are Panama, Liberia,
Honduras, and Costa Rica. Lebanon is sometimes included.

For cases sustaining the right of states to determine their own standards for
registration of ships, see *Muscat Dhows* case *(France* v. *Great Britain)* Permanent Court of Arbitration, Scott, *Hague Court Reports,* (1905) , p. 91; *Lauritzen*
v. *Larson,* 345 U.S. 571; *Constitution of the Maritime Safety Committee of the
Inter-Governmental Maritime Consultative Organization,* Advisory Opinion of 8
June 1960, I.C.J. Reports (1960) , p. 150.

[105] *The Virginius,* see in Moore, *Digest* II, pp. 898–901.

[106] Hyde, *op. cit.,* Vol. III, p. 1982, fn. 11.

[107] See comments in Hackworth, *Digest* II, pp. 371–74.

[108] Hackworth, *Digest* III, p. 11; Hyde, *op. cit.,* Vol. II, pp. 1081–82, fn. 3
(1082) ; see also generally, *Regina* v. *Leslie,* Great Britain, Court of Criminal
Appeal, 8 Cox's Criminal Cases, 269 (1860) .

outside interference with a private merchant vessel is appropriate or may be appropriate. (1) Where the merchant ship behaves in such a way that the suspicions of a man-of-war are aroused as to whether the vessel might be piratical, there is a limited right of interference. Under these circumstances visit and search are sometimes instituted, but if the suspicions of the warship are not sustained, it may be liable for damages.[109] (2) In time of war, of course, a belligerent right of visit and search exists some of the details of which will be noted in a later chapter.[110] (3) The coastal state may exercise control where a ship or aircraft is believed to have violated the regulations of a coastal state and where hot pursuit has been commenced when the offending ship or aircraft is within the national or territorial or contiguous waters of the coastal state. Hot pursuit must be uninterrupted. Also pursuit must cease when the offending craft enters the territorial sea of any other state.[111] (4) Where a private ship is responsible for damage done aboard another ship, there is a possibility of holding the foreign ship and, formerly, even its personnel liable. This last possibility is based upon the World Court decision in the famous *Lotus* case where, as a result of collision between a French and a Turkish ship on the high seas, the Turkish ship was sunk. When the French ship arrived in Turkey, the Turkish authorities arrested the French officer of the watch together with the Turkish captain. This was contested by France, but upheld by the Permanent Court of International Justice on the grounds that the damage was done on Turkish "territory." The decision has been widely criticized and the specific principle of disciplining the master in the courts of any but the flag state or of the master's own nationality has been prescribed by the 1958 Convention on the High Seas.[112]

Jurisdiction in Territorial Waters. When a merchant vessel enters the territorial or national waters of a foreign state, its

---

[109] The *Marianna Flora;* see above, fn. 94; see *High Seas Accord*, Arts. 21, 22.

[110] See below, Chapter Nine.

[111] See *High Seas Accord*, Art. 23.

[112] *The Lotus*, P.C.I.J. Reports, Series A, No. 10 (1927). See also J. L. Brierly, "The Lotus Case," *The Law Quarterly Review*, Vol. XLIV (April, 1928), pp. 154–63. *High Seas Accord*, Art. 11.

legal situation may undergo considerable change, even though
it is generally recognized that a servitude exists by which merchant vessels have a right of innocent passage through territorial waters. In theory a foreign merchant ship is subject to the
laws of the territorial state, but in fact the laws of the state of
the ship's registry continue to apply for most practical purposes.
The basic rule of territorial waters is seen in the following
statement of the U.S. Supreme Court:

> A merchant ship of one country voluntarily entering the territo-
> rial limits of another subjects herself to the jurisdiction of the latter.
> The jurisdiction attaches in virtue of her presence, just as with
> other objects within those limits. During her stay she is entitled to
> the protection of the laws of that place and correlatively is bound to
> yield obedience to them. Of course, the local sovereign may out of
> considerations of public policy choose to forego the exertion of its
> jurisdiction or to exert the same in only a limited way, but this is a
> matter resting solely in its discretion.[113]

Nevertheless, even though the territorial state may have jurisdiction if it desires to exercise it, frequently it will not do so.
In these instances the laws of the flag state apply and it is said
in such cases that concurrent jurisdiction exists. In the classic
case on this subject, *Regina* v. *Anderson,* an American seaman
aboard a British merchantman of Canadian registry committed
a murder while aboard ship well within French national waters. Since France did not assume jurisdiction, the British court
held that it had jurisdiction.[114]

In practice the principle usually followed is that the territorial state will exercise jurisdiction only in cases where the
"peace of the port" has been disturbed. While this seems simple
enough in principle, there appears to be wide diversity in application. Thus, in the *Anderson* case mentioned above, murder
aboard ship some 300 yards from the dock did not violate the
peace of the port as far as France was concerned. On the other
hand, a murder aboard a Belgian ship in New York harbor was

---

[113] *Cunard Steamship Co., Ltd., et al.* v. *Mellon,* 262 U.S. 100 (1923); quoted
also in Hackworth, *Digest* II, p. 208.

[114] *Regina* v. *Anderson,* Great Britain, Court of Criminal Appeal, 11 Cox's
Criminal Cases, 198 (1868).

viewed in the United States as disturbing the peace.[115] It may be added that, as a practical matter, the consul of the flag state exercises jurisdiction over such legal problems as may arise when the port state does not choose to exercise jurisdiction. The consul also assumes jurisdiction in regard to happenings aboard ship before entering territorial waters.

The Geneva Territorial Sea Accord of 1958 now spells out the prevailing rules for its adherents rather clearly. Innocent passage is guaranteed, but certain restraints are imposed, temporary suspensions of innocent passage may be made for security reasons, and ships must comply with coastal regulations.

As to civil jurisdiction the 1958 accord places merchant vessels (private and government owned) largely under the jurisdiction of the state of registry. A state, moreover, should not interfere with innocent passage, nor levy charges upon ships passing through its territorial waters (except for specific services). Illustrative of its provisions is the following statement:

The criminal jurisdiction of the coastal state should not be exercised on board a foreign ship passing through the territorial sea to arrest any person or to conduct any investigation in connection with any crime committed on board the ship during its passage, save only in the following cases:

a) If consequences of the crime extend to the coastal state; or
b) If the crime is of a kind to disturb the peace of the country or the good order of the territorial sea; or
c) If the assistance of the local authorities has been requested by the captain of the ship or by the consul of the country whose flag the ship flies; or
d) If it is necessary for the suppression of illicit traffic in narcotic drugs.[116]

There is one type of occasion where a merchant vessel appears to be largely free from the jurisdiction of the port state when in its territorial waters. This is in the case of *force majeure* when for reasons of distress a merchant ship must seek shelter. Under these circumstances port dues and customs du-

---

[115] *Wildenhus'* case, 120 U.S. 1 (1887).

[116] *Geneva Terr. Sea Accord*, Arts. 18–22; quotation in Art. 19. See also Whiteman, *Digest* IV, pp. 343–480.

ties do not apply to such vessels when they seek refuge in a foreign port.[117]

Finally, it may be mentioned that a merchant ship has no right to offer asylum to anyone while in territorial waters. This, of course, is logically consistant with other principles relevant to merchantmen.[118]

Jurisdiction over Public Vessels

Unlike the status of private vessels, most public vessels are subject only to the jurisdiction of the state to which they belong. This is entirely true of warships and ships performing some public functions,[119] and it is often true of state-owned ships used for ordinary commercial transportation.

In an early and classic case the U.S. Supreme Court held that a vessel which had formerly been the property of American shippers but which was seized by France and converted into a French warship could not be attached by the court and returned to its original owners when it put in at an American port. The reasons for this as seen by the court were stated as follows:

> It seems, then, to the court, to be a principle of public law, that national ships of war, entering the port of a friendly power open for their reception, are to be considered as exempted by the consent of that power from its jurisdiction.[120]

It is, of course, possible to exclude such vessels from a port by the simple expedient of not granting them permission to enter, as proper procedure requires that notification be given in advance of the projected stop. Moreover, the 1958 Geneva Ac-

---

[117] Hackworth, *Digest* II, pp. 277–82; Philip C. Jessup, *The Law of Territorial Waters and Maritime Jurisdiction* (New York: G. A. Jennings Co., Inc., 1927), pp. 194–208; *Geneva Terr. Sea Accord*, Art. 14 (3).

[118] Colombos, *op. cit.*, p. 287. There is perhaps one exception to this statement. See *High Seas Accord*, Art. 13, which states, *inter alia*, "Any slave taking refuge on board any ship, whatever its flag, shall *ipso facto* be free." See also Whiteman, *Digest* IV, pp. 645–48.

[119] See *High Seas Accord*, Arts. 8, 9. The status of ships of intergovernmental organizations appears to be undecided, see *ibid.*, Art. 7. Also Whiteman, *Digest* IV, pp. 633–40.

[120] *The Schooner Exchange* v. *McFaddon*, 7 Cranch 116 (1812).

cord on the Territorial Sea specifies that warships which do not "comply with the regulations of the coastal state" with reference to pertinent matters may be required "to leave the territorial sea," and submarines in territorial waters must surface and fly the national flag.[121]

Publicly owned vessels which, nevertheless, are not warships traditionally seem to have had almost exactly the same legal attributes as men-of-war. Thus, in the case of the *Berizzi Brothers Co.* v. *Pesaro,* as well as in many other instances, the U.S. Supreme Court held that a publicly owned merchant vessel was also immune from jurisdiction.[122] In 1926, however, a convention was drawn up which attempted to alter this state of affairs. The problem centers about the increase in the number of countries which have state-owned vessels in direct competition with private shippers. It has been felt that special privileges for public commercial vessels under these circumstances are highly questionable. As a result, a number of nations have signed the agreement mentioned above which attempts to put public and private commercial vessels on an equal basis. While it appears that the agreement has not been widely adopted,[123] there has been a significant change of position on this matter.

In U.S. court procedure a cue as to official policy is ordinarily taken from the executive branch, i.e., from the State Department, in cases where sovereign immunity is claimed. Accordingly, significance has been attached to the 1945 case of *Mexico* v. *Hoffman* in which the court took such a cue and stated:

. . . we think controlling in the present circumstances, is the fact that, despite numerous opportunities like the present to recognize immunity from suit of a vessel owned and not possessed by a foreign government, this government has failed to do so. We can only conclude that it is the national policy not to extend the immunity in the manner now suggested, and that it is the duty of the courts, in a matter so intimately associated with our foreign policy and which may profoundly affect it, not to enlarge an immunity to an extent

---

[121] Colombos, *op. cit.,* pp. 234–35; *Geneva Terr. Sea Accord,* Arts. 14 (6) , 23.

[122] *Berizzi Brothers Co.* v. *S. S. Pesaro,* 271 U.S. 562 (1926) .

[123] Convention cited in Hackworth, *Digest* II, pp. 463–65; 176 *L.N.T.S.,* 199 (1937) . Whiteman, *Digest* IV, pp. 399–404, 633–40.

which the government, although often asked, has not seen fit to recognize. . . .[124]

Seemingly as a base upon which this beginning might be generalized, in 1952 the Acting Legal Advisor to the U.S. Department of State in a letter to the Department of Justice reviewed the positions of a number of states on the two theories of immunity. He concluded that the restrictive theory was achieving increasing support, or, perhaps more precisely stated, except for the Soviet bloc there was "little support . . . for continued full acceptance of the absolute theory of sovereign immunity." For this and other reasons he stipulated that

It will hereafter be the Department's policy to follow the restrictive theory of sovereign immunity in the consideration of requests of foreign governments for a grant of sovereign immunity.[125]

Whether in practice American procedure has conformed to these guidelines is a matter of considerable debate,[126] but the

---

[124] *Republic of Mexico* v. *Hoffman* (*The Baja California*), 324 U.S. 30 (1945).

[125] "Changed Policy Concerning the Granting of Sovereign Immunity to Foreign Governments" (A letter to the Department of Justice from the Department of State's Acting Legal Adviser, Jack B. Tate), May 19, 1952, *Department of State Bulletin*, Vol. 26 (June 23, 1952), pp. 984–85; see conveniently in W. W. Bishop, Jr., *International Law Cases and Materials* (2nd ed.; Boston: Little, Brown & Co., 1962), pp. 568–70.

[126] Sovereign immunity in U.S. internal procedure is quite complicated. While the executive attitude is not binding on the judiciary, the courts nevertheless normally appear to follow executive policy. Interestingly enough, however, the absolute position taken in *The Pesaro* was despite a contrary Executive view. Many writers consider the State Department inconsistent, however, and there is much criticism of its sometime indication that while assumption of jurisdiction is appropriate, execution of judgment is not. See discussion of these and related problems as well as further source and case references in: W. W. Bishop, Jr., "New United States Policy Limiting Sovereign Immunity," *American Journal of International Law*, Vol. XLVII (January, 1953), pp. 93–106; L. M. Drachsler, "Some Observations on the Current Status of the Tate Letter," *American Journal of International Law*, Vol. LIV (October, 1960), pp. 790–800; V. G. Setser, "The Immunity of Waiver for State-Controlled Business Enterprises in United States Commercial Treaties," *Proceedings of the American Society of International Law* (1961), pp. 89–105; W. G. Griffin, "Execution against the Foreign Sovereign's Property: The Current Scene," *Proceedings of the American Society of International Law*, pp. 105–113; S. Timberg, "Expropriation Measures and State Trading," *Proceedings of the American Society of International Law*, pp. 113–121; R. Delson, "Applicability of Restrictive Theory of Sovereign Immunity to Actions to Perfect Attachment," *Proceedings of the American Society of International Law*, pp. 121–130; also "Remarks of William Harvey Reeves," *Proceedings of the*

guidelines appear to conform to developments in international legal doctrine. Indicative of this pattern is the pertinent section of the 1958 Geneva Territorial Sea Accord which, after specifying the rules applicable to all ships and the rules applicable to merchant ships (both categories as they pertain to innocent passage), states that "The rules contained in sub-sections A and B shall also apply to government ships operated for commercial purposes."[127] To the same end the 1958 Convention on the High Seas states that

Ships owned or operated by a State and used only on government non-commercial service shall, on the high seas, have complete immunity from the jurisdiction of any State other than the flag State.[128]

There are, however, varied deviations, disclaimers, and exceptions. The Soviet bloc nations do not recognize the applicability to themselves of the clauses in the Territorial Sea and High Seas Conventions noted above,[129] and U.S. court and Executive attitudes on sovereign immunity are anything but clear. Nevertheless, a recent and widely acclaimed treatise on the high seas states that

Under the prevailing authoritative general expectation, a state may apply policy to vessels engaged in commercial activities, but may not extend such authority to vessels regarded as performing a governmental function.[130]

Asylum. The question of asylum has frequently arisen with reference to warships. Although the United States is reluctant to acknowledge the concept in most instances, it is generally recognized that political refugees may be accorded asylum on ships of war. It also appears that slaves can be given asylum.

American Society of International Law, pp. 130–39; also remarks from the floor, *Proceedings of the American Society of International Law*, pp. 139–45. M. S. McDougal and W. T. Burke, *The Public Order of the Oceans* (New Haven, Conn.: Yale University Press, 1962), pp. 137–55. R. P. Borsody, "The American Law of Sovereign Immunity since the Tate Letter," *Virginia Journal of International Law*, Vol. IV, No. 1 (1964), pp. 76–97.

[127] *Genvea Terr. Sea Accord*, Arts. 21, 22.

[128] *High Seas Accord*, Art. 9.

[129] See conveniently in McDougal and Burke, *op. cit.*, pp. 1180–89. Ratifications and accessions as of February, 1962 are also listed on p. 1178.

[130] *Ibid.*, p. 153.

The United States allows such use to be made of its vessels only when the escapee's life is in immediate danger.[131] In Latin America where asylum retains a certain importance, its use has been restrained by convention and it is allowable only in "urgent cases."[132]

INTERNATIONAL SERVITUDES

The praedial servitude of Roman Law has been carried over in somewhat modified form into international law. There has been some debate as to whether such a concept really exists at all in international law,[133] but there is rather conclusive evidence now that it is quite valid.[134] An international servitude is merely a relatively permanent obligation on the part of a state to permit its property to be used for some specified purpose by another state. Reid defines an international servitude as

. . . a real right, whereby the territory of one state is made liable to permanent use by another state, for some specified purpose. The servitude may be permissive or restrictive, but does not involve any obligation upon either party to take positive action. It establishes a permanent legal relationship of territory to territory, unaffected by change of sovereignty in either of them, and terminable only by mutual consent, by renunciation on the part of the dominant state, or by consolidation of the territories affected.[135]

---

[131] Colombos, *op. cit.*, pp. 238–40; Hackworth, *Digest* II, pp. 639–42. Regarding slavery, see *High Seas Accord*, Art. 13; Whiteman, *Digest* IV, pp. 645–48; also this chapter above, fn. 118.

[132] See references in Hackworth, *Digest* II, pp. 646–49; 132 L.N.T.S. (1932–33), 323.

[133] *North Atlantic Coast Fisheries* case, Permanent Court of Arbitration; Scott, *Hague Court Reports*, 146 (1910).

[134] See in detail Helen Dwight Reid, *International Servitudes in Law and Practice* (Chicago: University of Chicago Press, 1932); F. A. Vali, *Servitudes of International Law* (2d ed.; New York: Frederick A. Praeger, Inc., 1958); see also Fenwick, *op. cit.*, pp. 386–407. See, however, discussion of this matter particularly from the standpoint of military servitudes in which the author concludes that "The concept of 'military servitudes' has been refuted by the recent practice of states." Albert J. Esgain, "Military Servitudes and the New Nations," in William V. O'Brien (ed.), *The New Nations in International Law and Diplomacy*, Vol. III, *The Yearbook of World Polity* (New York: Frederick A. Praeger Inc., 1965), pp. 42–97, quotation on p. 95.

[135] Reid, *op. cit.*, p. 25.

In theory such rights may arise in two ways: (1) by treaty, and (2) by prescription,[136] but it appears that as a rule the former pattern is much more common.

Examples of servitudes may be seen in the "perpetual" transit rights of the United States in Panama, Honduras, Mexico, and Nicaragua,[137] in the demilitarization obligations regarding the Aaland Islands,[138] in the Bolivian transit rights on the Amazon through Brazilian territory,[139] in the demilitarization obligations on certain areas ceded to Greece after World War II,[140] in the use of at least certain rivers by nonriparian states,[141] in aviation transit rights of certain limited sorts,[142] in the right of innocent passage in territorial waters and in certain straits,[143] and perhaps even in obligations to use only a certain amount of the water in certain rivers which flow through several jurisdictions.[144]

These examples are not all inclusive by any means. Authorities cite examples both historical and contemporary of many others. These serve, however, to illustrate the general concept of obligations not merely transitory under which states in some instances allow the use of their territory for certain purposes.

The political origin of servitudes is frequently in evidence. Thus, for a landlocked state transit rights may be of such impelling necessity that a servitude may be the only practical alternative to high and continued pressures for ports. Some-

---

[136] Vali, *op. cit.* (2d ed.) , p. 325.

[137] Reid, *op. cit.*, pp. 131–38.

[138] *Ibid.*, pp. 201–2; Vali, *op. cit.* (2d ed.) , pp. 264–70.

[139] Reid, *op. cit.*, pp. 154–55. On the question of transit rights, see also *Case Concerning Right of Passage over Indian Territory (Portugal v. India)* , I.C.J. Reports (1960) , p. 6, see also in *American Journal of International Law,* Vol. LIV (April, 1960) , p. 673.

[140] Fenwick, *op. cit.*, p. 407.

[141] Reid, *op. cit.*, pp. 146–66.

[142] *Convention on International Civil Aviation,* Art. 5.

[143] Reid, *op. cit.*, pp. 140–45; *The Corfu Channel* case, International Court of Justice, I.C.J. Reports (1949) , p. 4.

[144] See agreements governing use of waters of Rio Grande, Colorado and Tia Juana Rivers cited in Hackworth, *Digest* I, pp. 584–90; see also *Wyoming* v. *Colorado,* 259 U.S. 419 (1922) .

what similar pressures may influence establishment of a servitude such as that now applying to the Isthmus of Panama.[145]

JURISDICTION OVER PERSONS

A final area of jurisdiction remains to be surveyed in this chapter. This has to do with jurisdiction over private persons. These matters are of such a nature that some of them have and will come up in discussions in other chapters. For that reason, only elements for the most part not handled elsewhere will be surveyed here.

Nationality and Its Acquisition

A state has jurisdiction over various categories of persons, but foremost among these are its own nationals. The term "national" is used here rather than "citizen" because for international purposes it is a useful and precise concept which nevertheless excludes the internal constitutional problems inherent in citizenship.[146] Thus, for example, before the advent of Philippine independence, Filipinos were U.S. nationals but not its citizens.

Nationality is acquired in two basic ways: (1) by birth, and (2) by naturalization. The relevant legal aspects of both of these are governed by national law, but certain generalizations can be made.

Nationality by Birth. In the United States, Great Britain, and most Latin-American countries, nationality is basically governed by the principle of *jus soli,* that is, by the place of birth. Thus, persons born in the United States are citizens of

---

[145] For other material on servitudes, see W. E. Hall, *A Treatise on International Law* (5th ed.; Oxford: The Clarendon Press, 1904), pp. 159–60; Moore, *Digest* II, p. 18; Hackworth, *Digest* II, pp. 12–15; Hyde, *op. cit.,* Vol. I, pp. 510–15; see also *High Seas Accord,* Art. 3, which would appear to establish a docking and transit right for landlocked states where they and the appropriate coastal states are bound by the convention.

[146] The term *national* refers to a person over whom a state has sovereign jurisdiction. It includes citizens and also persons who do not enjoy whatever rights citizenship may convey, but whose primary allegiance, nevertheless, is to that state. The term does not include persons who are subject to foreign sovereigns, i.e., aliens, nor does it include stateless persons, i.e., those persons who are subject to no sovereign.

this country.[147] The prevailing view in Europe, Japan, the Philippines, and in some other areas is, however, somewhat different. In these places nationality at birth is governed as a rule by the nationality of the parents. Thus, a person whose parents are Filipinos is a Filipino at birth regardless of where he is born.[148] This is known as the principle of *jus sanguinis*. In most countries a combination of these two rules is in effect, however, and this is true of the United States.[149]

Naturalization. Nationality is also conferred by the legal process of assimilating persons into the body politic. This is known as naturalization and is almost wholly a matter of national law. Thus the United States sets its own rules and procedures by which aliens may become citizens,[150] as do other countries.

An exception to naturalization rights of every state may be seen, however, where states for one reason or another have attempted to impose their nationality on persons who are citizens of some other state. This would appear to be a justifiable cause for protest by states whose nationals have been the subject of such pressures.[151]

Finally it may be mentioned that in addition to individual naturalization proceedings, sometimes whole groups of people are granted citizenship or naturalization en bloc. This was done by an act of Congress with reference to Puerto Ricans born after 1879.[152]

Dual Nationality. There are situations where nationality overlaps. This may arise principally in two ways. Where conflicting theories of citizenship by birth obtain, and where naturalization in one jurisdiction is not complimented by its being relinquished in another, the end result may be a situation in which a person has conflicting nationalities. This is known as

---

[147] U.S., *Constitution*, Amendment XIV, Sec. 1.

[148] Philippines, *Constitution*, Article IV, Sec. 1 (3, 4).

[149] 66 U.S., *Statutes at Large* 163 (1952), Title III, Sec. 301.

[150] U.S., *Constitution*, Amendment XIV, Sec. 1; 66 *U.S. Statutes at Large* 163 (1952).

[151] Hackworth, *Digest* III, pp. 210–11; see references in Briggs, *The Law of Nations* (2d ed.; New York: Appleton-Century-Crofts, Inc., 1952), p. 461; Moore, *Digest* III, pp. 305–7.

[152] Hackworth, *Digest* III, p. 146; 54 *U.S. Statutes at Large,* 1139, Sec. 202.

dual nationality. By way of illustration, one might consider, for example a person born in the United States of Filipino parentage. He is entitled to citizenship under the laws of both countries and under some circumstances he may actually have dual nationality. When this happens, jurisdictional problems sometimes arise. For example, particularly during the Franco-Prussian War and World War I some persons of French, German, or Italian parentage who were born in and were citizens of the United States were nevertheless subjected to military conscription in France, Germany, and Italy respectively, and issues of this sort are still not yet wholly resolved.[153]

Naturalization may give rise to difficulties from another standpoint, however, if the naturalized person's state of origin does not recognize his expatriation. Fortunately, most states appear to recognize the right of expatriation for their nationals.[154]

Status of Women and Children. While the laws of the United States and of a few other countries place men and women on a substantially independent and equal footing in the matter of acquisition and loss of nationality, the commonly prevailing practice is that a woman, upon marriage, takes the nationality of her husband or follows his nationality should he undergo naturalization. A treaty arrangement has been entered into among a number of states to mitigate hardship in instances where, for example, a woman may lose her original nationality by marriage to a foreigner, but, under the laws of her husband's country, she does not acquire his nationality by marriage. In such instances the convention provides that the woman does not lose her original nationality.[155]

The nationality of children as noted above is ordinarily determined by their place of birth or the nationality of their parents. In at least some instances, however, an alien child may become a national—or may have its subsequent naturalization

---

[153] See references in Hackworth, *Digest* III, pp. 184–89; Moore, *Digest* III, pp. 532–51; Hyde, *op. cit.*, Vol. II, pp. 1140–43. See also *Kawakita* v. *United States*, 343 U.S. 717 (1952).

[154] See Hackworth, *Digest* III, pp. 161–207.

[155] *Convention on Certain Questions Relating to the Conflict of Nationality Laws*, The Hague, 1930, 179 L.N.T.S. 89, Arts. 8–11 (hereafter cited as *Nationality Convention*) ; see references in Oppenheim-Lauterpacht, *Treatise* I, pp. 654–56, fn. 3; Hackworth, *Digest* III, pp. 246–64.

much facilitated—by the naturalization of its parents.[156] Like
other matters pertaining to nationality, however, this is entirely
subject to national laws and to a few treaty arrangements.

   Statelessness.   Although much has been done by way of
trying to prevent loss of nationality in one state without simultaneous acquisition of nationality elsewhere,[157] there are instances in which this does happen. Such persons are said to be
stateless. As in examples cited above, a woman may occasionally find herself in this situation by virtue of marriage to an
alien. Similarly, a person may sometimes become stateless by
renouncing his allegiance or, as in the case of German Jews
during the Nazi era, by being deprived of nationality by the
state itself.[158] The International Law Commission has devoted
some study to the matter, but nothing more than draft conventions has resulted.[159]

   Aliens.   Persons who are not nationals of a given state are
considered as aliens. Most aliens are nationals of some other
state, but a few fall into the category of stateless persons described above. Aliens within the territory of a foreign state are
generally subject to its jurisdiction. There are, however, some
exceptions, and under any circumstances the state of which an
alien is a national may make inquiry by way of making sure
that its nationals are properly treated. Some aspects of the
treatment of aliens are considered elsewhere in this volume and
need not be duplicated here.[160]

Jurisdiction over Nationals and Aliens

   The principles governing jurisdiction over persons falling
into the various categories described above are not completely

---

[156] *Nationality Convention,* Arts. 13–16; Oppenheim-Lauterpacht, *Treatise* I,
p. 670; Hackworth, *Digest* III, pp. 235–46.

[157] *Nationality Convention,* see C. Seckler-Hudson, *Statelessness with Special
Reference to the United States* (Washington, D.C.: American University Graduate School, 1934).

[158] See *Stoeck* v. *Public Trustee,* Great Britain Chancery Division, 2 Ch. 67
(1921).

[159] See "Report of the International Law Commission" (5th Session), *American Journal of International Law,* Vol. XLVIII (January, 1954), esp. pp. 45–66
(documents section); also "Report of the International Law Commission" (6th
Session), *American Journal of International Law,* Vol. XLIX (January, 1955),
especially pp. 3–16 (documents section).

[160] Above, Chapter Four; below Chapter Ten.

uniform among the various nations. Certain principles, on the other hand, are universally recognized.

It appears that there are five basic principles governing penal jurisdiction. These are called (1) territoriality, (2) nationality, (3) protection, (4) universality, and (5) passive personality. It should be noted, however, that in applying any of these to aliens the Harvard draft convention specified that "no state shall prosecute an alien who has not been taken into custody by its authorities."[161]

Territoriality. The first of these, territoriality, is generally applicable and is of primary competence. Thus, every nation claims jurisdiction over crimes committed on its territory and over civil acts with application there. This applies regardless of the nationality of the person or persons involved. In *The Lotus* case the Court, going beyond the principle of territoriality, said that "in all systems of law the principle of the territorial character of criminal law is fundamental. . . ."[162]

Nationality. The second principle, nationality, is also generally utilized, though with varying comprehensiveness. It derives in some degree from the emphasis within the Italian school of international law, and, like the principle of territoriality, is also considered of primary competence. While nations as a rule are somewhat sparing in the laws which they impose on their nationals abroad, and this is particularly true of the United States and Great Britain, they are nevertheless free in principle to determine to what extent they will impose their laws on such persons. Thus, in the case of *Blackmer* v. *United States,* the U.S. Supreme Court said of the petitioner, who was living in France:

> By virtue of the obligations of citizenship, the United States retained its authority over him, and he was bound by its laws made applicable to him in a foreign country.[163]

Protection. The third principle, that of protection, is also widely used, but is less so than the first two and is considered

---

[161] Harvard Research, "Jurisdiction in Respect to Crime," *American Journal of International Law,* Vol. XXIX (Supplement, 1935), p. 445; also, Art. 12.

[162] *Ibid.,* pp. 445, 480–519. *The Lotus* case, P.C.I.J. Reports, Series A, No. 10 (1927).

[163] *Blackmer* v. *United States,* 284 U.S. 421 (1932); see also "Jurisdiction with Respect to Crime," *op. cit.,* pp. 519–42.

more auxiliary than primary in importance. Under this principle, jurisdiction is often exercised when an act, begun outside
the national territory, takes effect within that territory in a way
which is injurious to the state itself. This basis for jurisdiction
is said to have wider application elsewhere than in the United
States or Great Britain,[164] but it is applicable there to some
extent as well. Illustrative of the principle is the case of *United
States* v. *Rodriguez* in which the Court said:

We accordingly hold that #1546, Title 18 U.S.C.A. is constitutionally valid as applied to the crimes charged in the indictment,
committed outside of the United States, where the defendent is
subsequently apprehended within the United States. As a crime
against the sovereignty of the state, the very existence of the state
provides authority to Congress to prohibit its commission.[165]

Universality. The fourth principle, universality, is less
generally applied, but is nevertheless widely used and is considered as having auxiliary competence. It centers upon the idea
that a state may try a person for certain offenses committed
almost anywhere so long as the accused is in the custody of the
state which desires to exercise jurisdiction. Piracy clearly falls
into this category,[166] and it is probably correct to include certain crimes agains humanity and war crimes.[167]

---

[164] "Jurisdiction with Respect to Crime," *op. cit.,* pp. 543–63.

[165] *United States* v. *Rodriguez,* 182 F. Supp. 479, 494 (1960). See also
Strassheim v. *Daily,* 221 U.S. 280 (1911). The case of William Joyce, "Lord Haw
Haw" of World War II fame, is sometimes cited as an example of the principle
of protection. The question was whether an alien holding a British passport
while performing acts in Germany hostile to Great Britain could be convicted of
treason. British courts thought so, but it would appear that jurisdictionally this
is more akin to the nationality principle than to the principle of protection. See
Joyce v. *Director of Prosecutions,* House of Lords, The Times Law Reports, Vol.
LXII, No. 10 (1946), p. 208; reported conveniently in *American Journal of
International Law,* Vol. XL (July, 1946), p. 663.

[166] "Jurisdiction with Respect to Crime," *op. cit.,* pp. 563–92.

[167] "See Geneva Convention for the Amelioration of the Condition of the
Wounded and Sick in Armed Forces in the Field of August 12, 1949," (Department of the Army, Pamphlet No. 20–150 [Washington, D.C.: U.S. Government
Printing Office, 1950]), Art 49, which states, *inter alia,* "Each High Contracting
Party shall be under the obligation to search for persons alleged to have
committed, or to have ordered to be committed, such grave breaches, and shall
bring such persons, regardless of their nationality, before its own courts." Art. 50
states "Grave breaches to which the preceding Article relates shall be those
involving any of the following acts, if committed against persons or property

In *United States* v. *Smith* the Court recognized the applicability of the universality principle to piracy and stated:

the general practice of all nations in punishing all persons, whether natives or foreigners, who have committed this offence against any persons whatsoever, with whom they are in amity, is a conclusive proof that the offence is supposed to depend, not upon the particular provisions of any municipal code, but upon the law of nations, both for definition and punishment.[168]

Passive Personality. Finally the principle of passive personality is occasionally used. It is of less importance than the other bases for jurisdiction and is classified by the Harvard research group as being "probably not essential" but "admittedly auxi-

---

protected by the Convention: wilful killing, torture or inhuman treatment, including biological experiments, wilfully causing great suffering or serious injury to body or health, and extensive destruction and appropriation of property, not justified by military necessity and carried out unlawfully and wantonly."

See, *inter alia*, "International Military Tribunal (Nuremberg), Judgment and Sentences," 1946, in *American Journal of International Law,* Vol. XLI (January, 1947), p. 172; see especially pp. 248–49.

Note, however, that Art. 6 of the Genocide Convention states: "Persons charged with genocide or any of the other acts enumerated in Article III shall be tried by a competent tribunal of the State in the territory of which the act was committed, or by such international penal tribunal as may have jurisdiction with respect to those Contracting Parties which shall have accepted its jurisdiction." "Convention on the Prevention and Punishment of the Crime of Genocide," in *American Journal of International Law,* Vol. XLV (January, 1951), p. 7 (official document). If Art. 6 is to be taken at face value, it creates an interesting source of speculation about the jurisdictional base for the *Eichmann* case, unless, of course, that case can be considered merely as an exercise in war crimes jurisdiction. Does the *Eichmann* case fall primarily under the principle of universality or under passive personality? Is it good law? See *Attorney-General of the Government of Israel* v. *Eichmann,* Criminal Case No. 40/61, District Court of Jerusalem (1961), mimeographed unofficial translation, in *American Journal of International Law,* Vol. LVI (October, 1962), p. 805. See aso J. E. S. Fawcett, "The Eichmann Case," *The British Yearbook of International Law,* Vol. XXXVIII (1962), pp. 181–215; P. A. Papadatos, *The Eichmann Trial* (New York: Frederick A. Praeger, Inc., 1964); Helen Silving, "In Re Eichmann: A Dilemma of Law and Morality," *American Journal of International Law,* Vol. LV (April, 1961), pp. 307–58.

[168] *United States* v. *Smith,* 5 Wheaton 153 (1820). See also *People* v. *Lol-lo and Saraw,* 43 P.I. 19 (1922), where the Philippine Supreme Court stated: "The jurisdiction of piracy unlike other crimes has no territorial limits. As it is against all so may it be punished by all. Nor does it matter that the crime was committed within the jurisdictional 3-mile limit of a foreign state." Quoted and criticized in D. H. N. Johnson, "Piracy in Modern International Law," *Transactions for the Grotius Society,* Vol. XLIII (1957), pp. 63–85, quotation on p. 75.

liary."[169] Under this principle the nationality of the person injured by the offense can be the basis for assumption of jurisdiction by his state. In *The Lotus* case the Court stated:

it is certain that the courts of many countries which have given their criminal legislation a strictly territorial character, interpret criminal law in the sense that offences, the authors of which at the moment of commission are in the territory of another state, are nevertheless to be regarded as having been committed in the national territory, if one of the constituent elements of the offence, and more especially its effects, have taken place there. . . . Consequently, once it is admitted that the effects of the offence were produced on the Turkish vessel, it becomes impossible to hold that there is a rule of international law which prohibits Turkey from prosecuting Lieutenant Demons because of the fact that the author of the offence was on board the French ship.[170]

Certain Special Exceptions: Extraterritoriality: Exempt Persons. Although the matter is chiefly of historical importance, it may be mentioned that even up until the middle of the present century there were arrangements, particularly in some Muslim and Asian countries, whereby Western states could set up their own courts to try their own nationals. These special extraterritorial arrangements were referred to as extraterritorial jurisdiction or as capitulations.[171] It is believed that none of these are now operative.

It should also be recalled in passing that the heads of state, persons with diplomatic status, and officers and personnel of armed forces of a state are not ordinarily subject to the jurisdiction of any other state even though they may be located in such

---

[169] "Jurisdiction with Respect to Crime," p. 445.

[170] *The Lotus* case. In *The Cutting* case, Mexico, Bravos District Court, 1886 (see in U.S. Foreign Relations, 1886, p. 761; see conveniently in Briggs, *op. cit.*, pp. 571–75) , the court considered whether the offense of defamation could have been committed by a foreigner sometime resident of Mexico whose act of defamation was printed in Texas but nevertheless took effect in Mexico. The court said ". . . even supposing, without conceding it, that the penal offense of defamation was committed in the territory of Texas, the circumstance that the newspaper, El Paso *Sunday Herald,* was circulated in this town [in Mexico], of which circumstances Medina complained, and which was the ground of ordering the seizure of the copies which might be found in the office of Cutting, in this same town, properly constituted the consummation of the crime, . . ."

[171] Hyde, *op. cit.*, Vol. II, pp. 849–71.

state.[172] Provision for trying alien soldiers in the civil courts of the country where they are stationed is sometimes made by treaty.[173]

Interjurisdictional Cooperation

There are a number of ways in which states or jurisdictions within states cooperate with each other to serve the interests of justice. Some of these processes are based upon treaty law while others are more properly defined as cooperation based on comity. In this connection, extradition, letters rogatory, commissions to take testimony, and private international law will be briefly surveyed.

Extradition. The problem often arises as to how to get an offender into the jurisdiction which should properly try him for an offense. Several alternative approaches to the problem are possible. Thus, by the general application of the principle of universality of jurisdiction mentioned above there would be no difficulties except in the confusion, potential duplication, and resulting double or multiple jeopardy problems. An alternative, sometimes employed, is for a state to apply the criminal laws of others states as warranted. Still another alternative, extradition, is to send the escaped offender back to stand trial in the state properly having jurisdiction. It is a process quite similar to rendition as applied within the United States under the Constitution.[174] Extradition is commonly used and is formalized and applied on the basis of bilateral treaties which stipulate the offenses for which a person may be extradited. It is apparently used *only* when authorized by treaty. Exceptions to its use exist in the areas of political offenses for which extradition usually is not allowed.[175] Also, states relying heavily on the nationality basis of jurisdiction are sometimes reluctant to extradite their own nationals, preferring instead to try them in domestic courts for offenses committed abroad.[176]

---

[172] *Ibid.,* Vol. I, pp. 817–22, 1266–76, *et passim.*

[173] See, e.g., *Agreement Between the United States of America and the Republic of the Philippines Concerning Military Bases,* Manila, 1947, *T.I.A.S.* 1775, Art. XIII, Sec. 2; see further reference to this matter in Chapter Nine.

[174] U.S., *Constitution,* Art. IV, Sec. II (2).

[175] *In re Castioni,* Great Britain, Queen's Bench Division, 1 Q B 149 (1891).

[176] *Coumas* v. *Superior Ct. of San Joaquin Co.,* Supreme Court of California,

Letters Rogatory. It is sometimes necessary or desirable to procure testimony for a court proceeding in one country from a person located in another country. The appropriate procedure is for the court needing the testimony to contact the appropriate court or judicial authority in the other country and to ask that the desired testimony be taken and sent for use in the pending litigation. In accepting such a request a court must be governed by what its own national laws allow; obviously the honoring of letters rogatory is a matter of comity rather than of international law. Thus, by federal statute U.S. district and circuit courts may take and transmit testimony via letters rogatory only when "there be a suit pending in a foreign court out of which the letters rogatory issue," when "the government of the country of that court be a party to said suit or interested therein," and when "the suit be for the recovery of money or property."[177] The use of testimony obtained in this fashion in criminal cases in the United States appears to be constitutionally questionable because of the constitutional requirement that in criminal cases the accused has a right "to be confronted with the witnesses against him." It is perhaps possible that transmission of such information to a foreign court could be authorized by statute, however, but it is highly unlikely that it could be procured abroad and used in federal courts here. This, however, stems from American constitutional requirements and is not necessarily of general application.[178]

State courts, of course, operate under different statutes, and courts in other nations are similarly governed by local laws. Thus, the use of letters rogatory depends upon what the local courts are allowed to do. It should be added further that letters rogatory are used to transmit testimony and not as a device by which a court in one country can get a foreign court to serve its processes.[179]

Commissions to Take Testimony. Another device sometimes used to procure information for court proceedings may be

---

31 Cal. 2d 682 (1948) ; see also *Charlton* v. *Kelly,* 229 U.S. 447 (1913). For a summary of rules governing extradition, see Kurt von Schuschnigg, *International Law* (Milwaukee, Wis.: The Bruce Publishing Co., 1959) , pp. 224–25.

[177] Hackworth, *Digest* II, p. 112.

[178] U.S., *Constitution*, Amendment VI; Hackworth, *Digest* II, pp. 109–10.

[179] *In Re Letters Rogatory out of First Civil Court of City of Mexico,* U.S. District Court, Southern District, N.Y. 261 Fed. 652 (1919) .

mentioned. This is the commission to take testimony, which consists of a communication, for example, by a court in the United States to the appropriate U.S. consular official abroad, asking him to take certain testimony and transmit it back to the court. Obviously the effectiveness of such procedure is conditioned upon the consul's ability to persuade the proposed witnesses to testify. This procedure is clearly more a matter of extended national processes than of international comity.[180]

Private International Law. Problems often arise regarding the enforcement or even the mere recognition within one jurisdiction of the private legal acts and contracts made in some other jurisdiction. Thus, for example, the admission of a person to the United States as a nonquota immigrant may hinge upon whether his or her marriage to a citizen of the United States is recognized in this country as being valid.[181] Such matters as marriage, divorce, other contracts, wills, and enforcement of foreign court judgments are often to be legally considered in jurisdictions other than those in which they were constructed. It is not difficult to imagine the legal problems and complications which may result from refusal of a state to honor the legality of a marriage contracted elsewhere by persons who are nevertheless its residents. For the American student the full faith and credit clause of the Constitution coupled with an understanding of the case of *Williams* v. *North Carolina* point up some of the potential problems with clarity.[182]

Among nations, however, there is no full faith and credit clause and the validity of foreign contracts and judgments in any other states depends upon the attitude of the state where the judgment or contract is to be enforced. This is not, strictly speaking, a segment of public international law, but its relevance to the topic is at least peripheral. Questions of this sort are variously called the conflict of laws, private international law, and international private law.

The leading U.S. case on the subject emphasizes the point that enforcement of foreign judgments is a matter of comity

---

[180] Hackworth, *Digest* II, pp. 98–99.

[181] *Ibid.*, pp. 356–91.

[182] U.S., *Constitution*, Art. IV, Sec. 1; *Williams* v. *North Carolina*, 325 U.S. 226 (1945).

since no treaties apply. It also points to two basic considerations which courts use; these are (1) reciprocity, and (2) the fairness of the foreign trial. Thus, the U.S. courts will ordinarily honor judgments of a foreign country if that country honors American judgments; and if the foreign trial appears to have been fairly, reasonably, and properly conducted, American courts will ordinarily not feel compelled to retry the case.[183]

SUMMARY

Questions of jurisdiction are of fundamental importance in international law. Determination of what state has jurisdiction in any given matter depends in many instances upon the location of boundaries. The subject of jurisdiction may be subdivided into four main areas: (1) boundaries and acquisition of territory, (2) maritime jurisdiction, (3) international servitudes, and (4) jurisdiction over persons.

Territory may be acquired in five basic ways. These are (1) discovery followed by occupation, (2) prescription, (3) treaty, (4) conquest, and (5) accretion. Boundaries on land are determined according to a number of basic rules. These include (1) reference to maps and reference points, (2) *uti possidetis juris*, (3) *uti possidetis*, (4) the "water divide" of mountains, and as a rule, (5) the *thalweg* of rivers, straits, and other border waters. States also have jurisdiction over a territorial belt of water, their superjacent airspace, and their subsoil. The status of space and polar areas remains obscure, but it can be said that a rule is being formed governing the continental shelf and the conservation of coastal fisheries.

Jurisdiction on the high seas and aboard ship revolves around a few basic principles. The high seas are open for the use of all states. On the high seas merchant vessels are under the jurisdiction of the state in which they are registered, but in port they are subject to the laws of the port unless the port state

---

[183] *Hilton* v. *Guyot*, 159 U.S. 113 (1895) ; also Hackworth, *Digest* II, pp. 86–97. On the general subject of private international law, see Arthur Nussbaum, *Principles of Private International Law* (New York: Oxford University Press, Inc., 1943) ; also Martin Wolff, *Private International Law* (Oxford: University Press, 1945) ; see also Philip C. Jessup, *Transnational Law* (New Haven, Conn.: Yale University Press, 1956) .

waives jurisdiction. As a practical matter the port state usually exercises jurisdiction when it feels that the peace of the port has been disturbed. Public vessels, on the other hand, may be refused entrance to foreign territorial waters but if admitted they are not subject to local laws. Rules governing navigation, salvage, safety regulations and other matters exist; some are based on treaties while others are mere usages.

Despite the sovereign character of territorial jurisdiction, there are instances called international servitudes where for one reason or another an obligation exists to allow another nation to make certain use of particular territories. One of the best examples of this is perhaps the perpetual treaty right of the United States to the use of the Panama Canal Zone.

Jurisdiction over persons is governed by a number of considerations, the most important of which are location and nationality. The three other bases of jurisdiction are called universality, protection, and passive personality. Thus, a state may with very few exceptions exercise jurisdiction over any persons within its territory and over persons who hold its nationality. Nationality is determined by state law and may be procured by birth or by naturalization. States frequently cooperate in exchanging persons accused of crimes so that they can be tried, and courts often get foreign courts to take testimony for them, particularly in civil cases. Although not strictly a part of international law, enforcement of foreign judgments and recognition of foreign contracts depends upon comity.

CHAPTER 6

Treaties and Related International Legislation

THE LAW OF nations develops in a number of ways, but by far the most important contemporary device employed is what is generally called the "treaty." This chapter will be devoted largely to a discussion of treaties, but other legislative devices will be given brief comment as well.

INTERNATIONAL LEGISLATION IN GENERAL

The legislative procedure within the state is usually a process by which the main political forces can more or less readily pass laws—within the framework of specific substantive or procedural checks.[1] The legislative machinery for the international community, on the other hand, is far less unified and the process as a whole leaves much to be desired. Yet it clearly reflects the political complexion of the community of nations. Whereas the democratic state accepts the principle of majority rule or extraordinary majority rule for municipal legislation, and the dictatorial state abides by legislative processes which reflect its internal political complex, the international community in general follows the thesis that each state is free to adopt or reject any new rules that are proposed. It is perhaps doubtful

[1] For pertinent clauses in U.S., *Constitution,* see particularly Art. I, Secs. VII, VIII, IX; Amendments I–VIII.

whether a lone state of only modest endowment could successfully stand on this principle against the remainder of the international community if the latter were united and adamant in some objective, for power remains the foremost element in politics and legislation.

In this setting there are three basic ways by which international rules are formulated. These are (1) by specific agreement normally in treaty form, (2) by endowing an international organization (by treaty) with rule-making authority, and (3) by the slow process of custom.

Other legislative forces mentioned earlier in this work as sources of international law[2] such as court decisions, the writings of publicists, and principles of justice or natural law are of specialized character and will receive only brief and passing mention in this chapter.

Agreements and Treaties

Of the various international legislative processes, the establishment of law by treaty is the most important from a contemporary standpoint. The treaty process is relatively rapid and it has adequate flexibility. Furthermore, it is as explicit and definite as its formulators are able to make it and, if properly registered and drafted (as contrasted with rare oral accords), there is no question as to what the terms of the agreement are—though there may well be some controversy as to what the terms mean. Since treaties constitute the bulk of contemporary international legislation, the present chapter will be largely devoted to a treatment of them.

International Organizations with Rule-Making Authority

During the latter half of the 19th century international organizations, created by treaty, began to be established, and now there are several hundred in existence. Many—perhaps most—of these organizations have at least some sort of rule-making authority which may be called international administrative law. These agencies fall into the familiar dichotomy in

---

[2] See above, Chapter One.

which some are political while others are essentially technical, but both types have ordinance-making powers. This is an interesting and useful technique which, nevertheless, is controversial in some quarters because it appears to contravene the principle of sovereignty. It holds considerable importance for the future, however, and enjoys some current utility. It will be noted more fully later in this chapter.

Custom

Custom as a lawmaking process is not a rapid procedure. It would appear that establishment of a rule by custom within a decade is to approach top speed. Thus its utility is at best curtailed, and the peculiar character of the procedure seems to lend itself nicely to certain matters but appears utterly unfitted for others. The previous discussions of the development of the national sovereignty theory of airspace jurisdiction and of the developing continental shelf theory should suffice to illustrate the process,[3] and, therefore, no further attention will be given it in this chapter.

Court Actions and Other Lawmaking Processes

Without entering into the time-honored controversy as to whether courts find or make law, it may be merely indicated that the international political setting circumscribes severely whatever inventive instincts an international court may have. Moreover, the judicial process is more concerned with settlement of disputes, a matter which will be considered in a later chapter.[4]

The writings of publicists are influential in two ways: (1) they help to determine what prevailing practice is, and (2) they point to rules that should be adopted. Thus their influence is anterior to the actual legislative act—though intimately tied to it.

---

[3] See above, Chapter Five.

[4] See below, Chapter Eight. For comment on the political setting in which international courts operate, see Charles De Visscher, *Theory and Reality in Modern International Law,* trans. P. E. Corbett (Princeton, N.J.: Princeton University Press, 1957), pp. 327–61.

Similarly, principles of justice or natural law obviously influence the formulation of law, but it is difficult to comprehend them as in themselves a legislative process. Rather, they are situated together with numerous other elements within the political complex which lead to the formal legislative act. Thus, the moral principle that murder and theft are wrong is reflected not only in municipal law, but peripherally in extradition treaties, and in the recognized customary right of any state to punish a pirate. It is difficult and often misleading to push this distinction very far, but as a practical matter these elements need not be considered further in this chapter.

THE SCOPE OF MODERN TREATIES AND INTERNATIONAL ADMINISTRATIVE LEGISLATION

It is useful to survey here in fairly broad outline the breadth of coverage contemplated by contemporary treaties and related international legislation.[5] This matter will be suggested by the examples cited throughout the chapter, but there may be utility in a short direct comment.

Bipartite and multipartite accords, agreements which establish direct relationships, and treaties which charter major political or technical agencies are all part of the subject matter embraced within the scope of international legislation. It is useful, moreover, to think of the familiar dichotomy of the political and the technical when considering international agreements, for the former have a constitutional quality while the latter are more akin to ordinary municipal law.

Political Agreements

Political accords are both of traditional and of unorthodox character. Accordingly, alliances, boundary settlements, and peace treaties are among the more important traditional types.

---

[5] There are many outstanding treaty compilations. See, e.g., *The League of Nations Treaty Series;* also *The United Nations Treaty Series,* 555 volumes were available as of late 1967; also the U.S. government, *Treaties and Other International Acts Series;* also Manley O. Hudson, *International Legislation* (9 vols.; Washington, D.C.: The Carnegie Endowment, 1931–50) .

They clearly structure political settlements, but their form and pattern have been employed for centuries, even though the internal substance of each may be new and up to date.

The Charter of the United Nations and the basic documents of the Organization of American States, on the other hand, are the constitutions of major international agencies of far-reaching political importance. They represent, however, relatively new forms of international machinery.

Technical Accords

Beyond the scope of political agreements and major constitutional arrangements are a vast number of technical treaties. These serve the international community in very much the same way that police, social, economic, and other specialized technical legislation serve within the state. These also can be classed as partially traditional while others are essentially modern in character. Accordingly, consular, trade, extradition, and arbitration agreements represent types long familiar to international law. On the other hand, there are newer treaties which serve other purposes. Illustrative of this last group are agreements which attempt to limit hours of labor, to curb white slavery, to eliminate genocide, and to proscribe the use of white phosphorus in the manufacture of matches. There are agreements which protect birds, fish, whales, seals, and other creatures; still other accords are designed to improve diets, foster good health, transmit mail, improve radio communication, and facilitate air and railroad transportation.

Some of these activities are provided for in simple treaties while others are handled by international agencies which are created by treaties. All must be viewed together as part of the composite picture. Like their domestic counterparts, this legislation results from needs and pressures within the international community. It is not as extensive as municipal law nor is most treaty law universal in application, but it does represent the scope of enacted law within the international community.[6]

---

[6] See Charles G. Fenwick, *International Law* (3d ed.; New York: Appleton-Century-Crofts, Inc., 1948), particularly Chapter XXV.

TREATIES: TECHNICALITIES AND SCOPE

Treaties represent the most important form of modern international law. They will be discussed under four main topics. These are (1) terms and mechanics, (2) validity, (3) termination, and (4) interpretation.

Terms and Mechanics

Treaties constitute, as noted above, a relatively precise way of legislating within the international community. Mention will be made here of terms and classifications as they are characteristically employed.

Definitions and Nomenclature. The term "treaty" is used in two senses. As usually employed in this work it suggests, and may in fact be defined as, *any valid agreement between international persons—usually states.* As employed in precise United States constitutional usage, however, it refers to those international accords which have been submitted to the Senate for its advice and consent in conformity with required procedures.[7]

Careful definitions of the term "treaty" are found in a number of sources. The most widely quoted is perhaps that of the Harvard research group in international law which stipulated that "A 'treaty' is a formal instrument of agreement by which two or more states establish or seek to establish a relation under international law between themselves."[8] This omits agreements to which international organizations or other international persons are parties, and thus Oppenheim's definition seems more accurate. He states that "International treaties are agreements,

---

[7] U.S., *Constitution*, Art. II, Sec. II (2). On the U.S. treaty power generally, see C. H. McLaughlin, "The Scope of the Treaty Power in the United States," *Minnesota Law Review,* Vol. XLII, No. 5, (April, 1958), pp. 709–71; Vol. XLIII No. 4, (March, 1959), pp. 651–725.

[8] Harvard Law School Research in International Law, "Law of Treaties," in *American Journal of International Law,* Vol. XXIX (Supplement, 1935), p. 686 (hereafter cited as "Law of Treaties"). For general reference, see also drafts and commentary in *Yearbook of the International Law Commission,* 1951, Vol. II; 1952, Vol. II; and 1958, Vol. II. For latest efforts of the Commission, see conveniently "Draft Articles on the Law of Treaties," in *American Journal of International Law,* Vol. LX (January, 1966), pp. 164–73 (hereafter cited as "1965 Draft").

of a contractual character, between States, or organizations of
States, creating legal rights and obligations between the parties."[9]

Thus it may be reiterated that a treaty may be defined as a
valid agreement between international persons—usually states.
It should be added that it seems to serve no legally valid point
to insist that the treaty be "formal" or written, for oral agreements—though by nature more difficult to prove—are considered to have international binding force.[10]

The term "treaty," as noted above, is really a generic term
which applies to international agreements many of which are
called by some other name. Among the terms employed to
describe international agreements are "treaty," "convention,"
"additional articles," "final act," "general act," "declaration,"
"agreement," "protocol," *procès-verbal,* "exchange of notes,"
modus vivendi, compromis d'arbitrage, "pact," "covenant,"
"charter," "constitution," "statute," and "executive agreement." Some of these terms seem to have special meanings, but
since the terminology of leading authorities differs, it is questionable whether a detailed attempt at definitions here can be
truly definitive. Perhaps, however, the list of definitions in the
appendix to this chapter may be useful.[11]

Such terms as *covenant, charter, statute,* and *constitution* are
used to refer to treaties which create international organizations.

Finally, it must be realized that at best these attempted

---

[9] Oppenheim-Lauterpacht, *Treatise* I, p. 877.

[10] See, e.g., *Legal Status of Eastern Greenland,* P.C.I.J., Judgments, Sec. A B,
No. 53, (1933), p. 71 *et passim;* see also comments in Wesley L. Gould, *An
Introduction to International Law* (New York: Harper & Bros., 1957), pp.
303–04; also "Convention on Treaties," Art. 2, IV Hudson, *International Legislation,* pp. 2378–85, see conveniently in L. Pfankuchen, *A Documentary Textbook
in International Law* (New York: Farrar and Rinehart, Inc., 1940), pp. 459–64,
see however, statement in Harvard Research, "Law of Treaties," pp. 689–90, 729–
32.

[11] See Ernest Satow, *A Guide to Diplomatic Practice* (4th ed. by N. Bland;
London: Longmans, Green & Co., Inc., 1957), pp. 324–71; also D. McNair, *The
Law of Treaties* (New York: Columbia University Press, 1938), pp. 3–4; Harvard
Research, "Law of Treaties," pp. 710–22; G. G. Wilson, *International Law* (9th
ed.; New York: Silver Burdett & Co., 1935), pp. 208–11; Hackworth, *Digest* V, pp.
1–5, 390–433; Oppenheim-Lauterpacht, *Treatise* I, pp. 877–78, 890–91; Denys P.
Myers, "The Names and Scope of Treaties," *American Journal of International
Law,* Vol. LI (July, 1957), pp. 574–605. For list in chapter appendix, see pp.
199–200.

definitions are approximations. All involve the concept of agreement by international persons, though some are basic, and others are of more supplementary character.

The Principal Types of Accords. It has been customary to classify treaties in a number of ways which relate—or purport to relate—to their particular characteristics. Perhaps the most significant statement that can be made about such classifications is that for the most part they are of "limited usefulness."[12] Nevertheless, there may be passing utility in stating that there are six common distinctions. (1) *Bipartite* and *multipartite* treaties (sometimes called *bilateral* and *multilateral*) relate respectively to accords made by two and several powers. (2) *Equal* and *unequal* (sometimes also termed *unilateral* and *bilateral*) treaties refer respectively to whether the obligations are binding on one or both parties. (3) *Simple* and *conditional* are used to refer to whether the terms are absolute or somehow qualified. (4) *Executed* and *executory* relate to whether the terms of the treaty in themselves terminate the issue in question or whether on the other hand some continuous type of action is contemplated.[13] (5) *Lawmaking* and *contractual* (or other than lawmaking treaties) represent another distinction which, unlike the others, is of some importance and refers to whether or not the treaty lays "down general rules of conduct among a considerable number of States"[14] or merely establishes some sort of exchange or *quid pro quo*. (6) Finally, a useful distinction may be made between essentially *political* and essentially *technical* treaties.

It should be repeated that most of these distinctions are mere exercises in terminology and are not very important, nor are the terms themselves linguistically satisfying or logically sound. The concept of the lawmaking treaty vis-à-vis other treaties deserves additional mention, however.

Lawmaking Treaties and Contractual Accords. "Lawmaking treaties" and "contractual accords" are terms representing distinctions which are meaningful though far from precise. As the term "lawmaking treaty" is usually employed, it sug-

---

[12] Oppenheim-Lauterpacht, *Treatise* I, p. 878.

[13] Fenwick, *op. cit.,* p. 431; McNair, *op. cit.,* pp. 4–6.

[14] Oppenheim-Lauterpacht, *Treatise* I, pp. 878–79.

gests a broad multipartite accord which charts or at least confirms rules of conduct. Examples would include the Hague and Geneva conventions, the air law and telecommunications agreements, and such earlier accords as those coming out of the Congress of Vienna and the Paris Conference of 1856.[15] On the other hand, it has been aptly observed that a host of similar bipartite agreements such as those prescribing the scope of extradition have the collective effect of lawmaking treaties.[16] It is an important point, however, that the treaty is the only practical mechanism which can be used to change international law formally and quickly, and when it is so used, a lawmaking operation has taken place—whether between two states or two dozen.

One important difference between such treaty arrangements and municipal law is the matter of unanimity. A lawmaking treaty does not *in itself* extend to a nonsignatory state. On the other hand, a lawmaking treaty may merely formalize and articulate a rule which already exists as a matter of customary law. Moreover, and even less precise, it may represent a part of the process of such a rule's formulation, *de lege ferenda*. That is, of course, a different problem—but a related one.

By contrast, while it is sometimes argued that all treaties make law,[17] it is nevertheless apparent that a treaty formalizing a sale such as those by which the United States acquired the Louisiana territory and Alaska are in many respects much more like commercial contracts than legislation. Similarly, a boundary settlement or a commercial treaty often is more akin to an ordinary contract than to a legislative act. As a consequence, the term "contract treaty" may be appropriate to differentiate this type of agreement from the treaties which create international legislation. It should be apparent that there is no clear line of demarcation between these two types of agreements.

Mechanics of Enactment. The internal process by which a treaty is formulated varies from country to country, and there are even different procedures within the same country. In the

[15] *Ibid.*, pp. 878–80; Fenwick, *op. cit.*, pp. 428–30.
[16] Gould, *op. cit.*, p. 295.
[17] Oppenheim-Lauterpacht, *Treatise* I, p. 879.

last connection it may be recalled that in the United States a "treaty" must be approved by a two-thirds majority of a Senate quorum[18] (or two thirds of the members present if more than a quorum), whereas an "executive agreement" if properly authorized in advance is not subject to postnegotiation Senatorial approval at all.[19] Indeed, if the subject matter of the agreement falls within the areas where the President's constitutional authority is already sufficient, it is not even necessary to obtain prior legislative approval.[20] All of this is notwithstanding the fact that "treaties" and executive agreements appear to have the same binding status under international law.[21]

There are perhaps five basic aspects which are relevant to the enactment of treaties. These are (1) negotiation, (2) ratification, (3) reservations and understandings, (4) registration, and (5) date of effectiveness.

Negotiation. The process of negotiation may be carried out by any authorized person. Sometimes the head of state himself negotiates an agreement, as did President Wilson after World War I. At times the head of the government negotiates. In still other instances the foreign minister or foreign secretary, a diplomatic official or even an authorized foreigner performs this function, although it appears that the United States has never endowed a foreigner to act for it in this way.[22] There are even instances where unauthorized persons have negotiated agreements which were subsequently ratified.[23]

A person authorized to negotiate and sign an agreement is

---

[18] U.S., *Constitution*, Art. II, Sec. II (2).

[19] Hackworth, *Digest* V, pp. 407–29; *B. Altman & Co.* v. *United States*, 224 U.S. 583 (1912). According to the *Altman* case it would appear that the term treaty can be applied to executive agreements without doing violence to the Constitution. It is probable, however, that recent terminological usage does not conform to the Altman decision.

[20] Hackworth, *Digest* V, pp. 402–7; *United States* v. *Pink*, 315 U.S. 203 (1942); *United States* v. *Belmont*, 301 U.S. 324 (1937).

[21] *Altman* v. *U.S., op. cit.; U.S.* v. *Belmont, ibid.; U.S.* v. *Pink, ibid.*

[22] Charles Cheney Hyde, *International Law Chiefly as Interpreted and Applied by the United States* (2d ed.; Boston: Little, Brown & Co., 1945), Vol. II, p. 1419.

[23] For a discussion of the unusual circumstances attending negotiation of the peace treaty ending the Mexican War and its negotiator, N. P. Trist, see Jesse S. Reeves, "The Treaty of Guadalupe-Hidalgo," *American Historical Review*, Vol. X (January, 1905), pp. 309–24.

usually given what are called "plenary" or "full powers." This used to mean that the head of state had endowed the negotiator with full power to bind the state, but now it normally means that the negotiator has been duly designated to negotiate an agreement within the limits imposed by the constitution and the usual necessity for ratification, and with due attention to the wishes of the executive authority with whom he must usually keep in some sort of contact.[24]

In this connection, it is usually the practice for each state to receive a copy of the treaty for its archives in which its name appears first. This is known as the *alternat*.[25] Also, attached to the treaty itself is usually a signed copy of what in essence are the minutes of the negotiating sessions. These minutes, known as *protocols* or *procès-verbaux*, are often of value in determining the intent of the negotiators and other background data.[26] Another matter of form concerns the language of the treaty. Although in earlier times, Latin and later French were the prevailing diplomatic languages, there are no definite rules pertaining to the matter. Sometimes a treaty is written in two, three, or more languages, each of which is authoritative and occasionally a language foreign to both parties has been used. Often, however, the text of the treaty is in several languages, but one version is declared to be authoritative.[27]

Once negotiated, an agreement is usually signed by the negotiator. Depending upon a number of circumstances, the signature may range from a matter of utter insignificance to an act of major importance. For the most part, however, such signatures are unimportant, for the real binding significance is in the act of ratification.[28]

Ratification and Related Procedures. Although the signature of the negotiator clothed with plenary powers was once sufficient to bind the state and may still have binding force in some instances, the constitutional requirements of most states

---

[24] Hyde, *op. cit.*, Vol. II, pp. 1420–22.

[25] *Ibid.*, p. 1427.

[26] *Ibid.*, pp. 1427–28.

[27] *Ibid.*, pp. 1422–24. For references pertinent to multilingual problems see this chapter, *below*, fn. 138.

[28] Hyde, *op. cit.*, pp. 1428–29.

now give final importance to certain postnegotiation processes and to the final act of assent, a process known as ratification. While there is some distinguished argument to the effect that a treaty signed by a head of state with, however, improper attention to internal constitutional processes, is still legally binding,[29] this view seems to fly in the face of political realities which now, as translated into constitutional requirements, specify the ratification process in detail.[30]

In the United States, as noted earlier, a "treaty" must receive the assent—technically the advice and consent—of two thirds of a quorum of the Senate and then the final approval of the President. But it should be noted that the Senate action is not, technically speaking, ratification. In the case of "executive agreements" the advice and consent of the Senate is not required. Ratifications are then exchanged among the participating powers, and the treaty or agreement is proclaimed, and it is thus effectively solemnized.[31]

Closely related to ratification is the act of *adherence* by a third party. This is simply the formal act of a nonsignatory power by which it states that it too considers itself bound by a particular agreement with which it has been allowed to become associated. This procedure has application primarily to multipartite accords.[32]

Reservations and Understandings. In signing and ratifying treaties, states sometimes feel that they must clarify certain meanings or in some cases exclude themselves from the application of particular sections of the treaty. When a state specifies its "understanding" of the meaning of a certain word or clause, it does not ordinarily cause serious repercussions. Thus, for example, the United States might specify in ratifying a convention that it does so with the understanding that its relationship to the inter-American regional system will not be affected.[33]

---

[29] Dionisio Anzilotti, *Cours de droit international* (Paris: Recueil Sirey, 1929) , pp. 259–61.

[30] See, e.g., comments in De Visscher, *op. cit.,* pp. 248–49; see also Harvard Research, "Law of Treaties," pp. 756–59.

[31] Hyde, *op. cit.,* Vol. II, pp. 1444–49. See also "1965 Draft," Arts. 11, 12.

[32] Hyde, *op. cit.,* pp. 1447–48.

[33] See comments in Hackworth, *Digest* V, pp. 144–53; also Fenwick, *op. cit.,* p. 438.

A reservation is a more serious matter, however, and the whole subject of reservations has become the center of considerable controversy. If a treaty is bipartite, there is no real problem resulting from a reservation for, under these circumstances, it is realized that a reservation has the effect of altering the originally proposed agreement and the other party is then in the position of ratifying the agreement as reserved or of rejecting it.

On the other hand, real complications arise from reservations to multipartite accords. These complications result from lack of agreement as to which of three basic theories should be applied in such instances. One of these, the *inter-American view,* follows the practice of considering the treaty to be in force on an individual nation basis, that is, those states which accept another nation's reservations may do so while other states may not, depending upon individual national preferences. This position has been officially stated as follows:

With respect to the juridical status of treaties ratified with reservations, which have not been accepted, the Governing Board of the Pan American Union understands that:

1. The treaty shall be in force, in the form in which it was signed, as between those countries which ratify it without reservations, in the terms in which it was originally drafted and signed.

2. It shall be in force as between the governments which ratify it with reservations and the signatory States which accept the reservations in the form in which the treaty may be modified by said reservations.

3. It shall not be in force between a government which may have ratified with reservations and another which may have already ratified, and which does not accept such reservations.[34]

The second theory, often called *the traditional view,* is that represented by administrative procedure under the League of Nations and the Secretariat of the United Nations, and has been officially summed up as follows:

A State may make a reservation when signing, ratifying or acceding to a convention, prior to its entry into force, only with the

---

[34] Quoted in "Report of the International Law Commission," *American Journal of International Law,* Vol. XLV (October, 1951), p. 111 (documents section).

consent of all States which have ratified or acceded thereto up to the date of entry into force; and may do so after the date of entry into force only with the consent of all States which have theretofore ratified or acceded.[35]

A third position, often termed *the sovereign theory,* is adhered to especially by the Soviet bloc. Basically the theory states that every state has a right, inherent in its sovereignty, to make reservations to treaties. In relations with states objecting to the reservations, only those portions of the treaty objected to are held to be inoperative.[36]

Even these clear divergencies were not too disconcerting until 1951 when the General Assembly requested that the International Court of Justice give an advisory opinion on reservations to the genocide convention, and that the International Law Commission also study the matter of reservations to international conventions. The views of these two bodies were also contradictory. The Court adhered by a seven to five vote to what was essentially the inter-American practice while the International Law Commission's recommendations followed earlier League and United Nations administrative practices.[37]

The Commission also recommended what in the light of the prevailing confusion will probably need to become general practice, namely, that each convention be written to specify in its own terms the status to be accorded reservations.[38] This procedure, has often been followed and in such instances the legal complications are minimized.

Registration. Interest in the public registration of treaties is of fairly long standing,[39] but came to be of practical importance

---

[35] *Ibid.,* p. 110.

[36] *Soviet Textbook,* pp. 270–71; *Yearbook of the United Nations 1951* (New York: Columbia University Press, 1952) , p. 827. George Po-chung Chen, "A Study of Some Problems of Reservations to Treaties" (unpublished Master's thesis, Department of Government, Southern Illinois University, 1964) , pp. 7–9.

[37] "Report of the International Law Commission," *op. cit.,* pp. 106–7; see case of *Reservations to the Convention on the Prevention and Punishment of the Crime of Genocide,* advisory opinion, 1951; I.C.J., Pleadings, Oral Arguments, Documents, pp. 15–69. The court view did vary from the inter-American position to the extent that it insisted that reservations be not incompatible with the main substance of the treaty. For this reason Chen considers that there are essentially four theories, Chen, *op. cit.,* pp. 1–10. Cf. also modified position of the International Law Commission in "1965 Draft," Arts. 18–22.

[38] "Report of the International Law Commission," *op. cit.,* p. 114.

[39] See comments in Gould, *op. cit.,* pp. 328–29.

with the adoption of the Covenant of the League which stated that treaties would not be binding unless registered with the Secretariat.[40]

Obligations under the United Nations Charter do not appear to be quite as absolute. The charter merely states that treaties "shall as soon as possible be registered with the Secretariat and published by it," and that "No party to any such treaty . . . not . . . registered . . . may invoke that treaty . . . before . . . the United Nations."[41]

Date of Effectiveness. Treaties often stipulate the date or the acts which are to bring them into operation. Thus the United Nations Charter came into effect by its own terms when ratified by the five permanent members of the Security Council and "a majority of the other signatory states."[42]

Although U.S. constitutional interpretations specified that treaties once ratified should be considered as effective from the date of signature,[43] prevailing practice now rather clearly points to the date of final ratification or promulgation (where constitutionally specified), or the date or circumstances specified in the treaty itself as designating the date of effectiveness. Expressive of correct international usage is the inter-American "Convention on Treaties" which states that "Treaties shall become effective from the date of exchange or deposit of ratification, unless some other date has been agreed upon through an express provision."[44]

The Validity of Treaties

Perhaps the most basic of all foundation principles in international law is the assumption that "treaties are binding." Yet, as with contracts and even municipal legislation, there may be circumstances which have an invalidating effect. The present

---

[40] League of Nations, *Covenant*, Art. 18; see also McNair, *op. cit.*, pp. 154–60; also Harvard Research, "Law of Treaties," pp. 912–18.

[41] U.N., *Charter*, Art. 102. Also "1965 Draft," Art. 25.

[42] U.N. *Charter*, Art. 110 (3).

[43] *Haver v. Yaker*, 9 Wallace 32 (1869).

[44] Harvard Research, "Law of Treaties," pp. 779–812. "Convention on Treaties," Art. 8, see conveniently in Pfankuchen, *op. cit.*, p. 461. Also "1965 Draft," Arts. 23, 24.

section will consider two aspects of the problem: (1) the matter of why treaties are binding, and (2) what may be called the mechanics of validity, that is, the more common technical requirements for validity. These last, however, will be considered negatively, that is, from the standpoint of what properly may cause a treaty to be invalid.

The Binding Effect of Treaties. The question of why treaties are binding, the principle known as *pacta sunt servanda,* represents a philosophical issue which is full of engaging yet frustrating ramifications. The principle is sustained on a variety of grounds ranging from natural law to the consent theory. It is argued that this principle is pragmatically sound because no state wants to be branded as a treaty breaker. Yet it should be readily apparent that all of these explanations invite philosophical reservations. For purposes of this volume it may be argued that treaties are binding because one of the requisites of any sort of order would seem to be a principle of basic integrity without which society itself can scarcely exist. It is essentially a pragmatic political view, yet it contains elements of naturalistic, customary, consent, and reputation theses.[45]

Whatever may be the correct foundation for this principle, it represents, as noted above, perhaps the most important basic assumption of international law. It is an example of a "first principle" which probably cannot be proved, and in the last analysis it may be necessary to admit that its acceptance represents essentially an act of faith.

The Mechanics of Validity. There are perhaps seven[46] elements which from a technical standpoint condition the validity of agreements. These are (1) the capacity to contract, (2) the authority of the negotiator, (3) mutuality of consent, (4) freedom of the negotiator from duress, (5) absence of

---

[45] For a discussion of the principle together with matters affecting validity and related considerations, see John B. Whitton "The Sanctity of Treaties," *International Conciliation,* 1935, No. 313, pp. 395–430; also Josef L. Kunz, "The Meaning and Range of the term *Pacta Sunt Servanda,*" *American Journal of International Law,* Vol. XXXIX (April, 1945), pp. 180–97; also John P. Humphrey, "On the Foundations of International Law," *American Journal of International Law,* Vol. XXXIX (April, 1945), pp. 231–43.

[46] For other discussions, see Fenwick, *op. cit.,* pp. 431–44; Oppenheim-Lauterpacht, *Treatise* I, pp. 890–99; see Wilson, *op. cit.,* pp. 218–19, where only four relevant considerations are noted.

fraud, (6) absence of material error, and (7) consistency with superior norms or with certain earlier agreements. It should be noted that these elements refer merely to basic and original validity; subsequent termination of treaties, changes of circumstances, lack of performance due to impossibility, and related matters will be considered separately in this chapter.

The Capacity to Contract. The capacity to make treaties is generally conceded as a characteristic of entities endowed with international personality. It may, however, be a conditioned or qualified characteristic, or one of the parties may be of such a nature that the resulting agreement cannot be classified as a legal instrument under international law. For example, an agreement between a state and a tribal group does not ordinarily constitute an agreement of which international law can take cognizance.[47]

Of more practical moment are situations in which a state due to some prior commitment or other conditioning factor is legally barred from making certain types of agreements. A historical case in point was that of Cuba which, under the terms of the Platt Amendment contained in its 1903 treaty with the United States, could not impair its independence.[48] Another example of clear incapacity to contract is seen in the constituent states of the United States which under the Constitution are specifically barred from making international agreements without congressional authorization.[49] At the same time it must be realized that these comments must be seen in proper political context. Thus a vassel or constituent state emerging into full-blown statehood may sometimes make such an agreement, get away with it, and thereby chart its independence. It may be concluded, however, that as a general rule an agreement contracted by an entity of the sorts described above, has no validity or status under the law of nations.

The Authority of the Negotiator. The authorization granted the negotiator or governmental organ to make an

---

[47] *Island of Palmas* case, Permanent Court of Arbitration, see in Scott, *Hague Court Reports,* Second Series, 83.

[48] *Treaty between the United States and Cuba . . . ,* Habana, 1903, Arts. I, II, III, see in *U.S. Statutes,* Vol. 33, Part 2, p. 2251, also p. 2249.

[49] U.S., *Constitution,* Article I, Sec. X (3) .

agreement is a separate consideration. It was noted above that in the process of negotiation, considerable attention is paid to the exchange of credentials by the negotiators, and the practical importance of such attention is by way of making sure that the negotiator or governmental agency handling negotiations is properly authorized to negotiate, contract, or to do whatever else he purports to be competent to do. And to widen the possibilities, a treaty made by a governmental agency such as the Interstate Commerce Commission, which has no authorization whatever in the area of foreign affairs, would have to be considered as invalid.[50]

The problem of the improperly accredited negotiator may be of only minor practical value now since the exchange of ratifications would normally obviate it,[51] but the question of concluding a treaty by processes other than the proper constitutional ones is of more serious moment. Although some publicists maintain that the head of state's action binds the state externally regardless of constitutional processes,[52] it appears that a more imposing preponderance of authority as well as of practice stresses the contrary position.[53] Illustrative of the more correct view, the Inter-American Convention on Treaties stipulates that "Treaties will be concluded by the competent authorities of the States or by their representatives, according to their respective internal law,"[54] and the Harvard Research Draft Convention on Treaties stipulates:

A State is not bound by a treaty made on its behalf by an organ or authority not competent under its law to conclude the treaty; however, a State may be responsible for an injury resulting to another State from reasonable reliance by the latter upon a representation that such organ or authority was competent to conclude the treaty.[55]

---

[50] See Hackworth, *Digest* V, pp. 39–42; Harvard Research, "Law of Treaties," pp. 992–1009, example on p. 992.

[51] Fenwick, *op. cit.*, pp. 434–35.

[52] See Anzilotti, *op. cit.;* also see Harvard Research, "Law of Treaties," pp. 996–99.

[53] As illustrative, see Harvard Research, "Law of Treaties," pp. 999–1009.

[54] "Convention on Treaties," Art. I, conveniently in Pfankuchen, *op. cit.*, p. 459.

[55] Harvard Research, "Law of Treaties," Art. 21, p. 661, for discussion see pp. 992–1009.

It should be noted that the statement of the Harvard group speaks of the possible responsibility of the state for injuries resulting to another state from cancellation of an improperly concluded treaty. This simply means that there may be instances where a state has made an agreement which is somehow a variance with constitutional processes and that subsequently it refuses to be bound, but that at the same time the agreement has caused the other contracting state some expense while acting in good faith to execute its terms. Under such circumstances, if the constitutional requirement were not more or less obvious, the state in error might be liable for damages.[56] It is difficult to judge the strict legal validity of the Harvard group's position on this matter. While it does not appear to be particularly logical in relation to the basic issue involved, it should be evident that there is much to commend it merely as a policy procedure in the interests of amicable relationships.

Mutual Consent. Mutuality of consent is a basic principle of contractual validity, but its application to international agreements, while important, is somewhat strained. It may be noted that a treaty involves the assent of two or more parties—thus a one-sided declaration or doctrine is not in itself binding upon other parties; nor are mere preliminary negotiations, so-called *punctations*.[57] Yet the concept of consent is indeed tortured when it is argued that a vanquished power enters into a peace treaty voluntarily—its choice being to continue the lost struggle! Nevertheless, coercion of this type, which in effect forces the signing of a treaty, is not considered as invalidating the agreement, nor is the more subtle economic pressure.[58]

There are, however, obvious moral objections to forced acceptance of this type of treaty, and whether the principle of good faith can be strictly applied to such treaties seems a legitimate matter of conjecture. In addition there are generally accepted pacific principles such as the sections of the United Nations Charter which state:

---

[56] *Ibid.*, pp. 1008–9.

[57] See comments in Oppenheim-Lauterpacht, *Treatise* I, pp. 890, 316–17.

[58] See De Visscher, *op. cit.*, pp. 246–47; W. E. Hall, *A Treatise on International Law* (5th ed. by J. B. Atlay; Oxford: The Clarendon Press, 1904), pp. 327–28; McNair, *op. cit.*, pp. 129–30; Gould, *op. cit.*, p. 325; Hackworth, *Digest* V, pp. 158–59; Hyde, *op. cit.*, Vol. II, pp. 1379–81.

All Members shall settle their international disputes by peaceful means in such a manner that international peace and security, and justice, are not endangered.

All Members shall refrain in their international relations from the threat or use of force against the territorial integrity or political independence of any state, or in any other manner inconsistent with the Purposes of the United Nations.[59]

With these factors in mind, to what extent can it be maintained that forced treaties are valid? Unless one proposes to be doctrinaire at the expense of everything else, it must be admitted that there is no easy answer—indeed there is probably no satisfactory answer at all. On the one hand, there can be no doubt that power plays a dominant role in establishing legal relationships. Yet Lauterpacht's edition of *Oppenheim's International Law* states flatly that "duress in such cases must, it is submitted, be regarded as vitiating the treaty."[60] It is doubtful, moreover, whether under such circumstances states have ordinarily felt themselves bound beyond what their erstwhile adversaries could enforce. Accordingly, Brierly speaks of such peace treaties as being fundamentally different from other types of treaties,[61] and Fenwick, pointing to the historic tendency for states not to think of dictated peace arrangements as binding beyond the power of the former victor to enforce them, seems to argue that the principle of good faith cannot be applied to such arrangements for " 'Treaties of peace' belong to the time when war was a legalized procedure."[62]

It seems to the present writer that contemporary international legal relationships are such that both in historic and modern contexts forced treaties must be accepted as representing the current legal status quo, but that their stability and lasting power are intimately connected with the power to enforce them, and to the power relationship at any given moment. This, it is submitted, conforms to political-legal reality, and to historic practice.

---

[59] U.N., *Charter,* Art. 2 (3, 4).

[60] Oppenheim-Lauterpacht, *Treatise* I, p. 892.

[61] J. L. Brierly, *The Law of Nations* (5th ed.; Oxford: The Clarendon Press, 1955), p. 245.

[62] Fenwick, *op. cit.,* pp. 440–42, quotation on 442; see, however, De Visscher, *op. cit.,* pp. 246–47 for a different view.

Personal Duress. Theoretically at least, personal duress is something quite different from pressure brought upon the state itself. It is generally held that "all contracts are void which are made under the influence of personal fear."[63] Under such circumstances a treaty may be properly considered invalid by the state whose envoy or head was personally intimidated.[64] Perhaps the example most frequently cited of personal duress is Napoleon's threat to try Ferdinand VII of Spain for treason if he did not agree to a treaty providing for his own abdication. The Harvard research group observes that "the invalidity of the treaty has been affirmed by all writers who have discussed it."[65] Remedial procedure suggested as proper by the Harvard group is submission of the problem to "a competent international tribunal or authority."[66]

Fraud. Fraud does not appear to be a matter of practical concern in the enactment of treaties, for it has been observed that "In practice no instances of the actual employment of fraud in the negotiation of treaties are known, and there appear to be no decisions either of national or international tribunals involving the question."[67] It is widely recognized in theory, nevertheless, that fraudulent misrepresentation at the time of negotiation would constitute grounds for subsequent nullification of the treaty.[68] It is to be noted that mere nondisclosure of some motivating element such as internal weakness could hardly be characterized as fraud, while something having to do with the "subject-matter of the contract,"[69] for example, the presentation "of a forged or otherwise falsified map or document" as a basis for negotiation would clearly constitute fraud.[70]

---

[63] Hall, *op. cit.,* p. 328.

[64] See Harvard Research, "Law of Treaties," pp. 1148–61; Fenwick, *op. cit.,* pp. 438–40; Gould, *op. cit.,* pp. 321–25; Pfankuchen, *op. cit.,* pp. 464–65; Hyde, *op. cit.,* Vol. II, p. 379; Hackworth, *Digest* V, p. 159.

[65] Harvard Research, "Law of Treaties," p. 1156.

[66] *Ibid.,* pp. 1159–61, quotation on p. 1159.

[67] *Ibid.,* p. 1145.

[68] See *ibid.,* pp. 1144–48; Hall, *op. cit.,* p. 328; Oppenheim-Lauterpacht, *Treatise* I, pp. 892–93; Fenwick, *op. cit.,* p. 442; Gould, *op. cit.,* p. 34; Hackworth, *Digest* V, pp. 159–60.

[69] Fenwick, *op. cit.,* p. 442.

[70] Harvard Research, "Law of Treaties," p. 1146; see also Oppenheim-Lauterpacht, *Treatise* I, p. 893; Hall, *op. cit.,* p. 328.

It should be noted that the Harvard research group again suggests submission of the problem to a "competent international tribunal or authority" as the proper remedial procedure when fraud is alleged.[71]

Error. Error in assumptions antecedent to agreements may in practice be closely related to fraud; certainly many writers discuss them together.[72] Yet in principle the matters are quite different. It is quite generally recognized, however, that if in the negotiation and ratification of a treaty there has been some material assumption or consideration which, however, was incorrect, the treaty itself may be considered void, voidable, or at least "not binding." Accordingly, were a treaty entered into under impressions obtained from an incorrect map (there is no question here of a maliciously prepared and therefore fraudulent map) or from incorrect assumptions as to geographical phenomena or related matters, the treaty itself might be considered as not binding.[73] Here again the remedial procedure suggested by the Harvard group is submission of the matter to "a competent international tribunal or authority."[74]

Conformity with Superior Norms. Consistency with certain prior treaties and with general international law is a requirement widely recognized as necessary for the validity of treaties.[75] It is even held by some authorities that treaties stipulating immoral objects are not binding.[76] How much of this can be spelled out in accurate detail is a matter of some question.

It may be conjectured, however, that the following principles are relevant: (1) Generally in a treaty following, but in some measure inconsistent with an earlier agreement among *exactly* the same powers, the more recent treaty applies, *lex posterior*

---

[71] Harvard Research, "Law of Treaties," p. 1144.

[72] McNair, *op. cit.,* pp. 131–34; Oppenheim-Lauterpacht, *Treatise* I, pp. 892–93.

[73] Harvard Research, "Law of Treaties," pp. 1126–34; Hackworth, *Digest* V, pp. 160–61; Hyde, *op. cit.,* Vol. II, pp. 1381–83; McNair, *op. cit.,* pp. 131–34.

[74] Harvard Research, "Law of Treaties," p. 1126. For a discussion of the problem of correcting minor textual errors in treaties, most of which are merely typographical, see Hackworth, *Digest* V, pp. 93–101; Hyde, *op. cit.,* Vol. II, pp. 1382–83.

[75] See, e.g., Hall, *op. cit.,* pp. 328–29; Oppenheim-Lauterpacht, *Treatise* I, pp. 893–97; see also discussions in Fenwick, *op. cit.,* pp. 442–44; McNair, *op. cit.,* pp. 112–28; Gould, *op. cit.,* pp. 325–26.

[76] Oppenheim-Lauterpacht, *Treatise* I, pp. 896–97.

derogat priori.[77] (2) When a subsequent treaty violates rights of a third power under a prior agreement with one of the parties to the newer accord, the obligations of the earlier treaty are in general considered to have priority.[78] Illustrative of the prevailing view, the Harvard group stipulated:

If a State assumes by a treaty with another State an obligation which is in conflict with an obligation which it has assumed by an earlier treaty with a third State, the obligation assumed by the earlier treaty takes priority over the obligation assumed by the later treaty.[79]

It should be noted that this principle does not specifically state that the later treaty is void, but only that obligations under the earlier one take priority over those resulting from the more recent accord. In this connection Kelsen appears to hold that both treaties are valid, but that nonperformance under either constitutes an illegal act,[80] presumably with the obligation to make restitution for whatever wrongs may have been committed. The present writer must agree with the view that both agreements are binding, but is of the opinion that if a choice must be made the earlier agreement is generally to be followed, with the logical additional obligation to make restitution wherever damages are in order.[81]

(3) When a treaty is inconsistent with the Charter of the United Nations, the obligations of the Charter clearly take precedence if all signatories of the treaty are members of the United Nations. This is a widely held view[82] and it stems from the stipulation in the Charter that:

---

[77] See Hans Kelsen, *The Law of the United Nations* (London: Stevens & Sons, Ltd., 1950), p. 112; also Kunz, *op. cit.*, pp. 192–93; Harvard Research, "Law of Treaties," pp. 1009–16.

[78] Harvard Research, "Law of Treaties," pp. 1024–29; Oppenheim-Lauterpacht, *Treatise* I, pp. 814–15; McNair, *op. cit.*, pp. 116–28; Gould, *op. cit.*, pp. 325–26; Hackworth, *Digest* V, pp. 161–62.

[79] Harvard Research, "Law of Treaties," Art. 22 (c), p. 1024.

[80] Kelsen, *op. cit.*, pp. 113–14; also Kunz, *op. cit.*, pp. 192–93.

[81] It should be noted that this view appears to be consistent with the position taken by the Central American Court of Justice in the case of *Costa Rica* v. *Nicaragua*, see in *American Journal of International Law*, Vol. XI (January, 1917), pp. 181–229; also see Hackworth, *Digest* V, pp. 161–62.

[82] See Kelsen, *op. cit.*, p. 115; Oppenheim-Lauterpacht, *Treatise* I, pp. 895–96; Gould, *op. cit.*, p. 326.

In the event of a conflict between the obligations of the Members of the United Nations under the present Charter and their obligations under any other international agreement, their obligations under the present Charter shall prevail.[83]

(4) When an obligation under the Charter of the United Nations is inconsistent with an earlier accord which, however, represents a relationship between a U.N. member and a non-member, the situation is somewhat more complicated. It is here that Kelsen's argument is most convincing when he suggests, as noted above, that both agreements would be binding.[84] For the United Nations member, Article 103 stipulates that obligations under the Charter are to prevail. It would seem, therefore, that the proper view here is essentially the same as that specified in (2) above, that is, that both agreements are valid and that the state which is a signatory to both has to account for its deviation from either agreement. In the opinion of the present writer, political considerations would seem to suggest, however, that in this type of situation priority should be given to adherence to the obligations of the United Nations Charter because of its near universal application, but the binding character of the conflicting accord would seem to justify claims for damages from that quarter.

(5) When a treaty violates general conventional or customary international law, many writers consider the treaty to be invalid.[85] In this view an agreement to preempt a portion of the high seas, or an agreement between two states to divide between them the territory of a third state would be invalid. It is argued that these rules represent universal principles of international law; and even though not all states may have signed the allegedly superior conventions, they together with customary law represent rules to which treaties must conform. Certainly for signatories of a convention, the principles outlined above apply, but for nonsignatories to a near universal convention or for the general application of customary principles vis-à-vis conflicting obligations of a later treaty, none of the alterna-

---

[83] U.N., *Charter,* Art. 103.

[84] See above, fn. 80.

[85] Hall, *op. cit.,* pp. 328–29; Hyde, *op. cit.,* Vol. II, pp. 1374–75; Oppenheim-Lauterpacht, *Treatise* I, p. 897.

tive solutions is very satisfactory. It may be conjectured that were nine tenths of the maritime states including all of the great powers to agree to recognize the 12-mile limit, the lone protests of a minor power that its rights had been violated under the allegedly customary 3-mile rule would prove to be merely a gesture of futile impotence.[86] Perhaps the only solution which is even partially satisfactory is that a treaty which is in conflict with such norms as described above gives rise to the demand for redress by any injured party, but in itself is not invalid.

(6) Finally, it is sometimes argued that a treaty having for its substance an immoral object is not binding.[87] This would seem to assume that that which is immoral is also illegal. Since there is likely to be considerable variation in defining immorality, however, and since it is hardly valid to make an across-the-board formal liaison between morality and legality, the present writer doubts seriously the legal applicability of this general proposition, except in those cases where an immoral act is clearly an illegal act as well.

The Termination, Suspension, and Revision of Treaties

While regularized and politically adequate machinery exists for alteration or termination of municipal law, the procedures for achieving the same results with international treaties are far less uniform. In some respects the whole matter is unsatisfactory, and startlingly unrealistic. As is well known, municipal law in virtually all modern democratic states can be altered by a mere majority decision of the legislature. Even the more fundamental constitutional rules are subject to change by regularized

---

[86] This cannot be stated with finality, however, for the intensity of the precise political context would weigh significantly as would the vitality of the doctrinaire rule that no state may be bound without its own consent. Cf. Art. 2, No. 6 of the Charter of the United Nations states "The Organization shall ensure that states which are not Members of the United Nations act in accordance with these Principles so far as may be necessary for the maintenance of international peace and security." See also, *Covenant of the League of Nations*, Art. 17.

For a serious recent argument that there are in fact "norms with which treaties must not conflict," see Alfred Verdross, "*Jus Dispositivum* and *Jus Cogens* in International Law," *American Journal of International Law*, Vol. LX (January, 1966), pp. 55–63.

[87] Oppenheim-Lauterpacht, *Treatise* I, pp. 896–97.

processes such as those described in the U.S. Constitution,[88] although similar fundamental changes in Great Britain are consummated in the same way as any other legislation.

In International law, on the other hand, the problem is much more complex, and as already noted, much lack of realism is in evidence. Methods of termination fall into five main categories several of which may be subdivided into two or more lesser groups. These main categories are as follows: (1) Treaties may be terminated according to the terms of the treaty itself. (2) Treaties may be terminated by the agreement of the signatories—express or tacit. (3) If a treaty has been violated by one party, the other party may have the option of considering the treaty as void. (4) If some of the fundamental circumstances upon which a treaty is premised have changed, it may be permissible to consider the treaty to be terminated. (5) Finally, in the event of war, some treaties are considered suspended, others terminated, while still others, such as treaties governing the conduct of hostilities, are activated.

Within these five basic categories there are several processes which are quite adequate and satisfactory. On the other hand, there is no doubt that an impasse may result from a treaty without terms for revision for, as the great powers proclaimed in 1871 and the League Council reiterated in 1935:

. . . it is an essential principle of the law of nations that no Power can liberate itself from the engagements of a treaty, nor modify the stipulations thereof, except as the result of the consent of the contracting parties, by means of an amicable understanding.[89]

This represents the U.S. view as well, for in 1934 it informed the Japanese government that "Treaties can lawfully be modified or terminated only by processes prescribed or recognized or agreed upon by the parties to them."[90]

On the other hand, this legalistic state of affairs does not

---

[88] U.S., *Constitution*, Art. V. For a study of treaty termination in the United States, see Randall H. Nelson, "The Termination of Treaties and Executive Agreements by the United States: Theory and Practice," *Minnesota Law Review*, Vol. XLII (April, 1958) , pp. 879–906.

[89] See conveniently in M. O. Hudson, *Cases and Other Materials on International Law* (St. Paul, Minn.: West Publishing Co., 1951) , pp. 492–93; see also, *ibid.*, fn. 9 for League statement.

[90] Cited in Hackworth, *Digest* V, p. 298.

mean that adherence to the rules is alwsys satisfactory, nor does it mean that states always do in fact so adhere. The point to be emphasized, however, is that while some termination procedures are quite adequate, others are totally unsatisfactory, and that it is not realistic to think that any treaty can be binding forever. These procedures will be surveyed in the following paragraphs under the five main headings noted above.

  Termination under the Terms of the Treaty Itself. Many treaties are now drafted with self-contained terms under which termination is to be effected. In others the circumstances of effective termination are clearly implied. These treaties present no serious difficulties and the relevent procedures can be classed in three categories. These are termination by (1) performance, (2) arrival of the specified expiration date, and (3) renunciation in accordance with provisions.

  Termination by Performance. Some agreements, called executed treaties, are very much in the nature of commercial contracts. Under the terms of such accords some sort of exchange is effected and the only continuing importance of the treaty is as a record of the transaction. For example, under the terms of the Gadsden Purchase the United States acquired some 45,535 square miles of territory from Mexico in return for the sum of $10,000,000. Similarly, the United States purchased the Louisiana territory from France, Alaska from Russia, and the Virgin Islands from Denmark.[91]

  It may, perhaps, be improper to speak of these treaties as terminated, for they continue to be of importance in much the same sense that a deed of sale is important. Yet, action under the treaty has been terminated by the completed performance of the stipulated obligations.[92]

  Termination of Treaty at Date of Expiration. Many treaties are drafted for a certain number of years duration after which the treaty automatically lapses. Expressive of this type of arrangement is the pertinent clause of the Treaty of Chaumont which states that "the High Contracting Parties have agreed to

---

[91] For the texts of these treaties see respectively 6 Miller, *Treaties* . . . , pp. 293–302; 2 Hunter, *Treaties* . . . , pp. 498–515; 2 Malloy, *Treaties* . . . , pp. 1521–24; 39 U.S., *Statutes at Large,* Part II, pp. 1706–17.

[92] Harvard Research, "Law of Treaties," pp. 1171–73.

extend the duration of it to 20 years to take date from the day of its Signature."[93]

Very similar in character are treaties which are to prevail until some expected event has taken place. In this connection the Declaration Prohibiting the Discharge of Projectiles from Balloons states that "The Contracting Powers agree to prohibit, for a period extending to the close of the Third Peace Conference, the discharge of projectiles and explosives from balloons. . . ."[94] In this specific connection it is of interest to recall, however, that while the first and second peace conferences were held in 1899 and 1907 respectively, the projected Third Hague Conference would have taken place in about 1915. War had already broken out, however, and as a consequence, the "Third Peace Conference" was never held.[95]

Termination by Renunciation in Accordance with Terms. Closely related to the automatic expiration provisions surveyed above are clauses which permit renunciation. Such renunciation provisions are often conditioned upon the expiration of a certain extent of time. Typical of this type of arrangement, the North Atlantic Treaty provides:

> After the treaty has been in force for twenty years, any party may cease to be a party one year after its notice of denunciation has been given to the Government of the United States of America, which will inform the Governments of the other parties of the deposit of each notice of denunciation.[96]

Illustrative of the less conditional type of renunciation clause is that formed in the Declaration Prohibiting the Discharge of Projectiles from Balloons noted above. In another section of that treaty, which seems almost to take a right of renunciation for granted, it is stated that:

> In the event of one of the High Contracting Parties denouncing the present Declaration, such denunciation shall not take effect

---

[93] Art. XVI, see conveniently in James T. Watkins, IV and J. William Robinson, *General International Organization: A Source Book* (Princeton, N.J.: D. Van Nostrand Co., Inc., 1956), pp. 3–6.

[94] 36 U.S., *Statutes at Large*, Part 2, p. 2439.

[95] For further comment on this agreement, see *below*, Chapter Nine.

[96] Article 13, see conveniently in Louis L. Snyder, *Fifty Major Documents of the Twentieth Century* (New York: D. Van Nostrand, Co., Inc., 1955), pp. 145–48, quotation on p. 148.

until a year after the notification made in writing to the Netherlands Government, and forthwith communicated by it to all the
other Contracting Powers.[97]

Termination by Agreement of the Parties. It is clearly
recognized that treaties may be canceled by agreement of the
contracting powers.[98] Such agreements may be of three kinds
but in all instances the principle of *lex posterior* is applicable.
These three types are (1) specific termination by the parties,
(2) termination by implication, and (3) the problem of termination by desuetude. Finally consideration will be given to the
problem surrounding the contention that any state may unilaterally renounce its advantages under a treaty.

Specific Termination by the Contracting Parties. Powers
sometimes sign agreements by which they specifically abrogate
earlier accords. An example sometimes cited is that of the
Hay-Pauncefote Treaty which specifically abrogated the earlier
Clayton-Bulwer Treaty, the pertinent clause stating that: "The
High Contracting Parties agree that the present Treaty shall
supersede the afore-mentioned Convention of 19th April,
1850."[99] In this same connection the Convention on International Civil Aviation stipulates that:

> Each contracting State undertakes, immediately upon the coming
> into force of this Convention, to give notice of denunciation of the
> Convention relating to the Regulation of Aerial Navigation signed
> at Paris on October 13, 1919, or the Convention on Commercial
> Aviation signed at Habana on February 20, 1928, if it is a party to
> either. As between contracting States, this Convention supersedes
> the Conventions of Paris and Habana previously referred to.[100]

Termination by Implied Agreement. If a treaty contains
clauses which obviously supersede the terms of an earlier agreement, among the same signatories, it may imply that the earlier
accord or portions of it are to be considered as canceled. Ac-

---

[97] See above, fn. 94.

[98] See Harvard Research, "Law of Treaties," Art. 33 (a), pp. 1163–65; see also
Hackworth, *Digest* V, pp. 304–6; Fenwick, *op. cit.,* p. 451.

[99] *Ibid.;* Art. I, see in I Malloy, *Treaties . . . ,* p. 782; see reference in
Fenwick, *op. cit., passim.*

[100] *Convention on International Civil Aviation,* Chicago, 1944, Art. 80, Dept.
of State, Conference Series 64.

cordingly, the U.S. government viewed an 1830 treaty with the Ottoman Empire, and binding on Egypt after the end of Ottoman suzerainty, to have been impliedly abrogated by the Montreux Convention.[101]

Termination by Desuetude. It is theoretically possible that a treaty, like a rule of customary international law, may be allowed to lapse by mutual acquiescence in the nonobservance of its terms. This is obviously related to the matter of termination by implied agreement, but it is of course considerably more nebulous. The point is, however, that desuetude requires a sort of negative acquiescence by the contracting parties.

In the 1861 arbitral award in the *Yuille, Shortridge and Company Claims* case, the Senate of Hamburg said that an express act was required showing not only that the claimant state had disregarded the treaty, but also that the other party had pointedly failed to seek enforcement of its rights.[102]

Renunciation of Advantages. Related to the above is the question which arises from the view sometimes expressed that states may renounce unilaterally the advantages which they enjoy under a treaty.[103] While it seems unlikely that such a wish on the part of a beneficiary state would be objected to, it seems to be no different in principle than any other terms of agreement. Accordingly, the Harvard research group's view that no such principle of unilateral renunciation exists must be accepted,[104] and therefore, in order to renounce advantages under such a treaty there would be need for mutual consent—specific or implied—just as in any other agreement.

Termination of Violated Treaties by the Injured Party. When one party to an agreement has violated it or interpreted it in a way which appears to change its substance, the treaty is not considered to be automatically void, but merely voidable.

---

[101] Hackworth, *Digest* V, pp. 306–7.

[102] See Georg Schwarzenberger, *International Law* (2d ed.; London: Stevens & Sons, Ltd., 1949), Vol. I, p. 199; Gould, *op. cit.,* p. 338; see also in A. de Lapradelle and N. Politis, *Recueil des arbitrages internationaux* (Paris: Pedone, 1923), Vol. II, p. 105.

[103] Wilson, *op. cit.,* p. 223; see "Convention on Treaties," (Inter-American, 1928), Art. 14 (e), cited in Pfankuchen, *op. cit.,* p. 462; see also citation in Hackworth, *Digest* V, p. 298.

[104] Harvard Research, "Law of Treaties," pp. 1161–62.

That is, the injured state at its discretion may choose to consider that the treaty has been terminated, or to continue to consider it as binding and seek its enforcement.[105] In the interesting case of *Charlton* v. *Kelly* it was charged that the extradition treaty between the United States and Italy was void because Italy would not extradite its own citizens. Charlton thus tried to escape extradition to Italy to stand trial for the alleged murder of his wife while traveling in Italy. In view of the more extensive utilization of the nationality principle by Italy than by the United States,[106] Italian law made it illegal to extradite an Italian subject. Whether this attitude on the part of Italy be considered an interpretation or a violation, the Court thought a choice remained open to the United States, and it commented as follows:

If the attitude of Italy was, as contended, a violation of the obligation of the treaty, which, in international law, would have justified the United States in denouncing the treaty as no longer obligatory, it did not automatically have that effect. If the United States elected not to declare its abrogation, or come to a rupture, the treaty would remain in force. It was only voidable, not void; and if the United States should prefer, it might waive any breach which in its judgment had occurred and conform to its own obligation as if there had been no such breach.[107]

Of both theoretical and practical importance, the matter of voiding a voidable accord may raise a number of issues. For example, would violation of one section, especially one of small consequence, be justification for nullification of the entire agreement? Though an affirmative view invites abuse, and is by no means definitely correct, it appears to be widely held.[108] The Harvard research group was of the opinion that reasonable procedure would include referring the matter to a competent

---

[105] Hackworth, *Digest* V, pp. 342–48; Fenwick, *op. cit.*, pp. 452–53.

[106] For a discussion see above, Chapter Five.

[107] *Charlton* v. *Kelly*, 229 U.S. 447 (1913).

[108] For brief comment, see Fenwick, *op. cit.*, p. 452; Oppenheim-Lauterpacht, *Treatise* I, pp. 497–98. Another facet of the matter was seen in the U.S.–U.N. reaction of mid-1957 to the Communist buildup in North Korea in violation of the truce agreement. The U.N. Commander indicated that new weapons would be introduced until the balance contemplated by the agreement had been restored and until the Communist command demonstrated that it would adhere to the agreement. See in *New York Times*, June 22, 1957, p. 3.

international authority. The pertinent article of the Draft Convention drawn up by that group reads as follows:

> If a State fails to carry out in good faith its obligations under a
> treaty, any other party to the treaty, acting within a reasonable time
> after the failure, may seek from a competent international tribunal
> or authority a declaration to the effect that the treaty has ceased to
> be binding upon it in the sense of calling for further performance
> with respect to such State.[109]

This process would merely avoid the disadvantages of unilateral abrogation.

It may be mentioned, finally, that the problem is approached
from a somewhat different standpoint within the United Nations. A violator of the Charter is merely to be expelled from
the organization. In this connection the Charter states that:

> A Member of the United Nations which has persistently violated
> the Principles contained in the present Charter may be expelled
> from the Organization by the General Assembly upon the recom-
> mendation of the Security Council.[110]

Termination by Virtue of Altered or Unusual Circumstances.
It is unrealistic to assume that a treaty with no termination
clause would have to be enforced until the end of time, yet
there is no easy way to provide for unilateral termination in the
event that agreement to terminate cannot be achieved. There
are, however, at least two categories of instances where altered
or unusual circumstances allow for the possibility of termination. These may be classified as (1) a change of circumstances
which warrants invocation of the *clausula rebus sic stantibus,*
and (2) the impossibility of performance or *force majeure.*

Rebus Sic Stantibus. It is generally recognized that if
changes take place in the circumstances upon which an agreement rests, the treaty may be considered as not binding.[111] Recognizing the validity of this principle, Mr. Justice Davis of the
U.S. Court of Claims quoting Wharton, wrote:

---

[109] Harvard Research, "Law of Treaties," Art. 27, see on p. 1077 and comment
pp. 1077–94.

[110] U.N., *Charter*, Art. 6.

[111] See comment in Harvard Research, "Law of Treaties," pp. 1096–1126.

Abrogation of a treaty may occur by change of circumstances, as:

"When a state of things which was the basis of the treaty, and one of its tacit conditions, no longer exists. In most of the old treaties were inserted the *clausula rebus sic stantibus,* by which the treaty might be construed as abrogated when material circumstances on which it rested changed. To work this effect it is not necessary that the facts alleged to have changed should be material conditions. It is enough if they were strong inducements to the party asking abrogation.

"The maxim '*Conventio omnis intelligitur rebus sic stantibus*' is held to apply to all cases in which the reason for a treaty has failed, or there has been such a change of circumstances as to make its performance impracticable except at an unreasonable sacrifice."[112]

It may be further noted that the United States held that the International Load Line Convention of 1930 was rendered inoperative in mid-1941 by virtue of changes due to war conditions. The Attorney General's opinion states that:

In short the implicit assumption of normal peacetime international trade, which is at the foundation of the Load Line Convention, no longer exists.

Under these circumstances there is no doubt in my mind that the convention has ceased to be binding upon the United States. It is a well established principle of international law, *rebus sic stantibus,* that a treaty ceases to be binding when the basic conditions upon which it was founded have essentially changed. Suspension of the convention in such circumstances is the unquestioned right of a state adversely affected by such essential change.[113]

Despite these reasonably clear examples of the operation of the *clausual rebus sic stantibus,* there is no indication that the rule can be easily invoked. Furthermore, there is no clear rule as to when its invocation is justified. Accordingly, there is debate as to whether the changes must be "fundamental" or may be of lesser scope; whether absorption of a state transfers or nullifies treaties; and whether fundamental governmental changes may or may not justify invocation of the principle.[114]

[112] *Hooper* v. *United States,* 22 Court of Claims 408 (1887); quoted in Harvard Research, "Law of Treaties," pp. 1105–6.

[113] Quoted in Hackworth, *Digest* V, pp. 354–55.

[114] See discussion in Hyde, *op. cit.,* Vol. II, pp. 1523–41.

Because of these difficulties it may be well to cite the definition of one of the close students of the principle who states that:

It is believed that the following definition of *rebus sic stantibus* is the definition, and the only definition, which is recognized by States as a rule of customary international law under the title of the doctrine of *rebus sic stantibus:*

A treaty of perpetual or indefinite duration which contains no provision for revision or denunciation lapses, in the sense that stipulations which remain to be performed cease to bind the parties to the treaty, when it is recognized by the parties to the treaty or by a competent international authority that there has been an essential change in those circumstances which existed at the time of the conclusion of the treaty, and whose continuance without essential change formed a condition of the obligatory force of the treaty according to the intention of the parties.[115]

It should be mentioned, moreover, that the Harvard research group also felt that a decision by a competent international authority should be utilized in invoking the *clausula*. The rarity of cases in which the principle has been invoked has induced Brierly's observation that "There seems to be no recorded case in which its application has been admitted by both parties to a controversy, or in which it has been applied by an international tribunal." [116]

It may well be, however, that the Anglo-French-Turkish alliance of 1939 affords such an example. That agreement called for Anglo-French aid to Turkey in case of attack, and Turkish assistance in the event of war in the Mediterranean. With the entry of Italy into the war and the collapse of France, war had come to the Mediterranean, but under conditions radically different from those contemplated. Under these circumstances Turkey's decision to remain nonbelligerent until late in the

---

[115] Chesney Hill, *The Doctrine of "Rebus Sic Stantibus" in International Law* (Columbia, Mo.: University of Missouri, 1934), p. 83. The limitation of the *clausula* to unlimited or perpetual treaties raises some doubt. The International Law Commission noted in 1963 that such limitation was probably not warranted. See in "United Nations Report of the International Law Commission," *American Journal of International Law,* Vol. LVIII (January, 1964), pp. 283–91, especially pp. 288–89.

[116] Harvard Research, "Law of Treaties," Art. 28, p. 1096; Brierly, *op. cit.,* p. 261; see also *Case of the Free Zone of Upper Savoy and the District of Gex,* P.C.I.J. Series A/B, No. 46, 1932, pp. 155–58.

war seems to have had the sympathetic understanding of its allies.[117]

Impossibility of Performance or Force Majeure. Although one author has stated that *rebus sic stantibus* does not embrace the concept of impossibility of performance,[118] this concept, which is at least intimately related to the *clausula,* is also a clearly recognized condition under which treaties sometimes may be properly renounced. This includes impossibilities of several sorts—physical, economic, and judicial.[119]

Accordingly, if a state is bound by a defensive alliance with two other nations which subsequently go to war against each other, it is generally recognized that the third state is absolved from taking any part. This may be viewed as both a judicially and a physically impossible situation. Similarly, if a treaty concerns an island which subsequently disappears, or designates water rights in a river which is nonexistent, the pertinent treaty can hardly be considered as enforceable.[120]

Similarly, a treaty may be disregarded if it provides economic, military, or other terms which a state cannot meet without incurring mortal danger to the continuation of the very existence of the state itself.[121]

It should be added that these are essentially theoretical examples, but they perhaps illustrate the concept. It may also be noted that nonperformance under such circumstances is, like invocation of *rebus sic stantibus,* subject to controversy on the

---

[117] League of Nations Treaty Series, Vol. CC (1940–41) , pp. 169 ff. See George Lenezowski, *The Middle East in World Affairs* (2d ed.; Ithaca, N.Y.: Cornell University Press, 1956) , pp. 134–39 *et passim.* If not a full application of the *clausula rebus sic stantibus* in the sense of a formal abrogation, this instance nevertheless suggests similar practical dimensions. The writer is indebted to his colleague, Professor Abdul Majid Abbass, formerly ambassador of Iraq to the United Nations, for drawing this interesting historical instance to his attention.

For a recent study of this concept see Oliver J. Lissitzyn, "Treaties and Changed Circumstances" *American Journal of International Law,* Vol. LXI (October, 1967) , pp. 895–922.

[118] Hill, *op. cit.,* p. 79.

[119] Hackworth, *Digest* V, p. 356; Daniel Antokoletz, *Tratado de derecho internacional publico* (4th ed.; Buenos Aires: Bernabe y Cia, 1944) , Tomo III, pp. 265–66.

[120] Oppenheim-Lauterpacht, *Treatise* I, p. 945; Antokoletz, *op. cit.,* p. 266, *et passim.*

[121] Hackworth, *Digest* V, p. 356; Antokoletz, *op. cit., passim.*

grounds that such invocation was improper. Accordingly, in a case before the arbitral tribunal established to settle claims between Turkey and Russia, the court said:

> *The exception of "force majeure,"* cited as of the first impor-
> tance, may be pleaded in opposition in public as well as in private
> international law. International law must adapt itself to political
> necessities. The Imperial Russian Government expressly admits . . .
> that the obligation of a State to carry out treaties may give way "if
> the very existence of the State should be in danger, if the observance
> of the international duty is . . . 'self-destructive . . .'" . . . It
> would clearly be exaggeration to admit that the payment (or the
> obtaining of a loan for the payment) of the comparatively small
> sum of about six million francs due the Russian claimants would
> imperil the existence of the Ottoman Empire or seriously compro-
> mise its internal or external situation. The exception of *force maj-
> eure* cannot, therefore, be admitted.[122]

It should perhaps be added that the question of termination by virtue of dissolution of one of the contracting parties is a matter of some dispute in which even U.S. precedents are themselves quite contradictory.[123] Fenwick properly views this matter as a problem of state succession rather than as a termi- nation or obligation problem.[124]

The Effect of War on Treaties. Almost the entire scope of the question involved here is controversial.[125] It was formerly recognized that virtually all treaties were terminated or at least suspended between two states which were at war. In the Span- ish-American War, for example, the Spanish government issued a decree to the effect that all treaties with the United States were terminated.[126] Nevertheless, it is now generally recognized that certain treaties may remain in force, while others are terminated or suspended, and still others are activated. Al- though there is little dispute about the principle just enunci-

---

[122] Quoted in Hackworth, *Digest* V, p. 356, from Scott, *The Hague Court Reports* (1916), pp. 297, 317–18.

[123] Hyde, *op. cit.,* pp. 1529–35.

[124] Fenwick, *op. cit.,* p. 451.

[125] See comments in Harvard Research, "Law of Treaties," p. 1183 *et passim;* Cecil J. B. Hurst, "The Effect of War on Treaties," *The British Yearbook of International Law* (1921–22), p. 38.

[126] See discussion including comments on adjustments in the application of the Spanish decree in Moore, *Digest* V, pp. 375–80.

ated, there is real difficulty in determining precisely which treaties are to be abrogated and which are to be allowed to stand. There are some guideposts, however, and in this connection the Court of Appeals in New York held that:

International law today does not preserve treaties or annul them regardless of the effects produced. It deals with such problems pragmatically, preserving or annulling as the necessities of war exact. It establishes standards, but it does not fetter itself with rules. When it attempts to do more, it finds that there is neither unanimity of opinion nor uniformity of practice. "The whole question remains as yet unsettled" (Oppenheim, *supra*). This does not mean, of course, that there are not some classes of treaties about which there is general agreement. Treaties of alliance fall. Treaties of boundary or cession, "Dispositive" or "transitory" conventions survive. . . . So, of course, do treaties which regulate the conduct of hostilities. . . .[127]

In the same decision Judge Cardozo attempted to reduce the matter to a principle and in so doing observed that "provisions compatible with the state of hostilities, unless expressly terminated, will be enforced, and those incompatible rejected." [128]

It would seem that the change of conditions rendered by war is sufficient to allow legal latitude in this matter, but in practice four general guideposts emerge: (1) certain treaties come into full force, for example, treaties governing the rules of warfare; (2) certain other treaties are clearly terminated, for example, treaties of alliance; (3) certain other treaties, known as *pacta transitoria,* which are clearly of permanent character, are not interfered with, for example, boundary settlements which are not germane to the state of war; and (4) more generally, a treaty which is incompatible with the state of war cannot be expected to stand. This leaves much room for further dispute, the only general answer to which is that the law of the topic is admittedly unsettled.[129] In the opinion of the Harvard research

---

[127] *Techt* v. *Hughes,* Court of Appeals of New York, 229 N.Y. 222 (1920).

[128] *Ibid.;* see also Nelson, *op. cit.,* pp. 899–904.

[129] *Ibid.;* also Hurst, *op. cit.,* pp. 38–47; also Oppenheim-Lauterpacht, *Treatise* I, p. 949; also Vol. II (7th ed., 1952), pp. 302–6; also S. H. McIntyre, *Legal Effect of World War II on Treaties of the United States* (The Hague: Martinus Nijhoff, 1958), p. 355 where it is suggested that it does not appear that a single U.S. treaty was abrogated as a result of World War II. This would suggest a tendency to limit the traditional effect of war on treaties.

group, suspended treaties ordinarily should become operative on the conclusion of the war.[130]

Renewal of Treaties. It remains only to be mentioned that treaties or parts of treaties which have lapsed or the status of which has been rendered uncertain by war can be renewed by a new treaty the terms of which expressly so provide. It may also take place more or less automatically under terms of the original treaty itself as in treaties which specify that after a period of time the treaty may be renounced, but if it is not renounced, it is considered to be in effect for another specified period of time. Finally, it is sometimes suggested that tacit consent may renew or extend an expired treaty.[131]

The Interpretation of Treaties

The question of the rules to be applied to the interpretation of treaties is an interesting one, if for no other reason than the diversity of reactions found among the various publicists. Thus, while Brierly says that "There are no technical rules in international law for the interpretation of treaties," Hall, after listing some five interpretive rules, states that there are many rules which seem to have little clear application and then observes that "there is no place for the refinements of the courts in the rough jurisprudence of nations." By contrast Lauterpacht's edition of *Oppenheim's International Law* specifies some 16 rules of interpretation.[132]

The rules that are generally cited stem from earlier listings made by Grotius, Vattel, and others which are viewed critically by one writer as being "artificial maxims" developed with "assiduous nicety."[133] They were originally taken over from the

---

[130] Harvard Research, "Law of Treaties," Art. 35, p. 1183.

[131] Oppenheim-Lauterpacht, *Treatise* I, pp. 949–50; Hall, *op. cit.*, pp. 359–61.

[132] See respectively Brierly, *op. cit.*, p. 251; Hall, *op. cit.*, p. 341, fn. 1; Oppenheim-Lauterpacht, *Treatise* I, pp. 951–57. See also Ludwik Ehrlich, "L'Interpretation des traites," *Recueil des cours*, 1928, IV, Vol. 24, pp. 5–145. Cf. also Felix Frankfurter, "Reflections on Reading Statutes," (a Benjamin N. Cardozo Lecture printed in *The Record of the Association of the Bar of the City of New York*, Vol. 2 [June, 1947], pp. 213–37) . See conveniently in A. F. Westin, *The Supreme Court: Views from Inside* (New York: W. W. Norton & Co., Inc., 1961) , pp. 74–93.

[133] Tsune-Chi Yu, *The Interpretation of Treaties* (New York: Columbia University Press, 1927) , p. 27 *et passim*. For the main source of traditional

interpretive rules followed in Roman Law, yet some special points have been emphasized by national courts and a number of guideposts have been charted by international tribunals. The listings found in contemporary treatises are, as noted above, diverse, and there is no desire to add to what one writer has called "perhaps, one of the most confused subjects in international law today."[134] Accordingly, it is hoped that the following discussion may serve to simplify the problem.

Principles Underlying Interpretation. By way of achieving some sort of useful analysis it may be suggested that, in the view of the present author, there are two basic principles underlying all commentary on the interpretation of treaties. These are that (1) the object of interpretation is to arrive at the real and true meaning of those agreeing to the treaty,[135] and (2) it is to be presumed—in the absence of abundant evidence to the contrary —that the intent of a treaty is not to be nugatory, ineffectual, or absurd.[136]

Hierarchy and Rules of Treaty Interpretation. Within the scope of these principles, the more specific rules of interpretation and the hierarchy or priorities of their application which seem most satisfactory are those found in Professor Schwarzenberger's study which in this connection is based almost entirely upon usage of the Permanent Court of International Justice and the International Court of Justice. Though not an exact reproduction of his comments, the following statement derives largely from his treatment, the chief exception being an attempt to make certain seemingly appropriate simplifying consolidations. It seems proper to suggest that in attempting to arrive at what, in a combination of the two above-mentioned

---

canons of interpretation, see E. de Vattel, *The Law of Nations or the Principles of Natural Law Applied to the Conduct and to the Affairs of Nations and of Sovereigns,* 1758 edition (*The Classics of International Law,* trans. Charles G. Fenwick; 3 vols.; Washington, D.C.: The Carnegie Institution, 1916), Chapter XVII.

[134] Yi-Ting Chang, *The Interpretation of Treaties* (New York: Columbia University Press, 1933), p. 19.

[135] See, e.g., Schwarzenberger, *op. cit.,* p. 208; Harvard Research, "Law of Treaties," pp. 937–38 *et passim;* Hall, *op. cit.,* pp. 338–39; Fenwick, *op. cit.,* p. 445; McNair, *op. cit.,* p. 185 f.

[136] See, e.g., statement in Oppenheim-Lauterpacht, *Treatise* I, p. 955; Harvard Research, "Law of Treaties, pp. 939–40; Hall, *op. cit.,* pp. 338–39.

principles, may be called the nonnugatory meaning of the contracting powers, reference is to be had first to the terms of the
treaty in question (grammatical interpretation); secondly to a
systematic and logical analysis of the terms of the treaty in
dispute in relation to other terms of the treaty (systematic and
logical interpretation); thirdly, it is sometimes believed proper
to utilize historical data such as the records of the negotiations
(historical interpretation). Finally, it is sometimes proper to
try to interpret a treaty—not otherwise satisfactorily interpreted
—by reference to and analysis in the light of the function
which the treaty was designed to perform (functional interpretation).[137] Thus to illustrate, in interpretation of a disputed passage, nonnugatory meaning would first be sought in the
terms of the treaty itself, but if such search were not sufficiently
rewarding an attempt would be made to reconcile the phrase in
dispute with other phraseology of the treaty or recourse can be
had to rules of logic by which the disputed clause could be
interpreted restrictively or broadly or in other connections depending upon the logical way in which the clause itself should
seem to be interpreted. If still no solution is apparent, reference
may be had to the historical data which might reveal what the
negotiators had in mind, and finally, if nothing else works, the
total meaning and intent may be derived from the preamble
and other evidences showing what the treaty was supposed to
do, and the clause in dispute could then be interpreted in a way
which would be compatible with the treaty's objectives.

On the level of actual application, this hierarchy of general
interpretive rules may be broken down into a number of more
specific rules of interpretation. These will be summarized in
the following paragraphs.

Grammatical Interpretations. Terminological or grammatical interpretations may be arrived at by use of one or more of
the following eight rules. (1) terms are usually to be construed
as signifying their ordinary meanings. (2) No term is ordinarily to be considered as being superfluous. (3) It is not proper to
read into a treaty something which is not there. (4) Where two

---

[137] Schwarzenberger, *op. cit.,* pp. 208-23; G. Schwarzenberger, *A Manual of
International Law* (2d ed.; London: Stevens & Sons, Ltd., 1950), pp. 68-69
(hereafter cited as *Manual*).

or more languages are involved in a treaty, the one in which the treaty was drafted takes precedence, but (5) where two languages are both authoritative and where the breadth of meaning of a term is in dispute, the narrower meaning which can be made to harmonize with both versions is preferable. (6) Where a term in dispute has different meanings in the two countries, the meaning used in the country where the action it to take place should be followed. (7) Where wording is clear it is to be accepted as it stands, but (8) phraseology is not to be interpreted in a way which renders "contradictory or impossible consequences" or obviously goes beyond the original intent.[138]

Systematic and Logical Interpretations. Systematic and logical methods of interpretation may be applied when narrower grammatical interpretations are not sufficiently rewarding, which is to say that "the dubious word, sentence or passage has to be construed in its wider context." [139] Thus, (1) a meaning should be ascribed to a disputed clause which is reasonable in the light of other clauses of the treaty. (2) Obviously restrictive clauses should be interpreted restrictively, while (3) clauses which are broad in purpose should be interpreted extensively. (4) Special obligations take precedence over general references. (5) Similarly, a clause is sometimes interpreted *a contrario*, that is, in a self-evident way despite other clauses which might seem contrary to it, but which are not admissible if the intent of the specific clause is indeed self-evident. This is sometimes referred to as *expressio unius est exclusivo alterius,* that is, the express mention of one thing implies the exclusion of

---

[138] Schwarzenberger, *International Law, op. cit.,* pp. 209–11; see also Hall, *op. cit.,* p. 338 on specific rule No. "6." See also *Competence of the General Assembly for the Admission of a State to the United Nations,* Advisory Opinion of March 3, 1950, I.C.J. Reports, 1950, p. 4. The Court, quoting the P.C.I.J., said, "It is a cardinal principle of interpretation that words must be interpreted in the sense which they would normally have in their context, unless such interpretation would lead to something unreasonable or absurd," quotation on p. 8. See also *Polish Postal Service in Danzig,* P.C.I.J. Report, Series B/11 (1925), p. 39. On the subject of multiple language interpretation problems, see Jean Hardy, "The Interpretation of Plurilingual Treaties by International Courts and Tribunals," *The British Yearbook of International Law 1961,* Vol. XXXVII (1962), pp. 72–155. For treatment of a somewhat related topic, see Henry P. de Vries, "Choice of Language" under "Choice of Law and Language in European Contracts, A Symposium," *Virginia Journal of International Law,* Vol. 3, No. 1 (1963), pp. 26–34.

[139] Schwarzenberger, *Manual,* p. 69.

another. (6) On the other hand, the courts sometimes apply what may be called *a fortiori* reasoning to a clause and thus exercise jurisdiction over a matter not specifically mentioned in a treaty if it seems by its nature to be included in and of lesser scope than some power over which jurisdiction was specifically granted.[140]

Historical Interpretations. Historical interpretations are to be used with caution according to the International Court of Justice and it predecessor.[141] Where more primary sources of interpretation are not adequate to the task, however, and if "there is doubt as to the intentions of the parties which cannot be resolved by means of grammatical, systematic or logical interpretation of the treaty, the Permanent Court of International Justice did not hesitate to make full use of the method of historical interpretation."[142] Thus, (1) historical data, that is, the proceedings of the negotiations and related materials, can sometimes be used with justification to arrive at the true intention of the contracting parties; and (2) historical data may be especially useful in further confirming conclusions arrived at by other processes.[143]

Functional Interpretations. Finally, when other means of construction are unsatisfactory, functional interpretations may be employed. Yet they should not be used to read new provisions into a treaty. Thus, (1) it may sometimes be proper for a court to look directly into the functions which the treaty was designed to accomplish by (*a*) supplementary use of international customary law which seems to supplement obscure treaty provisions, and (*b*) by the use on rare occasions of other treaties of "parallel, supplementary or complementary character." (2) The preamble of a treaty as an indicator of purpose may sometimes be used to clarify the meaning of obscure terms.[144] It

---

[140] Schwarzenberger, *International Law, op. cit.,* pp. 211–17. It should be noted that Schwarzenberger specifies *systematic* on the one hand and *logical* on the other as two separate varieties of interpretation; for reasons of greater simplicity they are discussed together here.

[141] *Ibid.,* p. 217. For a diametrically opposed view see Yu, *op. cit.,* pp. 64–70 *et passim.*

[142] Schwarzenberger, *International Law, op. cit.,* p. 218.

[143] *Ibid.,* pp. 217–18.

[144] *Ibid.,* pp. 220–22, quotation on p. 222.

should be apparent that at least in part functional interpretation is merely a more remote application of the principle referred to above as systematic and logical interpretation.

Special Problems Pertaining to Interpretation. There are a number of rather specialized problems which arise in connection with treaty interpretation. Three such matters merit brief but special mention. These are (1) the effect of treaties upon third parties, (2) the problems peculiar to most-favored-nation clauses, and (3) particularly with reference to the United States, the problem of how treaties are to be interpreted when they conflict with municipal law.

Treaties and Third Parties. When a treaty makes certain stipulations of general application, or more particularly, is concerned with a state not a party to the agreement, the question arises as to the legal position of the third state under such treaty. In general the applicable rule is that treaties do not impose duties or benefits upon third parties, *pacta tertiis nec nocent nec prosunt.* Accordingly, as was noted above, a treaty obligation between two powers is not itself impaired by a later treaty between one of the original contracting powers and some other state the sense of which is somehow contrary to the earlier accord. In the same vein, virtually all publicists clearly recognize the rule that third states incur no obligations under treaties to which they have not acceded,[145] and this has been recognized on numerous occasions by the Permanent Court of International Justice.[146]

The question of whether a third state can derive rights as contrasted with obligations from an agreement to which it is not a party is a more complicated matter. While there is ample reason to assert that third states derive no rights where it is not intended that they should do so, there appears to be no reason why they cannot enjoy such rights if that was the intent of the agreement. Thus, while Secretary Hughes emphasized that third parties enjoy no legal rights under the treaties providing

---

[145] See, e.g., comment in Harvard Research, "Law of Treaties," p. 918 ff.

[146] See, e.g., *Case Concerning Certain German Interests in Polish Upper Silesia,* P.C.I.J., Judgments, Series A, No. 7 (1926), p. 29; *Case Relating to the Territorial Jurisdiction of the International Commission of the River Oder,* P.C.I.J., Judgments, Series A, No. 23 (1929), pp. 19–22.

for the Panama Canal,[147] nevertheless, the Permanent Court of
International Justice in the *Case of the Free Zones of Upper
Savoy and the District of Gex,* stated that:

It cannot be lightly presumed that stipulations favourable to a
third State have been adopted with the object of creating an actual
right in its favour. There is however nothing to prevent the will of
sovereign States from having this object and this effect. The question of the existence of a right acquired under an instrument drawn
between other States is therefore one to be decided in each particular case: it must be ascertained whether the States which have
stipulated in favour of a third State meant to create for that State an
actual right which that latter has accepted as such.[148]

The Harvard research group, though preferring the term "benefit" instead of "right," felt that the benefits to third states
while potentially valid were somewhat "precarious," and that
they can be held to exist only so long as the original contracting
parties "maintain the treaty in force between themselves."[149]
The draft article on the subject proposed by the Harvard group
is as follows:

A treaty may not impose obligations upon a State which is not a
party thereto.

If a treaty contains a stipulation which is expressly for the benefit
of a State which is not a party or a signatory to the treaty, such State
is entitled to claim the benefit of that stipulation so long as the
stipulation remains in force between the parties to the treaty.[150]

Most-Favored-Nation Clauses. A somewhat specialized
third power relationship is occasioned by utilization of what
are called most-favored-nation clauses. These are used particularly in commercial treaties, but also in some other accords. A
most-favored-nation clause between two states merely stipulates
that each state will grant the other commercial rights equal to
the most favorable rights granted to any other state. Accordingly if the United States and Canada have such an arrange-

---

[147] Cited in Hackworth, *Digest* V, pp. 221–22; see, however, Fenwick, *op. cit.,*
p. 450, where it is suggested that prescriptive use rights might evolve.

[148] *Case of the Free Zones of Upper Savoy and the District of Gex,* P.C.I.J.
Series A/B, No. 46 (1932), pp. 147–48, cited in Hackworth, *Digest* V, p. 219.

[149] Harvard Research, "Law of Treaties," p. 937.

[150] *Ibid.,* Art. 18, p. 661.

ment and Canada grants a special reduction of import duties on certain goods coming in from Ireland, the same rates would apply to similar goods from the United States. Such clauses are frequently applied to consular relationships as well as to other commercial matters.

Controversies have resulted, however, particularly before 1923, because the United States specified that its most-favored-nation clauses were conditioned upon a nation's meeting the reciprocal terms of a favor granted to any other nation. For example, the United States might agree to cut tariffs by 30 percent on certain Brazilian exports to the United States if Brazil would reciprocate in relation to certain U.S. exports to Brazil. The benefits of such an arrangement would be open to another country having a most-favored-nation relationship with the United States only if that country offered the United States substantially the same reciprocal benefits as those granted by Brazil. This was known as a *conditional most-favored-nation clause,* and was the source of much controversy. Not only was the principle problematical, but the administrative problem of determining whether a nation's concessions were or were not the equivalent of those specified in a treaty with another state, occasioned much difficulty.

In 1923 the United States began to move in the direction of the more widely followed policy in regard to most-favored-nation clauses. Instead of using the conditional type of clause, this country negotiated treaties containing what is known as the *unconditional most-favored-nation clause.* Accordingly, most-favored-nation treatment was not to be conditioned upon meeting special concessions—except of course for the general concession that each state would treat the other's commerce as favorably as that of the most favored nation. This policy has been continued with the reciprocal trade agreements of the 1930's.[151]

As noted above, the most-favored-nation clauses have appeared in consular treaties as well as in trade agreements. The United States has continued to apply them, however, in a con-

151 Hyde, *op. cit.,* Vol. II, pp. 1502–12; *Department of State Press Releases,* No. 435 (January 29, 1938), particularly pp. 148–51. See also Hackworth, *Digest V,* pp. 269–96.

ditional sense when they deal with consular matters. In addition such matters as diplomatic immunities, residence privileges of nationals, disposition of property, and some other concerns have also been included in the most-favored-nation treatment.[152]

Treaties and Municipal Law. The subject of the relationship of treaties and municipal law was noted in an earlier chapter,[153] but brief mention should be made here of the same problem, particularly in relation to the rulings of the U.S. courts. It should be emphasized that the problem in question here has little or nothing to do with whether domestic legislation can nullify the internationally binding effect of a bona fide treaty, for it clearly cannot do so.[154] Rather, it is a question of what internal legal relationship obtains when such a conflict exists. This is perhaps a more fitting topic for constitutional law than for international law, but in a discussion of the interpretation of treaties, it is well to bear in mind this particular relationship.

While the constitutions of certain countries give treaties preference over ordinary municipal law,[155] the rule applicable within the United States and some other jurisdictions is essentially that of *lex posterior,* that is, the most recently enacted legislation must prevail.[156] Accordingly, the Supreme Court speaking of treaties and acts of Congress, has said that:

When the two relate to the same subject, the courts will always endeavor to construe them so as to give effect to both, if that can be done without violating the language of either; but if the two are inconsistent, the one last in date will control the other, provided always the stipulation of the treaty on the subject is self-executing.[157]

---

[152] *Ibid.,* pp. 1512–15; *Santovicenzo* v. *Egan,* 284 U.S. 30 (1931).

[153] *See above,* Chapter Two.

[154] See discussion, *above,* Chapter Two; Hackworth, *Digest* V, pp. 194–95.

[155] See Louis C. Bial, "Some Recent French Decisions on the Relationship between Treaties and Municipal Law," *American Journal of International Law,* Vol. XLIX (July, 1955), pp. 347–48.

[156] On Austria, see Ignaz Seidl-Hohenveldern, "Relation of International Law to Internal Law in Austria," *American Journal of International Law,* Vol. XLIX (October, 1955), pp. 451–76.

[157] *Whitney* v. *Robertson,* 124 U.S. 190 (1888). Self-executing treaties are those the terms of which go into effect automatically upon ratification. Many treaties, however, are nonself-executing, and require legislation in order to make

It should be noted that the Permanent Court of International Justice ruled in 1925 that where treaty obligations and municipal law are at variance, the state is under obligation to make the necessary modifications in its municipal legislation.[158] The potential problems should be apparent.[159]

The Effect and Enforcement of Treaties. The obvious and primary effect of a treaty is to institute obligations and rights among the signatories. The rule, *pacta sunt servanda,* has already been discussed above, but it bears reiteration that this is the rule which stipulates that treaty obligations must be honored. Accordingly, the Permanent Court of International Justice observed that:

. . . It is a principle of international law that the breach of an engagement involves an obligation to make reparation in an adequate form. Reparation therefore is an indispensable complement of a failure to apply a convention and there is no necessity for this to be stated in the convention itself.[160]

The clarity of this pronouncement leaves little question as to the binding nature of treaty obligations. The matter of actual enforcement, however, goes somewhat beyond the mere recognition of the obligation to make reparation.

The subject of the enforcement of treaties is merely a part of the somewhat broader topic of the pacific and forcible settlement of international disputes which will be surveyed systematically and in some detail in a later chapter.[161] While it is superfluous to detail the subject here, a few remarks should, nevertheless, be directed toward the general problem of enforcement.

While breaches of treaty obligations undoubtedly do on oc-

---

them internally effective. Treaties involving the rights and duties of persons, activities of officers, and other internal matters normally fall into this latter category.

[158] *Exchange of Greek and Turkish Populations,* P.C.I.J., Advisory Opinions, Series B, No. 10 (1925) , p. 20.

[159] In 1952 and 1953 fears within the United States of the potential legal effect of newly enacted accords led to an unsuccessful movement to put curbs on the effect and the making of agreements. This was known as the Bricker amendment.

[160] *The Chorzow Factory* case, P.C.I.J., Series A, No. 9, Judgment No. 8 (1927) , p. 21, cited in Hackworth, *Digest* V, p. 165.

[161] *See below* Chapter Eight.

casion stem from willful and deliberate acts of unmitigated bad faith, it must be assumed that most violations stem from different interpretations of treaty meanings or from inadvertent circumstances. Thus, the "Permanent Court of International Justice has repeatedly emphasized that the breach of an international treaty obligation on the part of a sovereign State must never be presumed or taken for granted."[162]

The problem of enforcement may be simple and routine with nothing but minor technicalities being involved, or, on the other hand, it may entail the most complex and high-level political considerations. Accordingly, methods of settlement range from the mere exchange of diplomatic communications, to arbitral and judicial settlement, to threats of force, and even to war. Many questions are entirely resolvable by recourse to judicial or arbitral tribunals, yet some issues are of such fundamental import that states refuse to compromise their objectives.[163] Nevertheless, many states have assumed the obligation to submit at least certain disputes to judicial or arbitral settlement,[164] and a variety of other pacific avenues are also open to the state seeking to have its rights enforced. Yet it must be realized that some rights may be essentially unenforceable. As noted above, these enforcement techniques will be considered in a later chapter.

INTERNATIONAL LEGISLATION BY INTERNATIONAL AGENCIES

The legislative function in the international community, as has been pointed out above, is largely carried out by means of the treaty-making process. Some international organizations also possess legislative or at least quasi-legislative powers, and it is with these that this brief section is concerned.

As with other phases of international law, these functions of international organizations may be usefully considered under

---

[162] Schwarzenberger, *International Law, op. cit.*, p. 203.

[163] De Visscher, *op. cit.*, pp. 327–61.

[164] See, e.g., comment in Hackworth, *Digest* VI, pp. 60–66; see also Harvard Research, "Law of Treaties," Art. 36, p. 1204; and Harvard Research, "Extradition," *American Journal of International Law*, Vol. XXIX (Supplement, 1935), pp. 223–28.

two main categories: (1) the powers of political agencies, and (2) the powers of technical organizations.

Legislative-Type Functions of Political Organizations

The status of international society being as it is, the reluctance of states to grant full legislative powers to international organizations is understandable. It may even be considered somewhat remarkable that there has been any development at all along this line, and it must be emphasized that only a portion of what will be discussed here can be called true legislation. Major political organizations perform three activities, however, which seem germane to this discussion. These are (1) making recommendations, (2) providing for the drafting of conventions, and (3) making decisions of a more truly legislative character. It should be apparent, however, that rule-making authority is not likely to be as well developed in political organizations as in technical agencies.

Recommendatory Process. Both the General Assembly and the Security Council are empowered to make recommendations.[165] While such recommendations are not binding on the members and cannot be called legislation per se they are procedures of potential influence. Under the so-called "Uniting for Peace Resolution," the Assembly deems itself capable of recommending the use of armed force to quell aggression.[166]

Drafting of Conventions. Although the major political organs of the United Nations are not directly concerned with the drafting of conventions, this function is performed by the more technical groups. Accordingly, the Economic and Social Council may, *inter alia*, "prepare draft conventions for submission to the General Assembly."[167]

---

[165] U.N., *Charter,* Arts. 10, 11, 13, 14, 37, 38.

[166] See brief account in *Everyman's United Nations 1945–55* (5th ed.; New York: United Nations, 1956) , p. 19.

[167] U.N., *Charter,* Art. 62 (3). The International Law Commission, which began to function in 1949, is an example of such an activity of the General Assembly. The Commission has made studies and undertaken codification of the law in various substantive areas. Several of its draft codes have met with marked success. See the *Yearbooks of the International Law Commission,* published

Binding Regulations. In a very few instances political international organizations have been authorized to exercise limited rule-making authority. In this connection, the Security Council of the United Nations can take enforcement action which is binding upon member states.[168] The military aspects of such action are circumscribed by a number of limitations, and by the very nature of the Security Council plan, a permanent member is not bound without its consent.[169] In theory at least, the other members of that organization could be.

Other examples of limited rule-making authority in international organizations may be seen within the scope of regional developments. Two interesting examples are those of the Inter-American System and the European Community of the Inner Six. The Inter-American System functioning under the terms of the Rio Pact, allows the organization to determine by a two-thirds majority of the foreign ministers whether a state of aggression exists.[170]

The European Community of the Inner Six, operating through three principal treaties and their revisions, provides for limited rule-making authority governing matters pertaining to coal and steel, common market, and atomic energy interests of the community. It might be argued that these European Community activities are more in the realm of the technical than of the political, given the seeming long-range focus of European development, however, it is perhaps useful to think of it in both categories.[171]

---

annually since 1949; also see Luke T. Lee, "The International Law Commission Re-Examined," *American Journal of International Law*, Vol. LIX (July, 1965), pp. 545–69. The line of distinction between political and technical is blurred here. The International Law Commission is an instrumentality of the General Assembly, but its function is perhaps more technical than political in character.

The Special Committee on Principles of International Law concerning Friendly Relations and Cooperation among States which was created by the General Assembly in 1962 seems to have been designed as a somewhat more politically oriented body. See Lee, *op. cit.*, pp. 558–62.

[168] *Ibid.*, Arts. 39, 41, 42, 43, 49, *et passim.*

[169] *Ibid.*, Arts. 43, 27.

[170] *Inter-American Treaty of Reciprocal Assistance*, Rio de Janeiro, 1947, 62 U.S., *Statutes* 1681, Arts. 6, 17, see conveniently in F. H. Hartmann, *Basic Documents of International Relations* (New York: McGraw-Hill Book Co., Inc., 1951), pp. 287–94. See materials in Ruth C. Lawson, *International Regional Organizations* (New York: Frederick A. Praeger, Inc., 1962), pp. 313–60.

[171] Lawson, *op. cit.*, pp. 62–148. *European Organizations* (London: George Allen & Unwin Ltd., 1959), pp. 229–355; Ernst B. Haas, *The Uniting of Europe*

Legislative-Type Functions of Technical Organizations

Outside of the area of high political tensions there are numerous international organizations which perform varying technical tasks. Within the scope of technical organizations there are the same three types of rule proposing and making authority which were noted as being performed by political agencies. Since the principal concerns of these organizations are less centered upon matters of high tension, their rule-making potential is greater. It may be noted that primary examples are drawn from the World Health Organization because that agency has been endowed with rather extensive powers.[172]

Recommendatory Functions. Many technical international organizations have authority to make recommendations to member states, other international organizations, and even nonmember states in regard to matters within their purview. Accordingly, the Constitution of the World Health Organization provides that "The Health Assembly shall have authority to make recommendations to Members with respect to any matter within the competence of the Organization."[173] This authority is paralleled in many organizations, and, as noted above is not precisely legislative, yet it should be recognized in passing as having related qualities.

Drafting of Conventions. One of the preliminary steps in developing a legislative activity is to empower some agency to draw up and propose laws. This has been accomplished in the charters of several technical international organizations. The power is always circumscribed, however, by provision that conventions only become effective when adopted by the participating states. The pertinent section of the World Health Organization's Constitution is illustrative. It states that:

(Stanford, Calif.: Stanford University Press, 1958), *passim;* Donald C. Blaisdell, *International* Organization (New York: The Ronald Press Co., 1966) pp. 227–43; Henry L. Mason, *The European Coal and Steel Community, Experiment in Supranationalism* (The Hague: Martinus Nijhoff, 1955), *passim;* Werner Feld, *The Court of the European Communities: New Dimension in International Adjudication* (The Hague: Martinus Nijhoff, 1964) pp. 5–13.

172 Oppenheim-Lauterpacht, *Treatise* I, p. 981–86.

173 *Constitution of the World Health Organization,* Art. 23, see conveniently in P. B. Potter, *An Introduction to the Study of International Organization* (5th ed.; New York: Appleton-Century-Crofts, Inc., 1948), pp. 447–60.

The Health Assembly shall have authority to adopt conventions or agreements with respect to any matter within the competence of the Organization. A two-thirds vote of the Health Assembly shall be required for the adoption of such conventions or agreements which shall come into force for each Member when accepted by it in accordance with its constitutional processes.[174]

Clearly this is a step beyond the mere recommendatory process as described above.

Specialized Rule-Making Authority. A few international organizations have been authorized to make specialized rules and to apply them. Such rules have binding effect on all members, except that individual members may disallow the applicability of certain rules to them. Accordingly, the Constitution of the World Health Organization states that:

The Health Assembly shall have authority to adopt regulations concerning:
  a) Sanitary and quarantine requirements and other procedures designed to prevent the international spread of disease;
  b) Nomenclatures with respect to diseases, causes of death and public health practices;
  c) Standards with respect to diagnostic procedures for international use;
  d) Standards with respect to the safety, purity, and potency of biological, pharmaceutical and similar products moving in international commerce;
  e) Advertising and labelling of biological, pharmaceutical and similar products moving in international commerce.

Regulations adopted pursuant to Article 21 shall come into force for all Members after due notice has been given of their adoption by the Health Assembly except for such Members as may notify the Director-General of rejection or reservations within the period stated in the notice.[175]

Similar provisions are found in the basic document of the International Civil Aviation Organization.[176] Such provisions go well beyond the scope of the treaty drafting power and must be considered as a sort of international administrative law.

---

[174] *Ibid.,* Art. 19.

[175] *Ibid.,* Arts. 21, 22.

[176] *Convention on International Civil Aviation,* Arts. 37, 38, 54 (1).

SUMMARY

Law making in the international community is the result of
(1) development by custom, (2) endowing international agencies by treaty with rule-making authority, and, (3) legislation
by treaty. Of these the last is of the most practical contemporary importance. The scope of modern international
legislation is broad. It encompasses political accords such as
peace treaties as well as technical arrangements dealing with
such matters as extradition, consular affairs, transportation,
and public health.

The word "treaty" is a generic term for international
agreements of many specialized types going under many names.
Treaties are classified in a number of ways as (1) bipartite or
multipartite, (2) equal and unequal, (3) simple and conditional, (4) executed and executory, (5) lawmaking and
contractual (or other than law making), and (6) political and
technical.

Treaties are drawn up and put into force according to certain processes. These include negotiation, ratification, and
registration. When ratified with certain exceptions, a treaty is
said to have been ratified with "reservations." Such reservations
may or may not be accepted by the other parties. A state may
indicate its "understanding" of certain portions of a treaty at
the time of ratification, but that does not assume the importance of a reservation. In general, treaties take effect upon
ratification unless otherwise specified.

Treaties are assumed to be valid and binding under the
principle, *pacta sunt servanda* but there are certain conditions
which may affect adversely the validity of agreements. These
include questions as to (1) the capacity of the contracting
parties, (2) the authority of the negotiators, (3) the mutuality
of consent, (4) the freedom of the negotiator from duress, (5)
the absence of fraud, (6) the absence of error, and (7) consistency with superior norms.

Treaties may be terminated or revised in a number of ways.
These include (1) termination under the terms of the treaty
itself, (2) termination by consent of the parties, (3) termination by the injured party if the other party has violated the

agreement, (4) termination—at least theoretically—if the circumstances material to the agreement have changed, (5) termination by virtue of *force majeure,* and (6) termination or suspension of certain treaties because of war.

Once enacted, treaties must be interpreted. Although there are few "canons" of interpretation that are universally respected, the main objective in interpretation is to arrive at the intent of the contracting parties, and it is assumed that the intent was nonnugatory. Techniques for arriving at intent involve (1) scrutiny of terminology, (2) systematic and logical analysis of terms in the context of the treaty, (3) the use of historical data, and (4) analysis of the treaty in the light of the function it was designed to serve.

Closely related to the matter of treaty interpretation are questions dealing with the effect of treaties on third parties, the interpretation of most-favored-nation clauses, and the relationship of treaties to municipal law. In these connections (1) it is generally recognized that third parties are unaffected by treaty relationships to which they do not adhere; (2) the most-favored-nation clause now is usually applied on an unconditional basis by the United States except in relation to consular matters; and finally (3) while U.S. law and treaties are internally geared to the principle, *lex posterior,* this does not alter the internationally binding effect of treaties.

Enforcement techniques will be observed in a later chapter, but it may be noted here that techniques range from negotiation, to arbitration and adjudication, and to the use of force. In addition it must be realized that some agreements, like some laws, are essentially unenforceable.

Another form of international legislation may stem from powers granted to international organizations. Included are three levels of activity all of which have some bearing on the subject. These agencies may (1) make recommendations, (2) draft conventions which must be ratified before becoming effective, and finally (3) some organizations can make regulations which, unless specifically disavowed, are binding on their member states. The Security Council can bind all members to certain kinds of action, but the permanent members cannot be bound without their consent.

APPENDIX OF TERMINOLOGY DESCRIBING INTERNATIONAL AGREEMENTS

Accession refers to the process by which a third party can agree to be bound by an accord—usually a multipartite treaty.

Accord is a term employed broadly to mean treaty.

Cartels are agreements regulating certain relationships between belligerents in wartime.

Compromis d'arbitrage is "an agreement to refer to arbitration some matter . . . in dispute."

Concordat is a term referring to an agreement with the Vatican dealing usually but perhaps not always with religious matters.

Conventions are frequently multipartite accords.

Declarations are agreements which express existing law.

Exchanges of notes are often used to record agreements arrived at orally or by exchange of correspondence.

Executive agreements or merely *agreements* are identical to treaties for most purposes, but in U.S. constitutional usage they are contrasted with "treaties" and are international accords validated by processes other than submission to the Senate for advice and consent. These agreements are of two kinds: (*a*) those made by the Executive pursuant to authority granted by act of Congress, and (*b*) those made by the Executive by virtue of primary constitutional authority.

Final act is a summarization and enumeration of the proceedings of a conference, but each document included requires separate agreement.

General acts are like final acts except that ratification embraces all included agreements.

Lettres reversales seem almost archaic but appear to be statements with reference to an act of ceremony by which it is specified that an error is not to constitute a precedent or by which a concession is granted in return for some act.

Modus vivendi is a term used to specify an agreement of "temporary and provisional" character.

Pact is a term employed almost synonymously with treaty.

Pactum de contrahendo is a preliminary treaty which requires mutual consent. It deals with certain principal points but leaves other matters to later agreements.

Procès-verbal signifies "a formal record of proceedings" of a conference or congress.

Protocols are documents which amend or supplement other more basic treaties. The term is also used to designate the signed minutes of the proceedings of a conference.

Ratification is a final declaration of approval given to a treaty.

Sponsions are agreements made by agents not properly commissioned. They require ratification or tacit ratification in order to be valid.

Treaty is usually used to refer to accords of "particularly solemn character."

CHAPTER 7

Agents and Procedures of International Relationships

THE IMPORTANCE of adequate means of communication among nations is too obvious to need lengthy elaboration. Suffice it to note that every state must of necessity be concerned to know with some precision what is going on in at least some other states. Furthermore, the necessity for maintaining machinery through which communications can be accurately transmitted between states is of great importance. Finally there are problems—often minor—which arise in foreign countries which need the day-to-day attention of resident agents from the country whose nationals are involved.

Altogether there are numerous activities which fall to the lot of the foreign agents of modern states. It should be noted that these agents function nowadays in two types of settings: (1) in the conventional diplomatic and consular patterns, and (2) in the machinery of certain international organizations. In addition to a final summary section, discussion in this chapter will concern (1) the development of representative activities, (2) the functions of representative personnel, (3) the mechanics of representation, and (4) the termination of missions.

DEVELOPMENT OF REPRESENTATIVE ACTIVITIES

The representative functions of states have developed in certain well-defined patterns. Indeed, the law of diplomatic and

consular activities is one of the most precisely defined areas
within the entire field of international law. Considerations in
this section will center upon (1) the historical growth of diplomatic and consular institutions, (2) the right of legation, and
(3) procedures for maintaining international contacts.

The History of Diplomatic and Consular Institutions

Diplomacy was defined by Sir Ernest Satow as the "application of intelligence and tact to the conduct of official relations
between the governments of independent states. . . ."[1] It may
be more simply defined, however, as the art of influencing and
dealing with foreign governments by means short of war.
Consular functions are closely related to diplomacy, but center
upon the stimulation of commerce. Beyond that, however, both
embrace a multitude of activities.[2]

These two closely related areas of activity, that is, the diplomatic and consular fields, have somewhat separate origins and
current legal status, but it is significant that both are in at least
some respects virtually as old as recorded history.[3]

Diplomatic Development. Records of the use of diplomatic
agents are found in the annals of the ancient Greeks, and
scattered evidence is recorded of their use in much earlier
periods dating back as far as 2353 B.C. in China. In the Roman
period diplomatic personnel were both sent and received by the
Empire, though the Romans were more amenable to receiving
than sending them.[4]

Although many of the diplomatic practices and immunities
of today stem from similar practices in ancient eras, permanent

---

[1] Ernest Satow, *A Guide to Diplomatic Practice* (4th ed. by N. Bland;
London: Longmans, Green & Co., Inc., 1957), p. 1.

[2] Graham H. Stuart, *American Diplomatic and Consular Practice* (2d ed.;
New York: Appleton-Century-Crofts, Inc., 1952), pp. 170, 302, quotation on p.
302.

[3] *Ibid.*, pp. 114, 277; Hugo Grotius, *De iure belli ac pacis libri tres,* 1645
edition (*The Classics of International Law;* trans. F. W. Kelsey; 2 vols.; Oxford:
The Clarendon Press, 1925), pp. 438–49; Coleman Phillipson, *The International
Law and Custom of Ancient Greece and Rome* (London: Macmillan & Co., Ltd.,
1911), Vol. 1, pp. 147–56, 302–9.

[4] Phillipson, *op. cit.*, pp. 302–46; Stuart, *op. cit.*, pp. 114–18; Arthur Nussbaum, *A Concise History of the Law of Nations* (rev. ed.; New York: The
Macmillan Co., 1954), pp. 6–7.

missions were not employed until the Middle Ages. They were first used in the relations of the Roman Catholic Church with the Eastern Empire and the Holy Roman Empire. It was not until the latter Middle Ages, however, that resident diplomatic missions became relatively common. This practice was built up among the Italian states, and, with the emergence of the European state system, it came to prevail throughout Europe.[5]

It should perhaps be noted that many questions of protocol, immunity, rank, and related matters crystallized in this era. While some important changes have subsequently evolved, much of the contemporary pattern dates from the latter Middle Ages.

Consular Development. Both the Greeks and the Romans engaged personnel to handle consular matters, and later, during the Middle Ages, a number of outstanding codes of consular and maritime law emerged. The Crusades appear to have been particularly instrumental in bringing about circumstances under which consular institutions were widely employed. The functions of consuls, who represented private merchant groups, centered upon the settlement of disputes between nationals of the same country and they particularly dealt with the settlement of maritime or shipping problems. With the growth of permanent legations the functions of consuls shifted more in the direction of commerce and away from the judicial. Also, the consulates became more apparently state institutions.[6]

Today consular and diplomatic personnel tend to be closely allied. Foreign service personnel are frequently commissioned to exercise both diplomatic and consular functions, and, in the United States, the two services were merged in 1924.[7] Nevertheless, the procedures, rights, immunities, and prerogatives of diplomatic and consular personnel rest upon different bases, each being derived in part from its historic origins. The rights of the former are far more secure and are based upon general

---

[5] Stuart, *op. cit.*, pp. 118–21.

[6] Phillipson, *op. cit.*, pp. 147–56; Stuart *op. cit.*, pp. 277–91; Julius I. Puente, *The Foreign Consul: His Juridical Status in the United States* (Chicago: B. J. Smith Co., 1926), pp. 6–7; see also John H. Wigmore, *A Panorama of the World's Legal Systems* (St. Paul, Minn., West Publishing Co., 1928), Vol. III, pp. 875–929.

[7] 43 U.S., *Statutes,* p. 140.

international law while the status of consuls is based largely upon treaties and is more restricted.[8]

Means of Maintaining Foreign Contacts

States use several methods of maintaining the official international contacts which contemporary international relationships would seem to require. The most common of these are the usual diplomatic and consular establishments. Other procedures include (1) the use of conferences, (2) the use of international organizations as means of contact, and (3) the use of diplomatic establishments of third powers in conveying messages, handling routine business, and even for more serious negotiations. Before noting briefly these processes, however, the question of whether a "right of legation" exists will be considered.

Legation: A Competence or a Right?   It is often stated in commentaries on international law that a "right of legation" exists under which a state has some sort of obligation both to send (active right of legation) and to receive (passive right of legation) emissaries to and from other states.[9] Accordingly a U.S. State Department communication specified that:

> Every independent and full sovereign member of the family of nations possesses the right of legation, which is the right of a State to send and receive diplomatic envoys. This right has been accorded at times in a restricted form to Part-Sovereign and Semi-Sovereign States, the exact restrictions upon the diplomatic activity of each being determined by the instrument defining their international position.[10]

Whether a "right" of this sort can properly be held to exist is, however, a question that deserves some thought, for, as one recent writer has put it, "The right of legation is, however, discretionary, as no state is under any obligation either to send

---

[8] Stuart, *op. cit.*, pp. 289–91.

[9] See M. de Vattel, *The Law of Nations or Principles of the Law of Nature Applied to the Conduct and Affairs of Nations and Sovereigns* (New English edition by Joseph Chitty; Philadelphia: T. and J. W. Johnson, 1854), p. 452; Wesley L. Gould, *An Introduction to International Law* (New York: Harper & Bros., 1957), p. 264.

[10] See in Hackworth, *Digest* IV, p. 393.

or to receive diplomatic agents."[11] Nevertheless, it is contended that while no nation is under obligation to send diplomats or to receive permanent envoys, normally it is obliged to hear foreign official views. This has been stated as follows:

> The duty of every member [of the community of nations] to listen, in ordinary circumstances, to a message from another member brought by a diplomatic envoy is therefore, an outcome of its very membership of the international community, and this duty corresponds to the right of every member to send such envoys.[12]

On the other hand, some authorities have suggested that this alleged "right" is merely a "competence" which is a characteristic of sovereignty.[13] It may also be of interest to note in passing that the term "right of embassy" is used by Gentili to mean the right of the envoy to immunity, and Grotius used it both in the sense of the right to immunities, and in the more usual modern sense of the right to be admitted and heard.[14] It should be noted that Grotius qualifies this aspect of the right by stipulating that "The law of nations, in fact, does not enjoin that all be admitted, but it does forbid the rejection of ambassadors without cause," and Oppenheim seems to suggest that a rupture of diplomatic relations affords a situation in which no right of legation exists.[15] Finally, it must be realized that the nature of sovereignty would seem to leave to the state the right to determine the circumstances under which it can and will receive a foreign envoy, and even the individual whom it will receive.

Where, then, does this leave the "right of legation"? Clearly there is obligation neither (1) to send envoys nor (2) to re-

---

[11] Oscar Svarlien, *Introduction to the Law of Nations* (New York: McGraw-Hill Book Co., Inc., 1955), p. 236. The U.N. Convention specifies that "The establishment of diplomatic relations between states . . . takes place by mutual consent." *Vienna Convention on Diplomatic Relations*, 1961, Art. 2, see in *American Journal of International Law*, Vol. LV (October, 1961), pp. 1064–80 (hereafter cited as *U.N. Convention*).

[12] Oppenheim-Lauterpacht, *Treatise* I, p. 775.

[13] See Introductory Comment to Harvard Research Draft Convention on Diplomatic Privileges and Immunities in *American Journal of International Law*, Vol. XXVI (Supplement, 1932), pp. 31–32; also Oppenheim-Lauterpacht, *Treatise* I, p. 775; also Svarlien, *op. cit., passim*.

[14] Alberico Gentili, *De legationibus libri tres*, 1594 edition (*The Classics of International Law*, trans. G. L. Laing; 2 vols.; New York: Oxford University Press, Inc., 1924), pp. 57–58; Grotius, *op. cit.*, pp. 440–41 *et passim*.

[15] Grotius, *op. cit.*, p. 440; Oppenheim-Lauterpacht, *Treatise* I, p. 775.

ceive permanent emmissaries, and (3) under unusual circumstances (which would appear to be within the determination of the receiving state) a state may refuse to treat at all with the envoys of another state. From a practical standpoint this means that at any given time a state may set limitations which in effect bar the practical existence of any right of legation. To do so willy-nilly, however, would clearly contravene good faith, and in fact, the question is largely academic, particularly in the modern era of wireless communications. There is, thus, a competence on the part of states to send and to receive envoys and perhaps in theory an obligation to hear another state's message. As a practical matter most states exchange permanent representatives. It should be mentioned, also, that certain international organizations may also possess a right to send representative personnel for certain purposes.

Conventional Foreign Contacts. It needs only passing mention here that despite the qualified status of the right of legation, the usual machinery for ironing out differences between states, reporting to the home government, negotiating agreements, and handling routine matters of many sorts consists largely of the familiar diplomatic and consular establishments. These establishments are ordinarily coordinated within each nation under a special minister or department of foreign affairs, such, for example, as the U.S. Department of State. The U.S. government maintains an ambassador and his staff and several consular officers in virtually every country in the world, and nearly all nations have similar officials in the United States.[16] On the other hand, a small power may maintain only relatively few embassies or legations and consular establishments. The Republic of the Philippines, for example, maintained 18 diplomatic establishments and 15 consular establishments in 1956, several of which, however, were accredited to a number of states.[17]

---

[16] See Department of State, *Diplomatic List* (Washington, D.C.: U.S. Government Printing Office, October, 1957), published periodically. On U.S. establishments abroad, see Department of State, *Foreign Service List* (Washington, D.C.: U.S. Government Printing Office, July, 1957), published quarterly.

[17] See Abelardo G. Samonte and H. B. Jacobini, "Protective, Legal and Diplomatic Services," in H. B. Jacobini and Associates, *Governmental Services in the Philippines* (Manila: I.P.A., U.P., 1956), pp. 49–50, fns. 135, 136.

It may perhaps be noted that in addition to the more usual functions of these establishments, recent years have witnessed the sending of special missions—often closely related or attached to the diplomatic mission—which serve other purposes. Military missions and technical assistance missions are examples of these.[18]

Contacts through Conferences. Closely related to the usual diplomatic process is the use of the plenary conference or congress. These are usually utilized in connection with the negotiation of a major treaty. Examples include the Versailles Conference following World War I, the First and Second Hague Conferences, and the San Francisco Conference at which the United Nations was provided for. These do not serve the needs of daily contacts, but rather serve special purposes.[19]

Contacts in International Organizations. International organizations are often thought of either in connection with some specific technical function or in terms of the grand scope of incipient world government. It is perhaps on the more pedestrian level of another dimension of diplomacy, however, that the political international organization achieves its greatest contemporary utility. In this connection the United Nations provides constant machinery under which representatives of countries not otherwise in contact, may maintain liaison, and in which third states may promote settlement of disputes. Though perhaps there are fewer examples than might be desired, it may be possible that a pacific settlement of the Arab-Israeli difficulties may evolve through just such contacts. Another example may be seen in the airing of the U.S.-U.S.S.R. dispute over the Berlin blockade leading up to the temporary settlement.[20]

If this assessment of political international organization is substantially correct, there are some discomforting policy fac-

---

[18] See, e.g., discussions in National Policy Association Special Policy Committee on Technical Cooperation, *Technical Cooperation in Latin America* (Washington, D.C.: National Policy Association, 1950), pp. 113–18 *et passim;* see also H. B. Jacobini and T. H. Drews, "The Administration of Foreign Affairs," in E. O. Stene and Associates, *Public Administration in the Philippines* (Manila: I.P.A., U.P., 1955), pp. 356–62; also *Foreign Service List op. cit.*

[19] See comments in Satow, *op. cit.,* pp. 303–23; Stuart, *op. cit.,* pp. 200–201.

[20] See discussion by Philip C. Jessup, "The U.N. Begins to Show Power against Power," *New York Times Magazine* (October 23, 1949), pp. 12, 50, 51.

208 International Law: A Text

tors which need to be reflected upon. Synthesizing these it may simply be suggested that the most persistent and destructive conflicts since the founding of the United Nations have been in precisely those sectors where notable nonrepresentation obtains: Communist China, the two Vietnams, and the two Koreas.[21]

Third Power Contacts. There are a number of circumstances—fewer now perhaps than formerly—under which a state's contacts with another state are carried on with the assistance of a third state. For example, third party contacts may be useful (1) when two states are at war, (2) when two states or governments do not recognize each other, but need to negotiate a problem, and (3) when states, particularly small ones ordinarily not having much occasion for relationships, do not maintain direct diplomatic or consular contacts.

Examples may be seen of the first two in the contacts maintained by Switzerland and Sweden between the Allies and the Axis powers during World War II, and in the negotiations in Switzerland and Poland between the United States and Red Chinese governments.[22] An example of the third variety may be seen in the arrangement provided for by treaty, under which the United States will represent Philippine interests in countries where that Republic does not maintain its own diplomatic personnel.[23]

DIPLOMATIC AND CONSULAR FUNCTIONS

A survey of the international law of diplomatic and consular affairs may not appear to be the place for a discussion of functions, but brief mention would seem, nevertheless, to be in order for the status of personnel is related to their right to perform certain duties. These duties are indeed varied. The diplomatic functions are "to negotiate, to observe, and to pro-

---

[21] If, as is suggested above, the most significant role of the political international organization is as a universal on-going diplomatic conclave, efforts designed to keep various states—however untidy they may be—out of the United Nations are not only rather pointless and self-defeating, but essentially lethal.

[22] See comments in Stuart, *op. cit.*, p. 204; see newspaper accounts of U.S.–Red Chinese negotiations, e.g., see in *New York Times* (January 20, 1957), p. 22.

[23] *Treaty between the United States of America and the Philippines and Protocol Respecting General Relations,* Manila, 1946, 61 *U.S. Statutes at Large,* p. 1174, Art. III.

tect," while those of the consul are so "numerous and varied
. . . [that] . . . it would appear that he must not only be a
'Jack of all trades' but at the same time be a master of all of
them."[24] Although there is some overlapping between diplomatic and consular functions, it is convenient to review them
separately.

Diplomatic Activities

The trinity of diplomatic functions—negotiation, observation, and protection—covers a wide expanse of activity which
ranges from doing the amenities at a state dinner to delivery of
a declaration of war, and from negotiation of a treaty to providing passage home for destitute nationals.[25]

Negotiation and Representation. In order to maintain
peaceful and friendly relationships, the diplomat must work at
minimizing inconsequential friction, negotiating solutions for
more substantial differences, and otherwise oiling the cogs of
international relationships. Occasionally treaties are to be negotiated, and there are the day-to-day social contacts as well as
the more spectacular diplomatic and social occasions which
may be quite time-consuming but may be the stage for informal
discussions of some importance.[26]

Observation and Reporting. Somewhat removed from the
negotiation function of a diplomat are those phases of activity
which center upon his keeping the home government appraised
of pertinent events and attitudes in the country to which he is
accredited. As such he serves as the eyes and ears of his home
government and must keep it informed about anything and
everything which is of interest and importance. In addition he
may be expected to evaluate what he sees and hears as well as
merely to report it.

---

[24] Stuart, *op. cit.*, pp. 170, 302; *Elmer Plischke, Conduct of American Diplomacy* (New York: D. Van Nostrand Co., Inc., 1950), p. 232; Plischke speaks of
"representation, negotiation, observation, and protection." For an interesting
account in which the many facets of diplomatic activity are suggested, see W. L.
Beaulac, *Career Ambassador* (New York: The Macmillan Co., 1951).

[25] See comments in Samonte and Jacobini, *op. cit.*, pp. 53–55. *The U.N. Draft*,
Art. 3, specifies five functions: representation, protection, negotiation, reporting,
and promoting friendly relations.

[26] Stuart, *op. cit.*, pp. 170–72 *et passim*.

It is particularly important that diplomatic dispatches be honest and candid, and that the diplomatic pouch be secure. This information may or may not be seriously utilized by the home government but it is one of the ways in which a government can keep up on situations in other countries which may affect its interests.[27]

Protection of Nationals. The third major area of diplomatic activity is concerned with protecting the varied interests of fellow nationals. This practice is very much influenced by patterns of arbitration which, in this area are believed to date from the Jay Treaty of 1794.[28] Protection is based on the theory that there is a minimum standard of treatment to be accorded aliens—if they are admitted at all—and the state of which such persons are citizens is properly interested in seeing that they are accorded justice. As a practical matter the rights of such persons are usually based on treaties.[29] In this connection the Harvard draft convention on state responsibility, illustrative of proper procedure, states that:

> A state is responsible, as the term is used in this convention, when it has a duty to make reparation to another state for the injury sustained by the latter state as a consequence of an injury to its nationals.[30]

Procedures obviously vary, but as a rule they center upon bringing abuses to the attention of proper authorities. Sometimes, however, they have involved actual protective acts as well.[31]

In this connection mention must be made of the problem presented by the Calvo Clause. This is a device by which a foreign government requires an alien to renounce the protection of his own government in return for being awarded a contract or the right to work in a foreign nation. This clause, as

---

[27] *Ibid.*, pp. 172–76.

[28] F. S. Dunn, *The Protection of Nationals* (Baltimore, Md.: The Johns Hopkins Press, 1932) , pp. 52–53.

[29] E. Borchard, *The Diplomatic Protection of Citizens Abroad* (New York: Banks Publishing Co., 1915) , pp. 330–35, 402.

[30] Harvard Law School Research in International Law (draft convention), "Responsibility of States for Injuries to Aliens," Art. 1, *American Journal of International Law*, Vol. XXIII (Supplement, 1929) .

[31] Borchard, *op. cit.*, pp. 439–40 *et passim*, Stuart, *op. cit.*, pp. 180–85.

pointed out elsewhere in this volume, has not been generally accepted as valid.[32]

Consular Activities

As noted above, consular functions are not only carried out under less-protected status, but they are more diverse.[33] For purposes of convenience and brevity they can be usefully surveyed under four headings: (1) activities regarding commerce and trade, (2) activities pertaining to navigation and shipping, (3) activities concerned with passports, visas, and immigration, and (4) activities in the realm of general services to fellow nationals. These consular functions, incidentally, are almost entirely specified in treaties.[34]

Commerce. Promotion of trade is an important area of consular activity. In this category are consular studies and reports on economic conditions, aid to businessmen as to whether or not there is a market for their merchandise, finding new markets for national products, and assistance in instances where improper customs rules and other like impediments have injured economic relationships. Another activity is the certification of invoices, that is, specifying the nature and value of exports being sent to the home country.[35]

Navigation and Shipping. In keeping with their original functions, consuls exercise important activities in relation to shipping and navigation. These include settling disputes between ships' masters and seamen, making provision for destitute seamen, assuming jurisdiction over wrecked vessels of his nationality, taking over the papers of ships of his nationality while they are in his port, and being generally familiar with shipping laws and regulations. A consul's jurisdiction of a judicial nature often extends to events taking place aboard a ship of his nationality while in the port where he has jurisdiction.[36]

---

[32] See discussion above, Chapter Six.

[33] Samonte and Jacobini, *op. cit.,* pp. 55–56; Puente, *op. cit.,* pp. 53–113; Stuart, *op. cit.,* pp. 302–75.

[34] Puente, *op. cit.,* p. 56.

[35] Stuart, *op. cit.,* pp. 302–12; Puente, *op. cit.,* pp. 57–59.

[36] Puente, *op. cit.,* pp. 59–67; Stuart, *op. cit.,* pp. 312–21; see also *Wildenhus'* case, 120 U.S. 1 (1887).

Citizenship and Immigration. Consuls perform many
functions connected with citizenship and immigration. These
include registering births of children born to nationals while
abroad, occasionally the issuance of passports to nationals, issuing visas on passports of foreigners both for travel and for
immigration purposes, and checking prospective immigrants
for elegibility to enter under immigration laws. Citizens residing abroad must often register with the consulate.[37]

General Consular Services. Beyond what has been described above, consular officials are called upon to do an almost
endless variety of odd jobs. These include performing for nationals such varied activities as notarial services, protection
against denial of justice, acting as a post office for nationals for
receiving mail while abroad, procuring odd bits of information
for persons in the home country, helping tourists, aiding destitute nationals, recovering lost baggage, and witnessing and
certifying marriages.[38]

Other International Personnel

It may be added that there are various other categories of
international personnel, some national and some with functions pertaining to international organizations. Among the former are persons attached to regular diplomatic missions who,
however, do not perform regular consular or diplomatic functions. Among these are special attachés such as military, cultural, and information functionaries. Another category noted
earlier is that of technical assistance personnel who are sent
abroad to acquaint nationals of the host country with special
skills and procedures.

International organization personnel perform many varied
tasks. These include the representative function of persons sent
as delegates to organizations such as the General Assembly of
the United Nations, and a variety of technical personnel at-

---

[37] Stuart, *op. cit.*, pp. 349–75.

[38] See listing *ibid.*, p. 323 and generally pp. 322–48; also see Samonte and
Jacobini, *op. cit., passim;* Puente, *op. cit.*, pp. 67–113; Borchard, *op. cit.*, pp.
435–38.

tached to numerous international organizations and to United Nations technical assistance missions.[39]

THE MECHANICS OF REPRESENTATION

The practice of diplomatic and consular representation and its more recent derivative, international organization represen- tation, operate within a standardized pattern of procedure. The formalities attending the sending and reception of repre- sentatives, the hierarchical and rank patterns, and the expecta- tions as to behavior are all well established. Finally, the privi- ledges and immunities enjoyed by such personnel constitute a well-defined and exceedingly important aspect of the law of nations.

The Sending and Receiving of Representative Personnel

There are two aspects of this matter which will be noted here. These are (1) the acceptability of personnel to the gov- ernment to which they are to be sent, and (2) the procedure of accreditation and reception.

Agrément. "It is a general rule that no nation has a right to keep an agent within the limits of another without the consent of that other."[40] This principle, called the *agrément* or *agréation,* is based largely on the fact that a representative must be on reasonably good terms with both his own govern- ment and the government to which he is accredited if he is going to be of any service.[41]

The classic American case in point is the *Keiley* case. Mr. Anthony Keiley was refused first by Italy and later by Austria- Hungary on personal grounds. Italy objected to him because he had opposed Italy's acquisition of the Papal States, while Aus-

---

[39] See e.g., discussion in D.S. Cheever and H. F. Haviland, Jr., *Organizing for Peace* (Boston: Houghton Mifflin Co., 1954), pp. 354–97; E. F. Ranshofen- Wertheimer *The International Secretariat* (Washington, D.C.: Carnegie Endow- ment, 1945); E. P. Chase, *The United Nations in Action* (New York: McGraw-Hill Book Co., Inc., 1950).

[40] Thomas Jefferson quoted in Moore, *Digest* IV, p. 473.

[41] Satow, *op. cit.,* pp. 134–41.

tria-Hungary found that his marriage to a Jewess by a civil ceremony would render his position in Vienna "untenable and even impossible." While the United States found the Austro-Hungarian view to be highly objectionable, its right in the matter was clearly recognized.[42]

It is therefore understandable that U.S. practice, conforming to that of other powers, is exercised as follows:

Upon the appointment of an ambassador or minister by the President, inquiry is made through the Department of State of the head of the government to which he is to be accredited whether the appointment is agreeable to that government. Upon the receipt of a reply in the affirmative, the name of the ambassador or minister is sent by the President to the Senate for confirmation of his appointment in conformity with the provisions of Paragraph 2 Section 2, Article II of the Constitution of the United States.[43]

It may also be noted that the Convention Regarding Diplomatic Officers (inter-American, 1928) states in regard to this matter that "No State may accredit its diplomatic officers to other States without previous agreement with the latter."[44]

Closely related to the principle of the *agrément* is the principle that a minister who has become *persona non grata* must be withdrawn. For example, the Austro-Hungarian ambassador to the United States, Dr. Dumba, was no longer acceptable when it became clear that he was instigating strikes in American munitions plants during World War I. The United States felt that it could have given him his passports or asked his government to recall him, and "chose the latter course as the more considerate."[45]

Accreditation and Reception. Diplomatic and consular personnel are official representatives and their appointment and reception are attended by formalities, some of which are quite elaborate. Diplomatic officials are given what are known as *letters of credence* by their governments which state that the

---

[42] Moore, *Digest* IV, pp. 480–84.

[43] Cited in Hackworth, *Digest* IV, p. 446.

[44] *Convention Regarding Diplomatic Officers,* Havana, 1928, L.N.T.S. Vol. 155, p. 259, Art. 8, see conveniently in Llewellyn Pfankuchen, *A Documentary Textbook in International Law* (New York: Farrar and Rinehart, Inc., 1940) , p. 405; see also *U.N. Convention,* Arts. 4, 7.

[45] Hackworth, *Digest* IV, p. 450; see also *U.N. Convention,* Art. 9.

named official has been appointed at a specified rank and that it is hoped that the foreign government will give his acts full faith and credit.[46] If the diplomat is of *chargé d'affaires* rank, the letter of credence is addressed from the minister of foreign affairs of the accrediting country to the comparable official in the country to which the official is being sent. If the official is of higher rank, however, the letters are addressed from the head of the accrediting state to the head of the host state.

When the diplomat arrives at his post, protocol calls for his presenting a sealed copy of the letter of credence to the head of state (or foreign minister in the case of a *chargé d'affaires*). This is done after he has notified the ministry of foreign affairs of his arrival and a time has been set for the formal reception. The significance of the formalities is seen in the fact that a diplomatic officer's status is not official until accreditation and reception have been accomplished.[47]

Mention should also be made of a somewhat different sort of accreditation. In connection with conferences for the negotiation of special accords, envoys are sometimes specially commissioned for purposes of such negotiation. The credentials given to such officials include the so-called full powers. Reception entails an exchange of full powers credentials among the delegates.[48]

As with diplomats, the sending of consular officials is an act of the sovereign state. Reception of such officials also entails an exercise of sovereign rights on the part of the receiving state. It is in principle different from the procedure applied to diplomatic personnel, however, and should not be confused with it. Accordingly, the state sending a consular officer grants him a *commission* or a *patent* authorizing him to act for it in a particular district, and the state to which he is commissioned gives him a certificate, usually called an *exequatur*, allowing him to perform certain specified consular duties in its territory. A consular officer is therefore in a sense an agent of both nations. It may be noted that a state may exclude foreign consuls altogether or admit them to whatever extent it deems

---

[46] *Ibid.*, p. 439.

[47] See *In Re Baiz*, 135 U.S. 403 (1890) ; however, cf. *U.N. Convention*, Art. 13.

[48] See Oppenheim-Lauterpacht, *Treatise* I, pp. 780–81.

desirable, and, of course, particular persons may be rejected for any reason whatsoever, in conformity with the principle of the *agrément*.[49]

Rank and Hierarchy

In an egalitarian society, hierarchy and rank as marks of prestige often seem superficial and even degenerate. In the diplomatic world, however, these are matters of some concern, though far less so than in centuries past.[50]

Diplomatic Ranks and Hierarchy. Within different nations the top machinery for conducting foreign relations differs, yet the main outlines are significantly similar. The top hierarchy consists of the *head of state*, the *head of the government*, and the *minister of foreign affairs*. The distinction between the first two of these is lost in the United States where the President embodies both concepts. It may be distinguished easily in countries like Great Britain and Italy, however, where the Queen and President respectively represent the state while the prime minister and premier head their respective governments. Although there is some question about the relative status of top personnel, such matters are basically of little importance— except for the headaches which they give protocol chiefs and party hostesses. When such personnel are traveling abroad, they, and ministers of foreign affairs, are accorded full immunity and appropriate respect and ceremonial.[51]

When on rare occasions several heads of state, or of governments, or foreign affairs chiefs are simultaneously at the same capital, problems of precedence may arise. These are resolved by several means: (1) according to priority in terms of the alphabetical order of the names of the states, (2) by importance of the states, or (3) by alternating the honors.[52]

---

[49] Puente, *op. cit.*, pp. 20–31; Oppenheim-Lauterpacht, *Treatise* I, pp. 834–37; Charles C. Hyde, *International Law Chiefly as Interpreted and Applied by the United States* (2d ed., Boston: Little, Brown & Co., 1945), Vol. II, pp. 1314–17.

[50] Cf., however, John P. Armstrong, *Sihanouk Speaks* (New York: Walker & Co., 1964), pp. 77–101; here is an interesting account in which the contemporary importance of such matters emerges.

[51] Satow, *op. cit.*, pp. 5–24; Oppenheim-Lauterpacht, *Treatise* I, pp. 759–68; Gould, *op. cit.*, pp. 261–63.

[52] Satow, *op. cit.*, pp. 25–44.

Regarding the rank designations of the chiefs of diplomatic missions, it is interesting to note that while matters of rank and precedence have been regularized and standardized—and pacified since 1815—all kinds of absurd incidents had occurred prior to that time. Questions relating to which of several envoys should precede the others were especially taxing. Particularly distressing in this regard were the many Franco-Hispanic incidents. On one of these occasions, in 1661, Spanish and French personnel quite literally fought over the question of whose coach was to precede the other's in a London diplomatic procession.[53]

These difficulties were largely relegated to history when at the Congresses of Vienna and Aix la Chapelle a standardized procedure was agreed upon. Accordingly, diplomatic missions are to be headed by one of four ranks of diplomatic personnel. These are:

1. Ambassadors, legates, or nuncios.
2. Envoys extraordinary and ministers plenipotentiary, and papal internuncios.
3. Ministers resident.
4. Chargés d'affaires.

Within each rank, personnel take precedence according to the date of the official notification of their arrival. It may be added that the ranking diplomat at each capital is considered as the dean (*doyen*) of the diplomatic corps and on occasion he speaks for that group. It appears that in some countries the representative of the Vatican is automatically accorded the status of dean of the diplomatic corps regardless of date of accreditation.[54] It should be stressed that the four categories of ranks mentioned above pertain to chiefs of mission, although some countries including the United States now often accredit

---

[53] *Ibid.*, pp. 28–29.

[54] *Ibid.*, pp. 149–60, 338–39; Hyde, *op. cit.*, pp. 1222–25. Cf. *U.N. Convention,* Art. 14 which specifies three ranks omitting that of minister resident. Hackworth, *Digest* IV, pp. 636–37, 640–41. For an interesting account of a 1918 incident in which the U.S. ambassador to Russia, acting in concert with and as Dean of the diplomatic corps, protested the arrest of and contributed to the release of the Roumanian Minister, see in Herbert W. Briggs, *The Law of Nations* (2d ed.; New York: Appleton-Century-Crofts, 1952), pp. 770–71; original in *U.S. Foreign Relations,* 1918, Russia, I, pp. 477.

a person of ministerial rank as well as an ambassador to certain governments.

Below this top level, diplomatic personnel are designated in varied ways the most general term being "attaché" which is applied both to peripheral personnel, for example, military attachés, and also to persons employed directly in the work of the diplomatic mission per se, for example, political attachés. Personnel designated as counselor of embassy or secretary of the embassy are usually considered to outrank personnel designated simply as attaché.[55]

Consular Ranks. The ranks of consular personnel are less clearly defined in international practice than the ranks of diplomatic personnel. In general they are considered as subordinate in rank but circumstances attending a unified diplomatic-consulàr service such as obtains in the United States, and the practice of sometimes designating a person as having both diplomatic and consular status may obscure this distinction at times.

United States consular rank designations are as follows:

1. Consul general.
2. Consul.
3. Vice-consul.
4. Consular agent.

Of these the first two are full consular officers, while the latter two are of subordinate status. Usually the consul general heads up consular matters in a large district or a whole country; a consul has jurisdiction within a smaller district, a city, or a port; a vice-consul usually functions as assistant to a consul, but is occasionally given jurisdiction over a district; consular agents are used in separate localities, but under principal consular officials. While the United States commissions only its own citizens in consular capacities, many countries use nationals of the country where the post is located. Such personnel, particularly in posts of minor importance, are sometimes classed as *honorary consuls.*[56]

---

[55] Hyde, *op. cit.,* pp. 1225–27. Hackworth, *Digest* IV, pp. 637–39.

[56] Puente, *op. cit.,* pp. 12–19; Hyde, *op. cit.,* Vol. II, pp. 1312–13; Hackworth, *Digest* IV, pp. 655–66. Harvard Law School Research in International Law (draft convention) "Legal Position and Functions of Consuls," *American Journal of International Law,* Vol. XXVI (Supplement, 1932), pp. 221–22.

Behavior. Although the matter must of necessity be discussed later in connection with termination of missions, a word
needs to be said here regarding the conduct of representative
personnel. It is obviously not the ordinary function of diplomatic or consular personnel to foster bad relations or to impair
their personal effectiveness as representatives. Accordingly,
there are a number of practices in which they may not indulge,
among which are the following: they may not criticize the
personnel or policies of the government to which they are
accredited; they may not publish correspondence with the government to which they are accredited; and they may not serve
as centers of foreign espionage. To violate these principles is to
impair one's usefulness and to invite being asked to leave. In a
word, a diplomatic or consular official's recall may be requested
or in extreme cases he may be virtually expelled if he violates
these general rules. Classic examples include the recall of Lord
Sackville as a result of his vaguely disparaging comments about
President Cleveland in a letter to an alleged former British
subject; and the recall of Citizen Genet for making himself
obnoxious during the Washington administration. In a much
more recent case, the United States ambassador to the U.S.S.R.,
George Kennan, was specified as unacceptable to the U.S.S.R.
because of some remarks he made regarding that country while
in Berlin.[57]

Privileges and Immunities

One of the oldest segments of international law is that part
which guarantees the persons, property, and archives of representative personnel. Its status has been relatively secure
throughout the centuries because all states have needed the
protection for their own personnel and could scarcely hope to
enjoy it without reciprocation. Beyond that, the question of
good faith is involved, for immunities have been granted for so
long that they are now firmly grounded in customary law. The
political foundation for these privileges and immunities is thus

---

[57] See Moore, *Digest* IV, pp. 484–549; Charles G. Fenwick, *International Law*
(3d ed.; New York: Appleton-Century-Crofts, Inc., 1948) , p. 467; On the Kennan
incident, see *New York Times* (October 4, 1952) , pp. 1, 3.

both contemporary need for reciprocity and venerable custom.[58]

The details of the problem will be considered under four headings: (1) diplomatic immunities, (2) immunities of international organization personnel, (3) consular immunities, and (4) the problem of asylum.

Diplomatic Immunities. Since times of antiquity the representatives of foreign princes have been accorded immunities, and it has been observed that "Everywhere in antiquity ambassadors were considered inviolable." Both the protection of representative persons, and immunity from civil as well as criminal jurisdiction seem to have been involved.[59] In the early modern era these principles continued generally to prevail,[60] and the modern practice is in much the same vein. It is interesting and useful to note the view of one close student of the matter, however, that the establishment of ambassadorial immunities were "more as a result of political pressure than of any very strong respect for international law," but he goes on to state further "but what of that? The fact that they were established is enough, for precedents made the law."[61]

In a contemporary setting a brief survey of diplomatic immunities and privileges will be developed here under four headings: (1) protection, (2) franchise d'hotel, (3) immunity from criminal and civil jurisdiction, and (4) other privileges and immunities. In general this may be summed up by observing that the diplomatic agent is subject only to the law of the state which has accredited him.[62] While it is probably not proper to consider such rights to be based on the general principle of extraterritoriality, this tack is sometimes used. It seems more correct to employ the concept of mere exemption from local jurisdiction. It should be noted that these immunities pertain not only to the envoy himself, but to his staff, family,

---

[58] See, e.g., comments in Georg Schwarzenberger, *Power Politics* (New York: Frederick A. Praeger, Inc., 1951), pp. 207–11.

[59] Phillipson, *op. cit.*, Vol. I, pp. 328–41, quotation on p. 328.

[60] Gentili, *op. cit.*, pp. 57–58, 96–99; Grotius, *op. cit.*, pp. 441–46 *et passim;* E. R. Adair, *the Extraterritoriality of Ambassadors in the Sixteenth and Seventeenth Centuries* (London: Longmans Green and Co., 1929), *passim.*

[61] Adair, *ibid.*, p. 251.

[62] A. S. Hershey, *Diplomatic Agents and Immunities* (Washington, D.C.: U.S. Government Printing Office, 1919), p. 102.

and even in some instances to his household, and this ". . . is a necessary consequence of the conditions on which they are sent and received."[63]

Protection of diplomats against "interference with their security, peace or dignity"[64] is an obligation of the state to which they are accredited. Accordingly, in conformity with their obligations under international law, states in their municipal law provide protection to such persons.[65] For example, the U.S. federal law states:

> Whoever assaults, strikes, wounds, imprisons, or offers violence to the person of an ambassador or other public minister, in violation of the law of nations, shall be fined not more than $5,000 or imprisoned not more than three years, or both.[66]

This is one of those aspects of the law which tends to have almost a routine character about it. Normally the mutual desirability of maintaining these rights is of such obvious importance that there is no question of interference. It is in this sort of setting that what may be called apolitical or nonpolitical law emerges. Certainly much of the law of diplomatic and consular activities falls into this category. Nevertheless, there are occasional abberations, particularly where a state system seems to be significantly at variance and perhaps out of touch with much of the rest of the world.[67]

---

[63] Satow, *op. cit.*, pp. 174–241, quotation on p. 174.

[64] Harvard Law School Research in International Law (draft convention) "Diplomatic Privileges and Immunities," Art. 17 in *American Journal of International Law*, Vol. XXVI (Supplement, 1932), p. 90; see also *Yearbook of the International Law Commission*, 1958, Vol. II, pp. 16–19; also "Report of the International Law Commission" (9th Session), *American Journal of International Law*, Vol. LII (January, 1958), especially pp. 179–204; also "Report of the International Law Commission" (10th Session), *American Journal of International Law*, Vol. LIII (January, 1959), especially pp. 253–91; also *U.N. Convention*, Arts. 29, 31, 37, 38, 39.

[65] See Oppenheim-Lauterpacht, *Treatise* I, pp. 787–90; inter-American "Convention Regarding Diplomatic Officers," Art. 14; *Respublica v. De Longchamps*, U.S., Court of Oyer and Terminer at Philadelphia, 1784; I Dallas III; A. H. Feller and M. O. Hudson, *A Collection of the Diplomatic and Consular Laws and Regulations of Various Countries* (2 vols.; Washington, D.C.: Carnegie Endowment, 1933).

[66] 18 U.S.C.A. Sec. 112.

[67] Although the principal relevant difficulties between Red China and the United States centered upon mistreatment of consuls, that series represents a notable example of serious deviation. See Herbert W. Briggs, "American Consu-

Immunity of residence or franchise d'hotel is the immunity which attends the official property and residence of diplomatic personnel. In this connection the Harvard draft convention states:

A receiving state shall prevent its agents or the agents of any of its political subdivisions from entering the premises occupied or used by a mission, or occupied by a member of a mission, without the consent of the chief of the mission. . . .

A receiving state shall protect the archives of a mission from any violation. . . .[68]

On this same subject the inter-American convention states broadly:

Diplomatic officers shall be inviolate as to their persons, their residence, private or official, and their property. This inviolability covers: (*a*) All classes of diplomatic officers; (*b*) The entire official personnel of the diplomatic mission; (*c*) The members of the respective families living under the same roof; (*d*) The papers, archives and correspondence of the mission.[69]

Immunity from criminal and civil jurisdiction is a third broad area of protection enjoyed by diplomatic personnel. In brief this means that a diplomat cannot be arrested or tried under the jurisdiction of the state to which he is accredited for any crime which he allegedly may have committed, nor may he be made subject to any civil suit. This is not to say that diplomatic persons are unrestrained, for their own governments are under obligation to rectify transgressions, but it does mean that they are protected against action by the host government.[70] Illustrative of this situation, the pertinent article of the Har-

---

lar Rights in Communist China," *American Journal of International Law,* Vol. XLIV (April, 1950), pp. 243–58. For brief account of U.S. withdrawal of representatives to the Republic of Congo (Brazzaville) because of mistreatment of personnel see "Contemporary Practice of the United States Relating to International Law," *American Journal of International Law,* Vol. LX (January, 1966), pp. 91–92. For accounts of Red Chinese deviation in regard to diplomatic personnel from the U.S.S.R., France, and Eastern Europe, see newspaper accounts in early 1967, e.g., *St. Louis Post Dispatch,* February 7, 1967, p. 2A; February 8, 1967, pp. 1, 7; February 9, 1967, p. 2A.

[68] Harvard Research, "Diplomatic Privileges and Immunities," Arts. 3, 5; also *U.N. Convention,* Arts. 22, 24, 30.

[69] *Convention Regarding Diplomatic Officers,* Art. 14.

[70] Hershey, *op. cit.,* pp. 103–28.

vard Research draft convention states that "A receiving state shall not exercise judicial or administrative jurisdiction over a member of a mission or over a member of his family," and the pertinent inter-American convention provides that "Diplomatic officers are exempt from all civil or criminal jurisdiction of the state to which they are accredited. . . ."[71]

There are many historic examples with reference to civil action, but instances of criminality are perhaps less frequent. One case in point is that of the Spanish ambassador to England, Mendoza, who was involved in 1584 in a conspiracy to dethrone Queen Elizabeth I. In punishment he was merely sent away from England, and representations were made at Madrid.[72] An interesting case which would seem to illustrate proper procedure on both sides is the affair known as *Carlos Waddington's* case. It involved the son of the Chilean chargé d'affaires to Belgium who, in 1905, killed the secretary of the Chilean legation in Brussels. Although the chargé d'affaires waived immunity for his son, the Belgian government withheld action until the Chilean government had specifically consented to the waiver.[73]

Illustrative of the status of diplomatic immunity from civil suit, even in cases which are remote from the official character of the diplomat and his work, is the British case of *Dickinson* v. *Del Solar* which involved the insurance company with which the first secretary of the Peruvian legation in London was insured for public liability. The company tried to escape liability for damages caused by Del Solar's negligent driving by virtue of the first secretary's diplomatic immunity. The court stated, however, that:

Diplomatic agents are not, in virtue of their privileges as such, immune from legal liability for any wrongful acts. The accurate statement is that they are not liable to be sued in the English Courts unless they submit to the jurisdiction. Diplomatic privilege does not import immunity from legal liability, but only exemption from local jurisdiction. The privilege is the privilege of the Sovereign by

---

[71] Harvard Research, "Diplomatic Privileges and Immunities," Art. 19; *Convention Regarding Diplomatic Officers*, Art. 19.

[72] Hershey, *op. cit.*, p. 111; Oppenheim, Lauterpacht, *Treatise* I, p. 791.

[73] Satow, *op. cit.*, p. 198.

whom the diplomatic agent is accredited, and it may be waived with
the sanction of the Sovereign or of the official superior of the
agent. . . .[74]

It should be noted in passing that heads of states, should they
be traveling abroad, enjoy essentially the same status as diplomats, indeed, their position is more elevated. Illustrative of the
principle is the case of *Stratham* v. *Stratham and the Gaekwar
of Baroda* in which the prince of an Indian state was held
immune from being made a corespondent in a divorce case.[75]

Other privileges and immunities enjoyed by diplomatic personnel include their right to hold religious services of their own
faith at the embassy or legation provided they do not do so
flamboyantly; the right to travel unmolested—if admitted at
all—through third states to their destination; and the right to
exemption from customs duties for goods used or consumed by
diplomatic personnel. There is some question as to whether all
of these can be properly termed "rights" under international
law or whether certain of them—particularly the obligation of
third states to permit transit—may more properly be considered as grounded in comity.[76] It may also be noted that among
the areas in which immunities do not obtain are taxation of
property not used as diplomatic property or residence, which is
held by a diplomat in the country to which he is accredited.[77]

Immunities of International Organization Personnel.
While the privileges and immunities of diplomatic personnel
stem from their status as representatives of sovereign powers,
similar rights and immunities for personnel of international

---

[74] *Dickinson* v. *Del Solar,* Great Britain, King's Bench Division, 1 K. B. 376
(1929). Cf. *U.N. Convention,* Art. 31 where exceptions are made for certain
functions performed in private capacity by the diplomat to which civil jurisdiction may attach.

[75] *Stratham* v. *Stratham and Gaekwar of Baroda,* Great Britain, Probate,
Divorce and Admiralty Division, 1911, Probate 92.

[76] See in Satow, *op. cit.,* pp. 226–53; Harvard Research, "Diplomatic Privileges
and Immunities," Arts. 15, 20, 22; regarding status of transit, see Harvard
Research, "Diplomatic Privileges and Immunities," Art. 15 and comment, pp.
85–89; Moore, *Digest* IV, pp. 556–63; see *U.N. Convention,* Arts. 34, 35, 36, 40. In
Bergman v. *De Sieyes,* 71 F. Supp. 334 (1946), the U.S. District Court held that a
French diplomat accredited to Bolivia was immune from suit while passing
through the United States.

[77] Hershey, *op. cit.,* pp. 128–35.

organizations derive from treaties and conventions.[78] Illustrative of the basic law is the pertinent clause of the United Nations Charter which states that:

1. The Organization shall enjoy in the territory of each of its Members such privileges and immunities as are necessary for the fulfillment of its purposes.

2. Representatives of the Members of the United Nations and officials of the Organization shall similarly enjoy such privileges and immunities as are necessary for the independent exercise of their functions in connection with the Organization.[79]

A similar clause appeared in the Covenant of the League of Nations.[80] Also, similar statements are found in the Statute of the International Court of Justice and in the constitutions of the specialized agencies and the regional international organizations.[81] It should not be inferred, however, that representatives of all such organizations enjoy rights and privileges substantially equal to a full measure of diplomatic immunity. In the specialized agencies it is often true that immunities are somewhat more restricted. In regard to immunity from legal process, e.g., "in practice . . . [such] representatives have been accorded immunity from legal process in respect of their official acts only."[82]

To further spell out the scope of the immunities of interna-

---

[78] See C. M. Crosswell, *Protection of International Personnel Abroad* (New York: Oceana Publications, 1952), p. vi; see also M. Hill, *Immunities and Privileges of International Officials* (Washington, D.C.: Carnegie Endowment, 1947); also Josef L. Kunz, "Privileges and Immunities of International Organizations," *American Journal of International Law*, Vol. XLI (October, 1947), pp. 828–62; also Lawrence Preuss, "Immunity of Officers and Employees of the United Nations for Official Acts: The Ranallo Case," *American Journal of International Law*, Vol. XLI (July, 1947), pp. 555–78.

[79] U.N. *Charter*, Art. 105.

[80] *Covenant of the League of Nations*, Art. 7.

[81] *Statute of the International Court of Justice*, Arts. 19, 42; *Convention on International Civil Aviation*, Art. 60; *The Constitution of the International Labor Organization*, Art. 40; *Statute of the Council of Europe*, Art. 40; *Charter of the Organization of the American States*, Arts. 103, 104, 105; *Treaty Establishing the European Economic Community*, Arts. 211, 212, 216, 218. Special headquarters agreements and other similar devices are employed also within the framework of regional organizations. See Kuljit Ahluwalia, *The Legal Status, Privileges and Immunities of the Specialized Agencies of the United Nations and Certain Other International Organizations* (The Hague, Martinus Nijhoff, 1964), p. 55, *et passim*.

[82] Ahluwalia, *op. cit.* p. 164 *et passim*.

tional organization personnel, however, a number of agreements have been entered into. Pertaining specifically to the United Nations, a General Convention on the Privileges and Immunities of the United Nations was drawn up. This convention has not been widely accepted, nevertheless, the main center of United Nations activity has been removed from local jurisdiction by a special headquarters agreement between the United Nations and the United States.[83] Except as noted above, the privileges and immunities enjoyed by international organizations and some of their personnel bear a striking resemblance to diplomatic immunities in scope. Some are more easily likened to the immunities of consuls.[84]

Consular Privileges and Immunities. It is well recognized that while consuls do not enjoy diplomatic status, they do enjoy certain privileges and immunities. While this status may derive to some extent from general international law, it is mostly the result of treaty agreements, reciprocity, and comity. It will be remembered that the United States applies the most-favored-nation principle on a conditional basis regarding consular rights and privileges.[85] The status of consular rights and immunities will be discussed under the headings of protection of persons, protection of archives, and amenability to local jurisdiction.

Protection of the person of the consul and respect for his status are rights to which such personnel are entitled. Illustrative of prevailing practice the Harvard Research draft on consular matters states that:

A receiving state shall accord to a consul within its territory:
a) Respect and protection adequate for the exercise of his consular functions;
b) Subject to the condition of reciprocity, every exemption and

---

[83] I U.N.T.S. 15 and II U.N.T.S. 11.

[84] See *United States* v. *Coplon and Gubitchev*, 84 F. Supp. 472 (1949) ; also 88 F. Supp. 915 (1950). *Knocklong Corporation* v. *Kingdom of Afghanistan, New York Law Journal*, March 28, 1957, p. 13 (Co. Ct. Nassau Co., N.Y.; briefly reviewed in *American Journal of International Law*, Vol. LII (January, 1958), p. 139. See also case of *Reparation for Injuries Suffered in the Service of the United Nations*, Advisory Opinion of April 11, 1949, I.C.J. Reports, 1949, p. 174.

[85] See above, fn. 32; and above, Chapter Six.

immunity which it accords to any other consul of the same character and grade of service in the same place.[86]

An example of proper procedure in rectifying a violation is the instance in 1924 of the mob killing of the American vice-consul at Teheran. The Persian government acted with dispatch in arresting the guilty parties, and payments of $60,000 were made to the vice-consul's widow and $110,000 to the U.S. government for the expense of sending a warship to return the body. Some other courtesies were also extended.[87]

Inviolability of the consular archives and office represents another area of consular immunity. Accordingly the Harvard draft convention states:

A receiving state shall prevent the violation of consular archives by its agents of any character and it shall not require a consul to produce in court or elsewhere a document from such archives, or to testify as to their contents. The consul decides, subject to diplomatic recourse by the receiving state, whether a document is part of the archives.

A receiving state shall prevent the invasion of a consular office by its agents of any character, provided such office is used solely for consular purposes; and shall furnish special protection to such office and the property used in connection therewith when necessary to defend them from attacks directed against them because of their official character.[88]

This phase of immunity is believed to be more completely provided for in treaty law than is any other phase of consular immunities.[89] The general status of such matters has been nicely summed up by Puente, who says:

The rule has commended itself to universal acceptance that the archives and other official property of the consulate are *inviolable;* that is to say, absolutely exempt from seizure or examination by the

---

[86] Harvard Research, "Legal Position and Functions of Consuls," Art. 15; also "Consular Intercourse and Immunities," *Yearbook of the International Law Commission,* 1957, Vol. II, pp. 71–103.

[87] See in Stuart, *op. cit.,* p. 379. For instances of serious deviation from the norm, see this chapter above, fn. 67.

[88] Harvard Research, "Legal Position and Functions of Consuls," Arts. 16, 17.

[89] See Stuart, *op. cit.,* p. 380 quoting another source.

local authorities. This privilege belongs to the government which the foreign consul represents.

The *private* correspondence and personal effects of the consul are not so exempt, however, and must be kept separate from the *official* property of the consulate.[90]

Closely associated with this right are a number of other privileges. These include the privilege of displaying the national arms above the door of the consular offices, but the related privilege of displaying the national flag is apparently not firmly grounded and is subject to local regulations and to treaty arrangements.[91] Official communications with the consul's home government are inviolable, and the consul is exempt from the public service in the state to which he is assigned. Finally, consuls are usually given certain exemptions from local taxation. This is not universally accorded, but usually such immunity is granted on a reciprocal basis. Income taxes and custom duties are among the more common taxes from which consular personnel are usually exempted. The Harvard draft convention would exempt a consul from all local taxes or customs duties, but it suggests that it is not necessary to accord such privilege to noncareer consular personnel, particularly nationals of the receiving state.[92]

Amenability to local jurisdiction is a characteristic of consular status which distinguishes it from diplomatic status. Immunity ordinarily is granted in civil matters which are directly related to the exercise of official duties, and in criminal cases there is sometimes relief in cases involving misdemeanors, but in general there are not many benefits accorded consular personnel as far as immunities from civil and criminal jurisdiction are concerned.[93] The pertinent clause in the inter-American Convention Regarding Consular Agents states that:

---

90 Puente, *op. cit.,* p. 45.

91 For an example of such treaty right see "Republic of Costa Rica-United States of America, Consular Convention," in *American Journal of International Law,* Vol. XLIV (Supplement, April, 1950) , p. 90, Art. VI. For argument that the right to fly the flag is a part of international law, see Hackworth, *Digest* II, pp. 124–32.

92 See Puente, *op. cit.,* pp. 47–53; Stuart, *op. cit.,* pp. 385–87; Harvard Research, "Legal Position and Functions of Consuls," Arts. 23, 24, 25, 26.

93 See Harvard Research, "Legal Position and Functions of Consuls," Arts. 20, 21, 22; Stuart, *op. cit.,* pp. 388–91. The U.S.–U.S.S.R. Consular Treaty of 1967 is apparently an exception to the rule, as the criminal immunity of consular

In the absence of a special agreement between two nations, the consular agents who are nationals of the State appointing them shall neither be arrested nor prosecuted except in the cases when they are accused of committing an act classed as a crime by local legislation.

. . . .

In respect to unofficial acts, consuls are subject, in civil as well as in criminal matters, to the jurisdiction of the State where they exercise their functions.[94]

In the interesting and illustrative French court case of *Bigelow* v. *Princess Zizianoff* the question centered upon whether an offensive act by a consul was official and therefore exempt from court action or, on the other hand, whether it was unofficial and therefore the subject of local jurisdiction.

Bigelow, the U.S. passport officer at the consulate in Paris had refused a visa to Princess Zizianoff, and subsequently, by conversations with newspapermen had contributed material to an explanatory article published in an American newspaper sold in Paris. This account detailed spying activities, a deportation to Siberia, and performance of espionage activities in the United States. The court said:

we cannot discover a performance of an official act in the holding of such conversations. . . .

. . . the defendant is prosecuted, not for refusal of a passport, which would be an act in his consular capacity and would consequently be outside any jurisdiction of the courts, but only for having, in his communication of that decision of his country, delivered himself on the subject of said refusal of the above-described comments, which were not its necessary and indispensable corollary; and as in these comments, viewed as apart from or included in the official act itself, there is a serious wrong susceptible of injuring private interests and having a personal character; and this wrong, which is clearly unconnected with the duty performed by Bigelow and is not at all required in the examination of the said official act, would, if it is established, involve him in penal liability by reason of the criminal elements which it appears to contain. . . .[95]

---

officials is provided for; *New York Times*, March 17, 1967, pp. 1, 12. If most-favored-nation effect should stem from this accord, a significant change in consular immunities may be in the offing.

[94] *Convention Regarding Consular Agents*, Habana, 1928, Arts. 14, 17, see in 155 L.N.T.S. 291.

[95] *Bigelow* v. *Princess Zizianoff*, France, Court of Appeals of Paris, 1928, see in *American Journal of International Law*, Vol. XXIII (January, 1929) pp. 172–79. See also *Arcaya* v. *Paez*, 145 F. Supp. 464 (1956), where the court distinguished

Asylum. It was once the view in certain places that the section of the city in which a foreign envoy's residence was located might be a sanctuary from the host government, the so-called *franchise du quartier*. The rule which generally prevails today, however, is that a diplomatic or consular establishment may not be used as a place to afford asylum to offenders against the local government.[96] Illustrative of the general principle involved is the pertinent clause of the Harvard Research draft which states:

A sending state shall not permit the premises occupied or used by its mission or by a member of its mission to be used as a place of asylum for fugitives from justice.[97]

On the other hand, the practice of diplomatic asylum has persisted in some areas where governmental instability has given it a political foundation. Accordingly, the inter-American convention on asylum recognized no right of asylum for common criminals or deserters, but it did clearly recognize a right of political asylum under certain circumstances.[98] This qualified right has also been impliedly recognized as existing in Latin America by the International Court of Justice.[99]

United States policy has been one of being reluctant to recognize asylum as a right. There have been, however, practical variations of several sorts. In some areas where asylum exists in fact, the United States has insisted on the same rights in prac-

---

between diplomatic and consular immunities. It held that an action brought against a consul who had, subsequent to commencement of suit, been appointed and accepted in a diplomatic post, should not be dismissed. The court recognized that the action should not be allowed to proceed while the defendant held his diplomatic status, but that it could be continued upon termination of such status.

[96] Adair, *op. cit.*, pp. 198–229; Satow, *op. cit.*, pp. 219–25; Hershey, *op. cit.*, pp. 167–68; Puente, *op. cit.*, p. 46.

[97] Harvard Research, "Diplomatic Privileges and Immunities," Art. 6.

[98] *Convention Fixing the Rules to Be Observed for the Granting of Asylum* (1928), Arts. I, II, see in 132 L.N.T.S. 323. For further general comment, see Hyde, *op. cit.*, Vol. II, pp. 1284–90; Hackworth, *Digest* II, pp. 621–49.

[99] *Colombian-Peruvian Asylum Case,* I.C.J. Reports (1950), p. 266; *Haya de la Torre Case,* I.C.J. Reports (1951), p. 71. For a statement against diplomatic asylum, see Simon Planas Suarez, *El asilo diplomatico* (Buenos Aires: La Imprenta Lopez, 1953). For a good brief account of inter-American practice in regard to asylum, see C. Neal Ronning, *Law and Politics in Inter-American Diplomacy* (New York: John Wiley & Sons, Inc., 1963), pp. 89–105.

tice as other states enjoy which do recognize asylum as a right.[100] There is, moreover, much to suggest that asylum is a fact which, often, in those areas where it still exists, all parties want to tolerate, but few want to acknowledge.

The case of the Hungarian Cardinal, József Mindszenty, is interesting to note in this connection. In November of 1956, Cardinal Mindszenty was given asylum in the U.S. Legation in Budapest, and it appears that his asylum has not been the subject of nearly as much controversy as might have been expected. It is in all probability a good example of the sort of diverse mutual advantages which serve the interests of all parties. Within this sort of setting the phenomenon persists.[101]

TERMINATION OF A MISSION

As in the case of establishment of a mission, there are certain circumstances which ordinarily bring about the end of a mission. While there is some variation among countries in this regard, the principles are fairly standard, though specific classifications of such principles may vary. Discussion will be divided into (1) termination of diplomatic missions, and (2) termination of consular missions.

Termination of Diplomatic Missions

There are perhaps five basic ways in which diplomatic missions are terminated. These may be classed as follows: (1) termination by the envoy or his government, (2) termination by the host government, (3) termination by virtue of the goals of the mission having been accomplished, or by the expiration of its preset time limits, (4) termination by the death of certain of the principal parties, and (5) in some cases termination by virtue of principal governmental changes.[102]

---

[100] Ronning, op. cit., p. 92.

[101] See Daniel Schorr, "Cardinal in a Cage," The Reporter, November 24, 1960, pp. 39–40; also "The Status of the Cardinal," The Christian Century, April 15, 1959, pp. 445–46.

[102] Convention Regarding Diplomatic Officers, Art. 25; Satow, op. cit., pp. 274–75 lists 12 specific ways of termination, and Hershey, op. cit., pp. 24–27 lists 11 ways.

Termination by the Envoy or His Government. The envoy or his government can terminate the mission in various ways. A change of diplomats, severance of diplomatic relations, or merely the withdrawal or resignation of the envoy terminate the mission. This may be accomplished under friendly or unfriendly circumstances ranging from the mere routine reassignment of an envoy to a break in diplomatic relations or where still permissible, a declaration of war. Also, when a diplomat is raised in rank, the old mission terminates and a new one begins.

Termination by the Host Government. It is always within the power of the host government to terminate a mission accredited to it. As noted in the Harvard Research draft on diplomatic privileges and immunities, it may request withdrawal of diplomatic persons and eventually merely declare termination.[103] Beyond that it may end a mission by a declaration of war or by breaking off diplomatic relations, and sending the envoy his passports.

Accomplishment of Goals or Termination by Time Limit. A mission ends when it has accomplished its objective, for example, a diplomatic conference to negotiate a special convention ends when the matter has been negotiated or when the conference ends without having been able to agree. Similarly, a mission accredited for a certain period of time, say five years, ends at that time.

Death. A mission terminates, of course, when the envoy expires. Similarly, although it does not appear to pertain to countries lacking crowned heads, a mission terminates upon the death either of the accrediting sovereign or of the host sovereign.[104]

Principal Governmental Changes. When under normal circumstances one government falls and is replaced by another under the same constitutional system or the same monarch, there is no problem of the termination of diplomatic missions. On the other hand, if a monarchy changes to a republic or vice versa, if a state becomes extinct, if a monarch abdicates or is deposed, or if some other major change takes place, the mission

---

103 Harvard Research, "Diplomatic Privileges and Immunities," Art. 12.
104 Satow, *op. cit.*, pp. 274–75, 277–79.

normally ends.[105] These major changes are to be contrasted with relatively routine changes within the same constitutional pattern such as governmental changes within the framework of a parliamentary government; such routine changes entail no termination of diplomatic missions.

It is to be noted in passing that diplomatic immunities extend for a reasonable time after the termination of a mission, a time sufficient to "dispose of the affairs of his mission" and leave the country.[106]

Termination of Consular Missions

While much that has been noted above applies to consular missions as well as to diplomatic establishments, it may be well to note that the authorities list five basic ways of termination of a consular mission. These are (1) by virtue of the consul's death, (2) by the expiration of the term of appointment, (3) "if serving temporarily, by the *resumption of duty* by his chief, or by *appointment* of a new chief," (4) by the consul's resignation, and (5) by revocation of the consul's *exequatur*.[107]

SUMMARY

Communications among nations are handled in a number of ways, but certain procedures are generally utilized. The most important of these is the maintenance of diplomatic and consular representatives in other nations. The practice of using permanent embassies dates from the late Middle Ages, though special and commercial representatives had been used long before that time.

Diplomatic functions include representation, observation, and protection. Consular personnel are concerned with aid to commerce and navigation, and performing many services for nationals which range from helping them secure tickets to a

---

[105] *Ibid.*, p. 275; see however, *Convention Regarding Diplomatic Officers*, Art. 25, which specifically mentions death of head of state and change of government or political regime as not terminating missions; cited in Satow, *op. cit.*, p. 276.

[106] *Ibid.*, pp. 276, 179, 188; quotation on p. 276.

[107] Puente, *op. cit.*, pp. 30–31; also Oppenheim-Lauterpacht, *Treatise* I, pp. 843–44.

local opera to protecting them from violence. Consuls also have considerable interest in immigration matters.

In sending envoys abroad the acceptability of specific personnel must be ascertained in advance. This is known as the *agrément*. When actually sent, diplomatic personnel carry *letters of credence* and consular personnel have *patents* or *commissions*. Reception of such personnel includes a formal act of receiving diplomats and the issuance of an *exequatur* to consular personnel. Both diplomatic and consular personnel are given ranks. Chiefs of diplomatic missions are ambassadors, envoys extraordinary and ministers plenipotentiary, ministers resident, or chargés d'affairs. Consular ranks exist but are not as specific as diplomatic designations. Those used by the United States are consul general, consul, vice-consul, and consular agent. Diplomatic and consular officials enjoy considerable discretion but they nevertheless must behave in a way which does not antagonize the host government. Failure to do so may result in their recall or even expulsion.

Despite the limitations just mentioned, diplomatic, international organization, and consular officials enjoy varying degrees of immunity from civil and criminal jurisdiction. Such immunities are virtually absolute for diplomatic and some international officials, but are less comprehensive for consular personnel. Except in special circumstances, particularly in Latin America, no right of asylum exists.

Missions are terminated in a number of specific ways, but in general, diplomatic missions are terminated by (1) the envoy or his government, (2) the host government, (3) accomplishment of the mission's objectives or time limits, (4) death of envoy or either the accrediting or receiving monarch (if they are monarchs), and (5) principal governmental changes. The circumstances of termination of consular missions are similar.

CHAPTER 8

Modes of Redress Short of War

THE EXISTENCE of a legal system of substantive rights and obligations assumes that when violations obtain resort can be had to procedures of redress. In international law there have been traditionally three main remedial categories. These are (1) amicable methods of settlement, (2) nonamicable modes of redress which, nevertheless are short of war, and (3) war. In this chapter the first two of these will be considered.

It should be noted that both war and certain of the nonamicable modes of redress short of war are of dubious legality. While morally salutary, this legal consideration does not always seem to reflect reality; also, there are some legal loopholes which may allow forcible procedures to retain a degree of legality under certain circumstances. In this survey, therefore, these techniques will be considered, but the deviations of contemporary law and practice from traditional patterns will be carefully noted.

Distinction is often made between "justiciable" and "nonjusticiable" disputes, that is, between disputes which are amenable to judicial treatment, and disputes not subject to such settlement. History is full of disputes which are considered so important to one or more of the states concerned that they cannot be compromised in any way. The classic statement of this concept is Von Treitschke's comment that arbitration is applicable only "in cases of second—or third—rate importance," for, he goes on to state:

When a nation's existence is at stake there is no outside Power whose impartiality can be trusted. Were we to commit the folly of treating the Alsace-Lorraine problem as an open question, by submitting it to arbitration, who would seriously believe that the award could be impartial? It is, moreover, a point of honour for a State to solve such difficulties for itself. International treaties may indeed become more frequent, but a finally decisive tribunal of the nations is an impossibility. The appeal to arms will be valid until the end of history, and therein lies the sacredness of war.[1]

Despite the very real fact that these views still must command attention, there is no doubt that virtually all states are now legally obligated to seek redress by pacific means prior to using force. Various treaties have stressed this obligation,[2] including the Charter of the United Nations which states that:

All Members shall settle their international disputes by peaceful means in such a manner that international peace and security, and justice, are not endangered.

All Members shall refrain in their international relations from the threat or use of force against the territorial integrity or political independence of any state, or in any other manner inconsistent with the Purposes of the United Nations.[3]

Indeed a strict reading of these paragraphs would suggest that the use of force may not be resorted to, and that pacific means of redress are established as the only ones open to legal use. Nevertheless, to follow the logic of this position to its conclusion would lead to omitting consideration of force short of war, war, and neutrality, and to do so would be to abandon reality. It must be frankly recognized, however, that in discussing these forceful procedures one may in a sense be discussing the law applicable to procedures of dubious legality, for example, the laws of war applicable to the procedure of war which itself is normally illegal. Similarly, a discussion of forcible procedures short of war partakes of comparable difficulties.

---

[1] Heinrich von Treitschke, "Politics," *Introduction to Contemporary Civilization in the West* (New York: Columbia University Press, 1946), Vol. II, p. 770.

[2] See e.g., *Treaty for the Renunciation of War*, 94 L.N.T.S. 57, *Convention for the Pacific Settlement of International Disputes*, The Hague, 1907, 36 *U.S. Statutes at Large*, Part II, pp. 2199–2240; for texts of both the 1899 and 1907 conventions see J. B. Scott, *The Hague Conventions and Declarations of 1899 and 1907* (2d ed.; New York: Oxford University Press. Inc., 1915), pp. 41–88.

[3] U.N., *Charter*, Art. 2 (3, 4).

A further legal loophole in the armor of pacific settlement is the clear right of self-defense which still reposes in every sovereign state. In this connection the Charter of the United Nations states:

Nothing in the present Charter shall impair the inherent right of individual or collective self-defense if an armed attack occurs against a Member of the United Nations, until the Security Council has taken the measures necessary to maintain international peace and security. Measures taken by Members in the exercise of this right of self-defense shall be immediately reported to the Security Council and shall not in any way affect the authority and responsibility of the Security Council under the present Charter to take at any time such action as it deems necessary in order to maintain or restore international peace and security.[4]

Still another relevant consideration is the authorization under which the United Nations can itself employ forceful measures to enforce certain of its decisions, and under which members of the United Nations can legally employ such measures against transgressors. The Charter[5] provisions will be considered later in this chapter.

Whatever moral and legal restraints may be imposed upon states in the use of force only for matters of self-defense or in connection with United Nations action, these may at times become matters of semantics. This seems to apply particularly to self-defense, though possibly not to U.N. action. Thus it will be remembered that Germany's attack on Poland was launched with the justification of being a measure of protection.[6] The discussion thus far is by way of suggesting that both pacific and forceful procedures must be considered as techniques for redress because both are applicable in fact for they remain a part of the world's political fabric.

AMICABLE MODES OF REDRESS

It was noted above that virtually all states are under obligation to seek redress by pacific means. The principal procedures

---

[4] *Ibid.*, Art. 51.

[5] *Ibid.*, Arts. 41, 42.

[6] See above, Chapter Four, fn. 7.

in this category may be classified as (1) nonjuridical and (2) juridical modes of pacific redress.

Nonjuridical Modes of Pacific Redress

Nonjuridical techniques for settlement of disputes are those which seek to arrive at solutions by some sort of arrangement between the disputing parties without submitting the questions to tribunals for binding awards. The principal techniques in this category are (1) negotiation, (2) good offices and mediation, (3) commissions of inquiry, and (4) commissions of conciliation. In addition to these devices, attention will also be given to relevant procedures by international organizations.

Negotiation. By way of definition Hackworth states that " 'Negotiation' when employed as a mode of redress is the process by which states undertake to adjust differences by an exchange *inter se* of their views,"[7] and Judge Moore in his dissent in the *Mavrommatis* case stated:

> . . . in the international sphere and in the sense of international law, negotiation is the legal and orderly administrative process by which governments, in the exercise of their unquestionable powers, conduct their relations one with another and discuss, adjust and settle, their differences.[8]

It will be recalled that negotiation is one of the principal functions of diplomats. As a procedure, it is the least complicated method of pacific settlement and is ordinarily considered to be the first step in an attempt to adjust differences. Accordingly, many treaties for pacific settlement assume or specify negotiation as the first step in the settlement process. The Convention for the Pacific Settlement of International Disputes, for example, discusses the procedure of arbitration with reference to "international differences, which it has not been possible to settle by diplomacy. . . ."[9] Similarly the bilateral "Kellogg" conciliation and arbitration treaties speak of settlement devices "when ordinary diplomatic proceedings have

---

[7] Hackworth, *Digest* VI, p. 1.

[8] Quoted *ibid.,* p. 2; see *Case of the Mavrommatis Palestine Concessions,* P.C.I.J. Reports, Series A, Judgment 2 (1924) , pp. 62–63.

[9] *Convention for the Pacific Settlement of International Disputes,* Art. 41.

failed."[10] Finally, the Charter of the United Nations lists negotiation first among the pacific procedures which are to be employed.[11]

Negotiation can be a flexible process by which issues may be resolved. Yet it may be nothing more than the hollow procedural form by which the strong state pays formal homage to the obligation to employ pacific means. There is the further difficulty that internal political factors within a state may make reasonable concessions impossible for a politically oriented negotiator. Nevertheless, it may be assumed that most disputes are settled by negotiation.[12]

Good Offices and Mediation. These two moderating devices, which are very closely related and are almost always discussed together, are techniques by which a third state helps to bring two disputing states to an agreement.

Good Offices, according to Secretary of State Hay conveys two meanings: (1) "the unofficial advocacy of interests which the agent may properly represent, but which it may not be convenient to present and discuss on a full diplomatic footing," and (2) "it is allied to arbitral intermediation as the adviser of both parties."[13]

The first of these meanings refers merely to the act of a state in pressing some claim which it deems justifiable on behalf of another state and is not germane to the present discussion. The latter meaning involves the idea of bringing the disputants together. "Ordinarily," observes Professor Wilson, "good offices extend only to the establishing of basis for, and the commencement of, the negotiations."[14]

---

[10] *Treaty of Conciliation,* U.S. and Poland, 1924, U.S.T.S. 806, Art. I and similar accords; *Treaty of Arbitration,* U.S. and Poland, 1928, U.S.T.S. 805, Art. I and similar accords.

[11] U.N., *Charter,* Art. 33. it is interestingly parallel that in speaking of the international role of the Court of the European "inner six" a recent writer states that "most problems that have arisen between the Member States have been solved by negotiation." W. Feld, *The Court of the European Communities: New Dimension in International Adjudication* (The Hague: Martinus Nijhoff, 1964), p. 36.

[12] See, e.g., comment in Moore, *Digest* VII, p. 2.

[13] *Ibid.,* p. 3.

[14] G. G. Wilson, *International Law* (9th ed.; New York: Silver Burdett & Co., 1935), pp. 228–29. See Hackworth, *Digest* VI, pp. 24–28 *et passim,* where *inter*

Mediation is in a sense a specialized application of good offices. It consists basically of the direct participation of an agent of a third state in the negotiations between disputants in an effort to help steer them toward a solution of their differences.[15] The mediation by the United States of the Honduran-Guatamalan boundary dispute is a case in point. The United States sought to assist in part by drawing the disputants to an analysis of the economic problems of their frontier.[16]

Various international accords consider these two techniques in virtually the same breath. For example, in the Hague Convention for the Pacific Settlement of International Disputes the first substantive section is devoted to "Good Offices and Mediation," and an early article in that accord states that "In case of serious disagreement or dispute, before an appeal to arms, the *contracting* Powers agree to have recourse, as far as circumstances may allow, to the good offices or mediation of one or more friendly Powers."[17]

It should be noted that the convention authorizes any state to extend its good offices to disputants even in time of war and that "The exercise of this right can never be regarded by either of the parties in dispute as an unfriendly act."[18] Diplomatic annals are full of examples of these techniques.[19]

Commissions of Inquiry. There may be instances when a dispute could be settled quite easily if the facts were clarified. In contemplation of such circumstances the procedure of commissions of inquiry was given formal stature in 1899 and again in 1907 by the Hague Convention for the Pacific Settlement of International Disputes which states:

In disputes of an international nature involving neither honor nor vital interest, and arising from a difference of opinion on points

alia, the United States offer of good offices in the Tacna-Arica dispute is briefly commented upon.

[15] See comments in C. C. Hyde, *International Law Chiefly as Interpreted and Applied by the United States* (2d ed.; Boston: Little, Brown & Co., 1945), Vol. II, pp. 1563–68; also Oppenheim-Lauterpacht, *Treatise* II, pp. 10–11 *et passim.*

[16] See briefly in Hackworth, *Digest* VI, pp. 30–31.

[17] *Convention for the Pacific Settlement of International Disputes,* Art. 2.

[18] *Ibid.,* Art. 3.

[19] See, e.g., Moore, *Digest* VII, pp. 2–24; Hackworth, *Digest* VI, pp. 2–56.

of fact, the *contracting* Powers deem it expedient *and* desirable that the parties who have not been able to come to an agreement by means of diplomacy, should, as far as circumstances allow, institute an International Commission of Inquiry, to facilitate a solution of these disputes by elucidating the facts by means of an impartial and conscientious investigation.[20]

The concept has been carried further by bilateral accords among which the so-called Bryan treaties are the leading examples. These treaties, unlike the Hague Convention, do not exclude disputes which involve "honor" or "vital interests."[21]

In theory, a commission of inquiry does not make an award. It merely reveals the facts, and any further action is the responsibility of the disputants. The classic instance of this technique was that of the *Dogger Banks* case of 1908 between Russia and Great Britain. In 1904 Russian ships had fired on some British fishing vessels in the North Sea, but the facts being in dispute, the issue was turned over to a commission of inquiry. The commission in this instance was endowed with powers sufficiently broad to allow the assigning of responsibility which is somewhat in excess of the scope of authority ordinarily contemplated within the meaning of the term "commission of inquiry."[22]

Conciliation.   Standing on the border between juridical and nonjuridical modes of pacific settlement is the procedure known as conciliation. It embodies an arrangement whereby a dispute is submitted to a commission which clarifies the facts and renders an advisory award or proposals for settlement. The award, however, is not binding on either party.

Provisions for the creation of commissions of conciliation are found in a large number of bilateral agreements and multilat-

---

[20] *Convention for the Pacific Settlement of International Disputes,* Art. 9.

[21] See comment in Oppenheim-Lauterpacht, *Treatise* II, pp. 13–16.

[22] See text in Scott, *Hague Court Reports* (1916), Vol. I, pp. 403–12; also in *American Journal of International Law,* Vol. II (October, 1908), p. 931; also M. O. Hudson, *Cases and Other Materials on International Law* (3d ed.; St. Paul, Minn.: West Publishing Co., 1951), p. 51. Another case in point is the Commission of Inquiry and Conciliation set up to resolve the Chaco dispute between Bolivia and Paraguay. As with the Dogger Banks Controversy, the line between inquiry and settlement was blurred. See Hackworth, *Digest* VI, pp. 41–43 *et passim.*

eral conventions.[23] Illustrative of the device are the recommendations of the International Joint Commission set up between the United States and Canada under terms of a 1909 treaty. The recommendations of the commission were clearly specified as not being of a binding character. The treaty states that they "shall not be regarded as decisions . . . either on the facts or the law, and shall in no way have the character of an arbitral award."[24]

Political Settlement by International Organizations. Various procedures obtain for action by international organizations for the settlement of disputes. Processes both of the United Nations and of the Organization of American States will be noted briefly.

The United Nations Charter provides for a number of procedures for settlement of disputes. The Security Council may recommend methods of settlement and, in instances where peace is threatened, it may utilize varying degrees of pressure to ensure that its recommendations are sustained.[25] The General Assembly, under the Uniting for Peace Resolution, may also take action in the face of threats to the peace.[26] These forcible devices will be considered later in this chapter.

Regarding nonforcible methods, however, the Charter specifies that states involved in controversies should employ the various traditional devices for the resolution of disputes. Indeed, it urges settlement by these measures outside of the Organization's framework.[27] Beyond these there are various procedures by which the United Nations itself may promote settlement. In such matters the Charter emphasises the role of the

---

[23] See, e.g., *Pacific Settlement of International Disputes*, General Act, Geneva, 1928, 93 L.N.T.S. 343; also in *American Journal of International Law*, Vol. 26 (October, 1931) , p. 204; *Convention of Inter-American Conciliation*, 100 L.N.T.S. 399; see also Bryan and Kellogg treaties, this chapter, above, fn. 10; also *American Treaty on Pacific Settlement* (1948) .

[24] *Treaty between the United States and Great Britain Relating to Boundary Waters between the United States and Canada*, Washington, D.C., 1909; 36 U.S., *Statutes at Large*, 2448 (Quotation from Art. IX, p. 2451) ; Hackworth, *Digest* VI, pp. 4–5; *Digest* I, pp. 755–62; see also C. J. Chacko, *The International Joint Commission between the United States of America and the Dominion of Canada* (New York: Columbia University Press, 1932) .

[25] U.N., *Charter*, Arts. 33–51.

[26] See in *American Journal of International Law*, Vol. XLV Official Documents (January, 1951) , pp. 1–6.

[27] U.N. *Charter*, Art. 33.

Security Council which may investigate and make recommendations.[28] The General Assembly, however, may also consider such problems and may make recommendations for their resolution except that it may not make recommendations if an issue is currently under consideration by the Security Council.[29] The Secretary General, moreover, performs functions in this area both as a result of powers granted him in the Charter and by virtue of activities entrusted to him by the Council or the Assembly.[30]

Among the devices which can be employed are the sending of a United Nations Commissioner to a trouble spot thus creating a United Nations "presence," the employment of good offices, conciliation, mediation, and commissions of inquiry by an instrumentality of the United Nations, and the passing of an official pronouncement such as a cease-fire resolution or some other official indication of concern.[31] On this level, the United Nations functions largely through the avenues of publicity and the simple pressuring for maintenance or restoration of peace, and its efforts have often been successful.

A relatively clear and satisfactory example of pertinent United Nations action is seen in the *Iranian* case which arose following the end of World War II. While other foreign troops were withdrawn from Iran, the Russians continued to keep forces there with an apparent interest in oil leases and in Azerbaijan. This was brought to the attention of the Security Council by the Iranian ambassador through the acting Secretary General. Although the Council did little beyond keeping the problem on its agenda, the fact of United Nations concern together with the adverse publicity influenced the U.S.S.R. to withdraw.[32]

---

[28] *Ibid.*, Arts. 34, 36, 37, 38.

[29] *Ibid.*, Arts. 35, 10, 11, 12, 14.

[30] *Ibid.*, Art. 99; see also S. S. Goodspeed, *The Nature and Function of International Organization* (New York: Oxford University Press, Inc., 1959), pp. 347–53 *et passim.*

[31] See Goodspeed, *op. cit.*, pp. 167–217; also D. C. Blaisdell, *International Organization* (New York: The Ronald Press Co., 1966), pp. 91–105. Professor Blaisdell has included tables in his study, pp. 95–101, showing various actions of both Council and Assembly concerned with peaceful adjustment.

[32] For concise accounts of this incident together with other cases, see Goodspeed, *op. cit.*, pp. 179–80 ff., and F. H. Hartmann, *The Relations of Nations* (New York: The Macmillan Co., 1962), pp. 250–51 ff.

The inter-American system also possesses special machinery for the settlement of disputes. This consists of (1) the "Meetings of Consultation" composed of the foreign ministers of the American states, and (2) the Inter-American Peace Committee. The former can theoretically compel settlement of disputes among American states, while the latter has only voluntary application.[33]

The Costa Rican-Nicaraguan disputes of 1948–49 and 1955–56 afford an illustration of the application of an aspect of this machinery. Costa Rica informed the Chairman of the Council of the Organization of American States (OAS) that it had sustained an armed invasion from Nicaragua on December 10, 1948. The Council acting as provisional Organ of Consultation established an investigating committee and in due course heard and acted on the committee report by passing a resolution pointing to pacific settlement. In turn a Commission of Military Experts was sent to oversee the conformity to the terms of the resolution. An amity pact was suggested and by early 1949 such instrument had been signed and the difficulties were at least tentatively settled.[34] A somewhat parallel conflict broke out again between these two states in early 1955, and OAS action was again promptly instituted. Although the latter procedure was instituted along somewhat similar lines, the OAS activity was considerably more detailed and included direct aid to Costa Rica by member states under request from the OAS. Nevertheless, the amenities were maintained with Nicaragua and settlement took place in a face-saving atmosphere by early 1956.[35]

Juridical Modes of Pacific Redress

Juridical processes for the settlement of disputes embody the concept of submission of the question in dispute to a court, *ad*

---

[33] C. G. Fenwick, "The Inter-American Regional System," *Journal of International Affairs*, Vol. 7 (December, 1954), pp. 96–97; see also *Charter of the Organization of American States*, 1948, 119 U.N.T.S. 3.

[34] See Inter-American Institute of International Legal Studies, *The Inter-American System, Its Development and Strengthening* (Dobbs Ferry, N.Y.: Oceana Publications, Inc., 1966), pp. 122–24.

[35] *Ibid.*, pp. 132–34; J. C. Dreier, *The Organization of American States and the Hemisphere Crisis* (New York: Harper & Row, 1962), pp. 62–67. For

hoc or permanent, which then hands down a *binding* decision. Although very much alike in principle, the following discussion will consider separately the procedures of (1) arbitration, and (2) adjudication.

Arbitration. Arbitration is a process by which the parties to a dispute agree to submit the issues in question to one or more judges or umpires for a decision which is binding. Although such procedures are normally thought of as being concerned with law, the real issue is the fact that the disputants have submitted their dispute for a binding decision, and it is quite possible that an arbitral decision might be rendered in terms of equity or even perhaps in a spirit of compromise. Such decisions must be rendered, however, in conformity with the provisions of the original agreement setting up the arbitral arrangement. This agreement is known as the *compromis.*

The procedure of arbitration has been utilized through the ages. In ancient Greece and Rome, during the Middle Ages, and in modern times the process has found at least some favor.[36] While it has been argued, as noted earlier in this chapter, that only relatively minor disputes could be trusted to the hands of neutral arbitral boards, some awards have dealt with relatively important issues.[37] It may be suggested here, moreover, that the political context of a controversy may be more the real question than the intrinsic importance of the specific issue in dispute. Thus during the Nazi era the treatment of German minorities in Czechoslovakia and other similar countries was unresolvable while the question of German minorities in Italy was amicably handled. In a contemporary setting, settlement of minor issues between the United States and the Soviet Union has been made difficult and often impossible by the overall political atmosphere between the two states,[38] but as that atmosphere im-

---

accounts of other instances in which the machinery of the OAS has been employed, see these two works, *passim.*

[36] See J. H. Ralston, *International Arbitration from Athens to Locarno* (Stanford, Calif.: Stanford University Press, 1929), pp. 153–239; also C. Phillipson, *The International Law and Custom of Ancient Greece and Rome* (London: Macmillan & Co., 1911), 2 vols., *passim.*

[37] See comments in Oppenheim-Lauterpact, *Treatise* II, p. 34.

[38] See discussion in H. J. Morganthau, *Politics among Nations* (2d ed.; New York: Alfred A. Knopf, Inc., 1954), pp. 518–35 *et passim.*

proved in the mid-1960's, it was possible to negotiate agreements of considerable importance. Among these were the banning of the use of atomic arms in space.[39]

Arbitration has been provided for both on a permissive and
on an obligatory basis, and by treaties both multilateral and
bilateral in character. The modern impetus began with the Jay
Treaty of 1794.[40] More recently the United States has obligated
itself through several somewhat similar series of treaties—the
Root, Taft-Knox, Bryan and Kellogg treaties of 1908, 1911,
1913–14, and 1928 respectively—and other states have employed similar bilateral arrangements. On a multilateral level
the Hague Conventions for the Pacific Settlement of International Disputes, the General Treaty of Inter-American Arbitration, and the General Act of Pacific Settlement are the most
important accords.[41] It should be noted that the legal obligation
to arbitrate disputes over contract debts is nearly an absolute;
this is the enactment by treaty of a principle known as the
Drago Doctrine. There is, however, the exception that if the
debtor state will not arbitrate, other action may become justifiable.[42]

Arbitration is usually considered as an *ad hoc* affair in that a
dispute is, or several related disputes are, settled by a judge and
court which is specifically constituted for those particular cases
and is then disbanded. When another issue is to be resolved, a
new judge or set of judges is provided. *Indeed, this ad hoc quality is perhaps the principal characteristic which distinguishes
arbitration from adjudication.* Nevertheless, there is a permanent arbitral framework in existence which affords machinery
for arbitration. This is the Permanent Court of Arbitration

---

[39] "Treaty on Principles Governing the Activities of States in the Exploration
and Use of Outer Space, Including the Moon and Other Celestial Bodies,
American Journal of International Law, Vol. LXI (April, 1967), pp. 645–49.

[40] Ralston, *op. cit.,* p. 194, Oppenheim-Lauterpacht, *op. cit., passim.*

[41] 36 U.S., *Statutes at Large,* 2199–2240; 130 L.N.T.S. 135; 93 L.N.T.S. 343. See
also draft convention in "Report of the International Law Commission" (4th
Session), *American Journal of International Law,* Official Documents, Vol. XLVII
(January, 1953), especially pp. 3–23; also "Report of the International Law Commission" (5th Session), *American Journal of International Law,* Official Documents, Vol. LIII (January, 1959), especially pp. 232–52.

[42] *Convention Respecting the Limitation of the Employment of Force for the
Recovery of Contract Debts,* The Hague, 1907; 36 U.S., *Statutes at Large,* Part II,
p. 2241.

created by the Hague Convention of 1899 and continued by the Hague Convention of 1907. The term "Permanent Court" is somewhat misleading, however, for while there is indeed permanent machinery for setting up an arbitral tribunal, it consists merely of a council, an administrative bureau or secretariat, and a list of four judges from each signatory state from which the umpires or arbiters are to be chosen *ad hoc* and *de novo* for each separate case. These facilities were used consistently until 1932, there having been 20 cases arbitrated by that year, but it lay dormant from 1932 until 1955 when its services were again employed.[43] In addition to arbitral awards under the Hague machinery, many arbitral decisions have been made by other *ad hoc* tribunals. Prominent among these and illustrative are the United States–Mexican arbitrations from 1923 to 1934.[44] Indeed, it is important to realize that while the more universal machinery for arbitration has seen relatively little use, there were some 50,000 cases decided by *ad hoc* arbitral tribunals between 1920 and 1943.[45]

Procedurally, an arbitral arrangement ordinarily progresses through the following steps. Under the terms of a general treaty which authorizes arbitration or which makes it obligatory, a special agreement is made. The special agreement, known as the *compromis*, specifies exactly what is to be arbitrated and the scope of procedure to be employed. The selection of judges varies; sometimes only one judge is chosen who is agreeable to both sides; in other instances each side provides one or more judges who in turn together choose an additional judge who is agreeable to both sides. The procedure for selection of judges employed by the Permanent Court of Arbitration is as follows:

---

[43] *Convention for the Pacific Settlement of International Disputes* (1899 and 1907), Arts. 41–90; Oppenheim-Lauterpacht, *Treatise* II, pp. 38–41; W. L. Gould, *An Introduction to International Law* (New York: Harper & Bros. 1957), pp. 545–55.

[44] See Ralston, *op. cit.*, pp. 203–7; also A. H. Feller, *The Mexican Claims Commission 1923–1934* (New York: The Macmillan Co., 1935).

[45] See account quoted in W. B. Cowles, "Review of the United Nations Charter and the Adjudication of International Claims," *American Journal of International Law*, Vol. XLVIII (July, 1954), p. 460. It is interesting to note further that this account stipulates that the Permanent Court of International Justice has handled "less than one-tenth of one per cent, of the justiciable international cases arising since its establishment."

Failing the direct agreement of the parties on the composition of the Arbitration Tribunal, the following course shall be pursued:

Each party appoints two Arbitrators, of whom one only can be its national or chosen from among the persons selected by it as members of the Permanent Court. These Arbitrators together choose an Umpire.

If the votes are equally divided, the choice of the Umpire is intrusted to a third Power, selected by the parties by common accord.

If an agreement is not arrived at on this subject each party selects a different Power, and the choice of the Umpire is made in concert by the powers thus selected.

If, within two months' time, these two Powers cannot come to an agreement, each of them presents two candidates taken from the list of members of the Permanent Court, exclusive of the members selected by the parties and not being nationals of either of them. Drawing lots determines which of the candidates thus presented shall be Umpire.[46]

As noted above, arbitration implies that the decision of the tribunal is binding. In this connection the Hague Convention stipulates that "Recourse to arbitration implies an engagement to submit in good faith to the award."[47] There are, however, instances where the award has not been acceptable or where new evidence or other relevant exigencies have pointed to the desirability of revisionary hearings, or where the arbitrator has allowed his decision to stray from the framework established by the *compromis*.[48] In the U.S.–British boundary arbitration of 1831, for example, the award of the arbiter, the King of Holland, was set aside by both litigants.[49] Also by way of example, in the *Orinoco Steamship Co.* case the Court found certain aspects of the rejection by the United States of a prior arbitral award to be proper.[50]

It should be noted that the question of what disputes are

---

[46] Article 45.

[47] Article 37.

[48] See comments in K. S. Carlston, *The Process of International Arbitration* (New York: Columbia University Press, 1946), pp. 205–23 *et passim;* Moore, *Digest* VII, pp. 59–62.

[49] Moore, *Digest* VII, pp. 59–60.

[50] *Orinoco Steamship Company* case, Scott, *Hague Court Reports* (1916), Vol. I, pp. 226, 234.

subject to arbitration presents a serious problem. It is the difference between "political" and "legal," or "nonjusticiable" and "justiciable" disputes. This problem will be considered later in the chapter.

Adjudication. Very closely related to arbitration is the process known as adjudication. Indeed, in a broad sense, arbitration would appear to be a form of adjudication. Nevertheless, terminological usages would seem to indicate that the chief difference between the two is in the court to which the dispute is submitted. The term "adjudication" appears to apply when the court is a permanent one in which substantially the same personnel constitute the tribunal in all of its functions. While there have been several attempts to create such tribunals throughout the present century, there have been only three such courts actually constituted. These are the Central American Court of Justice, the Permanent Court of International Justice, and the present International Court of Justice. Of these only the last is extant. Besides these three there has been provision for creation of a number of somewhat specialized international courts, particularly in connection with Western-European agencies such as the European Coal and Steel Community, and the European Economic Community. These will also be noted briefly.

Serious attempts to establish international courts were made as early as 1907 when a draft convention was negotiated for the creation of a *Judicial Arbitration Court,* and when an *International Prize Court* was provided for. The draft convention was never carried beyond the recommendatory stage, however, and the prize court failed for lack of ratification.[51]

In the same year, however, the Central American republics adopted an agreement under which a *Central American Court of Justice* was created. It heard a total of 10 cases between 1909 and 1917, but its charter, which was to run initially for a 10-year period, was not renewed. There were various obstacles to the Court's successful operation, but the final case, a dispute between Costa Rica and Nicaragua, was particularly complex since it involved the legality of a treaty between Nicaragua and

---

[51] See comment in M. O. Hudson, *The Permanent Court of International Justice 1920–1942* (New York: The Macmillan Co., 1943), Chapters 4, 5.

the United States. The Court found that the treaty violated the rights of Costa Rica, but the situation was especially difficult since the United States was not a party to the Court and since the United States pressed for enforcement of the treaty.[52] In 1923 another Central American court was provided for, but the agreement was never implemented.[53]

The Permanent Court of International Justice was the first permanent court with substantially worldwide jurisdiction. Provision was made in the Covenant of the League of Nations for the creation of such a court and it was implemented in 1920 by the adoption of the Statute of the Court which went into effect in 1921. The Court decided its first case in 1923. The Permanent Court of International Justice, which could render both judgments and advisory opinions, decided a total of 57 cases. It ceased to function in 1945, the judges resigned in 1946 and the same year the final Assembly of the League dissolved the Court. This final action was taken pursuant to the recommendations of a committee of jurists at the San Francisco Conference.[54]

The International Court of Justice, created under the authority of the United Nations Charter, is the present international court. It operates under its Statute and is for all practical purposes the successor of the old Permanent Court of International Justice.[55] A principal difference between the two courts is the fact that the present one is an integral part of the United

---

[52] See Jean Eyma, *La cour de justice centre-Americaine* (Paris: E. Sagot and Cie, 1928) ; also A. S. de Bustamente y Sirven, *The World Court* (New York: The Macmillan Co., 1926) , Chapter V; also Hudson, *op. cit.,* Chapter 3; for *Convention for the Establishment of a Central American Court of Justice,* see *Foreign Relations of the United States 1907,* Part II (Washington, D.C.: U.S. Government Printing Office, 1910) , pp. 697–701. For Final Decision, and also Nicaraguan refusal to follow decision, see *Foreign Relations of the United States 1916* (Washington, D.C.: U.S. Government Printing Office, 1925) , pp. 853–61; for U.S. view on case see *Foreign Relations of the United States 1916,* pp. 831–32; for reference to final session of court see *Foreign Relations of the United States 1918,* p. 247.

[53] See comment in Hackworth, *Digest* VI, pp. 79–80.

[54] League of Nations, *Covenant,* Art. 14; Hudson, *op. cit., passim;* Oppenheim-Lauterpacht, *Treatise* II, pp. 44–48; M. O. Hudson, "The Twenty-Fourth Year of the World Court," *American Journal of International Law,* Vol. XL (January, 1946) , pp. 6–11.

[55] U.N., *Charter,* Arts. 92–96.

Nations system while the old court was less closely tied to the League of Nations.

The Court normally consists of 15 judges, no more than one of whom may be from any single state. There is also provision, moreover, for *ad hoc* national judges from countries involved in litigation before the Court which, however, do not have nationals among the 15 regular members of the Court. The regular judges are elected for nine-year staggered terms by "the General Assembly and the Security Council" from a list of persons nominated in most instances by the national groups in the Permanent Court of Arbitration. The Court, which sits at the Hague but may exercise "its functions elsewhere," decides only cases which are brought before it by states. It also gives advisory opinions on questions presented to it by instrumentalities of the United Nations. It is to be noted that states not members of the United Nations may be allowed to use its services.[56]

The jurisdiction of the Court includes three general categories of cases: (1) those brought by the mutual consent of disputing states, particularly cases "provided for in the Charter of the United Nations or in treaties and conventions in force"; (2) cases brought by one litigant against another when both have declared "that they recognize as compulsory *ipso facto* and without special agreement, in relation to any other state accepting the same obligation, the jurisdiction of the Court" in certain specified categories of disputes; and (3) cases referred to it by certain agencies of the United Nations for advisory opinions.[57]

By 1967 the compulsory jurisdiction clause referred to above (sometimes called the optional clause) had been accepted by some 45 states, but of these only 25 appear to have done so without substantial reservations. The U.S. reservation, generally known as the Connally Amendment, for example, excludes domestic disputes as determined by the United States itself, and according to the late Judge Hudson, the reservation of the state of Israel is so detailed and all inclusive that "it is

---

[56] *Statute*, Arts. 13–15, 22, 31, 34–35. See comment on *ad hoc* judges in I.C.J., *Yearbook 1954–55*, pp. 18–19 and in other yearbooks.

[57] *Statute*, Arts. 36, 37, 65.

difficult to foresee any disputes which may be dealt with under this declaration."[58]

The Court, as a court of law, is authorized to apply:

a) International conventions, whether general or particular, establishing rules expressly recognized by the contesting States;

b) International custom, as evidence of a general practice accepted as law;

c) The general principles of law recognized by civilized nations;

d) Subject to the provisions of Article 59, judicial decisions and the teachings of the most highly qualified publicists of the various nations, as subsidiary means for the determination of rules of law.[59]

At the same time the Court's scope of action is widened in theory by the statement that the provision just quoted above "shall not prejudice the power of the Court to decide a case *ex aequo et bono,* if the parties agree thereto." The exact meaning of this clause has been the subject of some controversy. It seems to mean, however, that the judge may with the prior consent of the parties to the litigation, utilize concepts not necessarily already imbedded in the law for purposes of arriving at a fair and just solution.[60]

It appears that by mid-1966 there were 120 states which were members of the Court, including 3 which were not members of the United Nations. These three are San Marino, Liechtenstein, and Switzerland.[61]

A European Community Court of Justice has been provided for the European Coal and Steel Community, the European

---

[58] I.C.J., *Yearbook 1965–66,* pp. 41–68; see pp. 67–68 for U.S. reservation, and pp. 52–53 for Israeli reservation. States signing declarations without substantial reservations are Belgium, China, Colombia, Denmark, Dominican Republic, Finland, Haiti, Honduras, Japan, Liechtenstein, Luxembourg, Mexico, Netherlands, Nicaragua, Nigeria, Norway, Panama, Philippines, Somalia, Sweden, Switzerland, Turkey, Uganda, United Arab Republic, and Uruguay. See M. O. Hudson, "The Twenty-Fifth Year of the World Court," *American Journal of International Law,* Vol. LI (January, 1957), p. 16 (hereafter cited as "Twenty-Fifth Year"). There are discrepancies in the sources; see p. 391, Exhibit 2.

[59] *Statute,* Art. 38.

[60] *Ibid.,* Max Habicht, *The Power of the International Judge to Give a Decision "Ex aequo et bono"* (London, Constable & Co., Ltd., 1935); see also comment in Gould, *op. cit.,* pp. 560–61.

[61] I.C.J., *Yearbook 1965–66,* pp. 25–29.

Economic Community, and the European Atomic Energy Community.[62] This tribunal is composed of seven judges who are assisted by two advocates-general, and a registrar. In addition each judge and advocate-general is aided by a permanent law clerk known as an attaché.[63]

One interesting aspect of the Court is that individuals as well as states may bring cases before it. Indeed, it appears that over half of its cases have arisen in this way.[64]

The Court's jurisdiction stems, as implied above, out of the three main treaties which structure the European Community of the "inner six," and in this sense it is clearly an international court. However, its role as administrative tribunal, and its litigation in the area of civil jurisdiction together with some aspects of its essential ethos suggest that it is less an international court than one would initially have supposed.[65] On the other hand, what has been called the "constitutional" aspects of the Court's jurisdiction are hard to distinguish from functions often performed by international courts. Nevertheless, the litigation's essentially international character is viewed by one careful observer as being minor, and an advocate-general has stated that the

. . . Court is not an international tribunal, but is concerned with the jurisdiction within a community which has been created by six states and which resembles more a federation than an international organization. . . . As for the sources of this law, nothing prevents

---

[62] See *European Yearbook* (The Hague: Martinus Nijhoff, 1955), Vol. I, pp. 375–81, 435–51 for "Treaty Establishing the European Coal and Steel Community," Arts. 31–45 and "Protocol on the Code of the Court of Justice"; for decisions of the court, see Cour de Justice, *Recueil de la jurisprudence de la cour* (Paris: Recueil Sirey, 1956, 1957), Vols. I, II; See "Convention Relating to Certain Institutions Common to the European Communities," Arts. 3, 4, *American Journal of International Law*, Vol. LI (October, 1957), pp. 1000–1004; also see "Treaty Establishing the European Economic Community," Arts. 164–188 *American Journal of International Law*, Vol. LI (October, 1957), pp. 865–937; also "Treaty Establishing the European Atomic Energy Community," Rome, 1957, Arts. 136–159 *American Journal of International Law*, Vol. LI (October, 1957), p. 865; for commentary, see Albert Van Hatta, "La cour de justice de la Communauté-Européenne du Charbon et de L'Acier," *European Yearbook*, Vol. II, pp. 183–222; for cases filed with the court (E.C.S.C.) see *European Yearbook*, Vol. III, pp. 381–90.

[63] Feld, *op. cit.*, pp. 14–33 *et passim*.

[64] *Ibid.*, p. 107.

[65] *Ibid.*, pp. 34–86; especially pp. 36–38.

that in a given case they may be sought in international law, however normally, and most frequently, they are found in the municipal law of the Member States.[66]

The European Court may well be the supreme tribunal of a nascent European federation. Its integration into the legal frameworks of the six participating states appears to be much more extensive than is the more customary role of the international court, and the use which has been made of it is considerable.[67] However conceived, the Court is an interesting variation on the international court theme.

The Obligation to Arbitrate or Adjudicate: A Critique. The obligation of states to seek a pacific solution for their differences has been noted above. At its cynical worst this may mean that a state can pay some sort of lip service to the concept and then under the shibboleth of self-defense take matters into its own hands. Under most circumstances, however, it can probably be assumed that it means that while a state may resort to force under extreme circumstances particularly where *self-defense really is involved,* modes of pacific settlement will be initially and exhaustively employed with full conscientiousness. It must be recognized, however, that despite the obligations noted above, the state retains a degree of ultimate discretion.

Arbitration and adjudication represent attempts to circumscribe the degree of discretion which is left to the state. Yet the political structure of international society is such that the attempt has met with only partial success at best. Thus, ordinary adjudication before the World Court and arbitration can be undertaken only with the prior consent of the litigants.[68]

Similarly, of the 120 members of the Court as of mid-1966, it appears that only 42 have accepted the compulsory jurisdiction clause—but many of these have qualified the obligation to exclude domestic matters. This is not to deny a certain importance to the optional clause, but rather to point to the exceed-

---

[66] Maurice Lagrange quoted *ibid.,* p. 90.

[67] *Ibid., passim.*

[68] *Eastern Carelia* case, P.C.I.J. Reports, Series B, No. 5 (1923), pp. 27–28. For recent application of the principle in Antarctic and aerial cases, see *Antarctica* case *(U.K.* v. *Argentina)*, I.C.J. Reports 1956, pp. 12–14; also *Aerial Incident of March 10th, 1953*, I.C.J. Reports 1956, pp. 6–8; also *Aerial Incident of October 7th, 1952*, I.C.J. Reports 1956, pp. 9–11; also *Antarctica Case (U.K.* v. *Chile)*, I.C.J. Reports 1956, pp. 15–17.

ingly spare *legal* obligation which actually obtains.[69] Earlier in
the chapter mention was made of some disputes characterized
as "legal" or "justiciable" while others have been classed as
"political" or "nonjusticiable," the latter not being amenable
to judicial determination. This distinction must still be borne
in mind.

It is no doubt unfortunate that the international community
retains so much of the sovereign state-oriented structure more
consistent with earlier eras. Yet it does and as long as this is a
political fact of life, the problem surveyed above will remain.
What is the core of the problem? In any attempt to analyze this
matter one must recognize that the state still represents the
fundamental unit of political organization, but beyond that *it
is the unit responsible for security organization.* It may be
submitted that as long as this remains the case, questions pertaining to state power, safety, and security—in a word to the
vital interests of the state—can be only conditionally subjected
to the obligation of juridical determination. In this connection
Judge de Visscher has observed:

. . . it must be admitted that an unreserved undertaking to submit
all disputes without exception to judicial settlement would hardly
accord with the present structure of international relations, which
favors leaving to the individual decision of States those of their
interests which they consider inseparable from their personality or
their power. The observation applies particularly to the mutual
relations of the great States, exposed as they always are to the
fluctuations of what is called power politics.[70]

NONAMICABLE MODES OF REDRESS

Suppose that the pacific procedures detailed above do not
suffice; suppose a state refuses to arbitrate and after a time even
to negotiate a real dispute. Under such circumstances what

---

[69] For declarations of acceptance of the compulsory jurisdiction clause, see
I.C.J., *Yearbook 1965–1966,* pp. 41–68; also in other issues of the *Yearbook;*
Hudson, "Twenty-Fifth Year." p. 17; Oppenheim-Lauterpacht, *Treatise* II, pp.
58–65. For recent additions and alterations regarding compulsory jurisdiction and
other recent data, see M. O. Hudson, "The Thirty-Sixth Year of the World
Court," *American Journal of International Law,* Vol. LII (January, 1958), pp.
1–15.

[70] Charles de Visscher, *Theory and Reality in Public International Law,* trans.
by P. E. Corbett (Princeton, N.J.: Princeton University Press, 1957), p. 348; see
also below, Chapter Eleven.

modes of redress are available? Or in another vein, suppose a
state defies a mandate by the United Nations Security Council.
Again the question may be posed: What modes of redress are
available?

With reference to most hypothetical situations of the sort
cited in the previous paragraph, there is certainly no easy
answer. The Kellogg Briand pact binds most states to "the
settlement or solution of all disputes or conflicts of whatever
nature or of whatever origin they may be, which may arise
among them" and it specifies that settlement "shall never be
sought except by pacific means."[71] Furthermore, as was noted
earlier in this chapter, all members of the United Nations are
obligated to

. . . settle their international disputes by peaceful means in such a
manner that international peace and security, and justice, are not
endangered.

4. All Members shall refrain in their international relations from
the threat or use of force. . . .[72]

At the same time, in the interests of enforcing certain of its
mandates, the Security Council is empowered to take action to
enforce the peace. Such action can be of a nonforcible character,[73] but also, under extreme circumstances, it may use force.[74]

Taken altogether these contractual obligations would seem
to suggest that most forcible procedures employed by individual states are improper, while those employed under the auspices of the United Nations are legitimate. This distinction
should be borne in mind while reading the remainder of this
chapter, particularly where the nonamicable procedures being
discussed are "nonpacific" as contrasted with those nonamicable procedures which, nevertheless, remain "pacific."[75] Yet it
must also be remembered that in addition to use of forcible
procedures under the United Nations Charter, the right of
self-defense still obtains in law as well as in fact, and that in a

---

[71] 94 L.N.T.S., 57, Art. 2.

[72] U.N., *Charter*, Art. 2 (3, 4) .

[73] *Ibid.*, Art. 41.

[74] *Ibid.*, Art. 42.

[75] The term "force short of war," often used in connection with this topic, is
not altogether satisfactory; on this subject, see Fritz Grob, *The Relativity of War
and Peace* (New Haven, Conn.: Yale University Press, 1949) , pp. 223–24 *et
passim.*

world where naked force still plays the role that it obviously does today, the occasional use of these forceful processes must be recognized as probable. Such processes will be discussed under four headings: "Strong Representations," "Severance of Diplomatic Relations," "Retorsion," and "Reprisals and Intervention." The nature of satisfaction will also be mentioned.

Strong Representations

The importance of negotiation was noted above. It is usual for such negotiations to be conducted within a framework of formal courtesy, yet at times the notes, counternotes, and protests take on a harsh tone. At what point they cease to be "amicable" and assume a "nonamicable" posture may be a matter of some dispute. Indeed, it might be argued that strong protests and the like remain technically amicable.

In August of 1946 after several American planes had been shot down over Yugoslavia, for example, the United States demanded and received an apology and assurances that such attacks would cease. Although force was neither used nor mentioned in the U.S. ultimatum, the tone of the American note was decidedly blunt.[76] What is important about this sort of communication, however, is that it portends worse things to follow if abuses persist.

A specialized category of note is the *ultimatum,* which is a term applied to a communication which stipulates that certain demands be met if some drastic action is to be avoided. The Austro-Hungarian ultimatum to Serbia prior to World War I is perhaps the classic instance of its use. While legal then, it would most probably be considered a legally improper act today for it involves a clear threat of force.[77]

Severance of Diplomatic Relations

When an abuse has become very serious, an injured state may register its disapproval by withdrawing its diplomatic con-

[76] *New York Times,* August 22, 1946, pp. 1, 3; September 2, 1946, p. 2.

[77] This ultimatum is reproduced in Louis L. Snyder, *Fifty Major Documents of the Twentieth Century* (New York: D. Van Nostrand Co., Inc., 1955), pp. 13–17.

tact from the state responsible for the abuse. According to Hyde, "Such action is not only expressive of national indignation, but also frequently serves to impress upon the latter the desirability of making amends." Since severance of diplomatic relations is often a prelude to war or some other forcible action it serves notice on the offending state that matters are assuming a posture of the utmost gravity. By way of example, Mexico severed relations with the United States in 1914 after the American occupation of Vera Cruz. Similarly the United States withdrew its minister from Venezuela in 1908 because of that government's dealings with Americans, because it would not arbitrate the differences between the two countries, and because of "the tone of the communications received from the Venezuelan government." More recently the United States severed relations with Cuba after sustaining prolonged abuse.[78] Severance of diplomatic relations is not the equivalent of nonrecognition, however. In the *Sabbatino* case the Court makes it clear that it considers severance of relations to be a less-constricting phenomenon than nonrecognition. In this connection it stated:

It is perhaps true that nonrecognition of a government in certain circumstances may reflect no greater unfriendliness than the severance of diplomatic relations with a recognized government, but the refusal to recognize has a unique legal aspect. It signifies this country's unwillingness to acknowledge that the government in question speaks as the sovereign authority for the territory it purports to control. . . . The possible incongruity of judicial "recognition," by permitting suit, of a government not recognized by the Executive is completely absent when merely diplomatic relations are broken.[79]

---

[78] Hyde, *op. cit.*, pp. 1656–57, quotation on 1656; Hackworth, *Digest* VI, pp. 147–49, quotation on 148; see *New York Times*, January 4, 1961, p. 1 *et passim*.

[79] *Banco Nacional de Cuba* v. *Sabbatino*, 376 U.S. 398, 410–11 (1964). See Oppenheim-Lauterpacht, *Treatise* I, p. 775 where it is stated that "however prolonged, interruption of diplomatic relations is not tantamount to withdrawal of recognition or a refusal to grant recognition." "Withdrawal of recognition" is not a widely used term, and indeed is often viewed as a logical inconsistency. See comments in Whiteman, *Digest* II, pp. 670–73; also P. C. Jessup, *A Modern Law of Nations* (New York: The Macmillan Co., 1948), pp. 57–58. T. C. Chen, *The International Law of Recognition* (New York: Frederick A. Praeger, Inc., 1951), pp. 259–64. In a sense the Court seemed to say in *Sabbatino* that only resort to war would create the equivalent of failure to recognize (p. 410); moreover there are instances in which governments have purported to withdraw recognition

It must be noted that severance of diplomatic relations is a perfectly legitimate action. While it is certainly nonamicable, it nevertheless remains "pacific."

Retorsion

Retaliatory action is sometimes taken by one state against another because of some unfriendly or unfair action taken by the latter. It is known as retorsion when neither the unfriendly act nor the retaliation is in itself an illegal act. Oppenheim states that "Retorsion consists in retaliation for a noxious act by a noxious act." This does not mean, however, that retorsion is necessarily "retaliation in kind" as has sometimes been asserted, though it certainly includes retaliation in kind.[80] Also, some authors use the term to include retaliation taken to remedy illegal acts of states—as contrasted with those which are legal but discourteous or unfair.[81] This seems to be too broad a definition of the term and one which makes its differentiation from reprisals meaningless.

There are some grounds for believing that retorsion which is in excess of being commensurate with the injury being reacted against is of questionable legality.[82] Since by definition neither action is illegal in itself, however, this view is difficult to accept.

Illustrative of what is usually classed as retorsion are the provisions recommended in 1870 by the President of the United States "to suspend the operation of any laws whereby the vessels of the Dominion of Canada are permitted to enter the waters of the United States," and some other trade restrictions should the Canadians "repeat their unneighborly acts toward our fishermen." Another example is the threat of tariffs on Russian

---

(Whiteman, *loc. cit.*, *et passim*). Both of these deny the "logic" involved in the argument that that which has been recognized cannot subsequently be denied the recognition which it was once granted. If, as may well be the case, the issue is more properly one of policy than of logic, this whole question might bear scholarly rethinking.

[80] Oppenheim-Lauterpacht, *Treatise* II, p. 135; Wilson, *op. cit.*, p. 237; Moore, *Digest* VII, p. 106.

[81] Hyde, *op. cit.*, pp. 1657-60.

[82] See e.g., comment in Julius Stone, *Legal Controls of International Conflict* (New York: Rinehart & Co., Inc., 1954), p. 289; see comments in Gould, *op. cit.*, pp. 589-90.

imports to Japan in retaliation for "excluding Japanese fishermen from the waters of Saghalien."[83]

Reprisals and Intervention

Reprisals have been defined as "coercive measures taken by
one state against another, without belligerent intent, in order
to secure redress for, or to prevent recurrence of, acts or omis-
sions which under international law constitute international
delinquency." They were defined by the tribunal in the Naulilaa incident as "an act of self help of the injured state, in
retaliation for an unredressed act of the offending state contrary to international law."[84] The distinction to be noted between retorsion and reprisals is that the latter is designed to
curb an illegal act and would itself be illegal were it not that a
prior illegality is thus being remedied, while the former is a
legal but damaging act in retaliation for a similar act by another state.

In past centuries it was not uncommon for a state to authorize its citizens who had suffered injury at the hands of a foreign
state or its nationals to prey upon the shipping of that state. To
legitimatize their activities along this line, so-called letters of
marque and of reprisal were issued. This practice has not been
utilized in modern times, however, and although authority for
such activity exists in the United States, it appears that this
country has never issued such documents. It may be noted too
that privateering—a less-objectionable near relation of private
reprisal—was considered outlawed in the mid-1800's, and this
position was rendered secure in the Declaration of Paris of 1856
and by subsequent practice.[85]

---

[83] Moore, *Digest* VII, p. 107; Hackworth, *Digest* VI, p. 149.

[84] A. E. Hindmarsh, *Force in Peace* (Cambridge, Mass.: Harvard University
Press, 1933), p. 58; *Naulilaa Incident*, 2 U.N. Reports 1019; for English translation and convenient reference see in H. W. Briggs, *The Law of Nations* (2d ed.;
New York: Appleton-Century-Crofts, Inc., 1952), p. 951; for a statement of the
view that the term reprisals is essentially undefinable see Grob, *op. cit.*, p. 237 *et
passim*.

[85] U.S., *Constitution*, Art. I, Sec. 8 (11); Moore, *Digest* VII, pp. 122–23; see
Declaration of Paris 46 *Brit. & For. State Papers*, 136; see comments in Wilson,
op. cit., pp. iv–v. For a discussion of private reprisals, see Hindmarsh, *op. cit.*,
pp. 43–56. On intervention, generally, see E. C. Stowell, *Intervention in International Law* (Washington, D.C.: John Byrne & Co., 1921).

In addition to the complete preclusion of private acts of reprisal, the proper exercise of reprisals, to be legitimate, should meet three requirements. These are (1) that the act or acts of the offending state be illegal, (2) that the reprisals be "preceded by a request for redress which has been unavailing," and (3) that there be at least a reasonable degree of proportion between the reprisal and the act which it seeks to redress.[86]

The increased necessity that ample opportunity for arbitration or other pacific means be attempted has been fully indicated at earlier points in this chapter. In the *Corfu Channel* case, despite some ambiguities in expression, it was rather clearly suggested again that forceful intervention is illegal. To what extent this excludes *all* forceful intervention, however, is not clear, for despite the obligation to eschew forceful means of redress, it is assumed here that in extreme cases reprisals are still legitimate, though this is not certain.[87] Finally, the United Nations Charter sanctions the employment of such procedures under certain circumstances when authorized by the United Nations Security Council. The United Nations military action in Korea is an extreme example of such procedure.[88]

Intervention as a term, it should be noted, does not carry a specific enough meaning to justify its discussion as a separate means of reprisal. Indeed, it is so broadly employed that it would appear to be at times not necessarily forcible, or even perhaps not necessarily nonamicable.[89] After discussion of the varied character of the definition, Thomas and Thomas define the concept in the following terms:

intervention occurs when a state or group of states interferes, in order to impose its will, in the internal or external affairs of another state, sovereign and independent, with which peaceful relations

---

[86] *Naulilaa Incident.*

[87] See A. V. W. Thomas and A. J. Thomas, Jr., *Non-Intervention the Law and Its Import in the Americas* (Dallas, Tex.: Southern Methodist University Press, 1956), pp. 136–38 *et passim;* see also Hackworth, *Digest* VI, pp. 152–53 and U.S. Naval War College, *International Law Situations 1938* (Washington, D.C.: U.S. Government Printing Office, 1940), pp. 43–88 for statement relevent prior to advent of U.N. Charter.

[88] U.N., *Charter,* Arts. 41, 42; for Council resolution authorizing Korean action; see *New York Times,* June 28, 1950, p. 6.

[89] Thomas and Thomas, *op. cit.,* pp. 67–74.

exist and without its consent, for the purpose of maintaining or altering the condition of things.[90]

In relation to this definition it appears that reprisals represent a variety of forms of intervention which, however, enjoy a degree of legality if employed strictly within the limitations noted above.[91] Generically, then, "intervention" is broader than the term "reprisals" and therefore it will not be discussed here as a separate concept.[92]

Specific types of reprisals which will be considered are (1) boycott or nonintercourse, (2) embargo, (3) display of force, (4) pacific blockade, (5) quarantine, and (6) other forcible techniques.

Boycott or Nonintercourse. There are several ways in which a state may retaliate against the illegal acts of another state. Some of these procedures involve no question of force on either side. Others, like pacific blockade and occupation, are highly charged and are at the very best of dubious legality. Nonintercourse and boycott are among the practices involving retaliatory actions which are nonforcible in a military sense, yet are acts which some observers have thought to be illegal except when they are performed by way of exercising legitimate reprisals.

Nonintercourse as a generic concept suggests action by which a nation seeks to bring another state to terms by means of suspending all or at least some aspects of their relationship. A classic example is seen in the 1798 Act of the United States Congress to suspend commercial relationships with France.[93] Such an act in ordinary times would normally involve violation of a commercial treaty—an obviously illegal act; yet as a rejoinder to an illegal act by another state, it appears to be entirely appropriate provided, of course, that it is proportionate to the original illegal act.

A *boycott* is a specialized variety of nonintercourse under

---

[90] *Ibid.*, p. 71.

[91] *Ibid.*, pp. 87–88.

[92] For an earlier discussion of intervention in relation to self-defense, see Chapter Four.

[93] Moore, *Digest* VII, pp. 148–51; I *U.S. Statutes*, p. 565; see also Hindmarsh, *op. cit.*, pp. 64–71.

which a state seeks to bring another state to terms by means of refusal to purchase its goods. As a political gesture it is sometimes considered to be of questionable legality,[94] but as an act of reprisal, in the language of the Lytton Commission, "it seems difficult to contest that the boycott is a legitimate weapon of defense against military aggression by a stronger country."[95] In this context, and bearing in mind both the necessity for a degree of commensurateness in all reprisals and the fact that it does not involve armed force, it is evident that the boycott as a form of state reprisal remains legitimate.[96]

On another level it may be reiterated that nonintercourse and boycott—"complete or partial interruption of economic relations"—may be required of members of the United Nations in support of Security Council action.[97]

Embargo. The technical term "embargo" is a confused one because its status as a reprisal is confused with usage of the term in a nontechnical sense. *As a reprisal* embargo means the detaining of merchant ships in port of a foreign state by another state as a means of curbing an illegal abuse. The embargo as a device for securing ships in anticipation of the outbreak of war is not considered to be a valid reprisal.[98] It is also to be differentiated from *arrêt de prince* and angary, neither of which is a form of reprisal.[99]

---

[94] See C. L. Bouvé, "The National Boycott as an International Delinquency," *American Journal of International Law*, Vol. XXVIII (January, 1934), pp. 19–42; for the view that commercial treaties do not offer a legal guarantee against boycotts, see C. C. Hyde & L. B. Wehle, "The Boycott in Foreign Affairs," *American Journal of International Law*, Vol. XXVII (January, 1933), pp. 1–10.

[95] Quoted in Bouvé, *op. cit.*, p. 42.

[96] See C. F. Remer, *A Study of the Chinese Boycotts with Special Reference to Their Economic Effectiveness* (Baltimore, Md.: Johns Hopkins Press, 1933), pp. 6–9; Remer describes the boycott as "nonviolent coercion."

[97] U.N., *Charter*, Art. 41.

[98] See J. Le Clére, *Les mesures coercitives sur les navirers de commerce étrangers angarie-embargo-arrêt de prince* (Paris: Librarie generale de droit et de jurisprudence, 1949), pp. 115–41 *et passim;* also Oppenheim-Lauterpacht, *Treatise* II, pp. 141–42, 334; also *Convention Relative to the Status of Enemy Merchant Ships at the Outbreak of Hostilities;* in Scott, *Proceedings of the Hague Peace Conferences* (New York: Oxford University Press, Inc., 1920), Vol. I, pp. 637–39, see conveniently in Wilson, *op. cit.*, pp. lxxi–lxxiii.

[99] Le Clére, *op. cit.*, pp. 171–75 *et passim.* For a discussion of angary, see Chapter Ten, below. *Arrêt de prince* is a device by which a state detains the ships of another state in order "to prevent the spread of news of political importance." Oppenheim-Lauterpacht speak of this as a form of embargo, but it is difficult to

.   Since the embargo does not constitute a threat against the
sovereignty or integrity of a state, it is highly doubtful whether
it could be classed as a violation of the Charter of the United
Nations as an employment of force, and it appears therefore
that the exercise of the embargo remains legally valid if employed within the restraining circumstances normally essential
to the propriety of reprisals. The relevant statement in the
Oppenheim-Lauterpacht *Treatise* is:

Now, as by way of reprisal all acts, otherwise illegal, may be performed, there is no doubt that ships of the delinquent State may be
prevented from leaving the ports of the injured State, for the
purpose of compelling the delinquent State to make reparation for
the wrong done.[100]

Display of Force.   On the periphery of forcible rectification of wrongs, and taking such varied forms that the term
has no technical status in international law, are the diverse
activities which may be called displays of force. In a very general sense they range from the more or less routine annual May
Day international muscle-flexing demonstrations in Moscow's
Red Square which are of a general character to the Dutch naval
demonstration in Venezuelan waters in 1908 and other like
demonstrations which are specifically pointed at a particular
nation and at a specific abuse. In the more restricted sense of
validly employed reprisals, the device has application to the
present discussion, but to do so properly a distinction must be
made between (1) displays of force as general political devices
and (2) displays of force as reprisals properly so-called. In the
former category are found innumerable instances of saber rat-
tling, designed presumably to suggest that a certain state—or
states generally—should be wary of crossing the objectives of
the state staging the demonstration. The modern Russian ar-
maments demonstrations, previously alluded to, are well-
known examples of the general posture, while the U.S. Navy
squadron's "goodwill" trip around the world in 1908 is usually
thought of as an example of its political use with reference to a
particular state. Neither, however, was a reprisal in the techni-

see it properly described by that term if embargo is used in its technical sense
as a form of reprisal. Oppenheim-Lauterpacht, *Treatise* II, p. 142.

[100] Oppenheim-Lauterpacht, *Treatise* II, p. 141.

cal sense of the term. Perhaps the most familiar example of the use of a show of force as a reprisal—albeit in a third-power relationship—was the sending of U.S. troops to the Mexican border in 1864 to stimulate dispatch in the evacuation of French troops.[101]

As a reprisal in the proper technical context, displays of force are on somewhat more precarious ground than other devices discussed so far. While they do not involve the *use* of force, per se, they do imply the *threat* of force. This, it will be recalled, is a procedure denied to members of the United Nations except as a collective device for enforcement of Security Council measures,[102] or, presumably, when in the face of an armed attack the inherent right of individual or collective self-defense is invoked.[103]

There are practical problems involved, however, for a threat can be subtly set in a cold war context and, indeed, it may be completely verbal—lacking entirely such spectacular accompaniments as naval demonstrations or the dispatch of troops to a border. The rash of Russian letters to NATO powers stating that should war break out the presence of U.S. bases on their territories would invite devastating bombardment illustrates this matter generally even though this instance cannot be considered as a reprisal.[104] Accordingly it is probably meaningless to say that these letters were illegal per se for in one sense they may be thought of as a friendly warning. In another sense, however, their portent can be considered more menacing than a fleet demonstration. The relativity of the pertinent elements should be apparent.

Whether legal or illegal and whether of general application

---

[101] Hindmarsh, *op. cit.*, pp. 61–64; see also A. P. Higgins and C. J. Colombos, *The International Law of the Sea* (London: Longmans, Green & Co., Inc., 1943), p. 304; see also Moore, *Digest* VII, pp. 107–9; on the U.S. attitude regarding French intervention in Mexico, see Moore, *Digest* VI, pp. 488–505. For a brief convenient reference to the naval demonstration of 1908, see T. A. Bailey, *A Diplomatic History of the American People* (5th ed.; New York: Appleton-Century-Crofts, Inc., 1955), pp. 571–75.

[102] U.N., *Charter*, Arts. 2 (4), 42.

[103] *Ibid.*, Art. 51. For consideration of the circumstances under which "preventive self-defense" might be considered as appropriate, see Chapter Four, above.

[104] See reference in *New York Times*, December 14, 1959, p. 4; December 15, 1959, p. 34.

or utilized as a form of reprisal, it is evident that the device is usable. In any careful attempt to determine strict legality, a specific example would need to be judged in relation to the aforementioned articles of the United Nations Charter.

Pacific Blockade. A pacific blockade is a blockade not considered as an act of war, imposed by one or more states on the ports of another state by which ingress and egress is denied to ships of the latter state as reprisal for a legal wrong.[105]

Although the legal status of pacific blockade has been the subject of some debate, there are many examples of its use since its initial utilization against the Ottoman Empire in 1827.[106] There is considerable difficulty, however, in determining when a blockade is pacific and when belligerent, and at times a distinction along these lines may be valueless.[107] Nevertheless, regardless of whatever difficulties in logic may obtain, it appears that the concept of pacific blockade has become fairly precise and that its utilization has been circumscribed by certain rules. The declaration of the Institute of International Law in 1887 appears to be expressive of the proper patterns and the bulk of opinion seems to support this view. The late Judge Moore has summarized these patterns as follows:

. . . pacific blockade should be recognized as permitted by the law of nations only under the following conditions: (1) That ships under a foreign flag should be allowed freely to enter in spite of the blockade; (2) that the blockade should be declared and notified officially and maintained by a sufficient force; (3) that ships of the blockaded power which should fail to respect the blockade should be sequestered, and that when blockade had ceased they should be restored with their cargoes to their owners, but without any damages for their detention.[108]

---

[105] See Moore, *Digest* VII, pp. 135–42; Oppenheim-Lauterpacht, *Treatise* II, pp. 144–49; A. E. Hogan, *Pacific Blockade* (Oxford: The Clarendon Press, 1908), p. 13 *et passim; Annuaire de la Institute de Droit International* (1887–88), pp. 300–301; Hyde, *op. cit.,* p. 1667; Wilson, *op. cit.,* p. 240; Hackworth, *Digest* VI, pp. 156–59.

[106] See Moore, *op. cit. passim.* Hogan, *op. cit.,* pp. 73–183.

[107] See, e.g., Grob, *op. cit.,* pp. 247–66 where there is strong criticism of most commentaries on pacific blockade.

[108] Quotation from Moore, *Digest* VII, p. 141; see *Annuaire* (1887–88), *op. cit., passim;* as examples of opinion see Hindmarsh, *op. cit.,* pp. 97–99; Oppenheim-Lauterpacht, *Treatise* II, pp. 146–47; also Fenwick, *op. cit.,* pp. 536–37; Wilson, *op. cit., passim.* Hackworth, *op. cit., passim.*

The further question arises, however, as to what the status of pacific blockade is in the light of the United Nations Charter and related obligations. This question can only be surveyed by asking whether pacific blockade constitutes force as meant by Article 2 (4), and it is most difficult to conceive of it in any other light. It must therefore be considered illegal except perhaps in the most extreme circumstances. Yet under circumstances of the greatest gravity it is to be presumed that it might still be validly employed—that is, to the extent to which the *Corfu Channel* case may be interpreted as not negating the validity of absolutely all forcible self-help.[109] Finally, it is certain that pacific blockade remains proper as a means of enforcement if utilized under Article 42 of the United Nations Charter.

Quarantine. The term quarantine has had until recently no meaning at all in international law. On October 23, 1962, however, the United States, acting in concert with the Organization of American States, proclaimed and proceeded to interdict the movement of certain offensive weapons from the U.S.S.R. to Cuba.[110] This action was neither a pacific blockade nor a wartime blockade, and has come to be called a quarantine.

Essentially it was a procedure by which the United States countered its principal power bloc adversary in a move which, if successful, would have made important changes in the defense capability of the western hemisphere and of the United States. Every precaution was taken to keep the action commensurate with the need and to evidence clear pacific intent. The quarantine was formally taken under regional defense arrangements,[111] but this tends to obscure the essentials. The real issue is whether a state (or states collectively) can take measured steps to prevent, in advance of actual launched attack, a buildup of military might in an adjacent area not hitherto heavily armed which in its honest judgment will seriously and irreparably in-

---

109 See Thomas and Thomas, *op. cit.*, pp. 136–38; *The Corfu Channel* case, I.C.J. Reports, 1949; see also Stone, *op. cit.*, pp. 196–98.

110 Proclamation 3504, "Interdiction of the Delivery of Offensive Weapons to Cuba," *American Journal of International Law*, Vol. LVII (April, 1963), pp. 512–13, reprinted from 27 Fed. Reg. 10401 (1962).

111 See in *The Inter-American System, op. cit.*, pp. 162–66.

jure its defense capability and effect a substantial change in the power balance.

Since the international machinery by which such deterence should ideally be regulated had been incapable of taking concerted action because of the veto, it is inconceivable that the traditional self-defense mechanisms do not obtain.[112] There is no other sanction consistent with minimum levels of world public order. As emphasized e'sewhere in this volume, as 'ong as the final obligations of security remain in the state, a degree of ultimate defense discretion remains there also.[113] As with other reprisals, of course, there are limits. These include commensurateness or proportionateness, and evidence of pacific intent. There is in addition the somewhat nebulous matter of the attitudes of other states. The quarantine appears to fall within the permissible limits.[114]

Other Forcible Techniques. Beyond what has already been discussed, note should be taken of techniques such as bombardment, landing of troops, temporary occupation—sometimes more protracted than temporary—and even so-called unde-

---

[112] U.N., *Charter,* Art. 53; see also discussion Chapter Four, above. The quarantine is probably best categorized as a form of reprisal. As such, however, it presupposes that the action reacted against was illegal. In a certain sense the U.S.S.R.'s activities were menacing only in greater degree than actions taken by both the U.S.S.R. and the United States at various times since 1946, some clearly illegal and others less evidently so, but not viewed as so mortally dangerous. If there is an overriding illegality in this action as well as in many of the others it is probably to be found as a violation of the Charter injunction that "All Members shall refrain in their international relations from the threat or use of force against the territorial integrity or political independence of any state, or in any other manner inconsistent with the Purposes of the United Nations." *U.N. Charter,* Art. 2 (4).

[113] See Chapter Eleven, *passim.*

[114] Among the pertinent accounts, see Myres S. McDougal, "The Soviet-Cuban Quarantine and Self-Defense," *American Journal of International Law,* Vol. LVII (July, 1963), pp. 597–604; C. Q. Christol and C. R. Davis, "Maritime Quarantine: The Naval Interdiction of Offensive Weapons and Associated Matériel to Cuba, 1962," *American Journal of International Law,* Vol. LVII (July, 1963), pp. 525–45; C. G. Fenwick, "The Quarantine Against Cuba: Legal or Illegal?," *American Journal of International Law* Vol. LVII (July, 1963), pp. 588–92; B. MacChesney, "Some Comments on the 'Quarantine' of Cuba," *American Journal of International Law,* Vol. LVII (July, 1963), pp. 592–97; L. C. Meeker, "Defensive Quarantine and the Law," *American Journal of International Law,* Vol. LVII (July, 1963), pp. 515–24; C. Oliver, "International Law and the Quarantine of Cuba: A Hopeful Prescription for Legal Writing," *American Journal of International Law,* Vol. LVII (April, 1963), pp. 373–77.

For an account which argues that the quarantine was not legally proper, see Q. Wright, "The Cuban Quarantine," *American Journal of International Law,* Vol. LVII (July, 1963), pp. 546–65.

clared war. These procedures differ from war only in the respect that neither side chooses to recognize the act as legal war.

Examples of these actions are myriad, one writer, for example, citing some 76 instances of such actions by the United States up to 1928.[115] Specific instances of classic stature would include the landing of U.S. troops at Tampico in reprisal for maltreatment of American servicemen, the occupation of Haiti to compel order, and bombardment of Corfu by Italy in reprisal for the murder of an Italian general officer. These engagements, serious enough in themselves, were once clearly allowable as enforcement procedures, and still repose in the arsenal of potential restraints. Still more enigmatic is "undeclared war" which in relation to reprisals may result when neither party wishes to acknowledge a state of war while at the same time neither is willing to capitulate to the demands of the other. The Sino-Japanese conflict of the 1930's is perhaps the best example of an undeclared war, yet it is questionable— despite its alleged causes—whether it can be seriously considered as a valid example of reprisals.[116]

Except under the most extremely imperative circumstances as outlined above, it would seem clear that all of these techniques are clearly illegal today as means of individual self-help.

Satisfaction

The object of seeking a settlement of differences may be termed satisfaction. If the problem involves a violation of law and demands for rectification of the problem, it is within the present scope of discussion. Satisfaction for injury takes a variety of forms including financial settlement for the family of a person wrongfully killed, a salute to the national flag, or punishment of an offending officer. On occasion mere winning of the case before a tribunal has been specified as satisfaction enough. Often the objective is to persuade an offending state to behave better in the future.[117]

---

[115] M. Offutt, *The Protection of Citizens Abroad by the Armed Forces of the United States* (Baltimore, Md.: Johns Hopkins Press, 1928, Series XLVI, No. 4).

[116] *Ibid.*, pp. 1–8; Moore, *Digest* VII, pp. 109–18; Hyde, *op. cit.*, pp. 1664–67. Also Grob, *op. cit.*, pp. 15–36 *et passim.*

[117] See Gould, *op. cit.*, pp. 597–99; also *Corfu Channel* case I.C.J. Reports, 1949, p. 4.

Forceful Procedures Employed by International Organizations. International agencies of several sorts function in the area of maintenance of world order. Among these are at least three categories: (1) defense alliances, (2) regional organizations of more than single purpose character, and (3) the United Nations.

Defense Alliances. Simple defense arrangements such as the North Atlantic Treaty Organization and the Warsaw Pact serve simply to structure calculated alliances. They are traditional, ordinarily unambiguous, and provide for retaliation in the face of attack. Perhaps their only new feature today is in the effort to harmonize with Article 51 of the United Nations Charter. The NATO pact, *e.g.,* provides that

> The parties agree that an armed attack against one or more of them in Europe or North America shall be considered an attack against them all; and consequently they agree that, if such an armed attack occurs, each of them, in exercise of the right of individual or collective self-defense recognized by Article 51 of the Charter of the United Nations, will assist the party or parties so attacked by taking forthwith, individually and in concert with the other parties, such action as it deems necessary, including the use of armed force, to restore and maintain the security of the North Atlantic area.
>
> Any such armed attack and all measures taken as a result thereof shall immediately be reported to the Security Council. Such measures shall be terminated when the Security Council has taken the measures necessary to restore and maintain international peace and security.[118]

Regional Organizations. More multiple purpose in character are regional organizations such, *e.g.,* as the Organization of American States.[119] Among the functions of the OAS is the maintenance of order in the Americas, and to this end it pro-

---

[118] *North Atlantic Treaty,* Art. 5. See conveniently in L. L. Snyder, *Fifty Major Documents of the Twentieth Century* (New York: D. Van Nostrand Company, Inc., 1955), pp. 145–48.

[119] *Charter of the Organization of the American States,* see in W. Sanders, "Bogota Conference," *International Conciliation,* No. 442 (June, 1948), pp. 418–33. Other regional organizations include the European "Inner Six" Community which in itself does not perform a security function, but is certainly multipurpose otherwise. Another such organization is the Organization of African Unity; see Boutros Boutros-Ghali, "The Addis Ababa Charter," *International Conciliation,* No. 546 January, 1964).

vides for self-defense under Article 51 of the U.N. Charter.[120] It seeks to resolve disputes among American powers,[121] but also has provision for dealing with threats to the western hemisphere which emanate from elsewhere. The pact stipulates that

If the inviolability or the integrity of the territory or the sovereignty or political independence of any American State should be affected by an aggression which is not an armed attack or by an extra-continental or intra-continental conflict, or by any other fact or situation that might endanger the peace of America, the Organ of Consultation shall meet immediately in order to agree on the measures which must be taken in case of aggression to assist the victim of the aggression or, in any case, the measures which should be taken for the common defense and for the maintenance of the peace and security of the Continent.[122]

The Organ of Consultation, consisting of the foreign ministers of the treaty powers, decides by a two-thirds vote. Provisionally and pending regular meetings, the Governing Board of the Pan American Union is authorized to act as an organ of consultation.[123]

Enforcement measures provided for within the orbit of the OAS range from the recalling of diplomatic mission chiefs to the use of armed force.[124] The Cuban missile crisis discussed above affords one enforcement illustration.

The United Nations. The great new hope of the world in 1945 was the United Nations. It was believed that that organization could forestall future wars and especially worldwide conflagrations. The pacific obligations of the Charter, binding on all member states, and the nonforcible procedures which can be utilized by the United Nations have been considered elsewhere in this text.[125] The purpose here is to note those forcible procedures which are available for resolution of disputes which the United Nations may employ. Given the high

---

[120] *Charter* (OAS), Arts. 24, 25; *Inter-American Treaty of Reciprocal Assistance* (known as the *Rio Pact*), Art. 3 (See *Rio Pact* conveniently in *Inter-American System, op. cit.* pp. 376–81).

[121] *Rio Pact*, Art. 7.

[122] *Ibid.*, Art. 6.

[123] *Ibid.*, Arts. 11, 12.

[124] *Ibid.*, Art. 8.

[125] This chapter, above, p. 256 ff., *et passim.*

hopes suggested above, those procedures have been something
of a disappointment, but those very limitations are nevertheless
a useful measure of the real character of contemporary international politics and law. However, even if not fully adequate,
U.N. enforcement devices have nevertheless functioned with
varying degrees of effectiveness.

Under the Charter, the Security Council has been given the
primary responsibility in matters of peace keeping and enforcement, and it may determine the existence of threats to the
peace and the action to be taken to resolve the pertinent problems.[126] A full measure of devices is available for enforcement,
and action by the Security Council is binding on all members
of the United Nations.[127] The Charter states

> The Security Council may decide what measures not involving
> the use of armed force are to be employed to give effect to its
> decisions, and it may include complete or partial interruption of
> economic relations and of rail, sea, air, postal, telegraphic, radio,
> and other means of communication, and the severance of diplomatic
> relations.[128]

> Should the Security Council consider that measures provided for
> in Article 41 would be inadequate or have proved to be inadequate,
> it may take such action by air, sea, or land forces as may be necessary
> to maintain or restore international peace and security. Such action
> may include demonstrations, blockade, and other operations by air,
> sea, or land forces of Members of the United Nations.[129]

Moreover, the Charter provides for drawing up agreements by
which the armed forces are to be made available for such
contingencies, for the creation and use of a Military Staff Committee, and for other categories of support for enforcement.[130]
Unfortunately, resort to the veto, and inability to structure the
contemplated military forces agreements have seriously limited
the Security Council's enforcement and peace-keeping potential.

In an effort to bypass the deadlocking effect of the veto in the

---

[126] U.N., *Charter*, Arts. 39, 40.

[127] *Ibid.*, Arts. 41, 48, 49.

[128] *Ibid.*, Art. 41.

[129] *Ibid.*, Art. 42.

[130] *Ibid.*, Arts. 43, 44, 45, 46, 47.

Security Council, the General Assembly, under the urging of the United States, approved a procedure, known as the "Uniting for Peace Resolution," under which the General Assembly could deal with problems of this sort.[131] It is well to note, however, that, while the procedure appears to be legal,[132] it does not bind the members of the United Nations in the same way that comparable action by the Security Council would.[133] Moreover, in all cases where United Nations peace-keeping or enforcement action has been undertaken, the troops were volunteered by states which were willing to participate.

If the whole matter of enforcement procedures is considered in perspective—liberal use of the veto, uniting for peace resolution and the subsequent Assembly enforcement role, and the *ad hoc* military unit arrangements—it is evident that virtually the entire enforcement mechanism has functioned in ways which were not originally contemplated.

In the Korean incident, the Security Council did authorize the United Nations effort, but this was possible only because the U.S.S.R. was absent at the time of the voting—a tactical error not likely to be repeated. In the subsequent Suez and Congo affairs ultimate action by the Security Council proved impossible because of the veto, and the action which did take place was effected under the authority of the General Assembly.[134]

---

[131] See in *American Journal of International Law*, Vol. XLV (January, 1951), pp. 1–6 (documents section).

[132] See, *e.g., Certain Expenses of the United Nations*, Advisory Opinion, I.C.J. Reports (1962), p. 151. See conveniently in *American Journal of International Law*, Vol. LVI (October, 1962), p. 1053.

[133] See discussion in J. W. Malderman, "Legal Basis for United Nations Armed Forces," *American Journal of International Law*, Vol. LVI (October, 1962), pp. 971–96, especially p. 995.

[134] *Ibid., passim;* E. M. Miller, "Legal Aspects of the United Nations Action in the Congo," *American Journal of International Law*, Vol. LV (January, 1961), pp. 1–28. W. E. Benton, "United Nations Action in the Suez Crisis," *International Law and the Middle East Crisis: A Symposium* (Tulane Studies in Political Science) Vol. IV, (New Orleans, La.; Tulane University Press, 1957), pp. 5–23; H. L. Mason, "The United Nations Emergency Force," *ibid.*, pp. 25–48. P. B. Potter, "Legal Aspects of the Situation in Korea," *American Journal of International Law*, Vol. XLIV (October, 1950), pp. 709–12. J. L. Kunz, "Legality of the Security Council Resolutions of June 25 and 27, 1950," *American Journal of International Law*, Vol. XLV (January, 1951), pp. 137–42. L. B. Sohn, "The Authority of the United Nations to Establish and Maintain a Permanent United Nations Force," *American Journal of International Law*, Vol. LII (April, 1958), pp. 229–40.

The significance of these developments is to underscore the traditional devices of international politics and law. The principle has been often mentioned in these pages that the location of ultimate responsibility for security circumscribes the real location of power, and thus molds the character of law. On this basis it is evident that while there have been some changes in the international security machinery, these changes are much less significant than a casual reading of the United Nations Charter would suggest.

SUMMARY

Modes of redress among states include two main categories aside from war. These have been termed (1) amicable modes of redress, and (2) nonamicable modes of redress short of war. There is a clear obligation in international law to exhaust all reasonable possibility of the former category before nonamicable and particularly forcible devices are employed, except of course that self-defense remains a valid basis for employment of force.

The principal amicable techniques are negotiation, good offices and mediation, commissions of inquiry, and conciliation as nonjuridical techniques, and arbitration and adjudication as juridical procedures. In addition the United Nations has special settlement procedures at its command. Although there is a clear obligation to use pacific means of settlement, there is only limited obligation to submit a dispute to arbitral or judicial settlement—and that is a self-imposed obligation wherever it exists. This situation perpetuates the distinction between "justiciable and nonjusticiable" controversies.

When the above devices do not work, resort is often had to devices which are nonamicable. Those nonamicable procedures which, nevertheless, are pacific and hence legitimate include strong representations, severance of diplomatic relations, retorsions, and certain reprisals including nonintercourse or boycott, and embargo. Techniques employing force include display of force, pacific blockade, and other forcible techniques such as bombardment, quarantine, and occupation. Some of these are on the periphery of force and the consideration which largely governs their legality centers upon whether the action is "pacific." Nonpacific devices may be employed under United Nations auspices, however, and in valid instances of self-defense. Other applications of them are either clearly illegal or dubious, but it is probably correct to suggest that such procedures are proper in circumstances of the utmost gravity. This, however, is not a certainty.

Satisfaction, that is, getting a suitable settlement of differences, is the objective of seeking redress. Satisfaction ranges widely and includes acknowledgment of an abuse, payment of an indemnity, making a settlement for the relatives of a wrongfully killed person, and salute to the national flag.

Forcible procedures are provided for in the basic charters of many international organizations both regional and universal as well as being the *raison d'être* for defense alliances. United Nations forcible devices were originally charted for the Security Council, but its effectiveness has been limited by the veto. Under the "Uniting for Peace Resolution" the General Assembly has undertaken to perform significant portions of this role when the Security Council is deadlocked.

CHAPTER 9

War

IT MAY WELL be that the most important problem facing the modern world is how to avoid major international strife. The appalling consequences of major war are such that intense desire for a pacific solution is understandable, for it is even possible that another major war will bring an end to the human race. Yet there is the relentlessness of history which seems to suggest that war is just one of many human practices which will be repeated, and perhaps humanity's greatest hopes must be pinned upon controlling it and keeping it in check. In law as in technique, war is not static. In its legal aspects it has undergone considerable change since the turn of the century, though perhaps not as much as has sometimes been suggested.

There are many aspects of war only a few of which fall within the province of a treatment of international law. The present discussion will be divided into four major parts in addition to a summary. These are (1) the nature of war, (2) commencement, suspension, and termination of war, (3) the legal effects of war, and (4) the rules of warfare.

THE NATURE OF WAR

War can be seen from many standpoints, yet it must again be stressed that here the object is to see it in the light of international law. Changes in international practices and even perhaps new conceptions of traditional practices have injected new concepts into the law, however, which have rendered clarity more difficult than was formerly the case. The present discussion will consider (1) definition of war, (2) political objectives of war, and (3) the legal status or the legality of war.

Definition of War

War is difficult to define because the term has both vernacular and technical meanings. If these were truly clear-cut there would be little problem, but this is not the case. War has been defined as "a condition of armed hostility between States."[1] This definition is perhaps as good as most, but it is not entirely satisfactory, for a state of war may exist without any armed conflict. For example, when Costa Rica declared war on the Axis in 1941 there was no clash of armies, yet the legal status of war obtained. Similarly, throughout much of the Sino-Japanese conflict there was ample evidence of conflict, but neither side recognized the existence of a "state of war." Finally, the matter is further complicated by the existence of civil war which is rarely if ever formally recognized or declared by the parent state, though it often comes to be tacitly recognized. Similarly, a conflict between states need not be openly declared in order to achieve the status of a war.[2] Finally, war has been outlawed, but as a physical phenomenon it has certainly not been abolished. It cannot, therefore, be stated now with certainty that war is a legal means of self-help. On the contrary its use with full legality is severely circumscribed, but what this may mean in terms of the occurrence of armed conflict is far from clear.

---

[1] C. C. Hyde, *International Law Chiefly as Interpreted and Applied by the United States* (2d ed.; Boston: Little, Brown & Co., 1945), Vol. III, p. 1686; see also John Westlake, *International Law, Part II War* (2d ed.; Cambridge, Mass.: Harvard University Press, 1913), Vol. II, p. 1; also Moore, *Digest* VII, p. 154; Oppenheim-Lauterpacht, *Treatise* II, p. 202; see also C. Eagleton, "The Attempt to Define War," *International Conciliation*, No. 291 (1933) for a survey which points to the many difficulties inherent in attempting to define war. For a statement of the view that war is not a status but rather a situation deriving solely from employment of armed force, see Hans Kelsen, *Principles of International Law* (New York: Rinehart & Co., Inc., 1952), pp. 26–28. See good discussion in J. Stone, *Legal Controls of International Conflict* (New York: Rinehart & Co., Inc., 1954), pp. 304–6.

[2] See Hyde, *op. cit.*, pp. 1688–89, 1692; Hackworth, *Digest* VI, pp. 161–66. See, however, F. Grob, *The Relativity of War and Peace* (New Haven, Conn.: Yale University Press, 1949), pp. 3–9, 189, *et passim*.

Thus war is a fact from which certain rights and obligations derive. It is usually to be defined, as noted above, as "a condition of armed hostility between States," but it may be a condition of formal hostility between states in which there is no actual armed conflict. Finally, an actual armed conflict may be treated as a minor affair, an incident, a police action, force short of war, or in some other way which does not achieve the status of war either in the eyes of the contenders or of other states. Presumably in a condition of this last character no war exists, yet it may be useful, as a device to further amplify the difficulties inherent in today's concept of war, to ask whether the soldiers contending in such an incident would be accorded rights of combatants in conformity with the laws of war. In the light of these remarks war may be defined qualifiedly as *a condition of armed and/or formal hostility between states.*

Intermediacy.   There has been considerable comment as to whether the dichotomy of war and peace is sufficiently realistic, and some writers have pointed out that legal theory does not quite conform to the facts of procedure. Thus a cold war situation is not war, yet it is not quite peace either. Terms such as "limited war," "force short of war," and "nonbelligerency" have been used to describe aspects of this intermediate status. These terms, like war, are themselves ambiguous. By way of illustration, the laws of war would seem to apply in a situation where "force short of war" is employed. Is such force then war?[3]

In this connection it has been suggested that a clearly recognized intermediate status between war and peace would allow us to think more clearly about the objectives in conflict. Accordingly, a state of peace, an intermediate status, and a state of war might be conceived of as formal postures rather than the traditional twofold idea of war or peace as a mold to which international relations are supposed to conform. This arrangement has been urged in part as a psychological device for forcing people to think more clearly about the character of conflict. An intermediate status would imply a somewhat dis-

---

[3] See particularly Grob, *op. cit.*, pp. 173–224 *et passim;* see also M. S. McDougal and F. P. Feliciano, "International Coercion and World Public Order: The General Principles of the Law of War," *Yale Law Journal,* Vol. 67 (April, 1958), pp. 774–79.

tant relationship and limited friction—even perhaps limited conflict—but the notion of all-out war or total conflict might be kept out of the picture, for it would pertain to the more extreme posture of war. Thus, conflict might be better kept in check and in closer relation to the political objectives which the use of force or friction or any other technique is intended to promote.[4] It must be emphasized that this sort of concept in a formal sense is foreign to contemporary international law, but it is at least useful to think about in order to help clarify the terribly confused conceptions of war and peace.

Political Objectives of War

The reasons for resort to war are probably myriad; they are in the political realm and range widely. Clausewitz in his classic statement that "War is nothing but a continuation of political intercourse, with a mixture of other means" has pointed to the heart of the matter.[5] Thus the quest for trade, territory, people, justice, revenge, or the needs of defense have all been responsible for armed conflict. Although it has been argued that the purpose of war is to overpower and defeat the enemy,[6] it is doubtful whether this view is sound. The object of war is to obtain some political end, and abject defeat of the enemy may or may not be a means to that end. For example, the United Nations objective in the Korean War seems to have been merely to contain the enemy, while the objective of the Allies in World War II was unconditional surrender.[7]

Whatever the real motives may be, it must be noted that the recent curbs placed on the legality of war and the seeming aversion of world public opinion for war have tended to restrict

---

[4] See P. C. Jessup, "Should International Law Recognize an Intermediate Status between Peace and War?" *American Journal of International Law,* Vol. XLVIII (January, 1954), pp. 98–103; also Grob, *op. cit., passim.*

[5] Gen. Carl Von Clausewitz, *On War,* trans. Col. J. J. Graham (New York: Barnes & Noble, Inc., 1956), Vol. III, p. 121.

[6] Oppenheim-Lauterpacht, *Treatise* II, pp. 208–9.

[7] See generally the discussion in Q. Wright, *A Study of War* (Chicago: University of Chicago Press, 1942), Vol. I, pp. 249–90; also McDougal and Feliciano, *op. cit.,* pp. 781–83; see also Von Clausewitz, *op. cit.,* pp. 131–40 *et passim;* also Henry A. Kissinger, *Nuclear Weapons and Foreign Policy* (Garden City, N.Y.: Doubleday & Co., Inc., 1958), *passim.*

the publicly announced reasons for resort to war to some variation of the right of self-defense.[8]

Legal Status of War

The traditional legal status of war under international law
was one which as a rule disregarded moral considerations. Although the doctrine of *bellum justum* was once thought applicable, when the principle of state sovereignty fully came into its
own, war became a fact of which the law merely took cognizance. It was not illegal, and might be legally utilized for
virtually any reason by almost any state.[9]

This was the situation until shortly after the end of World
War I. However, the Covenant of the League, the Pact of Paris,
and most recently the United Nations Charter have drastically
altered the letter of the law. By these agreements war has been
renounced as an instrument of national policy, and the Charter
of the United Nations states unequivocally:

3. All Members shall settle their international disputes by peaceful means in such a manner that international peace and security,
and justice, are not endangered.

4. All Members shall refrain in their international relations from
the threat or use of force against the territorial integrity or political
independence of any State, or in any other manner inconsistent with
the purposes of the United Nations.[10]

The war crimes trials further underline this position by giving
it acceptance by an international court. The court at Nuremberg spoke of aggressive war as "the supreme international
crime"; it stated:

To initiate a war of aggression, therefore, is not only an international crime; it is the supreme international crime differing only

---

[8] See above, Chapter Four, fn. 7; also Chapter Eight, fn. 6; *Treaty for the Renunciation of War*, U.S.T.S., No. 796; U.N., *Charter*, Art. 51.

[9] Charles De Visscher, *Theory and Reality in Public International Law*, trans. P. E. Corbett (Princeton, N.J.: Princeton University Press, 1957), pp. 16–19 *et passim;* Oppenheim-Lauterpacht, *Treatise* II, pp. 177–79.

[10] U.N., *Charter*, Art. 2 (3, 4); see also League of Nations, *Covenant*, Art. 12; also *Treaty for the Renunciation of War*, Arts. 1, 2.

from other war crimes in that it contains within itself the accumulated evil of the whole.[11]

This position has not gone unchallenged, for whatever impartiality may have existed, the fact that the judges were victors and the judged were the vanquished gave rise to some doubts.[12] Nevertheless, the apparently general acceptability of the judgments of the Nuremberg and Tokyo trials gives the procedure a reasonably firm status.[13]

There would appear to be two categories of war: (*a*) defensive and (*b*) aggressive. The latter is clearly illegal; the former, however, remains valid, for the Charter of the United Nations specifies that:

Nothing in the present Charter shall impair the inherent right of individual or collective self-defense if an armed attack occurs against a Member of the United Nations, until the Security Council has taken the measures necessary to maintain international peace and security. . . .[14]

As is suggested elsewhere in this volume, there has been a tendency for all states to allege self-defense whether or not it can be substantiated. Nevertheless, though questions of interpretation remain, the basic principle stands that now agressive war is illegal while defensive war is proper. To this it must

---

[11] See "International Military Tribunal (Nuremberg) Judgment and Sentences," *American Journal of International Law*, Vol. XLIII (January, 1947) , p. 186.

[12] See e.g., G. A. Finch, "The Nuremberg Trial and International Law," *American Journal of International Law*, Vol. XLI (January, 1947), pp. 20–37; for an extreme statement, see M. Belgion, *Victor's Justice* (Hinsdale, Ill.: Henry Regnery Co., 1949) , *passim*.

[13] See Q. Wright, "The Law of the Nuremberg Trial," *American Journal of International Law*, Vol. XLI (January, 1947) , pp. 38–72; also S. Glueck, *The Nuremberg Trial and Aggressive War* (New York: Alfred A. Knopf, Inc., 1946) , p. 91 *et passim*. For an analysis of the meaning of Nuremberg, see "Report of the International Law Commission," *American Journal of International Law*, Vol. XLIV (October, 1950) , especially pp. 125–34 (documents section) . For commentary on the precise definition of aggression and regarding offenses against peace see "Report of the International Law commission," *American Journal of International Law*, Vol. XLV (October, 1951) , especially pp. 118–32 (documents section) ; see also "Report of the International Law Commission" (6th session) , *American Journal of International Law*, Vol. XLIX (January, 1955) , especially pp. 16–23 (documents section) .

[14] U.N., *Charter*, Art. 51; see discussion in Chapter Nine.

be added that United Nations action on the field of battle is also legally proper.

It must be emphasized that clear determination along these lines is not an easy undertaking. War is rarely an enterprise which is immune from strong feeling. The possibilities inherent in internal subversion, civil war, and guerrilla conflict further complicate the matter. Moreover, when ideological and sometimes extreme ideological conflict obtain, and when emotional reactions are prevalent, the problem can become acerbated to a point where it may be most difficult to clarify the legal issues. The war in Vietnam is a case in point.[15]

Implications of This Principle. Logical consistency might allow one to argue that (1) if a certain war is wholly illegal, or (2) if one party to a war is an aggressor and the other is assuming a validly defensive posture, then (*a*) the laws of war and other rights of belligerents cannot accrue to either side in a wholly illegal war, or (*b*) to the aggressor in the second hypothetical instance above. This is in itself logical enough, for indeed a party ought not to be allowed to benefit from its own illegal acts, *jus ex injuria non oritur.* Nevertheless, there is an understandable hesitancy to push the matter to this ultimate conclusion, for the laws of war represent a sort of two-way street. If, for example, captured military personnel of one side are to be accorded the status of belligerents with the right to be treated as prisoners of war, it is unlikely that this can be achieved by putting the captured personnel of the enemy to death, even though they are from the aggressor nation. Simi-

---

[15] In the opinion of the present writer, the evidence suggests with reasonable clarity that the two Vietnams are in fact two legal international persons, that the conflict results largely from D.R.V. (Northern) attack and D.R.V. sponsored and supported attack, that the R.V.N. (South) is entitled to defend itself, and that U.S. and other assistance to the R.V.N., including measured air attack on the North, to counter this attack is an appropriate exercise of collective self-defense under Art. 51 of the U.N. Charter. However, failure to insist that the problem be considered by the Security Council as required by Art. 37 of the Charter of the United Nations appears to represent a procedural shortcoming. Soviet opposition to U.N. action in this matter helps to render the question of Security Council action essentially academic. See J. N. Moore, "The Lawfulness of Military Assistance to the Republic of Viet-Nam," *American Journal of International Law,* Vol. LXI (January, 1967), pp. 1–34. For a contrasting view, see Quincy Wright, "Legal Aspects of the Viet-Nam Situation," *American Journal of International Law,* Vol. LX (October, 1966), pp. 750–69. Arthur Larson, "Power and Law in World Affairs," *The Progressive,* November, 1966, pp. 12–15; December, 1966, pp. 35–37.

larly, even though an area is occupied by an aggressor, the inhabitants cannot expect to be treated in conformity with the rules if they do not themselves obey the traditional rules in relation to the occupying power. Thus, the rules of war have a political quality about them in the sense that they represent a mutual benefit. Accordingly, it appears that regardless of the legality of the war itself, the rules of warfare apply to hostile relationships generally, for if war has been legally outlawed, it certainly has not been factually abolished, and the mitigating effects of the rules are no less desirable in time of illegal war than in time of legal conflict.[16]

COMMENCEMENT, SUSPENSION, AND TERMINATION OF WAR

Wars begin in certain specific ways. Similarly, they are suspended and finally terminated by specific actions. Some of these are of special importance in the sense of being legally prescribed. Beyond that, there is legal significance in the existence of a state of war, hence there is importance in the exact duration of war. The present discussion will consider (1) commencement of war, (2) suspension of hostilities, and (3) termination of war.

Commencement of War

It was noted in an earlier chapter that there is a solemn obligation upon states to negotiate a controversy prior to using armed force. Should relationships continue to deteriorate sufficiently, there remains the possibility of conflict. Prior to 1907 it is believed that there was no obligation to declare war prior to commencement of hostilities, but in that year the Hague

---

[16] Q. Wright, "The Outlawing of War and the Law of War," *American Journal of International Law,* Vol. XLVII (July, 1953), pp. 365–76, especially pp. 370–71. R. W. Tucker, *The Law of War and Neutrality at Sea,* Naval War College, *International Law Studies,* Vol. XLX, 1955 (Washington, D.C.: U.S. Government Printing Office, 1957), pp. 1–11; Oppenheim-Lauterpacht, *Treatise* II, pp. 216–20; see Josef L. Kunz, "The Laws of War," *American Journal of International Law,* Vol. L (April, 1956), pp. 313–37. See *The Hostage* case (*U.S. v. List*), *Trials of War Criminals before the Nuremberg Military Tribunal* (Washington, D.C.: U.S. Government Printing Office, 1950), Vol. XI, pp. 1244–48.

Convention Relative to the Opening of Hostilities was drawn up, and that agreement, generally though not universally ratified, has established certain legal obligations.[17] Under its terms hostilities should not be commenced without "either . . . a reasoned declaration of war or . . . an ultimatum with conditional declaration of war." Neutrals are to be notified and the war is to be effective with reference to them only upon such notification. The requirements do not specify any time limit, thus the declaration may be well in advance or immediately preceding the actual attack.[18]

That the above requirements legally exist cannot be seriously questioned, but the facts of procedure suggest that compliance with the requirement to declare war has been more commonly avoided than adhered to. A study made in 1883 showed that between 1700 and 1870 out of a total of 117 wars only 10 had been formally declared. Moreover, the practices followed since the early 1930's suggest that this pattern remains. Accordingly, it must be reiterated that while the Convention of 1907 is still technically in force, it is of dubious importance, and some commentators have termed it obsolete.[19]

Since the requirement of a declaration has been as often honored in breach as in compliance, it is evident that the legal and practical effects of war commence in ways other than by declaration or by ultimatum and conditional declaration. There are two other ways commonly recognized: (1) "by the commission of hostile acts by one country" with a view to

---

[17] *Convention Relative to the Opening of Hostilities,* The Hague Convention No. III, 36 *U.S. Statutes* 2259; for comment on the pre-1907 rule, see Naval War College, *International Law Situations, 1933* (Washington, D.C.: U.S. Government Printing Office, 1934), p. 95; also Hyde, *op. cit.,* p. 1695. See above, Chapter Eight.

[18] See *Convention Relative to the Opening of Hostilities,* Arts. 1, 2; C. Eagleton, "The Form and Function of the Declaration of War," *American Journal of International Law,* Vol. XXXII (January, 1938), pp. 19–35. See E. Castrén, *The Present Law of War and Neutrality* (Helsinki: Annales Academica Scientiarum Fennicae, 1954), pp. 96–98 where it is stated that customary international law does not require a declaration of war; some powers, e.g., Italy, are not parties to Third Hague Convention.

[19] J. F. Maurice, *Hostilities without Declaration of War from 1700 to 1870* (London: H. M. Stationary Office, 1883), p. 4; L. Pfankuchen, *A Documentary Textbook in International Law* (New York: Rinehart & Co., Inc., 1940), p. 700; Q. Wright, *op. cit.,* Vol. I, p. 638; Stone, *op. cit.,* pp. 307–9; also Eagleton, *op. cit.,* pp. 19, 20, *et passim.*

making war and, (2) by a pronouncement of a state indicating that actions of another state have "brought into being a condition of war."[20] It must be noted that courts have sometimes disregarded the date of a declaration in favor of the date of actual hostilities in determining the exact moment of a war's beginning. Furthermore, they have sometimes specified that a state of war does not exist, despite the fact of hostilities, because the political branch of the government has not seen fit to so recognize it.[21] It may be added that civil wars present special difficulties because they are almost never declared wars. The American Civil War, for example, is held to have begun and ended in accordance with the proclamation and removal of blockade.[22]

Suspension of Hostilities

Suspension of hostilities must be differentiated from termination of war. The latter restores the state of peace but the former merely halts—sometimes only very temporarily—military action and does not necessarily carry with it the legal implication of termination of war.[23]

There are various devices employed in the area of temporary cessation of hostilities. Some arrangements apply locally, others generally, and the status of each is regulated by the terms of the accord itself. The descriptive terms are somewhat overlapping, but identification of the following terms seems useful: (1) armistice or truce, (2) suspension of arms, and (3) capitulations.

An armistice or a truce, not to be confused with a flag of truce, is an intergovernmental agreement to halt hostilities. It may or may not specify a time limit, and it may be general in scope or restricted to certain areas. Although it was once believed that armistices were such that hostilities could be rather summarily resumed by either side, it is now the general impres-

---

20 Hyde, *op. cit.,* pp. 1693–94.

21 See E. Borchard, "When Did the War Begin," *American Journal of International Law,* Vol. XLI (July, 1947), pp. 621–22 and cases cited there.

22 Hyde, *op. cit.,* p. 1698.

23 See *Commercial Cable Co. v. Burleson,* 255 F. 99 (1919).

sion that the terms of the armistice itself are the determining factors. They may, for example, so hamstring one party that hostilities cannot be resumed. This was particularly true of the armistice terminating hostilities at the end of World War I.[24]

Suspension of arms is a term employed to describe temporary local cessation of hostilities. It is brought about by the field commanders for some mutually beneficial purpose such as collection of casualities, burial of the dead, or even for a conference.[25]

Capitulations are agreements of field commanders for the surrender of towns, fortified places, or other areas. The term usually suggests a wholly military agreement for surrender on the one side with perhaps an understanding on the other as to security and treatment of troops and civilian population in such matters as their civil rights, property, keeping of arms, and other similar matters. Terms of such an accord must be agreeable to the respective governments. This matter, formerly of some importance, has lost its problem character with the vast improvement of communications. If, however, accords are made which are in excess of the commander's authority, they are known as *sponsions* or *sub spe rati*. Such accords must be ratified by their home governments in order for them to be valid, though, of course, their nature may be such that the act has accomplished *de facto* something which cannot be wholly rectified.[26]

Termination of War

Publicists generally agree that there are three ways in which a war may terminate. These are (1) by simple cessation of hostilities, (2) by subjugation, and (3) by a treaty of peace.

Termination by simple cessation of hostilities is uncommon today, but occasionally wars have ended in this fashion. The

---

[24] Moore, *Digest* VII, pp. 327–35; Hyde, *op. cit.*, pp. 1783–91; M. Greenspan, *The Modern Law of Land Warfare* (Berkeley, Calif.: University of California Press, 1959), pp. 385–92.

[25] Moore, *Digest* VII, p. 327.

[26] See Moore, *Digest* VII, pp. 321–26; G. G. Wilson, *International Law* (9th ed.; Boston: Silver Burdett & Co., 1935), p. 298; Hyde, *op. cit.*, pp. 1880–81, Greenspan, *op. cit.*, pp. 392–97.

war between Mexico and France ending in 1867 may be considered as ending in this way. There are, of course, some practical difficulties in specifying exactly the time of termination, for, as Secretary of State Seward indicated, "What period of suspension of war is necessary to justify the presumption of the restoration of peace has never yet been settled, and must in every case be determined with reference to collateral facts and circumstances." It may be added that termination in this fashion presumes settlement on an *uti possidetis* basis, that is, each side keeps what it has at the conclusion of hostilities.[27]

Termination by subjugation is also uncommon as a means of ending wars, and recent examples are of questionable value. The wars between Italy and Ethiopia in 1936, and Germany and Czechoslovakia (if it could be loosely called a war) ended in this way, but subsequent events altered the results. More permanent examples are seen in the processes by which both Italy and Germany became unified states. In 1859 the Kingdom of Sardinia absorbed the Two Sicilies, Tuscany, Modena, and Parma, and later in 1870, the Papal States, while in 1866 Prussia similarly absorbed Hannover, Nassau, Hesse-Cassel, and Frankfort am Maine.[28] Some sort of proclamation of annexation has often been used, but the essential legal consideration has been the fact of absorption. It may be questioned in light of the Paris Pact and the United Nations Charter whether this procedure could still claim legal validity, but it must be remembered that various states did recognize the Italian conquest of Ethiopia until the political tides turned in World War II. It may be instructive to speculate on the outcome of Italy's 1936 conquest if it had stayed out of World War II.

Termination by treaty of peace is the normal method by which wars end. The treaty of peace is not to be confused with a preliminary suspension of hostilities or armistice which is usually preliminary to the formal peace accord. The peace treaty restores peaceful relations and provides for many matters pertaining to settlement, including boundaries, indemnities,

---

[27] Moore, *Digest* VII, pp. 337–38; also Stone, *op. cit.*, p. 639; Oppenheim-Lauterpacht, *Treatise* II, pp. 598–99; see also Greenspan, *op. cit.*, pp. 603–4.

[28] Oppenheim-Lauterpacht, *Treatise* II, pp. 599–605; Stone, *op. cit.*, pp. 539–40; Hyde, *op. cit.*, pp. 2389–90; see also Greenspan, *op. cit.*, pp. 600–603.

exchange of prisoners of war, settlement of points of friction, and for such future mutual relationships as trade and resumption of agreements. The terms of the treaty may specify its own date of effectiveness, or it may provide for going into effect upon ratification. There is some question about the matter. Some writers feel that in the absence of express stipulation, a treaty of peace is effective retroactive to the date of signing, while others feel that the date of ratification is the moment of effectiveness. The latter view has been expressed earlier in this work.[29]

LEGAL EFFECTS OF WAR AND OF RESTORATION OF PEACE

As was noted above, war is a condition or fact from which certain legal implications derive. When war terminates and peace is restored, those legal effects of war end and the legal effects of peace again obtain. These matters will be considered in three categories: (1) general effects of war, (2) effect of war upon persons, (3) effect of war upon public and private property, (4) nonhostile relations of warring states, and (5) restoration of peace.

General Effects of War

In general, war has the effect of suspending the normal peacetime relationships between opposing belligerents, bringing into effect the pertinent wartime rules of international law, and instituting the rules of neutrality with neutral states. More specifically, (1) official diplomatic contacts are severed, and communications, commercial relations, and other contacts between belligerent personnel are suspended, and most peacetime treaties are suspended or even abrogated; (2) those agreements and general rules for the conduct of hostilities and other arrangements specifically designed to govern relationships in time

---

[29] Castrén, *op. cit.*, pp. 134–37; also this work, above, Chapter Six. Oppenheim-Lauterpacht, *Treatise* II, pp. 605–10; Stone, *op. cit.*, pp. 640–41; see also G. Schwarzenberger, *International Law* I (3d ed.; London: Stevens & Sons, 1957); see also Greenspan, *op. cit.*, pp. 588–600.

of war come into effect; (3) states remaining outside the conflict normally assume the position of neutrals and their rights
and duties as neutrals come into existence.[30]

Effect of War upon Persons

War has differing effects upon various categories of persons.
These may be considered in the following categories: (1) citizens, (2) enemy aliens, and (3) neutrals.

Citizens. Citizens of a state at war are, of course, governed
by their own municipal law. As far as international law is
concerned a state of war allows a state to require of its nationals
complete severance of foreign relationships. The United States,
for example, has generally allowed no trade with the enemy,
but European practice has tended to be less absolute in this
regard. A state may consider certain contracts between its citizens and enemy aliens to be invalid during the war; and,
similarly, all remittance of funds, including interest on debts,
may be suspended throughout the war. It should be stressed
that what is involved here is prevention of the transmission of
wealth during war which could indirectly serve to benefit the
enemy war effort. American practice has often provided for
protection of the alien's ultimate interests while preventing
wartime access to funds in this country.[31] Illustrative is the
following statement of the Court of Appeals of New York:

> The effect of war upon an existing contract between belligerents
> will vary with the nature of the obligation that is yet to be fulfilled.
> If the contract has been fully executed by the enemy before the
> outbreak of hostilities, if all that is left is a unilateral obligation for
> the payment of a debt, the obligation is suspended. The citizen must
> pay his debt when the war is at an end. On the other hand, if the
> contract is still executory at the beginning of the war, if there are
> mutual obligations that are yet to be fulfilled, the contract will be

---

[30] See above, Chapter Six; Hyde, *op. cit.,* pp. 1699–1772; Stone, *op. cit.,* pp.
417–50; Wilson, *op. cit.,* p. 251; O. Svarlien, *An Introduction to the Law of
Nations* (New York: McGraw-Hill Book Co., Inc., 1955), pp. 344–45; C. G.
Fenwick, *International Law* (3d ed.; New York: Appleton-Century-Crofts, Inc.,
1948), pp. 601–10.

[31] See generally Hyde, *op. cit., passim,* also C. G. Fenwick, *op. cit.,* pp. 608–9,
et passim.

terminated when the essential purpose of the parties would be thwarted by delay, or the business efficacy or value of their bargain materially impaired.[32]

Enemy Aliens. Enemy aliens domiciled or in temporary residence in a state with which their homeland is at war present a number of considerations. In general the state having such people within its borders has had rather wide discretion in dealing with them. Subject to the general rule of humanity, it was formerly proper to handle such aliens as the needs of the occasion seemed to demand. This situation has been changed somewhat by one of the 1949 Geneva conventions. Nevertheless, even the Convention allows rather severe action in the event of "absolute necessity." Accordingly, all aliens may be forced to register, their activities may be regulated, or they may even be interned or expelled. However, considerations of decency, justice, and humanity as well as the Convention would seem to temper the absoluteness of such discretion. Clearly it is not within the permissiveness of the law to exterminate enemy aliens for casual reasons and without trial. Accordingly, the German Federal Supreme Court recently upheld the conviction of a former officer who was immediately responsible for the execution of slave laborers during World War II.[33] Practice and treaty provisions generally allow such persons to remain in residence and to continue their normal activities so long as they behave themselves.[34]

Neutral Persons. Neutral persons domiciled or temporarily residents of a belligerent state are naturally subject to the dictates of local law. At the same time their home state retains an interest in them which they—so long as they remain its nationals—cannot deny. Although the extremities of permissive procedure are often moderated, a belligerent may expect neutral persons domiciled within its borders to be subject to

---

[32] *Neumond* v. *Farmers Feed Co.*, 244 N.Y. 202, 206; 155 N.E. 100 (cited in Hyde, *op. cit.*, p. 1708).

[33] Decision of the Federal Supreme Court (Germany), September 30, 1960. Reported in *American Journal of International Law*, Vol. LVII (January, 1963), p. 139.

[34] See below, this chapter, pp. 300–301 for discussion of humanity rule; Hyde, *op. cit.*, pp. 1721–25; *Geneva Convention Relative to the Protection of Civilian Persons* (1949); especially Arts. 27–46.

essentially the same restraints and regulations as citizens. Accordingly, an alien neutral may be taxed to support the war in the same pattern as citizens are taxed. Similarly, domiciled neutral persons may be subjected to the draft with the alternative of leaving the country. This last statement is probably an accurate portrayal of the general rule, but treaty arrangements, while sometimes reiterating this rule, occasionally modify it to prevent drafting of such persons.[35] Illustrative of such modifications are the pertinent articles of the Habana Convention on the Status of Aliens which states:

Foreigners may not be obliged to perform military service; but those foreigners who are domiciled, unless they prefer to leave the country, may be compelled, under the same conditions as nationals, to perform police, fire-protection, or militia duty for the protection of the place of their domicile against natural catastrophes or dangers not resulting from war.[36]

Effect of War on Public and Private Property

It is doubtful whether there is any real obligation not to seize enemy property within the national domain be it real or movable, public or private. A state has rather full power to prosecute a war as its needs dictate, and confiscation is allowable, except perhaps that certain publicly owned cultural treasures of art are usually considered exempt, and embassy buildings and archives remain inviolate.[37]

---

[35] Hyde, *op. cit.*, pp. 1744–56; see also this work, below, Chapter Ten.

[36] *Convention Regarding the Status of Aliens*, Havana, 1928; 46 U.S., *Statutes* 2753, Art. 3.

[37] There is, however, considerable ambiguity about this matter. The right to confiscate enemy property was clearly evident until about a century before World War I, but during that period, i.e., roughly 1814–1914 there appears to have been significant modification of the practice, and some authorities saw in this a change in law. However several authorities writing on this matter recognize that it is problematical whether "that practice has definitely crystallized into a customary rule of International Law." Oppenheim-Lauterpacht, *Treatise* II, p. 326; see also comment in Svarlien, *op. cit.*, p. 349; J. G. Starke, *An Introduction to International Law* (London: Butterworth & Co., Ltd., 1963), pp. 410–11. Pfankuchen, *op. cit.*, pp. 730–32. During World Wars I and II, practices were followed under which any real modification of the earlier rule seems to have been destroyed, and court decisions both early and late appear to underscore the right of confiscation. See, e.g., *Brown v. U.S.*, 8 Cranch 110 (1814), in which the Court said that "war gives to the sovereign full right to . . . confiscate the property of

Practice tends to be less severe than the permissive letter of the law. In American practice existence of a state of war does not institute confiscation, but merely allows it to the extent that legislation specifies.[38] In practice the United States formerly refrained from confiscating many categories of property, particularly that which was privately owned. After World War II, however, the Allied powers entered into an arrangement by which they agreed to keep certain categories of property and use it to satisfy the war claims of their own nationals. These arrangements were recognized in the peace treaties.[39]

Enemy property which is in an area occupied as a result of war by the opposing belligerent is subject to somewhat different rules. In general, private property remains unaffected. It is not to be confiscated, and pillage is prohibited. Property can be

---

the enemy," and over a century later, a British court said that "the right to seize private enemy property existed [at] . . . the beginning of the war with Bulgaria," *In re Ferdinand, Ex-Tsar of Bulgaria*, Great Britain, Court of Appeal, 1920, 1 Ch. 107 (see conveniently in Pfankuchen, *op. cit.*, pp. 725–30). In 1947 the U.S. Supreme Court said substantially the same thing, *Silesian American Corporation v. Clark*, 332 U.S. 429 (1947); see digest of this case in *American Journal of International Law*, Vol. XLII (April, 1948), p. 473. See also Alma Latifi, *Effects of War on Property* (London: Macmillan and Co., Ltd., 1909), p. 50. For assorted cases, incidents, and indications of practice, see Hackworth, *Digest* VI, pp. 199–237.

For details of the application of the Trading with the Enemy Act in the United States and for commentary on comparable acts elsewhere, see Martin Domke, *Trading with the Enemy in World War II* (New York: Central Book Co., 1943), *passim;* and Martin Domke, *The Control of Alien Property* (New York: Central Book Co., 1947), *passim.* The pattern which appears is one of many exceptions in practice to an assumption in theory that all enemy property could be taken. Whether this theoretical assumption is correct is, of course, the issue at hand. For statements of the position that the seizure of private enemy property is contrary to international law, see P. C. Jessup, "Enemy Property," *American Journal of International Law*, Vol. XLIX (January, 1955), pp. 57–62, see also references in the article; also G. von Glahn, *Law among Nations* (New York: The Macmillan Co., 1965), pp. 568–69; see also P. J. Eder, "Confiscation of Enemy Alien Property Held Unconstitutional by Colombian Supreme Court," *American Journal of International Law*, Vol. LIV (January, 1960), pp. 159–60; this appears to be a decision based upon constitutional considerations, however; see case in Colombia, 89 *Gaceta Judicial*, pp. 412–17. See also H. P. deVries, "The International Responsibility of the United States for Vested German Assets," *American Journal of International Law*, Vol. LI (January, 1957), pp. 18–28, especially p. 27.

[38] 56 *American Jurisprudence*, "War," #69, 77; *Brown v. U.S.*, 8 Cranch 110 (1814); Hyde, *op. cit.*, pp. 1726–43.

[39] See e.g., "Allied and Associated Powers and Italy; Treaty of Peace," Art. 79, *American Journal of International Law*, Vol. XLII (April, 1948) pp. 78–80 (documents section).

requisitioned, however, if military necessity demands it, but must be compensated for. Public property in occupied territory is subject to seizure if it is movable or in the form of funds or securities, but the occupying power has only usufructuary rights to public buildings, forests, real estate, and agricultural works. It should be added that property of local governments and of religious, educational, and charitable institutions, and articles of scientific and historical significance are not to be seized.[40] It remains to be added that except for cartel ships, hospital ships, vessels in nonhostile exploration or scientific work and small private coastal fishing or trading vessels, almost all enemy property on the high seas may be captured. The exceptions are noncontraband enemy goods on neutral ships, and—more as a matter of comity than law—artistic, historic, or scientific collections. The status of neutral property has been discussed at another place in this work.[41]

Nonhostile Relations of Warring States

As expected, most of the relationships of belligerent states are hostile. On the other hand not all relations are necessarily belligerent. Germane to this consideration are certain types of arrangements discussed earlier in this chapter under the general topic of suspension of hostilities. These arrangements assume contacts of one sort or another which keep open—or at least available to be opportunely opened—means of communication. Sometimes these contacts are kept open through the medium of diplomatic personnel of neutral states, but on occasion direct discussions take place between the belligerent envoys accredited to some neutral power. Although no formal state of war existed between Red China and the United States, the relationship since 1949 has often been not unlike a state of war. Negotiations of the last sort mentioned have been held both in Geneva and in Warsaw. Similarly, direct German and Ameri-

---

[40] *Annex to Hague Convention No. IV Respecting the Laws and Customs of War on Land and Annexed Regulations,* The Hague, 1907, 36 U.S., *Statutes* 2256, Arts. 46–56. On this subject, see Greenspan, *op. cit.,* pp. 278–310.

[41] See brief statement in Wilson, *op. cit.,* p. 270; see this work, below, Chapter Ten for treatment of neutral property.

can discussions were carried out during World War I concerning prisoners of war.

Nonhostile contacts in the field also occasionally take place. Sometimes these are initiated through use of a flag of truce, sometimes by naval flag signals, and sometimes by dropping leaflets from planes.[42] Certain specialized types of nonhostile relations are represented in (1) passports, safeguards, and safe conducts, (2) licenses to trade, and (3) agreements known as cartels.

Passports, safeguards, and safe conducts are specialized arrangements which are sometimes allowed between belligerents. *Passports* allow enemy personnel to travel generally in and out of occupied territory. The term *safe conduct* is usually applied to permission of a more restricted character such as a safe conduct for a messenger to go from point A to point B by a designated route. Even more restricted is the so-called *safeguard* which is defined by Hyde as "a form of protection granted by an officer, military or naval, for persons or property within the limits of forces under his command against the operations thereof." It may be given to a person or may be posted on the protected property itself.[43]

Licenses to trade are sometimes granted to neutrals or to personnel of the enemy state. If these are general in scope, they are granted by the head of state, while local licenses are obtained from an officer in the locality. Under these licenses trade may be carried on even through a state of war exists.[44]

Cartels are agreements between belligerents which regulate certain phases of their relations. The term applies particularly to arrangements for the exchange of prisoners, but also pertains to regulating other phases of nonhostile relationships. *Cartel ships* exchange prisoners of war and sometimes official communications.[45]

It need scarcely be reiterated here that arrangements of these kinds are highly dependent upon the exercise of good faith. In

---

[42] Hyde, *op. cit.*, pp. 1773–77; Wilson, *op. cit.*, pp. 294–95.

[43] Hyde, *op. cit.*, p. 1780, Moore, *Digest* VII, pp. 320–21; Greenspan, *op. cit.*, pp. 397–99.

[44] Wilson, *op. cit.*, p. 296.

[45] Hyde, *op. cit.*, p. 1782; Greenspan, *op. cit.*, p. 397.

time of war military needs, high tensions, suspicion, and hatred combine to make nonhostile contacts suspect from the start. It is therefore essential that personnel benefiting or operating under these arrangements perform in a fashion above reproach.

Restoration of Peace

It may be stated merely that a restoration of peace has the effect of ending the multiple legal effects of war, and those appertaining to a state of peace then are resumed. Various specialized terms are used to describe the results of peace following war, but these often serve more to obscure than to elucidate. The doctrine of *postliminium,* for example, suggests that except where occupied territory is absorbed by the victor, restoration of peace has the effect of restoring the *status quo ante bellum* within that territory as far as internal rights are concerned. What this has to do with international law is doubtful. The term *uti possidetis* describes a situation already noted elsewhere in this chapter, in which at the end of war the former belligerents keep what they have in the absence of treaty stipulations. Of more significance than these concepts is the persistent fact that wars usually end by treaties, the terms of which provide for property rights, boundaries, release of prisoners, liability of persons, and other details.[46]

THE RULES OF WARFARE

The rules of warfare consist of those general principles and specific rules governing the conduct of belligerents in battle. These rules have developed over long periods of time and many have been written into treaties, particularly certain of the Hague and Geneva Conventions.[47] The rules of warfare are a

---

[46] For comment on postliminium, see W. E. Hall, *A Treatise on International Law* (5th ed. by J. B. Atlay; Oxford: The Clarendon Press, 1904), pp. 486–95; also this chapter, above, pp. 287–88. Hyde, *op. cit.,* pp. 2419–20; also Wilson, *op. cit.,* pp. 290–91.

[47] See particularly *Hague Convention IV and Annex* previously cited; *Hague Convention No. III Relative to the Opening of Hostilities* (1907, 36 *Statutes* 2259); *Hague Convention No. V Respecting the Rights and Duties of Neutral Powers and Persons in Case of War on Land* (1907, 36 *Statutes* 2310); *Hague Convention No. VI Relative to the Status of Enemy Merchant Ships at the*

paradox. Nations at war are expected to behave according to these rules and this seems at times to be a needless restraint. At the same time, it must be realized that mutual advantages are served and that the rules are therefore based upon a political consensus. The rules regarding prisoners of war, for example, mean, in effect, that side A will take reasonably good care of prisoners of war if side B will reciprocate in kind, and there can be little objection to such an arrangement—indeed, the rule of humanity would seem to demand it. Similarly, other rules merely mitigate some of the potential rigors of war which are not militarily necessary or which fall below a minimum standard of civilized behavior.

The impression should not be left that these rules are always well observed, for they are not. On the other hand, it must be emphasized that the violations of rules are often much better publicized than are the instances of lawful behavior. If, for example, prisoners of war are taken in the desired fashion, no headlines are likely to result—only a back page notice that the son of some local resident is a prisoner of war. On the other hand, if a group of dead soldiers are found with their arms tied behind their backs, a big headline may well result. This kind of problem is compounded by the hatreds and fears that accompany hostilities as well as the further obscuring elements of honest mistakes on the one hand and reprisals on the other.

On another level the laws of war often seem to be well designed for a past war and some of the results may well appear as futile. For example, dumdum bullets are prohibited, but exploding bombs are quite legal. Similarly, it is a crime to poison the enemy's drinking water, but quite permissible to drop a bomb upon him.

Outbreak of Hostilities (1907; I, Scott, *Proceedings* 637)·; *Hague Convention No. X for the Adaptation to Naval War of the Principles of the Geneva Convention* (1907, 36 *Statutes* 2371) ; *Hague Convention No. XI Relating to the Exercise of the Right of Capture in Naval War* (1907, 36 *Statutes* 2396) ; *Hague Convention No. XIII Concerning the Rights and Duties of Neutral Persons in Naval War* (1907, 36 *Statutes*, 2415) ; *Geneva Convention for the Amelioration of the Condition of the Wounded and Sick in Armed Forces in the Field* (1949, *TOIA* Series 3362) ; *Geneva Convention for the Amelioration of the Condition of the Wounded, Sick, and Shipwrecked Members of the Armed Forces at Sea* (1949, *TOIA* Series 3363) ; *The Geneva Convention Relative to the Treatment of Prisoners of War* (1949, *TOIA* Series 3364) ; *The Geneva Convention Relative to the Protection of Civilian Persons in Time of War* (1949, *TOIA* Series 3365) .

The important point, however, is that the rules of warfare are neither a spectacular success nor a miserable failure. They do a pedestrian job of mitigating *some* of the horrors of war. They are in many respects international law at its worst, yet they still serve a useful but restricted purpose.[48]

The sanctions sustaining the laws of warfare may be briefly noted here. That is, in what ways are these rules enforced? At the outset it must be recognized that in many cases enforcement is impossible, but nevertheless, there are devices by which a degree of conformity with the rules can be urged. Some of these are through the good offices of neutral states, by protesting, by reprisals, and by the use of post-hostilities war crimes trials. It is not at all clear how effective these elements are; reprisals may, for example, merely afford an excuse to deviate from the rules where it serves a belligerent's advantage. And again, whether the threat of war crimes trials permeates into the thinking of the line trooper or field commander is at least moot.[49]

It is difficult to avoid the tentative conclusion, however, that a sort of inchoate sense of reciprocity does persist especially where there is a mutual stake in upholding the validity of a rule. Where on one side no quarter is given and no prisoners taken, the other side is likely to reciprocate in kind—and conversely if one's own personnel are to be treated properly when captured, it is only reasonable to assume that the same sort of treatment would need to be accorded the enemy. If this sort of

---

[48] Kunz, *op. cit., passim;* Castrén, *op. cit.,* pp. 3, 5–6 *et passim.* See also H. Kissinger, *op. cit.,* pp. 145–68 for a reasoned basis for limited war.

[49] It would be interesting to know how much attention is given to the rules of warfare in the training programs of armies. Recollections of wartime training and random questioning of veterans and military personnel suggest that the pertinent exposures have at most a minimal effect.

It is important to note that the 1949 Geneva Conventions all contain substantially the same requirement that "The High Contracting Parties undertake, in time of peace as in time of war, to disseminate the text of the present Convention as widely as possible in their respective countries, and, in particular, to include the study thereof in their programmes of military and, if possible, civil instruction, so that the principles thereof may become known to the entire population, in particular to the armed fighting forces, the medical personnel and the chaplains." "Wounded and Sick in Field," Art. 47; "Armed Forces at Sea," Art. 48; "Prisoners of War," Art. 127; "Protection of Civilian Persons," Art. 144; The phraseology of the last two conventions in this regard differs slightly from the other two specifying in particular that authorities entrusted with administering the matters considered in the convention be in possession of a text of the convention.

thing is not a sanction, at least it must be classed as a relatively persuasive influence, and there is evidence that a community of interest does exist in maintaining a certain minimum level of behavior. This, it may be emphasized, is in the nature of a political consensus, but there are other factors as well. For example, an interesting document drawn from the German war records shows a fascinating combination of fear of reprisals, selfish national advantage, expediency, legalistic considerations, and basic honor and decency all combining to induce a government to adhere to its wartime obligations under international law.[50]

The following treatment will consider (1) general principles, (2) categories of persons and their treatment, (3) proscribed practices, (4) the law of occupation, and (5) war crimes trials and other sanctions.

General Principles

Behind the specific rules of warfare are the three general principles of military necessity, humanity, and chivalry. These principles may seem to be contradictory, yet if understood in perspective they cut through much of the minutia of the specific rules and afford them a logical and abstractly understandable basis. These rules have been succinctly indentified in the U.S. Navy's *Law of Naval Warfare* as follows:

a) Military Necessity. The principle of military necessity permits a belligerent to apply only that degree and kind of regulated force, not otherwise prohibited by the laws of war, required for the partial or complete submission of the enemy with the least possible expenditure of time, life, and physical resources.

b) Humanity. The principle of humanity prohibits the employment of any kind or degree of force not necessary for the purpose of the war, i.e., for the partial or complete submission of the enemy with the least possible expenditure of time, life, and physical resources.

---

[50] See McDougal and Feliciano, *op. cit.*, pp. 811–14; see also what McDougal and Feliciano rightly term a "remarkable document," D-606, in *Nazi Conspiracy and Aggression*, Supplement A (Washington, D.C.: U.S. Government Printing Office, 1947), pp. 894–905. See comments in Stone, *op. cit.*, pp. 353–63; also Greenspan, *op. cit.*, pp. 9–11, 403–511.

c) Chivalry. The principle of chivalry forbids the resort to dishonorable (treacherous) means, expedients, or conduct.[51]

That these principles may sometimes be difficult to apply in specific cases or even at times to reconcile with one another should not obscure their general applicability. An attempt will be made to spell these principles out in more detail.

Military Necessity. The term "military necessity" is one which is often obscure. It has been used to describe several rather divergent ideas ranging from the German *kriegsraison* to considerably less extended positions. *Kriegsraison* is a concept by which the needs of the military situation are conceived of as allowing almost any action including the direct violation of rules of warfare. The position has been roundly condemned, and was rejected by the Nuremberg tribunal.[52] This position justifies anything and is therefore utterly incompatible with the idea of rules of warfare.

On the other hand, military necessity as defined in American practice assumes quite a different posture, one which does not contemplate violation of the laws of warfare. The American *Law of Naval Warfare* defines military necessity as noted above, and the general concept has been summarized in the following terms:

Military necessity is an urgent need, admitting of no delay, for the taking by a commander of measures, which are indispensable for forcing as quickly as possible the complete surrender of the enemy by means of regulated violence, and which are not forbidden by the laws and customs of war.[53]

---

[51] This Manual has been reproduced in an appendix to Tucker, *op. cit.*, pp. 357–422; quotation on p. 364. See similar statements in War Department Field Manual 27–10, *Rules of Land Warfare* (Washington, D.C.: U.S. Government Printing Office, 1940), pp. 1–2; Department of the Army Field Manual 27–10, *The Law of Land Warfare* (Washington, D.C.: U.S. Government Printing Office, 1956), pp. 3, 6.

[52] See W. G. Downey, Jr., "The Law of War and Military Necessity," *American Journal of International Law*, Vol. XLVII (April, 1953), pp. 251–54; also Stone, *op. cit.*, pp. 351–53; see also *The Hostage Case, Trials of War Criminals*, Vol. XI (Washington, D.C.: U.S. Government Printing Office, 1950), pp. 1253–56 *et passim*.

[53] Downey, *op. cit.*, p. 254; see also statement in *Law of Land Warfare*, pp. 3–4.

Similarly, Hyde states:

Military necessity, as understood by the United States, justifies resort to all measures which are indispensable to bring about the complete submission of the enemy as soon as possible, by means of regulated violence and which are not forbidden by the modern laws and customs of war.[54]

Conversely it does not allow wanton destruction of life or property, bad faith, or violation of the modern law of war. Accordingly, by way of example, a town of highly strategic importance to a military objective whose commander refused to surrender might conceivably be reduced to rubble with complete justification by the attacking force. To have destroyed the same town, however, after it had fallen as an act of retaliation for the fact that it had held out so long would be excessive. Similarly, 100 civilians killed incident to the taking of a military objective would be regrettable but justifiable, while the wanton killing on one person would be in excess of military necessity.[55]

Humanity. The principle of humanity is often even more difficult to be precise about than is military necessity. Indeed it is a principal mitigating factor already considered above in connection with military necessity. It was defined earlier as prohibiting the "employment of any kind or degree of force not necessary for the purpose of the war. . . ." Thus it may be said that considerations of humanity forbid useless cruelty—not to be confused with necessary deprivation such as withholding supplies from the civilians as well as the soldiers manning a military post. Similarly, it forbids wanton killing as described above. Although the principle is a general one and is widely applicable, it has been spelled out in many of the specific rules of warfare. Among them are the rules prohibiting the killing of prisoners, and the shelling of undefended towns.[56]

---

[54] Hyde, *op. cit.*, p. 1801.

[55] *Ibid.*, pp. 1801–2; Tucker, *op. cit.*, p. 386, fn. 9, 10. For a detailed analysis of the principle of military necessity including its historical background and its various manifestations, see W. V. O'Brien, "The Meaning of 'Military Necessity' in International Law," *World Polity*, Vol. I (1957), pp. 109–76. For a study which seeks to survey military necessity in relation to nuclear conflict, see W. V. O'Brien, "Legitimate Military Necessity in Nuclear War," *World Polity*, Vol. II (1960), pp. 35–120.

[56] *Annex to Hague Convention IV* (1907), Arts. 23, 25; *Geneva Convention on Prisoners of War* (1949), Art. 13.

There has been some debate as to whether a sharp decisive war is not more humane in the long run than one where momentarily more compassionate considerations mitigate. The question is a difficult one because it merges into the matter of new and more efficient weapons. In general it may be conjectured that improvement of weapons is not a consideration in this matter. Accordingly the creation and use of increasingly larger and more effective bombs, including atomic weapons per se, are probably not proscribed by the rule of humanity. Relevant aspects of this matter will be considered later in this chapter.[57]

Chivalry. There are certain restraints on combat which perhaps serve the convenience of both commanders in a conflict. Some of these restraints are closely associated with the most elemental levels of decency and honor. It is therefore asserted as noted above, that "The principle of chivalry forbids the resort to dishonorable (treacherous) means, expedients, or conduct."[58] In general this appears to mean that while many strategems and ruses of war are allowed, procedures which involve manifestly bad faith or treachery are not permissible. This admittedly is a distinction which is not entirely clear, but there are some helpful indices. It is, for example, quite proper to try to make the enemy think your troop concentrations are heavier than they really are by advantageous use of a small garrison; similarly it is acceptable to use feigned attacks, surprises, ambushes, and a variety of other similar devices to mislead the enemy. On the other hand, a blatant lie by a responsible commander in a matter of agreement with his opposite number, or improper use of a flag of truce involve treachery and are violations of the rule of chivalry.[59]

As with the principle of humanity, there are some examples of rules of chivalry or basic decency which have been written into the specific rules of warfare. While these will be considered in detail later on, it may be useful to cite a few of them here. Accordingly, the rules of warfare specifically prohibit killing or

---

[57] See below, especially pp. 315–16.

[58] See above, fn. 51.

[59] See *Law of Land Warfare* (1956), pp. 22–23; also *Rules of Land Warfare* (1940), pp. 10–12; Tucker, *op. cit.*, pp. 138–42; see also Stone, *op. cit.*, p. 337 fn. 10.

wounding persons who have surrendered, making improper use of a flag of truce, and killing or wounding treacherously enemy soldiers or other personnel. Another example may be seen in the special provisions for the protection of persons in occupied territory. For example, "Women shall be especially protected against any attack on their honour, in particular against rape, enforced prostitution, or any form of indecent assault."[60]

Altogether these are not an imposing array, but they do suggest a minimum level of good faith, honor, and decency, and even the most materialistic commander must behave honorably if he expects to benefit from reciprocal treatment.

Categories of Persons and Their Treatment

The laws of war single out various categories of persons and make special reference to how they must behave, and in turn, how they are to be treated. These may be considered as follows: (1) combatants and noncombatants, (2) prisoners of war, (3) the sick, the wounded, and the dead (4) specially protected categories, and (5) spies, war traitors, war rebels, and hostages.

Combatants and Noncombatants. Enemy belligerents fall into two basic classes: noncombatants and combatants. The former are those persons who, in general, cannot or do not participate directly in the hostilities, for example, the older males, most women, the clergy, and children. These people are entitled to a certain immunity from the rigors of war, but they certainly are not altogether immune. Military necessity may require imposing many curbs upon such people, but unnecessary restraint is unwarranted.[61]

The other group, combatants, comprises the persons with whom this section is more closely concerned. It consists of the armies, militia, and volunteer groups, and includes even the so-called *levées en masse* about which more will be said later. In order to be eligible for the protection of the laws of war, it is necessary for combatants:

---

[60] *Annex to Hague Convention IV*, Art. 23; quotation from *Geneva Convention on Protection of Civilian Persons*, Art. 27.

[61] See Moore, *Digest* VII, pp. 172–73; Hall, *op. cit.*, pp. 397–98.

1. To be commanded by a person responsible for his subordinates;
2. To have a fixed distinctive emblem recognizable at a distance;
3. To carry arms openly; and
4. To conduct their operations in accordance with the laws and customs of war.[62]

The term *levée en masse* applies to a spontaneous defense of territory by the population against invading forces. Even though these people may not have had time to organize themselves into appropriately led and uniformed units, they are to be treated as combatants, providing they carry arms openly and conduct themselves in accordance with the laws of war.[63]

Although the above categories would seem to include naval personnel as well, it may nevertheless be useful to point out specifically that sailors and officers on warships, and merchant vessels converted into warships, marines, and land or air troops aboard ships enjoy combatant character. In addition, the crews of enemy merchantmen, particularly those which have engaged in hostilities, would appear to be properly classed as combatants.[64]

Prisoners of War. In centuries past the treatment of captives has varied widely. They were until the middle 1600's ordinarily made slaves, but that practice was largely discontinued following the Peace of Westphalia. By perhaps the 18th century the general rule was emerging that captives should be treated with some concern for humane principles. A U.S.–Prussian agreement of 1785 was probably the first treaty providing for proper treatment, and in the 19th century it became generally recognized that prisoners of war should be treated and maintained on a standard similar to that of the captor's own troops. By 1874 there was sufficient general interest so that a conference

---

[62] *Annex to Hague Convention IV*, Art. 1; See also *Geneva Convention on Prisoners of War* (1949), Art. 4; and other conventions.

[63] *Annex to Hague Convention No. IV*, Art. 2; also *Geneva Convention on Prisoners of War*, Art. 4 (A-6).

[64] See *Hague Convention No. XI*, Arts. 5, 6; *No. X*, Art. 14; *Geneva Convention on Prisoners of War*, Art. 4 (A-5); see also Hackworth, *Digest* VII, pp. 451–52; also Tucker, *op. cit.*, Appendix, p. 399; C. J. Colombos, *The International Law of the Sea* (4th rev. ed.; London: Longmans, Green & Co., Ltd., 1959), pp. 501–02.

was held in Brussels which drew up a convention relative to the treatment of war prisoners. Although it did not go into effect, it was quite influential. Finally the Hague Conventions of 1899 and 1907 included some formal provisions which reflected the law then thought to be in force.[65] In 1929 another somewhat fuller agreement was signed to supplement the Hague articles, and it was hoped that this would compensate for inadequacies noted during World War I. That these arrangements were not entirely satisfactory is attested by the various war crimes trials dealing with treatment of prisoners, but certainly much must be said too by way of praising the treatment accorded prisoners.[66] In 1949 still another agreement was drawn up which is now generally in effect. It may be added that although the convention may not bind nonsignatories, a certain minimum level of treatment is assumed to be binding anyway under the general customary rules of international law.[67]

Circumstances and Personnel. According to the 1949 convention, the circumstances under which the terms of the convention apply are widely inclusive. The convention applies not only in a declared war, but also in an unrecognized war, in occupying territory regardless of whether the invading force meets opposition, and in a war with a belligerent not a party to the agreement, provided that the latter accepts and applies its provisions. A certain level of humanity is even provided for in civil wars.

Personnel entitled to treatment as prisoners of war are: regular armed forces personnel, militia personnel, volunteer corps

---

[65] See W. E. S. Flory, *Prisoners of War* (Washington, D.C.: American Council on Public Affairs, 1942), pp. 7–23; Oppenheim-Lauterpacht, *Treatise* II, p. 368; Fenwick, *op. cit.*, p. 574; for U.S.–Prussian Treaty, see 8 U.S., *Statutes*, 84; *Annex to Hague Convention No. IV*, Arts. 4–20. For some interesting case materials, see Judge Advocate Section, Hq. 3rd Army (S. W. Wurfel and W. G. Downey), "Cases and Materials on the Laws of War and Related Subjects" (mimeographed, 1951), Chapter III.

[66] *Convention Relating to the Treatment of Prisoners of War* (Geneva, 1929), 47 *U.S. Statutes* 2021; see also *High Command Case*, IX *Trials of War Criminals passim;* See also J. L. Kunz, "Treatment of Prisoners of War," *Proceedings of the American Society of International Law* (1953), p. 100.

[67] *Prisoners of War Convention* (1949) Art. 142; For commentary on the 1949 convention see Kunz, *op. cit.*, pp. 99–111. Flory, *op. cit.*, pp. 15–23, 158; see also *The High Command Case* (*U.S. v Von Leeb, et al.*); *Trials of War Criminals. . . .* p. 3 *et passim;* see also lengthy and detailed treatment of the whole area of prisoners of war in Greenspan, *op. cit.*, pp. 95–153.

of a belligerent whether recognized or not, crew and officers of civil aircraft and of the merchant marine, persons who have spontaneously taken up arms to combat an invader, authorized civil persons who accompany the armed forces such as war correspondents or contractors, and under certain circumstances former members of the armed forces of an occupied country, and high civil government personnel.

It may be reiterated that the usual criteria to which military personnel must conform in order to be treated as prisoners of war are that they be responsibly commanded, wear a fixed emblem, carry arms openly, and follow the rules of warfare. Noncombatant categories mentioned above are not required to have met these requirements, nor must more be expected of the persons in spontaneous uprisings (*levée en masse*) than that they carry their "arms openly" and respect "the laws and customs of war."[68]

Treatment of Prisoners of War. The 1949 convention on prisoners of war, even more than earlier arrangements, provides in considerable detail for the humane treatment of prisoners. Without going too greatly into these details, the following generalizations apply: Prisoners of war are considered to be in the custody of the state and not of the army or unit which captures them. They are to be treated humanely and are entitled to the same maintenance as troops of the same rank of the capturing country. Adequate provision is to be made for their health. They may be confined only to the extent necessary to assure their retention and must not be punished except for acts committed after their capture. An unsuccessful attempt to escape is grounds only for disciplinary punishment, although personnel of the detaining power are authorized to use force to prevent escape, and it is presumed that a person could be justifiably shot while in the act of attempting an escape. In the event that a prisoner's home country allows the practice, he may promise not to try to escape and may then be given partial or complete freedom. This is known as *parole,* and a person making such a promise is honor bound to keep his promise.

---

[68] *Prisoners of War Convention* (1949), Arts. 2, 3, 4; *Law of Land Warfare* (1956), pp. 25–28. *Rules of Land Warfare* (1940), pp. 16–18; Tucker, *op. cit.,* pp. 111–16.

Although the 1949 convention does not specify punishment in this matter, the 1907 Hague Convention states that a parolee who is subsequently captured bearing arms forfeits his right to treatment as a prisoner of war.

Prisoners are not to be forced to do degrading work, but enlisted personnel may be required to do work which does not directly aid the capturing country's war effort, and officers may volunteer for suitable work. Prisoners of war are not only entitled to regular pay commensurate with their rank, but also for work performed. Prisoner personnel may be required to give information only to the extent of telling their names, date of birth, serial numbers, and rank. They are to be allowed periodically to communicate with their relatives, and agents of a "protecting power" and the Committee of the Red Cross are to be permitted to visit all such personnel. Further clauses provide for health, spiritual matters, segregation of the sexes, and a number of other considerations.[69]

Punishment of Prisoners of War. Prisoner of war status in general is not penal, but it is obvious that discipline can be enforced. Also, disciplinary measures may be imposed upon prisoners who try to escape but fail, though if escape is made good but the former prisoner becomes a prisoner of war on a later occasion, no punishment for the former escape may be

---

[69] *Prisoners of War Convention* (1949), particularly Arts. 12, 13, 15, 17, 21, 25, 29, 30, 34, 42, 49–57, 60, 62, 70, 71, 78, 92, 93, 126, *et passim;* see *Annex to Hague Convention IV*, Arts. 4–20; for discussion of parole see Flory, *op. cit.*, pp. 116–31. For a discussion of the use of prisoners of war for labor purposes, see H. S. Levie, "The Employment of Prisoners of War," *American Journal of International Law,* Vol. LVII (April, 1963), pp. 318–53. Regarding the development of standards of treatment and related matters, see Levie, "Penal Sanctions for Maltreatment of Prisoners of War," *American Journal of International Law,* Vol. LVI (April, 1962), pp. 433–68.

Throughout the Vietnamese conflict there has been much dispute as to the procedures for treatment of prisoners of war. In mid-1966 the North Vietnamese put captured U.S. pilots on display and it was reported that they might be tried for war crimes. After protest and adverse reaction, humane treatment was assured. The Red Cross leveled charges of mistreatment against both North and South Vietnam as well as against the National Liberation Front. The early practice by the United States of turning its prisoners over to the Republic of Vietnam was also the subject of criticism. See numerous newspaper accounts, e.g., *St. Louis Post Dispatch,* July 28, 1966, p. 6B; July 8, 1966, p. 8B; July 29, 1966, p. 8A; August 31, 1966, p. 6C; March 14, 1967, p. 8A. See article by Richard Dudman, "Nüernberg Trials No Basis for Hanoi Action on Flyers," *St. Louis Post Dispatch,* July 24, 1966, pp. 1C, 3C.

meted out. In general a prisoner is subject to the same rules applicable in the armed forces of the detaining power. Categories of punishment are (1) disciplinary and (2) judicial.[70] The former are relatively mild and are proscribed as follows:

1. A fine which shall not exceed 50 per cent of the advances of pay and working pay which the prisoner of war would otherwise receive under the provisions of Articles 60 and 62 during a period of not more than thirty days.
2. Discontinuance of privileges granted over and above the treatment provided for by the present Convention.
3. Fatigue duties not exceeding two hours daily.
4. Confinement.
   The punishment referred to under (3) shall not be applied to officers.
   In no case shall displinary punishments be inhuman, brutal or dangerous to the health of prisoners of war.[71]

In more serious offenses judicial proceedings are provided for and punishment may include capital punishment, except that the execution may not be carried out until six months after the protecting power has been informed of the details. Procedures are provided for to assure a fair trial and "No Prisoners of war may be tried or sentenced for an act which is not forbidden by the law of the Detaining Power or by international law, in force at the time the said act was committed." The convention also provides many other guarantees to prevent abuse.[72]

Repatriation. Prisoners of war are to be repatriated "without delay after the cessation of active hostilities," and special provisions provide for early repatriation of prisoners whose health is precarious.[73] The issue of repatriation has been a controversial one for a number of reasons, and in fact does present some practical difficulties. The Soviet Union made little or no attempt to repatriate prisoners of war after World War II, taking the position that it was not a party to any of the prisoner of war agreements. The inhumanity of such a position

---

[70] See generally *Prisoners of War Convention* (1949), Arts. 82–108.
[71] *Ibid.*, Art. 89.
[72] *Ibid.*, Arts. 99–108, quotation in Art. 99, also *passim.*
[73] *Ibid.*, Art. 109–19.

leaves the impression that not even a semblance of good faith
was employed, for it may be conjectured that a customary rule
of international law requires reasonably prompt repatriation.[74]

Of a more complex character is the problem presented at the
end of the Korean War. The United Nations command was
clearly bound by the obligation to repatriate the prisoners of
war. Yet many had specifically asked not to be turned back
because they feared for their lives. There is no very satisfactory
answer to this problem, but considerations of humanity coupled with past practices relative to asylum may afford some sort
of solution in future situations of this sort. It has been suggested that guides in the form of the Korean solution may be
the most fruitful. This has been summarized as follows:

Its essential principles are four. First, "screening" (that is, the
registration of prisoners' objections to repatriation) should be
under the control of neither belligerent, but of a neutral authority.
Second, before the prisoners' choice is regarded as final they should
be taken out of the control of the belligerent captors into that of a
neutral authority. Third, a sufficient interval should be allowed to
permit the state whose personnel are involved to give explanations,
and information and assurances to them, before final choice. Access
should be allowed to that state's representatives for this purpose,
but in the presence of the neutral authority and of the opponent.
Fourth, prisoners who finally refuse to return home should be
released as soon as States willing to admit them for permanent
residence can be found.[75]

Inspection and Supervision. It is exceedingly difficult to
develop absolutely surefire procedures, but every reasonable
attempt has been made to give adequate protection to prisoners
of war. By way of inspection, the "protecting power," that is,
the neutral power which takes over the obligation to watch the
affairs of a certain belligerent, may visit prisoners of war at any
time. Similarly the International Commission of the Red Cross
has the same rights. Normally such personnel may visit prisoners of war at any time and with no restrictions on the frequency
of the visits. The only qualification is that "Visits may not be

---

[74] See Flory, *op. cit.*, pp. 135–37.

[75] Stone, *op. cit.*, pp. 664–65. See also J. Mayda, "The Korean Repatriation
Problem and International Law," *American Journal of International Law*, Vol.
XLVII (July, 1953), pp. 414–38.

prohibited except for reasons of imperative military necessity, and then only as an exceptional and temporary measure."

Relative to the exchange of information on prisoners of war, it may be mentioned that each belligerent must establish a special prisoner of war bureau, and a central prisoner of war information bureau is to be created—*ad hoc* for each conflict—in a neutral power. Through these mechanisms information on prisoners of war is exchanged among belligerents and internal supervision is effected.[76]

The Sick, the Wounded, and the Dead. It is not clear whether rules for the protection of the sick and wounded were at all well established as a matter of strict law prior to the establishment of conventions. In any event whether due to law or merely to humanitarian instincts, some attention was given to the matter.[77] In the Union regulations during the Civil War, for example, protection was given to wounded enemy personnel and to enemy medical personnel. Also, enemy wounded were to be given medical attention if possible. At the Geneva Conference of 1864 the first treaty governing the matter was adopted and four years later additional articles were drawn up which considered the problem in relation to sea warfare. These articles did not become effective, but in 1907 a naval warfare agreement was enacted which purported to adapt to naval conditions the rules of the Geneva Convention for Amelioration of the Condition of the Sick and Wounded on Land. Finally, at the Geneva Conference of 1949 two agreements were adopted dealing with the matter of sick, wounded, and related personnel in land warfare and in sea warfare.[78]

The conventions provide for many details which cannot usefully be noted here, but the general principles can be surveyed briefly. In general, states are to give medical treatment and humane care to sick and wounded enemy personnel who are

---

[76] *Geneva Convention on Prisoners of War*, Arts. 8, 122–32, quotation in Art. 126.

[77] Hyde, *op. cit.*, p. 1867; Fenwick, *op. cit.*, p. 576.

[78] "Instructions for the Government of Armies of the United States in the Field, War Department General Order 100," (1863) ; see in Wilson, *op. cit.*, pp. vi–xxxvi, Arts. 53, 71, 79; *Convention for the Amelioration of the Condition of the Wounded in the Field* (Geneva, 1864) ; see in Moore, *Digest* VII, pp. 235–61; see also pp. 372–78; *Hague Convention No. X;* Geneva conventions (1949) on wounded and sick on land and sea (see fn. 47) .

their prisoners of war. Enemy medical personnel are not to be made prisoners of war, but if retained are to be used in caring for enemy wounded. Personnel of private relief societies such as the Red Cross are also protected. Hospital areas are not to be bombed or otherwise attacked. Similarly, injured, sick, or ship-wrecked naval personnel are to be treated humanely and are to be sought out if possible after a battle.

As with hospital areas, hospital ships are protected, provided they conform to certain rules. They must have been announced 10 days prior to their use and they must be properly marked. Similar protection is accorded to medical aircraft and to ships used exclusively to transport medical supplies.

In order to indicate clearly the character of medical person-nel and facilities, provision is made for painting hospital ships and hospital areas in a particular fashion and for the wearing of distinctive armbands by medical personnel. The red cross on a white field is the usual symbol, but the red crescent or red lion and sun on a white field are also proper. States are also to notify the enemy through the proper channels mentioned above, of the wounded, the sick, and the dead.[79]

With reference to the dead, every state is to try to make proper identification and investigation of the bodies, and to bury them individually if possible. On land they are to be buried with records kept of individual graves and, if possible, with the rites of their religion. The dead are not to be despoiled or pillaged. Notification is to be made to the home country.[80]

Other Specially Protected Categories. Two categories of es-pecially protected personnel are medical personnel, as noted above, and chaplains. Such persons normally are not supposed to be equipped for combat, and are not to be considered as prisoners of war. They may be detained to minister to the needs of prisoners of war, however, and "as a minimum" under such circumstances, they are to receive "the benefits and protec-tion" of the prisoner of war convention.

It should be mentioned that women members of the armed forces are also specially protected to the extent that they, as

---

[79] *Geneva Convention on Wounded on Land,* 1949, Arts. 12, 19, 20, 24, 26, 28, 33–44, *et passim; Geneva Convention on Wounded at Sea,* 1949, Arts. 12, 22–45, *et passim.*

[80] *Ibid.* (Land), Arts. 15, 17; *Ibid.* (Sea), Arts. 18, 20.

prisoners of war and in other ways, are to be "treated with all consideration due their sex."[81]

Spies, War Traitors, War Rebels, and Hostages. There are several special categories of persons whose activities or utility are such that they are singled out for relatively severe treatment. In many cases this must be considered as justifiable, but of hostages nothing more can be said except that the entire process is at best abominable, if ever defensible at all.

Spies. Spies are persons who act "clandestinely, or on false pretenses" to obtain or to seek to obtain information within a belligerent area of operations for use by the opposing belligerent. Spying is not a perfidious activity and therefore not in itself a crime or a disgrace. A spy who is caught may, after trial and conviction, be severely punished not because spying is illegal but rather to render the process dangerous and difficult. If, however, a person is able to rejoin his own army after serving as a spy, but is subsequently captured, he may not be punished for his earlier acts of spying.[82] American practice as reflected in the articles of war is as follows:

Any person who in time of war shall be found lurking or acting as a spy in or about any of the fortifications, posts, quarters or encampments of any of the armies of the United States, or elsewhere, shall be tried by a general court martial or by a military commission, and shall, on conviction thereof, suffer death.[83]

War Treason. War treason is a term applied to certain acts of persons in occupied territory which seriously compromise their protected status. The people in an occupied area must in general obey the law established by the occupying power. Accordingly, punishment may be meted out to those who sabotage its position and even the death penalty is appropriate where the occupying army's positions are endangered.[84] American practice is reflected in the following statement:

War Treason. Examples of acts which, when committed by inhabitants of territory under hostile military occupation, are pun-

---

[81] *Ibid.* (Land), Arts. 12, 21, 24. *Ibid.* (Sea), Arts. 36, 37; *Prisoners of War Convention,* 1949, Art. 33.

[82] *Annex to Hague Convention IV,* Arts. 29, 30, 31; see Hackworth, *Digest* VI, pp. 304–8; Rules of Land Warfare, pp. 58–59; Hyde, *op. cit.,* pp. 1862–65.

[83] Cited in Hackworth, *Digest* VI, p. 305.

[84] See Fenwick, *op. cit.,* pp. 573–74; Hackworth, *Digest* VI, pp. 308–9.

ishable by the occupying belligerent as treasonable under laws of war, are as follows: Espionage; supplying information to the enemy; damage to railways, war material, telegraphs or other means of communication; aiding prisoners of war to escape; conspiracy against the occupying forces or members thereof; intentional misleading of troops while acting as guides; voluntary assistance to the enemy by giving money or acting as guides; inducing soldiers of the occupying forces to act as spies for the enemy, to desert, or to surrender; bribing soldiers in the interest of the enemy; damage or alteration to military notices and signposts in the interest of the enemy; fouling sources of water supply and concealing animals, vehicles, supplies, and fuel in the interest of the enemy; knowingly aiding the advance or retirement of the enemy; and circulating propaganda in the interest of the enemy.[85]

War Rebels. War rebels are persons who, in an occupied area, take up arms against the occupying forces or against the authorized government. Such persons may be punished, and American practice authorizes, but apparently does not require, the death penalty.[86]

Hostages. In times past it has been permissible for an army to take members of the civilian population and hold them as hostages for the general pacific and lawful behavior of the occupied population. American rules of warfare subscribed to this practice and allowed punishment including putting to death of such persons if unlawful behavior continued.[87] There is now much evidence to suggest that the practice is proscribed. This is the opinion of Lauterpacht and is hinted in certain war crimes trials. On the other hand the *List case* gives rise to the contrary or traditional view. The practice of taking hostages, whatever its former legal status, is an abhorrent one, and the Geneva Convention of 1949 now flatly states that "the taking of hostages is prohibited."[88]

---

[85] Hackworth, *Digest* VI, p. 308.

[86] *Ibid.*, p. 309.

[87] Hyde, *op. cit.*, pp. 1902–3.

[88] Oppenheim-Lauterpacht, *Treatise* II, pp. 589–92; *Geneva Convention on Protection of Civilians*, Art. 34. See *The High Command Case, Trials of War Criminals*, Vol. IX, pp. 528–29. For a direct consideration of hostage matters, see *The Hostage Case, Trials of War Criminals*, Vol. XI, pp. 1248–54 *et passim;* see also, Greenspan, *op. cit.*, pp. 413–17.

Proscribed Practices

Aside from the treatment of particular categories of persons, the law of nations provides a number of rules which limit the employment of certain devices and techniques. These matters will be considered in connection with (1) land warfare, (2) nuclear weapons, (3) warfare at sea, and (4) warfare in the air and space.

Warfare on Land. An accurate statement of prohibited techniques is difficult to establish. While the Hague Convention specifies that "the right of belligerents to adopt means of injuring the enemy is not unlimited" and then proceeds to list proscribed techniques,[89] practice seems to suggest that the limitations are in reality not very great. Nor are many of them really very meaningful in a broad context. For example, commentary on small incendiary and expanding bullets as being cruel out of proportion to military utility—a reasonable and humanitarian position in itself to be sure—is not particularly impressive when seen in comparison with flame throwers, explosive artillery, antiaircraft shells, blockbuster bombs, guided missles, and atomic bombs. In general it may be said that a few restraining rules exist, but that these have very little effect on the increasing ability of belligerents to destroy each other.

In brief the principal land warfare convention states the rules as follows:

In addition to the prohibitions provided by special Conventions, it is especially prohibited:

  a) To employ poison or poisoned weapons;
  b) To kill or wound treacherously individuals belonging to the hostile nation or army;
  c) To kill or wound an enemy who, having laid down arms, or having no longer means of defense, has surrendered at discretion;
  d) To declare that no quarter will be given;
  e) To employ arms, projectiles, or material of a nature to cause unnecessary suffering;
  f) To make improper use of a flag of truce, the national flag,

---

[89] *Annex to Hague Convention IV*, Arts. 22–28. See detailed discussion of "Methods and Instruments of Warfare," in Greenspan, *op. cit.*, pp. 313–77.

or of the military insignia and uniform of the enemy, as well
as the distinctive badges of the Geneva Convention;

g) To destroy or seize the enemy's property, unless such destruction or seizure be imperatively demanded by the necessities
of war;

h) To declare abolished, suspended, or inadmissible in a court
of law the rights and actions of the nationals of the hostile
party.

A belligerent is likewise forbidden to compel the nationals of the
hostile party to take part in the operations of war directed against
their own country, even if they were in the belligerent's service
before the commencement of the war.

.   .   .   .

Article 25.   The attack or bombardment, by whatever means, of
towns, villages, dwellings, buildings which are undefended is prohibited.

Article 26.   The officer in command of an attacking force must
before commencing a bombardment, except in cases of assault, do
all in his power to warn the authorities.

Article 27.   In sieges and bombardments all necessary steps must
be taken to spare, as far as possible, buildings dedicated to religion,
art, science, or charitable purposes, historic monuments, hospitals,
the places where the sick and wounded are collected, provided they
are not being used at the same time for military purposes.

It is the duty of the besieged to indicate the presence of such
buildings or places by distinctive and visible signs, which shall be
notified to the enemy beforehand.

Article 28.   The pillage of a town or place, even when taken by
assault, is prohibited.[90]

Special conventions outlaw the use of incendiary bullets over
400 grams, dumdum bullets, asphyxiating gases, and biological
warfare.[91] It may be added further that there is some belief that
techniques such as destroying the productivity of land are pro-

---

[90] *Ibid.*, Arts. 23, 25, 26, 27, 28.

[91] *Declaration Renouncing the Use, in Time of War, of Exploding Projectiles
under 400 Grammes Weight* (St. Petersburg, 1868), see in *British Sessional
Papers,* House of Commons, 1868–69, Vol. LXIV, pp. 659–64; *Hague Declaration
Concerning Expanding Bullets* (1899); see L. Pfankuchen, *A Documentary
Textbook of International Law* (New York: Rinehart & Co., Inc., 1940), pp.
768–69; *Protocol for the Prohibition of the Use in War of Asphyxiating
Poisonous and Other Gases, and of Bacteriological Methods of Warfare* (1925),
see in Pfankuchen, *op. cit.,* pp. 769–71. Note that the United States is not bound
by any of these accords per se, but a good case can be made for the view that
these rules are binding in custom as well as by convention.

scribed by the customary rules stemming from the principle of humanity.[92]

Nuclear Weapons. The further question of whether nuclear weapons are or are not legally proscribed must also be considered. It has been argued by some commentators that their enormity and indiscriminate ability to destroy, place such weapons outside the bounds of legitimacy.[93] Others have found these devices to remain within the bounds of legality.[94] Contentions of illegality have in times past, however, been directed against many weapon innovations. Nevertheless, the judgment of the powers as to whether such force is necessary in battle rather than representing superfluous destruction is a subjective consideration upon which legality hinges. Moreover, the fact that the nations have argued indecisively over whether a convention outlawing the bomb should be drawn up further underscores this view. As a practical matter it may be conjectured that decisions as to the use of nuclear weapons in wartime will be based on military considerations, retaliatory prospects, and related circumstances to a greater extent than upon legal disputation. However that may be, it is useful to consider other evidence which can be focused upon this problem. In doing so, it appears that there are at least two considerations of legal significance. These can be categorized as (1) the proportionality of nuclear response, and (2) initiation of nuclear holocaust.

Proportionality of Nuclear Response. As noted above, it is difficult to see the concept of nuclear response completely outside of the context of the improvement of weaponry.[95] Accord-

---

[92] Hyde, *op. cit.*, pp. 1806–9.

[93] Greenspan, *op. cit.*, pp. 368–77; Castrén, *op. cit.*, pp. 204–7. E. Margolis, "The Hydrogen Bomb Experiments and International Law," *The Yale Law Journal,* Vol. LXIV (April, 1955), pp. 629–47.

[94] G. Schwarzenberger, *The Legality of Nuclear Weapons* (London: Stevens & Sons Ltd., 1958), *passim;* Tucker, *op. cit.*, pp. 54–55. Oppenheim-Lauterpacht, *Treatise* II, pp. 350–52. See, moreover, *Law of Land Warfare,* p. 18 where use of atomic weapons is viewed as not being "violative of international law in the absence of any customary rule . . . or . . . convention." See also discussion in Stone, *op. cit.*, pp. 342–48; also M. S. McDougal and N. A. Schlei, "The Hydrogen Bomb Tests in Perspective, Lawful Measures for Security," in M. S. McDougal and Associates, *Studies in World Public Order* (New Haven, Conn.: Yale University Press, 1960), pp. 763–843.

[95] See comments in R. R. Baxter, "The Role of Law in Modern War," *Proceedings of the American Society of International Law* (1953), pp. 91–92 *et passim.*

ingly, if nuclear power is used to propel a better tank engine it seems doubtful that a serious critic would find it an improper implement of war. Suppose, however, that the nuclear power is involved in a tactical explosive which in a limited physical battlefield setting is significantly more effective against a legitimate military target than are other weapons which, nevertheless are concerned with the same tactical problem. Is such a device to be categorized as illegal per se or ought it be considered in some other framework? It should be noted that except where a specific device has been outlawed, it has been the general rule that the way in which a weapon is applied, not the weapon itself, is the phenomenon regulated by law. At this juncture, therefore, it must be assumed that the legality of nuclear devices in war is essentially a matter of proportion, and relativity of the specific application.[96] As a field weapon it must be in proportion to the legitimate objective sought. As a reprisal it must be in proportion to the action which it seeks to punish.[97] For reasons to be noted below, it is becoming apparent that legitimate use of all out nuclear bombardment could be justified, if at all, only as a reprisal for a comparable nuclear attack or, at least in theory, an action of equal intensity and horror, an example of which is hard to imagine.[98]

Initiation of Nuclear Holocaust. Growing awareness of what is involved in full-scale nuclear war has increased the general aversion to it. Initiating the use of major nuclear weapons[99] appears in this context to be outside the range of any imaginable measure of proportionality. If this is correct, it must then be concluded that this level of nuclear application is illegal. If law develops by the arrival at significant levels of consensus as well as by other means,[100] it then follows that certain other developments need to be noted. These develop-

---

[96] See discussion of this problem in O'Brien, *op cit.* (1960), pp. 35–120.

[97] See discussion of reprisals, above, Chapter Eight.

[98] The potentialities of bacteriological warfare as sometimes described offer an example which might be thought comparable.

[99] The use of the term "major nuclear weapons" in the text suggests the use of relatively large bombs used particularly in population centers. The term is in contrast with the concept of tactical field weapons used against military objectives.

[100] See discussion, below, Chapter Eleven.

ments are not in themselves conclusive, but altogether they constitute the sort of setting which at most might indicate a particular legal conclusion, or, which may at least point to an emerging conclusion, *de lege ferenda.*

In 1961 the General Assembly of the United Nations adopted a resolution taking the position that the use of nuclear and thermonuclear weapons would violate the United Nations Charter and the laws of humanity because, seemingly, such weapons are "directed not against an enemy or enemies alone but also against mankind in general."[101] Here both an all-out response and a lack of proportionality are taken for granted. The legal significance of this resolution was nullified however, by the 20 votes registered against it.[102]

In 1963 the "Test Ban Treaty" was signed.[103] This agreement, initially among the United States, the U.S.S.R., and Great Britain, outlawed the testing of nuclear devices in space or under the high seas. In addition, while it allows continued testing and explosions in national territory, such activities must not result in any contamination outside that territory. In itself this treaty clearly does not outlaw nuclear war,[104] but it does show growing concern of a highly specialized sort.

Also in 1963 the District Court of Tokyo handed down a decision in the so-called *Shimoda* case in which it found that the atomic bombing of Hiroshima and Nagasaki was contrary to the law of nations.[105] The Court's conclusion seems to be based upon two considerations: (1) as essentially undefended

---

[101] "Declaration on the Prohibition of the Use of Nuclear and Thermonuclear Weapons," *Resolutions Adopted by the General Assembly during its Sixteenth Session*, Vol. I. General Assembly, *Official Records:* 16th Session, Supplement No. 17 (A/5100), pp. 4–5. See also "The Urgent Need for a Treaty to Ban Nuclear Weapons Tests under Effective International Control," *ibid.*, p. 4.

[102] See E. Schwelb, "The Nuclear Test Ban Treaty and International Law," *American Journal of International Law*, Vol. LVIII (July, 1964), pp. 645–46.

[103] "Treaty Banning Nuclear Weapon Tests in the Atmosphere, in Outer Space and Under Water," *American Journal of International Law*, Vol. LVII (October, 1963), pp. 1026–28.

[104] Schwelb, *op. cit.*, pp. 643–45.

[105] See English translation in *The Japanese Annual of International Law for 1964*, pp. 212–52. See digest in *American Journal of International Law*, Vol. LVIII (October, 1964), p. 1016. For a detailed discussion of this interesting case, see R. A. Falk, "The Shimoda Case: A Legal Appraisal of the Atomic Attacks upon Hiroshima and Nagasaki," *American Journal of International Law*, Vol. LIX (October, 1965), pp. 759–93.

cities having only slight military significance, indiscriminate or area bombardment (as contrasted with precision bombing) was not legally proper. Atomic bombing (of the sort used against Japan) was by its nature of indiscriminate character. (2) International law prohibits the use of devices which are excessively cruel and which cause unnecessary suffering. Since the Court felt that these qualities are characteristic of the atomic bomb, it considered its use to be illegal.[106] Nevertheless, the primary consideration was whether the atomic bombing of Japan was proper, not whether nuclear weapons per se were legally interdicted. Nor does it appear that the reprisal factor was considered by the Court.

Finally, in early 1967 an international agreement was signed which bans virtually all use of nuclear arms in space,[107] and there is also a regional accord which seeks to bar the use of nuclear weapons in a large zone of the western hemisphere, especially in Latin America.[108]

In these contexts therefore, it appears that certain tentative conclusions are appropriate. In judging the legality of the use of nuclear devices of limited and tactical character, the key question is that of proportionality. When considered in the context of reprisals, the question of proportionality is again of first concern. The responsibility to third parties for damages resulting from any nuclear explosion seems clear. Finally, it is difficult to imagine circumstances which would legally justify the initial use of major nuclear devices in modern war.

Warfare at Sea.   The rules limiting the scope of action in sea warfare are not perhaps as definite as those pertaining to land warfare. There are nevertheless some well-defined rules in that sphere as well.

Legitimate *warships* are in general those properly commissioned and officered and staffed by naval personnel. These may

---

[106] Falk, *op. cit.*, p. 776.

[107] "Treaty on Principles Governing the Activities of States in the Exploration and Use of Outer Space, Including the Moon and Other Celestial Bodies," *American Journal of International Law*, Vol. LXI (April, 1967), pp. 644–49, especially Art. IV, p. 645.

[108] *St. Louis Post-Dispatch*, February 16, 1967, p. 22A. "United Nations: Treaty for the Prohibition of Nuclear Weapons in Latin America," *International Legal Materials*, Vol. VI (May–June, 1967), pp. 521–34.

include properly converted merchant ships, but not privateers which were abolished by the Declaration of Paris and by general adherence to its principles by other powers. The circumstances attending the proper conversion of merchant ships are as follows: the ship must be "under the direct authority, immediate control, and responsibility of the Power whose flag it flies," it must "bear the external marks which distinguish the war-ships of their nationality," it must be "commanded by a commissioned man on the list of the officers of the fighting fleet," "the crew must be subject to military discipline," the ship must follow the laws and customs of war, and it must have been announced in the list of warships.[109]

A category of ship which has been particularly controversial is the submarine. Its controversial character stemmed from the improbability that it could conform to some of the other procedures required by international law. At the present writing it is probably correct to state that in general these underwater craft are supposed to conform to the general rules of international law as though they were surface ships. Nevertheless, there are important ambiguities. Accordingly, the Submarine Rules of 1936 state:

1. In their action with regard to merchant ships, submarines must conform to the rules of international law to which surface vessels are subject.

2. In particular, except in the case of persistent refusal to stop on being duly summoned, or of active resistance to visit or search, a warship, whether surface vessel or submarine, may not sink or render incapable of navigation a merchant vessel without having first placed passengers, crew and ships papers in a place of safety. For this purpose the ship's boats are not regarded as a place of safety unless the safety of the passengers and crew is assured in the existing sea and weather conditions, by the proximity of land, or the presence of another vessel which is in a position to take them on board.[110]

---

[109] *Declaration of Paris,* see conveniently with comment in Pfankuchen, *op. cit.,* pp. 890–93; also Moore, *Digest* VII, pp. 535–43; *Hague Convention VII Relating to the Conversion of Merchant Ships to War Ships.* The U.S. is a formal signatory of neither accord; see Tucker, *op. cit.,* pp. 40–41.

[110] "Procès-Verbal Relating to the Rules of Submarine Warfare" (1936), *American Journal of International Law,* Vol. XXXI (July, 1937), pp. 137–38 (documents section).

The difficulty remains, however, that if a submarine is to be effective it may be impossible for it to do such things as searching for survivors when the submarine's own security is jeopardized, and it appears, accordingly, that the rules specified above have often been disregarded.[111] Moreover, in the cases of Grand-admirals Dönitz and Raeder, the Nuremberg Tribunal recognized that the deviation from the letter of the law had been general, and did not see fit to apply it. The Court said "In the actual circumstances of this case, the Tribunal is not prepared to hold Dönitz guilty for his conduct of submarine warfare against British armed merchant ships." Later in the judgment, however the Tribunal indicated that it felt that Dönitz' violation of the Protocol of 1936 had been established, but due to British and American deviations, "the sentence of Dönitz is not assessed on the ground of his breaches of the international law of submarine warfare."[112]

Specially proscribed techniques in naval warfare include the use of certain types of weapons and the employment of bombardment under certain circumstances. With reference to weapons, specifically mines and torpedos, the Hague Convention (VIII) makes the following stipulations which are the only specific conventional rules on the subject:

Article 1. It is forbidden:
1. To lay unanchored automatic contact mines, except when they are so constructed as to become harmless one hour at most after the person who laid them ceases to control them;
2. To lay anchored automatic contact mines which do not become harmless as soon as they have broken loose from their moorings;
3. To use torpedoes which do not become harmless when they have missed their mark.

Article 2. It is forbidden to lay automatic contact mines off the

---

[111] Tucker, *op. cit.*, pp. 72–73, 333; see also discussions in Colombos, *op. cit.*, pp. 443–48; Oppenheim-Lauterpacht, *Treatise* II, pp. 489–93; see also pertinent remarks in "International Military Tribunal (Nuremberg) Judgment and Sentences," *American Journal of International Law*, Vol. XLI (January, 1947), pp. 303–6; see also comment in Castrén, *op. cit.*, pp. 282–89.

[112] *Trial of the Major War Criminals before the International Military Tribunal* (Nürnberg: International Military Tribunal, 1948), Vol. XXII, pp. 557–62 quotations, at pp. 558 and 559. See also Vol. XIV, p. 196 ff. and Vol. XIII, pp. 247–95, 351–91.

coast and ports of the enemy, with the sole object of intercepting commercial shipping.

Article 3. When anchored automatic contact mines are employed, every possible precaution must be taken for the security of peaceful shipping.

The belligerents undertake to do their utmost to render these mines harmless within a limited time, and, should they cease to be under surveillance, to notify the danger zones as soon as military exigencies permit, by a notice addressed to ship owners, which must also be communicated to the Governments through the diplomatic channel.[113]

It is generally presumed that many of the more general rules such as those limiting the use of poison gas, bacteriological warfare, dishonorable devices, denial of quarter, and so forth also apply to naval warfare.[114]

Bombardment is limited by the terms of the Ninth Hague Convention of 1907. In abbreviated form it specifies that undefended places are not to be bombarded, that religious, artistic, scientific, and charitable properties, historic monuments, and hospitals should be spared, and if possible a commander should warn the authorities of a place before bombarding it. The people should mark such places with "large, stiff rectangular panels divided diagonally into two colored triangular portions, the upper portion black, the lower portion white." Finally, pillage is forbidden.[115]

Blockade will be discussed in the chapter on neutrality. Here it may be merely noted that blockade is a procedure used to keep vessels from entering or leaving a particular enemy port or area. A blockade should be made known to all states and, in order to be legal, it must be effective to the extent that an attempt to run it presents real danger.[116]

Stratagems or *ruses* in naval warfare as in land warfare are legal so long as they do not partake of treachery or perfidy.

---

[113] *Hague Convention VIII Relative to the Laying of Automatic Submarine Contact Mines,* 36 *U.S. Statutes* 2332, Arts. 1, 2, 3; also in Tucker, *op. cit.,* p. 409.

[114] Tucker, *op. cit.,* pp. 409–10, and 422, fns. 42 and 43.

[115] *Hague Convention IX Concerning Bombardment by Naval Forces,* quotation in Art. 5.

[116] See discussion below Chapter Ten; see U.S. Naval law statement in Tucker, *op. cit.,* pp. 412–14.

Perhaps the most important device properly imployed as a ruse
in naval warfare is the use of false colors. The only qualifications are that the ship show its true colors before going into
combat, and, of course, that improper use of such symbols as
the red cross and the flag of truce is forbidden. Improper use of
a flag of truce, it would appear, always involves perfidy.[117]

Air and Space Warfare. There is very little specific mention
of aircraft in the wartime conventions on international law.
The Geneva Conventions pertaining to the sick and wounded
provide for the marking and use of medical craft; the Fourth
Hague Convention prohibits "The attack or bombardment, *by
whatever means,* of towns, villages, dwellings, or buildings
which are undefended," and finally there is the anachronistic
Fourteenth Hague Convention by which "The Contracting
Powers agree to prohibit, for a period extending to the close of
the Third Peace Conference, the discharge of projectiles and
explosives from balloons or by other new methods of a similar
nature." It is unlikely that this last accord, to which 28 states
are parties, would be invoked. It is at least theoretically possible, however, that it might be invoked should war occur between two of the ratifying powers, if neither were joined by a
nonsignatory power.[118]

In 1922 a group of air warfare rules were drawn up by a
commission of jurists. The document was never ratified, but
seems to suggest, along with other indications that in general
and where applicable the other rules of warfare apply to aircraft. It may be noted as an exception to this generalization

---

[117] See Tucker, *op. cit.,* p. 414, also fns. 42–44 on p. 422; Colombos, *op. cit.,*
pp. 432–34.

[118] *Geneva Convention for Wounded in the Field* (1949), Arts. 36, 37; *Geneva
Convention for Wounded at Sea* (1949), Arts. 39, 40; *Annex to Hague
Convention IV,* Art. 25 (italics supplied; the expression "by whatever means"
includes aircraft). *Hague Declaration XIV Prohibiting the Discharge of Projectiles and Explosives from Balloons,* 36 *U.S. Statutes* 2439; this last Declaration has
been cited as a complete dead letter in Greenspan, *op. cit.,* p. 332. Moreover, it is
significant that the recent Defense Department publications ignore the 14th
Convention entirely; see e.g., Tucker, *op. cit.,* pp. 143–49. Some measure of the
lack of vitality which these rules have in the area of air warfare may be seen in
the fact that the war crimes trials did not consider aerial bombardment at all.
See McDougal and Feliciano, *op. cit.,* pp. 641–42 especially fn. 381. See also Stone,
op. cit., pp. 525–59 *et passim.*

that naval aircraft do not appear to enjoy the right of warships to use false markings.[119]

One matter which pertains only to aircraft is the rule, noted earlier, that the airspace over a nation is under that nation's sovereignty. Accordingly, no military action may take place over a neutral state.[120] The related question, germane to considerations of space, may be raised as to where the upper limits of sovereignty lie. As long as only a few miles of airspace are in question the old rule cannot be seriously questioned, but once distances peculiar to considerations of space are employed, its validity is easily shaken. It must be presumed that in the absence of some agreement, sovereignty will extend upward as far as the subjacent state can exercise effective control, or short of that point only to an extent deemed consistent with its security. It may be further presumed that war in space will be governed by other rules of warfare insofar as they are applicable.[121] Finally, it will be recalled that the recent treaty prohibiting nuclear weapons in space severely limits the belligerent use of that medium.[122]

The Law of Occupation

There are two aspects of occupation which need to be briefly noted. These are (1) occupation of territory of an opposing

---

[119] See "General Report of the Commission of Jurists at the Hague, 1923," Art. 19; *American Journal of International Law*, Vol. XVII (October, 1923), pp. 242–60 (documents section); Tucker, *op. cit.*, p. 422, fn. 43. It is interesting to note that in the *Shimoda* case the Court gave some credence to these draft articles. See Falk, *op. cit.*, p. 770.

[120] See above Chapter Five, see *Convention on International Civil Aviation*, 1944, Dept. of State Publication 2282, Arts. 1, 3, 9; for discussion, see J. M. Spaight, *Air Power and War Rights* (3d ed.; London: Longmans, Green & Co., Inc., 1947), pp. 420–60; also C. P. Phillips, "Air Warfare and Law," *George Washington Law Review*, Vol. XXI (January, 1953), pp. 311–35; also Part II in Vol. XXI (March, 1953), pp. 395–422.

[121] See H. B. Jacobini, "Effective Control as Related to the Extension of Sovereignty in Space," *Journal of Public Law*, Vol. VII (Spring, 1958), pp. 97–119; see discussion in M. S. McDougal and L. Lipson, "Perspectives for a Law of Outer Space," *American Journal of International Law*, Vol. LII (July, 1958), pp. 407–31. See also discussion in Chapter Five.

[122] See this chapter, above, fn. 107.

belligerent, and (2) what has been called "friendly occupation," that is, the sending or stationing of troops in a friendly
power at its request or with its approval.

Belligerent Occupation.   Various phases of belligerent occupation have already been noted and will not be considered
here. The basic principle governing this relationship is that
belligerent occupation does not in itself affect legal sovereignty.
But as a practical matter, real control is exercised by the occupying power. Expressive of the position is the U.S. Army's view
that:

> Being an incident of war, military occupation confers upon the
> invading force the right to exercise control for the period of occupa-
> tion. It does not transfer the sovereignty to the occupant, but simply
> the authority or power to exercise some of the rights of sovereignty.
> The exercise of these rights results from the established power of the
> occupant and from the necessity of maintaining law and order,
> indispensable to both the inhabitants and to the occupying force.[123]

In order that territory may be considered as occupied it must be
"actually placed under the authority of the hostile army," and
under such circumstances the occupying power is obliged to
make every reasonable effort to "restore and insure . . . public
order and safety. . . ." Accordingly, military government is
established, and it is obvious that order may be imposed.

In such occupation the occupying power is to respect "the
laws in force in the country," if at all possible. The people
are not to be forced to reveal information regarding their army
nor are they to be required to take an oath of allegiance to the
enemy power. Also, family honor, lives, religious views, and
private property are to be respected, and pillage is outlawed.

As the administrative power, however, the occupying state
may continue to collect taxes and similar charges as the normal
devices for defraying the state's ordinary financial expenses.
Other assessments established by the occupying power may be
made for administration of the territory itself. If assessments
are made, however, they are to be upon the written order of the
commander-in-chief, and each payee is to be given a receipt.

---

[123] *Laws of Land Warfare* (1956), p. 140; also in nearly identical form in
Hackworth, *Digest* VI, p. 385; from *Rules of Land Warfare* (1940), pp. 73–74;
see generally *Annex to Hague Convention IV*, Arts. 43, 55.

Similarly, where a requisition is made upon a commune or upon inhabitants, it must be for military necessities only and is to be paid for in cash or with a receipt which can be converted shortly.

It has already been noted that the occupying power can take such things as cash and movable property belonging to the state whose territory it occupies, and such devices as news transmission devices may be seized even if privately owned, but must be returned at the end of hostilities with compensation. Similarly, submarine cables between occupied and neutral territory can be destroyed only "in the case of absolute necessity," and they too are to be restored with compensation.

Besides private property, the buildings of the occupied power and such nonmovable assets as forests, real estate, and agricultural works are considered as usufruct and are to be protected. Similarly, property of communes, religious, charitable, and educational institutions, works of science and art, and historic monuments are to be respected. Finally, penalties "pecuniary or otherwise" are not to be imposed on the population because of individual acts for which they "cannot be regarded as jointly and severally responsible."[124]

These statements summarize the only general accord on the subject, but it is doubtful whether some of these rules are likely to be followed in certain types of conflict. Moreover, certain of the rules appear to be generally bypassed. In these connections it may be doubted whether the U.S.S.R. would feel religiously bound to honor the private property clauses, particularly since it does not consider itself to be a party to the treaty. Similarly, the hostages clause seems to have been widely disregarded in emergencies, but it must be remembered that absolute prohibition of taking of hostages dates only from 1949.[125]

Friendly Occupation. For various reasons the troops of one

---

[124] See *Annex to Hague Convention IV*, Arts. 42–56; see also Hackworth, *Digest VII*, pp. 385–414, on the subject of occupation see D. A. Graber, the *Development of the Law of Belligerent Occupation 1863–1914* (New York: Columbia University Press, 1949) ; also E. Fraenkel, *Military Occupation and the Rule of Law* (New York: Oxford University Press, 1944) ; also Gerhard von Glahn, *The Occupation of Enemy Territory . . . A Commentary on the Law and Practice of Belligerent Occupation* (Minneapolis, Minn.: University of Minnesota Press, 1957) ; for a good brief account see Svarlien, *op. cit.*, pp. 374–95.

[125] *Geneva Convention on Civilian Persons* (1949) , Art. 34.

country may be stationed in the territory of a friendly power. When this takes place the legal status of the guest troops may be entirely governed by an agreement. On the other hand, if no such agreement exists it is generally recognized that the troops are under the law of the state to which they belong and are not subject to the jurisdiction of the host state.[126]

War Crimes Trials and Other Sanctions.

Elsewhere in this volume there have been discussions of the problems of enforcement.[127] War crimes, however, represent rather specialized problems, and it is therefore useful to comment briefly on these matters. Consideration can be divided into the two categories of (1) customary sanctions, and (2) war crimes trials.

Customary Sanctions. It is almost axiomatic that many war crimes go unpunished and even perhaps undetected. The nature of war makes this almost inevitable. However, when offenders are discovered they can be punished. It is more likely, however, that when illegal acts are discovered, reprisals are taken because the guilty parties are unknown. In extreme cases this may degenerate—as did much of the activity in the Pacific in World War II—to a conflict in which no quarter is given on either side. In less extreme cases a protest is made or an act of reprisal makes its point and conflict returns to more normal patterns.[128]

War Crimes Trials. Following the end of World War II

---

[126] A. King, "Jurisdiction over Friendly Foreign Armed Forces," *American Journal of International Law*, Vol. XXXVI (October, 1942), pp. 539–67; also see A. King, "Further Developments Concerning Jurisdiction over Friendly Foreign Armed Forces," *American Journal of International Law*, Vol. XL (April, 1946), pp. 257–79; for an expression of the contrary view that the primary jurisdictional immunity obtains, see G. P. Barton, "Foreign Armed Forces: Qualified Jurisdictional Immunity," *The British Yearbook of International Law 1954*, Vol. XXXI, pp. 341–70. See also Svarlien, *op. cit.*, p. 385; Hackworth, *Digest* VI, pp. 414–15. see *Schooner Exchange* v. *McFaddon*, 7 Cranch 116; see also above, Chapter Five, fn. 149. On the matter of status of forces agreements, see J. H. Rouse and G. B. Baldwin, "The Exercise of Criminal Jurisdiction under the NATO Status of Forces Agreement," *American Journal of International Law*, Vol. LI (January, 1957), pp. 29–62.

[127] See, e.g., Chapter Eight; pp. 297–98; *et passim*.

[128] For a discussion of reprisals, see above, Chapter Eight.

the essentially new device of war crimes trials came into existence. While references to these trials are found throughout this chapter and elsewhere in this volume, it is useful to summarize their role, for they have given a certain legal precision to some acts previously of somewhat obscure legal character. In essence the trials recognized the illegal nature of three categories of acts: (1) conspiracy to perpetrate aggressive war and more narrowly, aggression, (2) war crimes, and (3) crimes against humanity. Beyond these, the trials spelled out the responsibility which every individual must ultimately bear, at least in some measure, for his own involvement in acts which are improper including participation in organizations dedicated to illegal purposes.[129]

These trials have taken several forms. The best known are the initial Nuremberg and Tokyo trials which were carried out under the auspices of international tribunals. Subsequent trials took place under tribunals set up in the separate national zones of Germany, under the authority of Control Council Law #10. Still others were held before courts set up by other individual states.[130]

As noted earlier, the virtue of these trials has not gone uncontested,[131] but there is no doubt that the findings of the principal tribunals now represent firm law.[132] It is not clear, of

---

[129] See Telford Taylor, "Nuremberg Trials," *International Conciliation,* No. 450 (April, 1949) ; also Solis Horwitz, "The Tokyo Trial," *International Conciliation,* No. 465 (November, 1950) ; "International Military Tribunal (Nuremberg) Judgment and Sentences," *op. cit.* For other references in this chapter, see footnotes 11, 12, and 13. For the *Eichmann* case and some other pertinent references, see above, Chapter Five, fn. 167.

For an account of the trial of Japanese officers by the U.S.S.R., see *Materials on the Trial of Former Servicemen of the Japanese Army Charged with Manufacturing and Employing Bacteriological Weapons* (Moscow: Foreign Languages Publishing House, 1950) .

[130] Taylor, *op. cit.,* pp. 244–56.

[131] See, e.g., p. 281.

[132] See, e.g., "Report of the International Law Commission," reported in *American Journal of International Law,* Vol. XLIV (October, 1950) , especially pp. 125–34 (documents sections) .

The 1966 revision of the French Army Laws recognizes the individual responsibility of combatants quite clearly. In considering the rights and responsibilities of superiors to subordinates the rules state: "The chief has the right and the duty of requiring obedience of his subordinates; nevertheless, he cannot order them to fulfill acts the execution of which would involve their penal responsibility." The laws then list war crimes, domestic and constitutional offenses, and illegal acts against life, freedom, and property.

course, what use will be made of these precedents in the future, particularly if, as it may be conjectured, unconditional surrender is not likely to be a consistent concomitant of termination of conflict. Perhaps their chief value is to help clarify the obligations of states, of statesmen, and of combatants before the bar of history.

SUMMARY

War is a legal status stemming from hostility which is usually but not always armed. It has been one of the many devices used in international relations to attain political objectives. War is an ambiguous concept, however, and it is technically no longer legal except for defensive purposes, but it remains a sort of illegal fact. Laws of war govern almost all armed hostility whether or not this conflict is legal. War is supposed to begin only with a declaration or an ultimatum with conditional declaration, but this rule is often disregarded. Hostilities may be temporarily suspended by means such as agreements of commanding officers or by armistices. More permanently, wars may be terminated by simple cessation of hostilities, by subjugation, or by peace treaty.

In regard to the rights and responsibilities of subordinates, the laws state:

". . . the subordinate who executes an order prescibing the accomplishment of an illegal act envisioned in Article 21–3 of the present regulation, would fully engage his penal and disciplinary responsibility.

"If the subordinate believes himself to be confronted with such an order, he has the duty to communicate his objections to the authority which has given it, indicating expressly the illegal significance which he attaches to the order in dispute.

"If the order is maintained and if, in spite of the explanations or the interpretations which have been given him regarding it, the subordinate persists in his dispute, he appeals, prior to any execution, to the authority of the superior echelons which he has the possibility of contacting.

"In default of this last possibility, or if, although confirmed by the superior authority, the order still seems to him to be tainted with illegality, the subordinate need not execute it, without being excused, however, from the sanctions which not executing the order implies in the case where, afterwards, the latter [i.e., not executing the order] cannot be justified by an exact evaluation of the illegal character of the contested order."

See "Décret No. 66–749 portant règlement de discipline générale dans les armées. Du 1er Octobre 1966 (A) " in *Bulletin Officiel* (BOC/SC, 24 Octobre 1966–No. 43 bis) , Arts. 21, 22, pp. 862, 863 (Translated by the author.)

The legal effects of war include the suspending of normal pacific relations, and validating the acts of belligerency. Some nonhostile arrangements are continued or allowed, however; these include cartels, licenses to trade, and similar processes. Individual persons are subject to wartime requirements based on the status of their country. Citizens may be required to sever all relations with enemy persons. Enemy aliens are usually accorded some privileges, but may be severely curtailed in their activities if necessary. Neutrals are often privileged, but may be required to assume some obligations such as submitting to tax requirements or may even be drafted subject to allowing them to leave. The effect of war on property varies. In general, public immovable property, private property, and the property of religious, charitable, and educational institutions and of local communities may not be touched in occupied areas, while state funds and movable property may be. Enemy property of all sorts except embassy buildings and historic, religious, or similar items may be taken if within the boundaries of a state at war. This is usually not severely carried out. Property of the enemy at sea may be seized except noncontraband aboard a neutral vessel. The effect of the restoration of peace is to restore the peacetime rights and to abolish the wartime legal regime.

The rules of warfare rest uneasily upon their mutual utility to the belligerents and upon the sanction of reprisals and war crimes trials. The laws of warfare center upon the principles of necessity, humanity, and chivalry. Personnel in warfare are classified as combatants and noncombatants. Combatants are subject to the rules of warfare while noncombatants are generally protected. Prisoners of war are to be treated humanely and are to be repatriated at the war's end. Wounded and sick of both sides are to be treated, and medical personnel and chaplains are especially protected. The dead are to be buried. The enemy country is to be formally informed of prisoners of war, sick and wounded, and the dead. Spies, war traitors, and war rebels may be punished if caught. Taking of hostages appears to be abolished in law.

Prohibited devices and techniques in land warfare are: use of small expanding and incendiary bullets, dumdum bullets, gas, biological warfare, poison arms or poison, killing or

wounding the enemy treacherously, killing or wounding a surrendered person, allowing no quarter, using weapons which
inflict excessive injury, using improperly a flag of truce or other
flags, needless destruction of property, abolishing all rights of
enemy persons in the courts, compelling enemy persons to take
part in the war, attacking undefended towns, and pillaging. A
commander is, if possible, to warn a town before bombarding
it, and he should spare as far as possible the religious, historic,
and other like property. Ruses of war are allowable. There is
some reason to believe that destruction of the productivity of
land is also outlawed.

In the first edition of this work it was observed that "Though
still moot to an extent, the use of atomic weapons cannot be
considered as proscribed at the present writing." In 1967 this
must be modified. The permissibility of tactical nuclear devices
of limited character depends upon their proportionality to the
legitimate goal sought. Moreover, it is probably correct to state
that the initial use of major nuclear bombs in warfare is no
longer legal, except perhaps as reprisal for equally horrendous
acts.

Prohibited techniques at sea include using privateers or
other unregistered ships; laying unanchored contact mines
which are effective more than an hour after the person laying
them has lost control of them or as soon as they break loose, or
torpedos which remain effective after missing their mark; and
bombardment of undefended places including those solely de-
fended by harbor mines. A naval commander, like his land-
based colleagues, is to warn of bombardment if possible, and
should spare religious, educational, and like property if possible. Pillage is forbidden. Statagems and ruses are allowable,
and apparently at sea this includes use of false colors so long as
true standards are raised before commencing to fire. Warfare in
the air or in space is less amenable to traditional rules, but such
rules would seem to apply where practicable.

Occupation of territory does not itself transfer sovereignty.
An occupying power is to restore and maintain order and in
general to respect existing laws. It may collect existing taxes for
administrative purposes. Other assessments are unusual but
may be made in emergencies on the order of the commanding

officer. Payment and receipts are to be used. The occupying power may take public movable property but not private property or public immovable property. Religious, charitable, or educational properties are to be protected. Where occupation of a friendly power takes place, rules are often established by treaty; otherwise foreign troops are under the jurisdiction of their own country.

Sanctions in war are of two sorts: traditional procedures and the newer war crimes trials. The former center upon protests and reprisals. War crimes trials have helped to define the illegality of some sorts of belligerent behavior.

CHAPTER 10

Neutrality

LIKE WAR, NEUTRALITY has been pushed into a difficult posture due to developments since World War I.[1] Some modern writers have argued with considerable logic that the obligations of the League Covenant and of the United Nations Charter make it legally questionable for a state to remain neutral. On an ethical level it has even been suggested that neutrality is immoral since the neutral stands idly by while others fight for right. Also, the changing orientation of the United States from the leading professional neutral to leader of the West may have seemed in a way to underwrite these newer views, for moralizing one's own nation's position is a time-honored practice.

It must be noted, nevertheless, that if the mantle of neutral leadership was relinquished by the United States, it was assumed by India in the form of a policy of "neutralism," which, however, emphasizes a neutral relationship toward the East-West cold war, but would presumably be applied in a hot war context as well. In addition, World War II and the Korean conflict bear witness to the fact that nations do still remain neutral in war.[2] Neutrality, therefore, will be discussed here in

---

[1] See e.g., Oscar Svarlien, *Introduction to the Law of Nations* (New York: McGraw-Hill Book Co., Inc., 1955), p. 373; C. G. Fenwick, *International Law* (3d ed.; New York: Appleton-Century-Crofts, Inc., 1948), pp. 621–22; also C. G. Fenwick, "The Legal Aspects of Neutralism," *American Journal of International Law*, Vol. LI (January, 1957), pp. 71–74.

[2] Fenwick, "The Legal Aspects of Neutralism," *op. cit., passim.*

a relatively traditional context, taking into account, however, the changes brought about by the more recent developments. Discussion will be organized around: (1) the nature and status of neutrality, (2) neutral rights and duties, and (3) problems regarding neutral citizens, trade, and the seizure of property.

NATURE AND STATUS OF NEUTRALITY

The present section will consider the character of neutrality, trace its development, and briefly assess its contemporary status.

Characteristics and Definition of Neutrality and Related Concepts

In attempting to isolate the essence of neutrality it is to be stressed that authoritative discussions center upon the importance of two elements: (1) nonparticipation in an existing conflict, and (2) impartiality. Some writers insist that the essence of neutrality is the mere fact of nonparticipation in a conflict and that impartiality is essentially a neutral obligation.[3] Others emphasize impartiality as an integral aspect of the concept of neutrality along with the fact of nonparticipation,[4] and in this last connection the U.S. Army basic field manual on the *Rules of Land Warfare* states:

Neutrality on the part of a state not a party to the war consists in refraining from all participation in the war, and in exercising absolute impartiality in preventing, tolerating, and regulating certain acts on its own part by its subjects and by the belligerents.[5]

[3] See Hans Kelsen, *Collective Security under International Law* (Naval War College, *International Law Studies*, 1954; Washington, D.C.: U.S. Government Printing Office, 1956), pp. 154–64; Robert W. Tucker, *The Law of War and Neutrality at Sea* (Naval War College, *International Law Studies, 1955;* Washington, D.C.: U.S. Government Printing Office, 1957), pp. 196–99; E. Castrén, *The Present Law of War and Neutrality* (Helsinki: Annales Academiae Scientiarum Fennicae, Ser. B, Tom. 85, 1954), p. 422.

[4] Oppenheim-Lauterpacht, *Treatise* II, pp. 653–56; Q. Wright, "The Present Status of Neutrality," *American Journal of International Law,* Vol. XXXIV (July, 1940), pp. 392–94.

[5] See in Hackworth, *Digest* VII, p. 343 (quoting Army F. M. 27–10, 1940, p. 90).

The distinguishing point may seem to center upon the question of whether a state is really a neutral if it does not behave impartially, yet manages to stay outside a conflict. The question is misleading, however, for it centers upon matters of policy rather than matters of law. Such a nation remains "neutral" in the popular sense of the term yet its right to be treated as a neutral has been at the very least seriously impaired. Thus the comment by the distinguished Harvard Research group that "The principle itself is inherent in the nature of neutrality."[6] It is therefore assumed in this discussion that impartiality is not merely a duty of a neutral state, but rather that it is an integral feature of the concept of neutrality. Accordingly, neutrality may be *defined* as *impartial nonparticipation in a war between other states.*

Neutralization.   Neutrality differs from neutralization in that the essence of neutrality is impartial nonparticipation which, however, may be renounced in favor of another policy. Neutralization, on the other hand entails the permanent obligation of a state to retain its neutrality. Thus, for example, the status of Switzerland, Austria, and Laos is governed by treaties under which these states agree to remain neutral and other states have agreed to respect their neutrality.[7]

Nonbelligerency.   The term "nonbelligerency" must also be differentiated from neutrality. It has been argued that this concept enjoys no status in international law,[8] yet as a practical matter the term "nonbelligerency" suggests real meaning and a certain legal importance. Accordingly, if a state remains outside a conflict it may perhaps profess to be "neutral" even if it fails to behave impartially, yet as such it does not enjoy the full

---

[6] Harvard Research in International Law, "Rights and Duties of Neutral States in Naval and Aerial War," *American Journal of International Law,* Vol. XXXIII (Supplement, 1939) , p. 233.

[7] Hackworth, *Digest* VII, p. 344; also Vol. I, pp. 66–74; Josef L. Kunz, "Austria's Permanent Neutrality," *American Journal of International Law,* Vol. L (April, 1956) , pp. 418–25; Hans J. Morgenthau, "The End of Switzerland's 'Differential' Neutrality," *American Journal of International Law,* Vol. XXXII (July, 1938) , pp. 558–62; League of Nations, *Official Journal* (1920) , pp. 57–59. John J. Czyzak, "The International Conference on the Settlement of the Laotian Question and the Geneva Agreements of 1962," *American Journal of International Law,* Vol. LVII (April, 1963) , pp. 300–17.

[8] Josef L. Kunz, "Neutrality and the European War 1939–1940," *Michigan Law Review,* Vol. XXXIX (March, 1941) , pp. 747–51.

rights of a neutral. Moreover, states have at times quite candidly proclaimed a nonbelligerent status while others have assumed it in fact. Thus the term "nonbelligerency" refers to the status of formally staying out of a conflict while nevertheless distinctly favoring one of the belligerents. Italy, Spain, and the United States all assumed essentially this posture at one time or another during World War II. It must be emphasized, however, that the continued noninvolvement of a state operating on these premises depends entirely upon whether the less-favored belligerent thinks it expedient to make war on the offending nonbelligerent.[9]

History of Neutrality

Neutrality as a concept is of relatively recent origin. Until perhaps the 16th century no such right could be held to exist. Up to that time a nation electing to remain at peace was looked at askance for it was assumed that if it were not an ally or at least a sympathetic and helpful associate, it must be an enemy. In the early years of the modern era the right of neutrality began to take form, but it must be noted that the modern emphasis on impartiality was not yet well developed.[10] Accordingly, Grotius believed that a nonparticipant status might exist, but that a state had a duty not to aid an unjust cause. It was his view, however, that if the justice of one belligerent did not seem to overshadow that of the other, both were to be treated the same.[11]

A century later Bynkershoek's writings suggest that the moral judgment factor was declining, though Vattel still clung to the notion that the justice of the cause of one belligerent

---

[9] Tucker, *op. cit.*, p. 199 (fn.) ; see R. R. Wilson, " 'Non-Belligerency' in Relation to the Terminology of Neutrality," *American Journal of International Law,* Vol. XXXV (January, 1941) , pp. 121–23; also comment in E. Borchard, "War, Neutrality, and Non-Belligerency," *American Journal of International Law,* Vol. XXXV (October, 1941) , p. 624; N. Orvik, *The Decline of Neutrality, 1914–1941* (Oslo: Tanum, 1953) , pp. 195–215.

[10] Hackworth, *Digest* VII, pp. 344–46; Oppenheim-Lauterpacht, *Treatise* II, pp. 624–25.

[11] Hugo Grotius, *De jure belli ac pacis libri tres,* 1645 edition (*The Classics of International Law,* trans. F. W. Kelsey; 2 vols.;. Oxford: The Clarendon Press, 1925) , Vol. II, pp. 786–87.

would, without impairing neutral status, allow a nonparticipating state to aid mildly the just and thereby hinder the wicked.[12] During the 18th century neutrality took on even more of an impartial posture. As with other phases of law, neutrality did not evolve in a political vacuum, and much of the stabilizing of neutral rights was associated with the willingness and ability of neutrals to use force to maintain their status. The various armed neutralities, which operated off and on throughout part of the 17th and 18th centuries stressed neutral rights of trade, but questions of commerce have remained contentious.[13]

Rules regarding blockade and the status of neutral goods and neutral shipping which had been urged earlier were firmly established in 1856 when the Declaration of Paris was signed. It provided with reference to neutrality (1) that a blockade must be real and not merely a "paper blockade" in order to be legitimate, (2) that "the neutral flag covers enemy's goods" except contraband, and (3) that neutral goods are exempt from seizure on enemy ships.[14]

The importance of neutral duties emerged concretely from the British-American controversy regarding the outfitting of ships in Britain for the Confederacy during the American Civil War, the famous *Alabama Claims* case.[15] In that case the duty of a neutral to police its own nationals to assure neutrality was brought out.

---

[12] C. Van Bynkershock, *Questionum juris publici libri duo,* 1737 edition (*Classics of International Law;* trans. J. de Louter; 2 vols.; Oxford: The Clarendon Press, 1930), Vol. II, pp. 60–61; E. de Vattel, *Le droit des gens, ou principes de la loi naturelle, appliques a la conduit et aux affaires des nations et des souverains,* 1785 edition (*Classics of International Law;* trans. C. G. Fenwick; 3 vols.; Washington, D.C.: Carnegie Institution, 1916), p. 268.

[13] W. S. Carpenter, "The United States and the League of Neutrals of 1780," *American Journal of International Law,* Vol. XV (October, 1921), pp. 511–22; C. J. Kulsrud, "Armed Neutralities to 1780," *American Journal of International Law,* Vol. XXIX (July, 1935), pp. 423–47; see also, *Official Documents Bearing on the Armed Neutrality of 1780 and 1800* (Washington, D.C.: Carnegie Endowment, 1917); also *Extracts from American and Foreign Works on International Law Concerning the Armed Neutrality of 1780 and 1800* (Washington, D.C.: Carnegie Endowment, 1917).

[14] *Declaration of Paris,* 46 *Br. and Foreign State Papers,* p. 136; see conveniently in G. G. Wilson, *International Law* (9th ed.; New York: Silver Burdett & Co., 1935), pp. iv–v.

[15] *The Alabama Claims* case, I Moore's *International Arbitrations,* pp. 495–682.

In 1907 at the Hague Conference neutrality was the subject of two conventions.[16] These two conventions together with some more recent variations constitute the present formal law of neutrality. Nevertheless the impact of total war has had the effect of changing the substance of neutral trade rights, particularly with reference to contraband. This question will be dealt with later, but it may be noted here that while the goods which could justifiably be labeled as usable in war were limited even a few decades ago, today a reasonably good case can be made for the position that almost any commodity has a wartime application when the whole population and fiber of a nation is geared to war. Thus while the formalities of neutrality may be much the same as they were in 1907, their real substance has undergone considerable change.

Beyond that, the circumstances under which neutrality is a legally justifiable posture have also undergone change. Thus, there are situations under the terms of the United Nations Charter where neutrality is legally excluded. This matter, which will be discussed in more detail shortly, has had the effect of changing the modern setting of neutrality.

Finally, it must be reemphasized that neutrality and neutrals do not exist in a vacuum. The rights of neutrals emerged under the impact of power, and such factors as the armed neutralities and the intense pressure from the United States were important elements in its development. Today, many of the great traditional champions of neutrality have themselves become the primary participants in power politics. In the United States, for example, an active wartime and cold war posture has replaced active neutrality, leaving in the camp of neutrality only relatively weak powers. Unless these powers emerge as strong states and actively champion neutral rights, or unless while remaining weak they have a strong bargaining position, the scope and meaning of neutrality can be expected to become perhaps even more restricted.[17]

---

[16] *V Convention Respecting the Rights and Duties of Neutral Powers and Persons in Case of War on Land*, 36 U.S. *Statutes* 2310; *XIII Convention Concerning the Rights and Duties of Neutral Powers in Naval War*, 36 U.S., *Statutes* 2415; see conveniently in Wilson, *op. cit.*, pp. lxviii–lxxi and lxxx–lxxxv respectively.

[17] See Orvik, *op. cit.*, especially pp. 38–72.

The Present Status of Neutrality

The question now arises as to the strictly legal contemporary status of neutrality in the light of the United Nations Charter and related accords. In this connection it has often been argued that war is now illegal, that collective defense is now an obligation, and that it logically follows that neutrality is obsolete.[18] This position, while partially valid, is applicable only in certain circumstances, and it is the scope of this validity which is to be noted here.

In the first place, it should be observed that there appears to be no obligation to avoid neutrality under the terms of the Paris Peace Pact. That accord would seem to justify nonneutral action on the part of a third power but does not require the eschewal of neutrality.

On the other hand, the obligations formerly of the League Covenant and now of the United Nations Charter are of much greater importance. In the interests of brevity it may suffice to point out regarding the League that while the restraints on neutrality were important, neutrality did not disappear as a valid position. Under many circumstances it remained quite possib!e, and it continued to be widely employed.[19]

Under the United Nations Charter important restraints on neutrality continue to obtain—at least in theory. The Charter states that:

Article 41. The Security Council may decide what measures not involving the use of armed force are to be employed to give effect to its decisions, and it may call upon the Members of the United Nations to apply such measures. These may include complete or partial interruption of economic relations and of rail, sea, air, postal, telegraphic, radio and other means of communication, and the severance of diplomatic relations.

.   .   .   .

----

[18] See *above*, fn. 1.

[19] *Treaty for the Renunciation of War*, 46 *Statutes*, 2343; Tucker, *op. cit.*, pp. 166–88; Philip Jessup, *Neutrality Its History, Economics and Law* (New York: Columbia University Press, 1936), Vol. IV, pp. 86–123; J. F. Lalive, "International Organization and Neutrality," *British Yearbook of International Law*, 1947, pp. 74–77.

Article 48. 1. The action required to carry out the decisions of the Security Council for the maintenance of international peace and security shall be taken by all the Members of the United Nations or by some of them, as the Security Council may determine.

2. Such decisions shall be carried out by the Members of the United Nations directly and through their action in the appropriate international agencies of which they are members.

Article 49. The Members of the United Nations shall join in affording mutual assistance in carrying out the measures decided upon by the Security Council.[20]

These articles, together with others providing for armed action by member states, clearly indicate that there are circumstances in which a member nation may not legally remain neutral. In these circumstances, however, the Security Council must act to determine a threat to the peace and must provide for punitive action. To do so the Big Five must be in agreement. It is thus theoretically a legal possibility to preclude neutrality altogether on the part of United Nations member states, yet from the standpoint of practical international politics, unanimity of the Big Five is a rare thing and the requirement of neutrality is likely to obtain only in minor disputes.[21] Accordingly, neutral status may persist even in United Nations circles.

Moreover, while the Charter suggests that nonmember states can be compelled to "act in accordance with" the principles of the Charter "so far as may be necessary for the maintenance of international peace and security," it is doubtful whether there is legal recognition for such procedures in international law.[22] Nevertheless, however remote the possibility, a politically concerted stand by the United Nations including the Big Five would tend to have that practical effect. It must be emphasized, moreover, that neutrality is not politically defenseless, for a huge block of humanity is clustered ideologically around India

---

[20] U.N., *Charter*, Arts. 41, 48, 49.

[21] U.N., *Charter*, Chapter VII; also Art. 27; Lalive, *op. cit.*, p. 79.

[22] U.N., *Charter*, Art. 2 (6); Lalive, *op. cit.*, p. 85. For a discussion of the whole problem of neutrality in the face of action by the League of Nations and now the United Nations, see H. J. Taubenfeld, "International Actions and Neutrality," *American Journal of International Law*, Vol. XLVII (July, 1953), pp. 377–96.

and its policy of "neutralism" which is certainly a near relative
of neutrality.

Thus in summary neutrality clearly remains a legal possibility (1) for members of the Big Five at their discretion, (2) for
other members of the United Nations when the Security Council has not acted, (3) for nonmember states under almost any
circumstances except perhaps in the highly unlikely possibility
that the totality of United Nations force were to be politically
applied to curbing a nonmember's right to remain neutral.

NEUTRAL RIGHTS AND DUTIES

Once a state has determined that it wishes to remain neutral,
it is normal but not necessary for it to proclaim publicly its
neutral status. In so doing it implies that in order to be entitled
to the rights of a neutral it must assume the duties of one as
well. Rights and duties are very closely related in that, for
example, while a neutral has a *right* to expect belligerents not
to utilize its territory for belligerent purposes, it has a commensurate *duty* to see to it that no such offensive use is made of
its domains.

Neutral Rights

The essence of the rights of neutrals, as they are usually
considered in international law, centers upon the obligation of
belligerents not to do certain things which would compromise
either the neutral's sovereignty or its neutrality. The logical
consistency of these concepts was formerly subject to question,
however, for as long as it was legal to declare war for any
purpose, the neutral had no real legal assurance that its neutrality would be respected—except perhaps in the case of the
existence of a treaty of neutrality or neutralization. Today the
obligation is much more nearly an absolute one, but obviously
it is still tied to the neutral obligation of impartiality. These
rights are largely codified in the Fifth Hague Convention of
1907.[23]

---

[23] 36 U.S., *Statutes* 2310.

Inviolability of Neutral Territory. The basic neutral right is the inviolability of territory. Indeed, all other rights can be viewed as mere corollaries of that principle. Accordingly, the pertinent Hague Convention states that "The Territory of neutral powers is inviolable,"[24] and the 13th Hague Convention states that "Belligerents are bound to respect the sovereign rights of neutral powers and to abstain, in neutral territory or neutral waters, from any act which would, if knowingly permitted, by any Power, constitute a nonfulfillment of neutrality."[25] The Harvard research draft convention restates the rule in the following terms: "A belligerent shall not commit within neutral territory any act the toleration of which by a neutral state would constitute a nonfulfillment of its neutral duty."[26]

The Corollary Rights. As noted above the rule of inviolability is in itself very broad and the other specific rights can be viewed as a mere spelling out of the pertinent details. This is the approach adopted in the present text. Accordingly, a neutral power has a right to expect that no troops, convoys, or munitions be conveyed across its territory except perhaps for wounded or sick personnel; that its territory not be used as a base of operations; that no device for "communicating with belligerent forces on land or sea" be built on its domains nor that even the use of such a device be allowed unless it is open to use by the general public; that troops for use of the belligerent not be recruited or organized on its territory; that no prize court be set up on its territory, and finally that there are to be no acts of hostility committed in neutral territorial waters.[27] Although not a part of treaty law, it has been opined that a neutral has a right to expect that its flag will not be employed by belligerent merchant ships.[28] This is a debatable point, how-

---

[24] *Ibid.*, Art. I.

[25] 36 U.S., *Statutes* 2415, Art. I

[26] *Draft Convention on Rights and Duties of Neutral States in Naval and Aerial War, American Journal of International Law,* Vol. XXXIII (Supplement, 1939), (hereafter cited as "Harvard Neutrality Draft"), Art. 15.

[27] See *Hague Convention V*, Arts. 2, 3, 4, 14; *Convention XIII*, Arts. 2, 4, 5, 8; *The Steamship Appam,* 243 U.S. 124 (1917); *The Florida,* 101 U.S. 37 (1879).

[28] "Harvard Neutrality Draft," Art. 20; see also comment, pp. 353–59.

ever, and it is probable that to state it thus would be excessive.[29]

Finally, neutrals have the right to maintain relations with the belligerents except of course that these relations must not be of a character which violates the neutral's duty of impartiality or of rendering material aid to either side.[30]

Neutral Duties

In a sense the obligations of neutrals are largely a sort of converse restatement of the rights of neutrals and of the general principles of neutrality. There are four aspects of these duties, however, and they may be categorized as follows: (1) impartiality, (2) nonassistance to the belligerents, (3) strict regulation of the use of port and shipping facilities, and (4) enforcement of rights.

It may be noted that neutral states try to assure correct behavior along these lines by issuing *neutrality regulations* which specify the pertinent details and include rules for the governance of their nationals. It may also be noted that often these regulations are in excess of the requirements of international law.[31]

Impartiality. Although it has been emphasized that impartiality is a characteristic of neutrality, it must also be considered as an absolute obligation of neutral behavior. It is not too much to say that whether or not a state follows a course of strict impartiality determines whether its claim of neutrality is to be taken seriously. Accordingly both of the 1907 Hague conventions which are concerned with neutrality stress the obligation of the neutral to treat the belligerents impartially in the application of its regulations regarding use of commercial telegraphic facilities, private sales of munitions, and the length of

---

[29] See C. J. Colombos, *The International Law of the Sea* (4th rev. ed.; London: Longmans Green & Co., Ltd., 1959), pp. 432–34.

[30] Castrén, *op. cit.*, pp. 469–70.

[31] See Hackworth, *Digest* VII, pp. 373–79; C. C. Hyde, *International Law Chiefly as Interpreted and Applied by the United States* (2d ed.; Boston: Little, Brown & Co., 1951), Vol. III, pp. 2316–20; F. Deak and P. C. Jessup, *A Collection of Neutrality Laws, Regulations and Treaties of Various Countries* (2 vols.; Washington, D.C.: Carnegie Endowment, 1939).

stay for ships and other relevant matters regarding use of neutral ports.[32] A more generalized statement which is probably in conformity with existing legal obligations is that of the Harvard Research draft convention which stipulates:

A neutral State, in the exercise of its neutral rights and in the performance of its neutral duties, shall be impartial and shall refrain from discrimination between belligerents.[33]

Nonassistance. Although it is sometimes thought that a neutral may do nothing which aids either belligerent, it is probably much more correct to state that there are certain types of assistance which may not be rendered. In most cases these are acts of the state and are to be contrasted with acts of private persons. Accordingly, neutral states may not sell munitions or war supplies nor extend or guarantee loans to a belligerent power. Of even more specific application is the obligation of neutrals not to sell, outfit or allow to be outfitted or sold to a belligerent power any vessel of war. This last rule was first specified in the *Alabama Claims* case and was later written into the 13th Hague Convention of 1907.[34] The principle has sometimes been applied to aircraft, but it is not clear whether such extension represents a valid legal obligation.[35]

Strict Regulation of Use of Neutral Ports and Other Facilities. There are certain specified activities which it must be noted are really forms of assistance to the belligerents and which may be rendered provided they are impartially applied. These, however, are rather rigidly governed by the stipulations of the 13th Hague Convention and may be summarized as follows: belligerent warships—except those employed for religion, science, or philanthropy—may use neutral ports for only a limited time, usually 24 hours at a time; no more than three such ships of a single belligerent may be in the same port at the same time; ships may be revictualed only to the extent of their

---

[32] *Hague Convention V*, Art. 9; *Hague Convention XIII*, Art. 9.

[33] "Harvard Neutrality Draft," Art. 4.

[34] *Hague Convention XIII*, Arts. 6, 7, 8; Hague Convention V, Arts. 6, 7, 8; also Castrén, *op. cit.*, pp. 477–78; *Alabama Claims* case, *op. cit.*; "Harvard Neutrality Draft," Arts. 5, 7.

[35] See "Harvard Neutrality Draft," Art. 99 and comment pp. 770–72; cf. *Hague Air Rules,* 1923, Arts. 44, 45, 46.

peacetime standard; and in general they are to obtain only
sufficient fuel to carry them to their nearest home port. Modifications of these rules allow ships to remain longer than specified
if lack of seaworthiness or weather conditions make it necessary
or if refueling has not been accomplished within 24 hours.
Also, prize ships may be admitted under stress of weather or
unseaworthiness, but it must be noted that these are emergency
circumstances which allow of only limited time. In addition
there are certain obligations imposed on the departure of
warships from neutral ports. If ships of two opposing belligerent powers are in a neutral port at the same time, 24 hours
must elapse between their departure, and, if a merchant ship of
one belligerent and a warship of an opposing state are simultaneously in a port, the same rule applies except that the merchant ship is to leave first.[36] It should be noted also that a
neutral must intern and maintain troops if they cross to its
territory, unless they are escaped prisoners of war in which case
they are to be left at liberty.[37]

Enforcement of Rights. The final aspect of neutral obligations to be considered here involves the duty of a neutral to
utilize the "means at its disposal" to see that the rights discussed earlier in this chapter are not violated. Thus, for example, a neutral has a *right* to expect that there will be no belligerent radio station erected on its territory and at the same time
the neutral has a *duty* to prevent such construction. Accordingly, the neutral is bound to resist the movement by a belligerent of troops or supplies across its territory, to oppose erection
of a wireless station on its domains, and to stop the formation of
corps of combatants or of recruiting. Furthermore, the neutral
must resist violations of its territorial waters and must not
allow prizes to be condemned in its ports.[38] In this connection
the 13th Hague Convention states:

A neutral Power is bound to exercise such surveillance as the
means at its disposal allow to prevent any violation of the provisions

---

[36] *Hague Convention XIII,* Arts. 12, 14, 15, 16, 17, 21.
[37] *Hague Convention V,* Arts. 11, 12, 13.
[38] *Ibid.,* Arts. 2, 3, 4, 5; *Hague Convention XIII,* Arts. 2, 3, 4, 5, 25.

of the above Articles occuring in its ports or roadsteads or in its waters.[39]

It should be noted, however, that a neutral's obligation is qualified. It must use only the "means at its disposal" to prevent violation. In an illustrative case arising out of the War of 1812, the Portuguese were not held responsible for failure to enforce pacific behavior by neutral ships in their port of Fayal partially because Portuguese defenses were inadequate to the task.[40]

PROBLEMS REGARDING NEUTRAL CITIZENS, TRADE, AND SEIZURE OF PROPERTY

The real problems of neutrality have often been more the result of private citizens' activity than of official state policy, for many restraints that apply to neutral states do not necessarily apply to the private citizens of neutral states. Moreover, problems of trade are becoming more absolute, that is, trade with belligerents is becoming more circumscribed as wars become more "total" in character. Finally problems arise over the seizure of neutral property. These matters will be discussed under the three categories of (1) neutral citizens, (2) problems of trade, and (3) seizure of property.

Neutral Citizens

A sharp distinction must be made between acts which a neutral state may perform without placing its neutrality in jeopardy, and the behavior of individual citizens of the neutral state. Thus, in general while a neutral state may not sell munitions or arms to belligerents, the private citizen is free to do so subject of course to the fact that if he is caught his goods will be confiscated. Even then he is not to be personally treated as if he were a belligerent. Accordingly the Fifth Hague Convention states:

[39] *Hague Convention V*, Arts. 2, 3, 4, 5; *Hague Convention XIII*, Art. 25.

[40] *The General Armstrong*, U.S.–Portugal, Claims Arbitration, 1852; 2 Moore, *International Arbitrations*, 1094.

Article 7. A neutral Power is not called upon to prevent the export or transport, on behalf of one or other of the belligerents, of arms, munitions of war, or, in general, of anything which can be of use to an army or a fleet.

Article 8. A neutral Power is not called upon to forbid or restrict the use on behalf of the belligerents of telegraph or telephone cables or of wireless telegraphy apparatus belonging to it or to companies or private individuals.

Similarly, the 13th Hague Convention stipulates that

A neutral Power is not bound to prevent the export or transit, for the use of either belligerent, of arms, ammunitions, or, in general, of anything which could be of use to an army or fleet.[41]

It must be noted, however, that states often do prohibit their nationals from engaging in trade—or certain kinds of trade—with the belligerents. When they do so, such regulations must not discriminate between the belligerents. In this connection the Harvard Research draft specifically recognizes the right of a nation to restrict trade in arms and other commodities and to take other measures to better safeguard its neutral status.[42]

There is one area of private trade in which the neutral state is obliged to take restrictive measures. In the previously cited *Alabama Claims* case it was recognized that the outfitting in neutral territory of warships for belligerent use in time of war was improper, and this rule was later written into the 13th Hague Convention in the following terms:

A neutral Government is bound to employ the means at its disposal to prevent the fitting out or arming of any vessel within its jurisdiction which it has reason to believe is intended to cruise, or engage in hostile operations, against a Power with which that Government is at peace. It is also bound to display the same vigilance to prevent the departure from its jurisdiction of any vessel intended to cruise, or engage in hostile operations, which had been adapted entirely or partly within the said jurisdiction for use in war.[43]

---

[41] *Hague Convention V*, Arts. 7, 8; see also Art. 18; *Hague Convention XIII*, Art. 7.

[42] *Hague Convention V*, Art. 9; *Hague Convention XIII*, Art. 9; "Harvard Neutrality Draft," Arts. 11, 12, 13; see also Deak and Jessup, *op. cit., passim.*

[43] *Hague Convention XIII*, Art. 8.

The Harvard Research draft incorporates this principle and as noted earlier, applies it to aircraft as well. In this last connection, the Hague Air Rules of 1923 had taken the position that a government must not sell such craft to belligerents, but that neutral citizens might do so.[44] It must be doubted whether the rule is clearly incorporated into international law to the extent of being applicable to aircraft.

Finally it must be noted that if a citizen of a neutral country commits hostile acts such as enlisting in the forces of a belligerent power, he of course forfeits all claim to being treated as a neutral. On the other hand he is to be treated no more severely than "a national of the other belligerent state."[45]

Problems of Trade

One of the most pressing difficulties inherent in the concept of neutrality centers upon the conflict between the right of neutrals to trade and the right of belligerents to prevent—if they can—war supplies from reaching the enemy. The problems which result will be noted in three categories: (1) neutral ships and neutral goods, (2) contraband, and (3) blockade.

Neutral Ships and Neutral Goods. Although a state of war poses difficulties for neutrals, it does not put a stop to all trade. On the other hand, restraints exist and these have become more stringent as wars have become more nearly total. The basic principles are, however, as follows: (1) neutral goods which are not contraband are not liable to confiscation even on enemy ships; (2) neither neutral nor enemy owned goods except contraband are subject to seizure on neutral vessels.[46]

On the other hand, a neutral vessel may jeopardize its immunity by rendering "unneutral service." This would appear to include transportation of a belligerent military detachment, conveying of military information, taking part in hostilities, or serving under the control of or as chartered by a belligerent.

---

[44] "Harvard Neutrality Draft," Arts. 31, 99; *Hague Air Rules,* 1923, Arts. 44, 45, 46.

[45] *Hague Convention V,* Arts. 16, 17; see generally Hackworth, *Digest* VII, pp. 609–16.

[46] *Declaration of Paris;* also see Hackworth, *Digest VII,* pp. 1–14.

Another common cause for confiscation of a neutral ship is resistance to legitimate search.[47]

Contraband. Among the limitations clearly recognized as restraining neutral trade is the matter of goods which may not be sold to belligerents. Such goods are known as contraband. It was once thought possible to point with some degree of precision to this restriction and to observe the categories of (1) goods always subject to seizure, or "absolute contraband"; (2) goods sometimes subject to seizure, or "conditional contraband"; and (3) goods which were "not to be declared contraband of war." Indeed, it was once judicially ascertained that these categories were quite rigid and that a belligerent could not arbitrarily reclassify goods from the category of conditional contraband to absolute contraband.[48]

Precise international lists were established by the Declaration of London of 1909. Although it never went into effect, it was probably a fairly accurate expression of prevailing concepts at the time of its drafting. In practice, however, belligerents drew up and proclaimed their own contraband lists, but there were many differences between neutrals and belligerents over specific items. Thus, for example, foodstuffs have been the subject of such controversy, but Hyde states:

> As war is now conducted, it is a probability rather than a possibility that foodstuffs imported into belligerent territory will serve a military end and so be used for a hostile purpose, if there is a general shortage of such articles.[49]

It may be further noted that only goods destined for use by a belligerent can be classed as contraband. Yet it has been recognized that goods may be seized if formally consigned to a neutral port, but are obviously to be transshipped or conveyed overland to the belligerent. This is known variously as the *doctrine of continuous voyage* or the *doctrine of ultimate des-*

---

[47] See as illustration *The Declaration of London* 1909 (cited conveniently in Wilson, *op. cit.*, pp. lxxxvi–c), Arts. 45, 46, 47, 63. Note that the Declaration did not go into effect itself, but is valuable as a statement of rules many of which are valid customary law. See Hackworth, *Digest* VII, pp. 99–114.

[48] See *Declaration of London*, Arts. 22–44; see also "Harvard Neutrality Draft," Annex 1; also *The Prometheus,* Hong Kong Supreme Court, 2 Hong Kong L. R. 207 (1906) ; see comment in Hackworth, *Digest* VII, pp. 15–29.

[49] Hyde, *op. cit.*, Vol. III, p. 2122.

tination.[50] This principle has been carried so far as to limit the imports of certain items by neutrals substantially to their peacetime intake. While this cannot be said to enjoy clear validity, neither can it be categorized as a wholly unreasonable restriction.[51]

In the last analysis the right of belligerents to prevent useful war goods from reaching their enemies is the core of the contraband idea. While it is certainly a valid concept, it is difficult to reconcile it with the neutral right to trade, particularly in a total or near total war situation. As the political power of neutrals has waned, the scope of pertinent neutral rights of trade has been circumscribed. Accordingly, contraband now appears to be highly flexible and may potentially include almost anything.[52] Sometimes, it may be added, belligerents merely "preempt" goods and do not confiscate them. Under this practice they buy the goods rather than confiscate them.[53]

Blockade. Another device of belligerent control is the blockade. It is merely the proclamation and enforcement by one belligerent of the prohibition of any trade with a particular enemy coast or port. Although it was once debatable as to whether a blockade had to be enforced in order to be valid, the Declaration of Paris established that "Blockades, in order to be binding, must be effective—that is to say, maintained by a force sufficient really to prevent access to the coast of the enemy."[54]

In order to impose a blockade it must be announced and individually communicated to neutral states and to the local authorities of the blockaded areas with indication as to its extent and its time of beginning. Furthermore, a time must be

---

[50] *The Springbok*, 5 Wallace 1 (1866); *The Peterhoff*, 5 Wallace 28 (1866); *The Kim*, High Court of Justice, Probate, Divorce and Admiralty Division 1915; L. R. Probate 215; see discussion in Hyde, *op. cit.*, Vol. III, pp. 2129–58; also, Hackworth, *Digest* VII, pp. 34–63.

[51] See comment in C. G. Fenwick, *International Law, op. cit.*, pp. 640–41; *The Kim, op. cit.*; see also supplement to the *American Journal of International Law*, Vol. X (April, 1916), p. 96.

[52] See *Law of Naval Warfare* (U.S.) #631 and fns. 18–26 (found in appendix of Tucker, *op. cit.*); also, Julius Stone, *Legal Control of International Conflict* (New York: Rinehart & Co., Inc., 1954), pp. 481–83.

[53] See comment in G. G. Wilson, *op. cit.*, pp. 345–46; W. E. Hall, *International Law* (5th ed.; Oxford: The Clarendon Press, 1904), p. 665.

[54] *Declaration of Paris* #4.

specified in which neutral vessels may leave unmolested. Exception is usually granted to ships not aware of the existence of the blockade, though it is to be presumed that this sort of ignorance is rare today. A ship violating the blockade is subject to confiscation unless, as just noted, it is truely unaware of the existence of the blockade. Finally, capture of a ship for blockade violation is proper only if caught in the act. If a ship escapes and is later found plying other seas it cannot properly be captured for its earlier blockade running activity.[55]

Procedures for Seizure and Condemnation of Vessels

If neutral vessels run blockades, carry contraband, or otherwise behave in an unneutral fashion, they and their goods or certain of their cargo are ordinarily subject to confiscation. In addition, neutral vessels and railroad rolling stock are sometimes legitimately requisitioned for belligerent use. These procedures will be discussed as (1) visit, search and seizure, (2) prize courts and prize procedure, and (3) angary and requisition.

Visit, Search, and Seizure. In order to eliminate trade and transportation which is beneficial to its enemies, a belligerent may use its warships to stop and search all merchant vessels on the high seas. Neutrals are obliged to submit to this procedure, and the U.S. naval regulations express this concept in the following terms:

The belligerent right of visit and search may be exercised anywhere outside of neutral jurisdiction upon all merchant vessels and aircraft in order to determine their character (enemy or neutral), the nature of their cargo, the manner of their employment, or other facts which bear on their relation to the war.[56]

The visiting officer looks at the ship's papers and then, if there is any doubt or suspicion, he may search the vessel for contra-

---

[55] See *Declaration of London,* Arts. 1–21; "Harvard Neutrality Draft," Arts. 68–82 and accompanying comment; *Laws of Naval Warfare* (U.S.), #632; Hyde, *op. cit.,* Vol. III, pp. 2177–2223; Hackworth, *Digest* VII, pp. 114–34; Edgar Turlington, *The World War Period,* Vol. III of the Jessup *et al.* series, *Neutrality: Its History, Economics and Law,* pp. 34–66.

[56] *Law of Naval Warfare* (U.S.), #502 (a).

band. If there is no evidence of unneutral service the vessel is normally released. If, on the other hand, there is further suspicion, the craft is taken into one of the captor's ports and the question of whether it may properly be confiscated is determined by a prize court.[57]

Modern practice appears to allow taking a vessel into port for search in view of the hazards of search on the high seas. While this practice has not perhaps been clearly sanctioned by law, it is widely employed and may probably be considered as proper. American practice, for example, provides as follows:

> If visit and search at sea of a neutral merchant vessel is deemed hazardous or impracticable, the neutral vessel may be escorted by the summoning vessel or by another vessel or by aircraft to the nearest place where search may be made conveniently.[58]

Another disputed practice is that of visiting merchant ships under convoy of a neutral warship. The practice is certainly awkward, but cannot clearly be classed as legally improper.[59]

Procedure for visit and search varies somewhat from nation to nation but appears to be relatively uniform. United States procedure, for example, is specified in some detail, and it is indicated that tact is essential. When a vessel is stopped, it is boarded by an officer who should first examine the ship's papers, after which, if there is any question, the ship may be searched and its personnel questioned. Finally, except when "military security prohibits" it, the officer is to make an appropriate entry in the ship's log.[60]

Prize Courts and Prize Procedure. If it is determined that a neutral ship should be captured, it is then taken or ordered to go to a port of the capturing belligerent state where it is turned over to a prize court. In the event that military necessity requires it, neutral prizes are sometimes destroyed, and the legal

---

[57] See *ibid.*, #502 (b); "Harvard Neutrality Draft," Arts. 49–55; Colombos, *op. cit.*, pp. 688–729; Hackworth, *Digest* VII, pp. 175–270.

[58] *Laws of Naval Warfare* (U.S.), #502 (b-5); see Colombos, *op. cit.*, pp. 707–10 for a summary of prevailing practice.

[59] See Colombos, *op. cit.*, pp. 694–700; also Tucker, *op. cit.*, pp. 334–35. See also, however, *Declaration of London*, Arts. 61, 62; "Harvard Neutrality Draft," Arts. 56, 57, 58.

[60] *Laws of Naval Warfare* (U.S.), #502 (b); also Colombos, *op. cit.*, pp. 700–01.

implications of such destruction are not absolutely clear. A recent commentator has stated:

As matters presently stand it does not appear possible to define with any real precision the circumstances in which neutral prizes lawfully may be destroyed. Undoubtedly it remains true, however, that the destruction of neutral prizes involves a much more serious responsibility for a belligerent, as well as for a belligerent commander, than does the destruction of an enemy prize. If it is later found that either the vessel or the cargo was not liable to condemnation indemnification of the innocent property must be made. For this reason, among others, the destruction of neutral prizes ought to be avoided whenever possible.[61]

It is clear that in the event of such destruction, the belligerent is obliged to secure the safety of all personnel and of the ship's papers. Although there have been many violations, this general principle would seem to apply to procedures to be employed by submarines and airplanes as well as by surface ships.[62]

In port the vessel—or its papers if the ship has been destroyed—is turned over to a prize court which looks into the propriety of the seizure and inquires into whether the vessel and/or its cargo or a portion of the latter may properly be confiscated. This function is performed in the United States by the federal district courts. Decisions are rendered in conformity with the belligerent state's prize regulations which, however, are generally presumed to conform to international law. An attempt was made in 1907 to create an international prize court. The statute was drawn up but it was not ratified and therefore did not go into effect.[63]

An indication of the scope of rules applicable in prize pro-

---

[61] Tucker, *op. cit.*, p. 352.

[62] *Laws of Naval Warfare* (U.S.), #503 (e); *London Naval Treaty of 1930,* 46 U.S. Statutes 2858, Art. 22; "Procès-verbal Relating to the Rules of Submarine Warfare Set Forth in Part IV of the Treaty of London of April 22, 1930," London, 1936, in *American Journal of International Law,* Vol. XXI (Supplement, 1937), pp. 137–39; Tucker, *op. cit.*, p. 352; see also "Harvard Neutrality Draft," Arts. 54, 55, 109; *Hague Air Rules of 1923,* Arts. 49–60.

[63] See U.S., *Constitution,* Art. III, Sec. 2 (1, 2); 36 *U.S. Statutes* 1091; Hyde, *op. cit.*, Vol. III, pp. 2363–84; Hackworth, *Digest* VII, pp. 270–341; Colombos, *op. cit.*, pp. 730–60. Regarding international prize court, see M. O. Hudson, *The Permanent Court of International Justice 1920–1942* (New York: The Macmillan Co., 1943), pp. 71–79.

ceedings may be garnered from the brief statement in the Harvard Neutrality Draft. Although it is only a draft convention, its rules of prize law may be considered to be substantially correct and in general conformity with international law. It stipulates as follows:

A prize court shall be bound by the following rules:

a) A vessel which intended to run a blockade, may be condemned together with its cargo.

b) Cargo destined for a blockaded port by sea, may be condemned; the vessel may also be condemned if the destination of the cargo was known to the owner, charterer or master of the vessel.

c) The presence of an uncertified vessel within a blockade zone is presumptive evidence of an intention to break the blockade; the presumption may be rebutted by proof that neither the vessel nor the cargo was in fact destined for a blockaded port or place by sea.

d) A certified vessel seized in a blockade zone may be condemned together with the cargo on board, unless it is proved that the vessel entered the blockade zone by mistake or in distress.

e) Cargo destined for belligerent territory either directly or through a neutral port, may be condemned in so far as it is composed of arms, ammunition or implements of war, or of other goods shipped in violation of a neutral State's prohibition under Article II. If more than half of the cargo by value, weight, volume or freight is composed of goods which may be condemned, the rest of the cargo and the vessel are similarly subject to condemnation.

f) Any commodity in a cargo destined for a neutral State upon whose imports of that commodity a quota has been fixed under Article 47, but not included within a portion of the the quota allocation to the State from which the commodity was shipped, may be condemned.

g) Enemy vessels and such parts of their cargo as are of enemy ownership may be condemned; the disposition of neutral cargo is not affected by the fact that it is carried in a belligerent vessel, but neutral cargo belonging to the owner, charterer, or master of a vessel which, under Article 64 or 65 a belligerent may treat as an enemy vessel, may be condemned.

h) Cargo destined for unblockaded belligerent territory or for a

neutral port affording convenient access to belligerent territory and not subject to condemnation under preceding paragraphs of this article, may be preempted by the capturing
belligerent upon payment of the market price current in its
territory on the date of the arrival of the prize in port, plus
ten per cent.

i) When a vessel's cargo is subject only to preëmption, the vessel must be released and the capturing belligerent must pay
damages for the delay.

j) Enemy ownership or origin of cargo on a neutral vessel does
not affect the disposition of the cargo: "free ships make free
goods."

k) When a vessel has been captured and brought into port for
prize proceedings and the prize court finds that there was no
probable cause for the capture, damages must be paid for
losses suffered by the vessel and by the owners of the cargo.

l) A vessel which has been diverted to port in violation of the
provisions of Article 61 (3), regardless of the nature of its
voyage or of its cargo, shall be released and the capturing
belligerent must pay damages for the delay.

m) Postal correspondence on a captured neutral vessel is inviolable, unless it is being carried to or from a blockaded
place on a vessel which is subject to condemnation for
breach of blockade.

n) Postal parcels may be treated as cargo.[64]

Finally it should be noted that ships are often not accorded
neutral status if they were purchased from a belligerent after

---

[64] "Harvard Neutrality Draft," Art. 63; for U.S. rules see 56 *American
Jurisprudence, War* #180–203 and 93 C.J.S., War #27–32; also *U.S. Code, 1952,*
Title 34, Chapter 20. Certain terms in the draft convention cited may need
clarification. *Certified vessel* refers to a vessel cleared by a neutral state as
performing purely neutral functions and marked in a particular way. It carries a
certificate of neutrality. An *uncertified vessel* is one to which no such official
commitments and markings attach. The term *quota* indicates that limited
quantity of certain goods recognized by a belligerent state as reasonable con-
sumption by a particular neutral. The presumption is that a great increase in
such imports would indicate transshipment to an enemy belligerent. *Preemption*
refers to the practice on the part of a belligerent of taking neutral cargo destined
for a nonblockaded port, but paying for it at the market price plus 10 percent. In
addition to the above it may be useful to note a procedure used by the British
during World War I and known as the *"navicert system."* Under this plan a
neutral ship or cargo might be certified in a British or allied port by a British
official as not being destined for an enemy port. Such ships and cargo were then
less likely to suffer delays at sea at the hands of the British.

the outbreak of war. Attempts were made to establish the ruling that if a vessel were transferred less than 30 days before the outbreak of war, such transfer would not be recognized, but this rule has not generally been accepted. United States practice appears to emphasize whether or not the sale was bona fide as the criterion rather than utilizing an arbitrary time limit.[65]

Angary and Requisition. Although it was once thought to be virtually obsolete, it is now clear that a belligerent may seize neutral vessels in its ports and also railroad rolling stock within its territory. This is generally known as the right of angary, but the term is loosely applied to include types of requisitioning which are perhaps not properly termed as angary. Regarding angary the Harvard draft convention states:

A belligerent may, within its territory or within territory held in military occupation, in case of urgent necessity, requisition a neutral vessel privately owned and operated, or cargo owned by nationals of a neutral State, if the vessel or the cargo was brought into such territory voluntarily and not as the result of compulsion or pressure exercised by the belligerent or by an allied belligerent; provided that this privilege may be exercised by a belligerent only if it pays the fair market value, under prevailing conditions, of the vessel or cargo requisitioned.[66]

The general principle here is not subject to dispute, but there is question as to whether or not a vessel may be seized on the high seas and brought before a prize court and, while before the court, be confiscated under the right of angary. Such a procedure was held to be valid under certain circumstances by a British prize court during World War I, but it is not a practice which neutrals find satisfactory. Railroad rolling stock is also subject to seizure if it is urgently needed by the belligerent. It is clear that reasonable compensation must always be given in such cases and the ships and equipment should eventually be returned. Neutrals also enjoy the right in emergencies to seize

---

[65] Tucker, *op. cit.*, pp. 78–81; Hyde, op. cit., Vol. III, pp. 2078–84; Colombos, *op. cit.*, pp. 499–501; see also, however, "Harvard Neutrality Draft," Art. 67; *Declaration of London*, Arts. 55, 56.

[66] "Harvard Neutrality Draft," Art. 21.

the merchant ships and railroad materiel of belligerents, subject to the obligation to compensate the owners and ultimately
to return the equipment.[67]

Finally it should be noted that angary is in a modern setting
closely related to or identical with the sovereign right of a state
to seize private property and is therefore not really very startling. Yet in a wartime context it has been the source of much
belligerent-neutral friction.[68]

SUMMARY

Neutrality is still a valid concept in international law although its admissability has been somewhat circumscribed by
agreements. In essence it involves (1) nonparticipation in a
war and (2) impartiality. It differs from neutralization which
is permanent neutrality, and from nonbelligerency which involves nonparticipation in a war but favoritism to one side.
Neutrality is of relatively recent origin. It was not until about
the 16th century that it came into use. More recently it has
been under fire because it is alleged that legal abolition of war
and the United Nations obligations have made it obsolete.
While this may be true in some instances, it is not always or
even generally the case.

Neutrality, like other aspects of international law, does not
exist in a political vacuum, and throughout its history there has
been much tension between neutrals and belligerents. Ham-
mered out on the anvil of politics, however, have been a number of neutral rights and neutral duties. Neutral rights center
upon inviolability of territory. This excludes from neutral territory enemy wireless stations, recruiting, forming of combatant
units, belligerent transit, prize courts, and use of its flag by
ships of belligerent registry. Conversely, belligerents are obligated not to do these things. In addition, a neutral has a right
to maintain relations with belligerent powers.

---

[67] *The Zamora*, G. B., Jud. Comm. of Privy Co., 1916, L.R. 2 A.C. 77;
Hackworth, *Digest* VI, pp. 638–55; *Digest* VII, pp. 529 ff.; Hyde, *op. cit.*, Vol. III,
pp. 1760–70; Colombos, *op. cit.*, pp. 505–13. *Hague Convention V*, Art. 19. See
J. E. Harley, "The Law of Angary," *American Journal of International Law*, Vol.
XIII (April, 1919), pp. 267–301.

[68] See Tucker, *op. cit.*, pp. 348–49 (fn. 41).

Neutral duties include the obligation of impartiality; of non-assistance to the belligerents in regard particularly to the sale of munitions, ships, and war supplies; the obligation not to allow the sale of warships to belligerents by persons based on neutral territory; and the obligation to regulate the use of its ports and docking facilities by belligerents. In this last connection no more than three belligerent ships of the same nationality may be in a port at the same time; ships may stay only a limited time, usually 24 hours, and may not return for three months; refueling and provisioning such ships is limited to peacetime standards, and sufficient fuel to return to the nearest home port. Repairs, further time, and other deviations are sometimes allowed if weather conditions or inability to service the ships in the limited time require it, but such deviations must be impartially applied. Other port restrictions include clearing belligerent ships of different warring nationalities at 24-hour intervals and allowing merchant ships to leave first. A further obligation obtains to intern belligerent troops if they enter neutral territory, except that this does not apply to escaped prisoners. A neutral must utilize the means at its disposal to see that its neutral rights are not violated.

Trade has been the source of much neutral-belligerent controversy. In general, neutral citizens may trade with belligerents and there is no obligation for neutral states to prevent such activity—except for the sale of warships which is prohibited. Sale of munitions does not transform a neutral person into a belligerent, but performance of certain types of unneutral acts does. An example of the latter is enlisting in the belligerent force, in which case a person is to be treated as a belligerent. Neutral goods are not liable to capture on enemy ships unless they are contraband; and neutral ships cover both enemy and neutral goods except contraband. Neutral ships are not to carry contraband, that is, goods of military use, to belligerent countries. This often includes trade with nearby neutral ports from which goods are easily transshipped or shipped overland to the belligerent; this is known as the doctrine of continuous voyage and ultimate destination. A neutral may not trade at all with a blockaded enemy port.

Neutral vessels are subject to seizure if they engage in unneutral service, and contraband goods are always subject to seizure if destined for a belligerent port. If suspected of nonneutral service of some sort, ships may be stopped and searched. If there is then evidence of unneutral service, they may be seized and taken to a belligerent port. In port they are turned over to a prize court which attempts to determine whether the seizure was proper and whether the ship, its cargo, or a portion of the latter, or both ship and cargo may be confiscated. It remains only to note that both belligerent and neutral states may at times seize the merchant ships and railroad rolling stock of the other if in its own ports or territory. This is known as the right of angary and must be followed by paying of proper compensation.

CHAPTER 11

Prospects for the Future

AT SOME PERIODS of modern history the rules of international law seem to have been much more stable and reliable than during other eras. The basis for this is in principle relatively simple. When the rules of international law which originated in Europe were applicable only to western Europeans who enjoyed similar value systems, a much higher degree of uniformity could be expected than in an era when these rules apply to a world society, the members of which often seemed to have more attitudes at variance than in common. Also, eras when technology was relatively stable, probably have been politically and legally less upsetting than eras renowned for their remarkable technological changes. In these connections it must never cease to be realized that law bears a very close—often direct—relationship to the patterns of politics, and accordingly, periods of political unrest are also periods of legal turmoil.

In dealing with the future prospects for international law, therefore, one must bear in mind the probable degree of homogeneity in future international society, together with the technological problems and the degree of political intensity present in that society. None of these can be determined with a high degree of certainty, but some patterns of development do appear and can therefore be considered.

What kind of a future, then, can be said to lie ahead for the law of nations? This question has been restated repeatedly for at least a half century, and speculative commentary has wandered in a variety of directions. These have included codification, the need for new foundations, the necessity to limit sovereignty, the desirability of international organization, and the attempt to emphasize the individual, and human rights. All these and other elements have been the subjects of revisionary commentary. That each of these may have some individual merit is not to be seriously questioned. Few of these elements really come to grips with the nature of international law, however, and consequently with its basic problems.

Law, as Professor Corbett has pointed out, consists of those norms which the ruling element wishes to enforce.[1] And while it may or may not embody justice, it does reflect the political fabric of the community from which it derives. Thus law may develop a certain autonomy, but it can never be expected to be independent of its base. This factor is often inadequately stressed in discussions about law in international society.

Directions of Development

Between the theoretical extremes of the Austinians and the world federalists, international law has wended its nonspectacular way. It has perhaps suffered as much from those who asked too much of it as from those who asked and expected too little.[2] Fear for the future has compelled some advocates of change to urge world government as the only alternative to annihilation, while others have sought refuge in revitalized national power.[3] Between these extremes, international law as a practical and necessary device has often been lost sight of. Despite pronounced revisionary literature, it must be realized that as a practical matter international law has really not

---

[1] P. E. Corbett, *The Study of International Law* (Garden City, N.Y.: Double-day & Co., Inc., 1955), p. 3.

[2] See, e.g., comment in J. L. Brierly, *The Law of Nations* (5th ed.; Oxford: The Clarendon Press, 1955), p. v; also J. L. Brierly, *The Outlook for International Law* (Oxford: The Clarendon Press, 1944), pp. 1–2. For an eloquently balanced statement, see J. L. Kunz, "The Swing of the Pendulum: From Overestimation to Underestimation of International Law," *American Journal of International Law*, Vol. XLIV (January, 1950), pp. 135–40.

[3] See, e.g., E. Reves, *The Anatomy of Peace* (8th ed.; New York: Harper & Bros., 1946) as a logical argument for world government. See argument in H. Kissinger, *Nuclear Weapons and Foreign Policy* (Garden City, N.Y.: Doubleday & Co., Inc., 1958) for revitalizing the power position of the West.

changed so very much over the past half century. To be sure, it has taken on some new concepts and has sloughed off others, but its general position has remained much the same. It is, in the now classic words of Brierly, "neither a myth on the one hand, nor a panacea on the other, but just one institution among others which we can use for the building of a better international order."[4]

Within this framework, then, it may be useful to survey a few of the avenues thought by some publicists to be useful for the future development of the law of nations.

Codification. Codification is the process by which states draw up multilateral treaties which restate in clear and systematic form the prevailing rules of customary and other law.[5] The term is sometimes loosely expanded to include agreements which create new law, but this process goes well beyond codification in its more proper sense. Much has been said regarding the value of codification, and many examples of past progress along such lines have been noted in the preceding chapters. It is important for the student of international law to realize, however, that codification is a useful technique, not a panacea. It can only clarify, organize, and systematize the law, but it cannot rechart the world's legal system. It is one thing to restate an agreed principle, but it is quite another to achieve agreement on some new principle, particularly if it is of far-reaching importance. When such major changes are made, the crucial activity is political agreement, not technical codification.

Advancing Arbitration and Adjudication. In a widely heralded speech in 1959, Vice President Nixon suggested greater

---

[4] Brierly, *Law of Nations,* p. v, *passim.*

[5] Perhaps the classic attempts at individual codification are the works of Bluntschli, Fiore, Field, and Levi. Alejandro Alvarez, who once advocated this approach has more recently questioned its utility in unsettled times, see A. Alvarez, *La Codification du droit international,* (Paris: A. Pedone, 1912), and A. Alvarez, "Introduction" to M. Cruchaga Tocornal, *Derecho Internacional* (Santiago, Chile: Editorial Nascimento, 1944) Tomo I, pp. LXIV–LXVI. See above, Chapter Six for a discussion of the treaty process as the main technique for legislating in the international community. For a series of recent efforts, see the "Reports of the International Law Commission," in the official documents section of the *American Journal of International Law* in the following designated issues: (January, 1950, October, 1951 and January of 1953, 1954, 1955, 1956, 1957, 1958, 1959, 1960, 1961, 1962, 1963, 1964, 1965, 1966, 1967). The United Nations Conference on the Law of the Sea held in Geneva in 1958 was grounded on earlier International Law Commission Studies; see *American Journal of International Law,* Vol. LII (October, 1958), pp. 830–67.

use of the International Court of Justice as a device for the settlement of disputes. Such an approach is highly favored by many students of international affairs, and the American Society of International Law supports this view.[6]

Adjudication and related techniques have long been considered of importance in furthering the utility of international law. Here again only modest encouragement can be given to hopes for marked advancement along these lines. To be sure, the techniques are advantageous enough in themselves, and it is only common sense to insist that they be used whenever possible. It is evident that most disputes could and should be submitted to adjudication or arbitration. But as long as the state bears the primary responsibility for security, which as a practical matter includes "vital interests" of various sorts, there will remain an area in which these devices are not likely to be used. If a new order of security maintenance were to emerge, this principle would undergo change—but until such new political context evolves, top security matters will inevitably remain outside this sphere.[7]

Regionalism and Universality. There has been much discussion of the essential universality of international law. On the other hand, in the western hemisphere in particular, there has been much discussion of the existence of a regional American international law. Today further thought is necessarily being given to whether international law can be regional or whether it must have a universal character.[8] There can be little

---

[6] For Mr. Nixon's comments see *New York Times*, April 14, 1959, pp. 1, 20; text on p. 20; for comment dealing especially with the U.S. position, see H. W. Briggs, "The United States and the International Court of Justice: A Reexamination," *American Journal of International Law*, Vol. LIII (April, 1959), pp. 301–18; also Lawrence Preuss, "The International Court of Justice, The Senate, and Matters of Domestic Jurisdiction," *American Journal of International Law*, Vol. XL (October, 1946), pp. 720–36; for a pertinent recording of the "sense of the meeting" of the American Society of International Law, see *Proceedings of the American Society International Law* (1959), p. 330.

[7] For a brief and sound discussion of the nature of vital interests, see Brierly, *The Outlook for International Law, op. cit.,* pp. 31–45.

[8] For a recent statement see M. S. McDougal and H. D. Lasswell, "The Identification and Appraisal of Diverse Systems of Public Order," *American Journal of International Law*, Vol. LIII (January, 1959), pp. 1–29; see A. Alvarez, *Le droit international américain son fondement—sa nature* (Paris: A. Pedone, 1910); for a discussion of various Latin-American viewpoints, see H. B. Jacobini, *A Study of the Philosophy of International Law as Seen in Works of Latin American Writers* (The Hague: Martinus Nijhoff, 1954), pp. 126–36; for comment in the present volume see above, Chapter II.

real question, however, that international law can and does develop within parochial frameworks as well as in a universal context. Thus a Western area is developing which has a high level of internal cooperation; on the other hand, the Soviet bloc seems to have experienced a somewhat similar development. Between these two areas there is much less mutuality, but there is certainly some, and it appears to be increasing. Similarly, within the western hemisphere there is renewed evidence of special cooperation despite examples of conflict, and Western Europe has made considerable progress in the same direction. It is entirely possible that specialized systems of regional international law may develop quite fully in the near future. Indeed, the polarization of present-day international society suggests that legal regionalism within a broad worldwide system of international law may very well be a characteristic of the international law of the future.

The Individual and Human Rights. Another interesting aspect of the future of international law is seen in the possibility that states and other traditional international entities will increasingly share international personality with man as an individual. Under some circumstances such persons as diplomats, heads of state, pirates, and military men have traditionally been accorded such personality. Much comment and some international activity point to an increasingly important place to be taken by individual men as persons and subjects of international law in the future.[9] This is not only of passing interest, for it must be realized that if a time arrives when international society can touch the individual without proceeding through the state as an intermediary, a great step toward world government will have been taken.

A related matter is the question of what rights a person has as a human being aside from his rights as a citizen or a resident of the state. Stemming out of the slaughter of minorities in World War II, and amplified by related contemporary problems, there have been various attempts directed at developing a minimum standard of justice in the human rights area. The

---

[9] See, e.g., P. C. Jessup, *A Modern Law of Nations* (New York: The Macmillan Co., 1950), pp. 15–42 *et passim*. For an attempt to survey the extent to which the view is held in a particular regional setting see Jacobini, *op. cit., passim.*

United Nations Universal Declaration of Human Rights, while
not binding as such, is indicative of the general concept, and
the genocide convention is a specialized example of a treaty
which attempts to protect a civil right. Also, some writers have
sought a naturalist base for international law as a barrier to
such atrocities.[10] In the last analysis, however, these are avenues
which potentially come into conflict with the national rights of
sovereignty and will do so as long as sovereign states exist. It is
unfortunate perhaps, but undoubtedly it is also significant that
the Universal Declaration of Human Rights, while of moral
value, has been accorded little if any legal utility. The genocide
convention which outlaws the killing or damaging of any "national, ethnical, racial or religious group" is at least to some
extent an exception. This accord is not self-executing, however,
and enforcement is left to the courts of the country where the
acts take place under the terms of such implementing legislation as the state itself may pass. While an important gesture has
been made by adopting this treaty and although it certainly has
legal importance, the mechanics of enforcement suggest that
the state is well supplied with effective loopholes. Thus, while
some advance has certainly been made, it is probably far more
spectacular than real.

New Foundations and International Government

A logical and important remedy for the problems of the law
of nations has been seen in the concept of "new foundations of
international law." This idea, which is normally synonomous
with some sort of arrangement for world government, is in a
class by itself far removed in importance from the remedies
mentioned above. Detailed systems vary somewhat, but they all
come to grips more or less with the fundamentals of security.
They point toward a transfer of sovereignty—and hence problems of security—from the existing nation state to some sort of
world state, or in some cases to larger but nonuniversal states.[11]

---

[10] See, e.g., H. Lauterpacht, *International Law and Human Rights* (New
York: Frederick A. Praeger, Inc., 1950) ; the Universal Declaration of Human
Rights is reproduced on pp. 428–34.

[11] Classic examples include E. Reves, *op. cit.;* C. K. Streit, *Union Now with
Britain* (2d ed.; New York: Harper & Bros., 1941) ; for a recent example, see G.

International law would then emerge in most of the projected systems as "world law," the law of a sovereign world community. Its utility would be considerably altered and it would be a much more powerful influence on the conduct of international relationships. But the political and organizational context in which the law is rooted would have undergone fundamental change, and the law as a derivative entity, would merely reflect the new political environment.

To structure logically such a system and to bring it into actual existence are two quite different matters, however. One is an intellectual accomplishment while the other is a political attainment. The latter has many implications, but first of all world government must become politically palatable before it can become a reality. The fact that it may be in the long run the only logical solution to the world's most pressing problems, is irrelevant so long as this fact is not widely appreciated.

It has been suggested that the future of international law is closely linked with that of international organization.[12] Thus it may be argued—and the author is in agreement—that international organization offers a solution to many world problems, and only in such a setting is it possible that international law can develop as has municipal law. But the future is not the present, and since world society is not so organized, international law is *ipso facto* less well structured. The relation between law and its political and constitutional antecedents is immutable—and often direct.[13]

International Administrative Organization. Related to, yet differing fundamentally from, political international organizations are international administrative agencies. These include such organizations as the Universal Postal Union, the International Civil Aviation Organization, and the World Health Or-

---

Clark and L. B. Sohn, *World Peace through World Law* (Cambridge, Mass.: Harvard University Press, 1958) ; see "Convention on the Prevention and Punishment of Genocide," *American Journal of International Law*, Vol. XLV (January, 1951) , pp. 7–10 (documents section) .

[12] P. E. Corbett, *Law and Society in the Relations of States* (New York: Harcourt, Brace & World, Inc., 1951) , pp. 12–13.

[13] For further discussion of this point, see A. Alvarez, *Despues de la guerra* (Buenos Aires: Imprenta de la universidad, 1943) , p. 288 *et passim.* For consideration of related matters, see various studies in M. S. McDougal, *Studies in World Public Order* (New Haven, Conn.: Yale University Press, 1960) .

ganization. Much evidence points to a future international
society even more dependent upon the services of these international administrative agencies than is true of the present-day
community of nations. Technological problems in areas such as
air traffic, disease, and radio can be expected to multiply over
the years and to a considerable extent these problems can and
will probably be entrusted to international agencies.[14]

The rules and regulations emanating from such agencies are
not ordinarily conceived of as being of great importance in
areas touching sovereignty and security. They are of first-rank
importance, however, as far as disease control, literacy, and
related interests are concerned.

Forces in the Lawmaking Process

The politics of lawmaking is normally subjected to the new
forces which find their way into the political arena. These are
rarely easy to evaluate although identification of them may be
relatively simple. Among those which may be considered here
are (1) the impact of the new nations, (2) what may be loosely
called a new law evolving technique of the General Assembly,
(3) the element of security, and (4) the politics of law.

The New Nations. A current roster of the United Nations
membership reveals many state names unknown throughout
most of the world until recently. These new states together with
many older members of the international community evidence
a restlessness and dissatisfaction with the world legal system.
Much is said about an international legal system of Western or
European or great state origin governing an international community, a majority of the members of which have their roots
in non-Western societies or which have come into existence
since the law was formed.[15] This is said to be particularly

---

[14] For examples of such activities see above, Chapter Six.

[15] R. P. Anand, "Role of the 'New' Asian-African Countries in the Present
International Legal Order," *American Journal of International Law,* Vol. LVI
(April, 1962), pp. 383–406; Robert L. Friedheim, "The 'Satisfied' and 'Dissatis-
fied' States Negotiate International Law: A Case Study," *World Politics,* Vol.
XVIII (October, 1965), pp. 20–41; John H. Hazard, "The Sixth Committee and
the New Law," *American Journal of International Law,* Vol. LVII (July, 1963),
pp. 604–13; Jorge Castañeda, "The Underdeveloped Nations and the Development
of International Law," *International Organization,* Vol. XV (Winter, 1961),
pp. 38–48.

significant since a general maxim of international law postulates that each new state must take the law of nations as it finds it upon emerging as a full-fledged member of the society of nations. Whether this is as fundamental in fact as it sometimes appears to be in word is difficult to determine. It is not difficult to recall similar themes with different place names, for states seeking to change the status quo have traditionally argued in this general vein. And indeed, how does any legal pattern become altered but by some such interplay of interests followed by accommodation? What factors appear to motivate these states and what can be expected to evolve from the ensuing interplay?

Persistent themes in the modern world common to all the new states and to most of the older ones are anticolonialism and the principle of nonintervention. Yet these together have sometimes presented strange pictures particularly when combined with the mandate for pacific settlement. If consideration is given, *inter alia*, to the Chinese attack on India, the Indian method of acquiring Goa, the Indo-Pakistan conflict over Kashmir, the Indonesian acquisition of West Iran and later its confrontation with Malaysia, the Egyptian intervention in Aden, the Arab-Israeli difficulties, and the increased Chinese control in Tibet, it is not evident that the voice of the new and refurbished states bespeaks peace and nonintervention with more dignity and detachment than does that of any other collection of countries. Nor is there convincing evidence that the new states have shown less concern with sovereignty than the old, nor, when it involved self-limitation, less concern with nuclear defense. But it can also be argued that the new states have used pacific devices. Thailand allowed suit to be brought against it in regard to the Temple Preah Vihear[16] and accepted an adverse ruling of the Court despite the fact that it had ample power to take the land in question; African states have used the Court regarding South-West Africa;[17] and China and Burma appear able to live in peace. All of this serves, however, only to show balance in the picture, for if the behavior of the

---

[16] *Case Concerning the Temple of Preah Vihear (Cambodia v. Thailand)*, I.C.J. Reports (1962), p. 6.

[17] *South West Africa* cases *(Ethiopia v. South Africa; Liberia v. South Africa)*, I.C.J. Reports (1962), p. 319; I.C.J. Reports (1966), p. 6.

new states is different, it is at most only a matter of modest degree.

There is, nevertheless, frustration on the part of the new states when they are confronted with certain norms of international law. One writer observes that "there is, among the relatively new countries generally, less acceptance of the provisions of classic international law than among the older states."[18] Moreover, the newer states are said to manifest a revisionist political orientation when involved in the task of codification of the law.[19] Also, one can detect a restlessness in such countries when faced with some aspects of international relations which run completely counter to their needs or to their underlying convictions. Anything that the Republic of South Africa does, e.g., appears to be suspect in many parts of Africa.[20] Despite the few variations which do obtain, it appears that—rather than being antilegal or seriously deviationist in their behavior—the new and small states are among those the most committed to the ideals of the law of nations.[21]

Accordingly, it is not clear that the behavior of these states is really generically different from that of other revisionist states throughout history. If, as one writer points out, Guatemala is reluctant to allow the Belize question to go to the World Court to be judged on its legal merits, but would be willing to do so if the case were decided *ex acquo et bono*,[22] how does this differ in essence from the unwillingness of the U.S.S.R. to adjudicate debt and confiscation problems or of the United States to relinquish the Connally Amendment? In the last analysis it is indeed clear that the new states are pressing for revisions in international law, but it is not evident that there is anything constitutionally deviationist about their behavior.

---

18 Castañeda, *op. cit.*, p. 40.

19 See, e.g., remarks in Friedheim, *op. cit.*, *passim*.

20 See Robert O. Keohane, "Political Influence in the General Assembly," *International Conciliation*, No. 557 (March, 1966), p. 27, where an account of voting behavior is quoted. A new state representative was said simply to cast his vote opposite to the way the votes were cast by the representatives of Portugal and South Africa.

21 Anand, *op. cit.*, pp. 388–90 *et passim*.

22 Castañeda, *op. cit.*, pp. 41–2.

The General Assembly and Customary Law. One of the time-honored principles of international law stipulates that no new rule of international law may be imposed upon a state without its consent.[23] This is a legal monument to sovereignty, but it is also an awkward impediment. Strictly interpreted it means that one state may stand out against the entirety of the international community in a matter of a new legal reform. By this light a state has only to refrain from formally acceding to a new conventional rule in order to be free of its restraints. It may be doubted whether in application this rule has ever been as absolute in fact as it can be stated in theory. Nevertheless, it remains an uncertain aspect of the law of nations which leaves much to be desired, for few laws, whether criminal or civil, public or private, municipal or international, can rest ultimately upon such a complete and overwhelming consensus that *absolutely* all must have agreed to the regulation in advance of its application. Nor can it be argued with any cogency that the principle of simple majority rule suitably applies either. Here it must be asked, a majority of what—states, states which are U.N. members, people, adult people, literate people, wealth (however defined), power (also however defined)? Yet somewhere between majority and unanimity lies a point where international legal decision making may stand. What is significant is that while this point is formalized in municipal law, it is not yet precise enough in international law to be articulated.

It will be recalled that in general there are three ways in which new rules of international law are formulated: by custom, by treaty, and by limited rule-making authority vested through treaty in international organizations.[24] It appears now that there is also an emerging variant of custom by which the consensus of the community of nations can be garnered to indicate that custom has indeed been crystallized on some particular point of law. This consensus-compiling function has come to center in the General Assembly of the United Nations, but as with the more traditional matter of determining when custom has become law, there is no clear guideline as to what

---

[23] See discussion *above*, Chapter Six.

[24] See *above*, Chapter Six.

sort of preponderance serves to indicate consensus. Clearly, if it were to be seriously argued that a majority of the Assembly could determine such a matter, the entire development of this interesting process could easily be aborted. If carefully nurtured, however, it will be interesting to watch this process both as a passive exercise in jurisprudence, and, from a more activist standpoint, as a device by which the law of nations may be made into a more precise and adequate instrument.

Accordingly, a recent writer speaking of these matters states that while he believes that the General Assembly has some capacity to speak authoritatively on matters of international law, he does not feel that an Assembly declaration, approved but only with many opposing votes, falls into that definitive category. The 1961 declaration concerning the use of nuclear weapons, for example, was adopted by the Assembly with opposition votes cast by 20 states including the United States, the United Kingdom, and France. On the other hand, the 1963 outer space declaration which enjoyed approval "by acclamation" was seen as an example of the Assembly's authoritative expression.[25]

If one goes beyond the mere recognition of a customary rule and tries to view the Assembly as a device for making law, it is not difficult to discount its validity on relatively clear-cut constitutional grounds,[26] but if, somewhat less spectacularly, the Assembly actions are seen as devices by which the political ethos is moved into a context in which a new political orientation can and does emerge, then, in effect if not in word, a new lawmaking device is being created.[27] This is what appears to be

---

[25] Egan Schwelb, "The Nuclear Test Ban Treaty and International Law," *American Journal of International Law*, Vol. LVIII (July, 1964) , pp. 645–46.

[26] A Philippine move at the San Francisco Convention to give the General Assembly the power to make law was decisively defeated 26 to 1. See 9 *U.N.C.I.O.* Docs. 316,70 (1945) ; Richard A. Falk, "On the Quasi Legislative Competence of the General Assembly," *American Journal of International Law*, Vol. LX (October, 1966) , p. 783; K. Skubiszewski, "The General Assembly of the United Nations and the Power to Influence National Action," *Proceedings of the American Society of International Law*, 1964, pp. 153–54.

[27] See G. R. Lande, "The Changing Effectiveness of General Assembly Resolutions," *Proceedings of the American Society of International Law*, 1964, pp. 162–70, Skubiszewski, *op. cit., passim;* Falk, *op.cit., passim;* see also Richard A. Falk, "The Adequacy of Contemporary Theories of International Law—Gaps in Legal Thinking," *Virginia Law Review*, Vol. L (1964) , pp. 231–65.

developing, and it may in time prove to be one of the most exciting jural developments of modern times.

Security. Undoubtedly the main factor in the whole question of the development of international law in the highly political areas of activity revolves around the nature of security and sovereignty.[28] The entity responsible for these matters today is the state. As long as this remains true, there is little that the law can do to mitigate the effects of the highest levels of political relations among states. The reason for this is simply that as long as security is a state responsibility, the state and its agents cannot shirk that responsibility. Thus if war is prevented it is not law which will do it, but rather the circumstances of politics.

On the other hand, law will continue to smooth the relations of states on a less highly charged level. Thus the real crux of the matter is not how international law as such can be made more effective, but a frank recognition that the heart of the problem of international relations is not primarily legal but political.[29] A remedy for the hazards of the contemporary world lies in the creation of new procedures and institutions leading toward world government, or in a careful utilization of power politics within the existing state system.

The Politics of Law. As has been emphasized earlier, law is a formalized derivative of politics. If this is realized and appreciated, it is inescapable that law cannot rise far above its political base. This then puts the reforming emphasis where it should be—in the realm of politics, and not on the law's doorstep. While it has been argued with some persuasiveness that the source of jural law is public opinion,[30] this view must be accepted cautiously. Where public opinion is the prime mover of political power as it is in a democracy, such a view may withstand serious scrutiny, but elsewhere it is true only to whatever extent public opinion can be equated with real political power. Thus law is not a device which reforms society, but

---

[28] See discussion in Corbett, *Law and Society* . . . , pp. 86–87.

[29] See discussion in Charles de Visscher, *Theory and Reality in Public International Law,* trans. P. E. Corbett (Princeton, N.J.: Princeton University Press, 1957) , pp. 286–96.

[30] Q. Wright, "International Law and Power Politics," *Measure,* Vol. II (Spring, 1951) , pp. 137–38.

rather it is a system which comes to mirror the existing political milieu. It is a sort of regularized reflection of the society itself. When question is raised as to whether international law can prevent war, the answer must invariably be a substantial though qualified negative. In Professor Brierly's words, "law does not create order, [but] it can be used, as it is habitually used within the state, to underpin the fabric of order once this has been established.[31] It must be reiterated that the solution to major problems lies in achieving a political consensus in the international community which points toward some other organizational form for the international community—presumably some sort of federation—and at such time international law will adapt to reflect the new political consensus. Otherwise a solution lies within the orbit of a careful marshaling of the political forces within the present structure of world society—and it is probable that this will be the framework of international society for the foreseeable future.[32] In any event, the political complex is the motivating force, and the resulting legal patterns are merely derivative.

A Modest Future for International Law

It has been suggested that it is reasonable to expect international law to undergo modest refinements in the areas of international administrative organization and in such matters as codification and the adjustment of disputes through wider use of adjudication. Perhaps regional advancements will be seen in greater numbers than formerly. Certainly the developments leading toward a common market in Europe and toward closer consultations in the inter-American system are suggestive—but not conclusive. The seeming advances in the control of the Antarctic region may also be a case in point. Moreover, a broader, unwritten and even unspoken, sense of understanding of where the brink lies on the part of the Soviet Union and the United States may be a hopeful sign. Yet these bespeak larger sovereignties, more refined cooperation, and perhaps greater

---

[31] Brierly, *The Outlook for International Law, op. cit.,* p. 95.

[32] H. J. Morgenthau, *Politics among Nations* (2d ed.; New York: Alfred A. Knopf, Inc., 1954) , Chapter XXIX *et passim.*

wisdom, but they do little in the way of effecting radical changes in the structure of the international community. Moreover, increasing numbers of sovereign states, each jealous of its sovereign prerogatives, and new and revitalized great states or potential great states willing to use force when it seems to serve their interests, do not assure a better or a greatly altered community of nations. Finally, it has become increasingly clear that the United Nations, as an institution, can rise only slightly higher than the level of the states which comprise it.

It will be surprising, therefore, if advances of a more far-reaching character are made in the next few years. Thus one may conjecture that sovereignty will remain in the states and under those circumstances, as has been pointed out above, the political complexion of the international community will remain much as it has been for centuries. If this is true, then it follows that international law will remain much the same. As such, international law will remain a most important device for regularizing procedures, but its utility on the higher levels of politics will not be great. If this fact can be widely grasped, international law will not continue to suffer one fate which has so often beset it, that is, the disillusionment resulting from excessive expectations. It can be viewed then in proper perspective: as an aid in smoothing international relationships, and even as a useful ancillary device to assist in maintaining peace—but of use only within the prevailing pattern of world politics.

SUMMARY

The future of international law has been considered from several points of view. Techniques of codification, wider use of arbitration and adjudication, and advancing the position of the individual and of human rights have all been suggested as avenues to a wider utility for international law. There has been recent comment regarding the importance of universality as a base for international law, and it has been noted that universality is often impractical in theory and that there is evidence of a rise in regional usages.

There has been much commentary regarding new foundations of international law. Normally this means a new international system involving world government. It is doubtful if there are any close students of international affairs who do not recognize the need for some sort of development along these lines. Yet there are serious barriers remaining to its accomplishment. International administrative agencies, however, represent one aspect of international organization which will probably be even more widely used in the foreseeable future. Perhaps the most interesting innovation, one which bears watching, is the limited ability of the General Assembly to act by declaration to determine the existence of customary law. This in time could have far-reaching implications.

Meanwhile, until some system of real world government comes into existence, and out of it a far more comprehensive system of world law, it must be realized that the future of international law within the present international state system will be a modest one. The real problem is that so long as responsibility for security remains in the states, international law will reflect that underlying political reality and will serve only the same purposes which it has served during the modern era—little more or little less.

Selected References

THERE ARE several unusually comprehensive bibliographies available to the reader. Moreover, the careful student recognizes in footnote references an ideal source of useful materials, particularly if several texts are consulted.

The following list will therefore include only a very small number of selected sources and will stress materials in English which, for the most part, are accessible and reasonably up to date.

Digests, Major Treatises, Periodicals, Major Compendia, and Reference Aids

ACADEMIE DE DROIT INTERNATIONAL. *Recueil des cours.* Published since 1923.

American Journal of International Law. Published since 1907. (Also Proceedings since 1907.)

British Yearbook of International Law. Published since 1920.

Canadian Yearbook of International Law. Published since 1963.

Grotius International Yearbook. (Grotius-Annuaire International.) Published since 1913.

Grotius Society, Transactions of the. Published since 1916.

HACKWORTH, G. H. *Digest of International Law.* 8 vols. Washington, D.C.: U.S. Government Printing Office, 1940–44.

Harvard International Law Club Journal. Published since 1959.

"Harvard Law School Research in International Law," *American Journal of International Law.* Special Supplements, 1929, 1932, 1935, 1939.

HYDE, C. C. *International Law Chiefly as Interpreted by the United States.* 3 vols. 2d ed. Boston: Little, Brown & Co., 1945.

Indian Journal of International Law. Published since 1963.

Inter-American Juridical Yearbook. Published since 1948.

International and Comparative Law Quarterly. Published since

1952. (*International Law Quarterly*, 1947–51, and *Journal of Comparative Legislation and International Law*, 1896–1951, merged to form *International and Comparative Law Quarterly*.)

International Conciliation. Published since 1907.

INTERNATIONAL COURT OF JUSTICE. *Report of Judgments, Advisory Opinions, and Orders.* Published since 1947. (Also related Documents.)

International Law Association, Reports. Published since 1873.

International Law Reports. Published under various titles and with supplementary volumes covering most of the period from 1919 to the present.

International Law Studies. Published by the U.S. Naval War College under various titles since 1901.

International Legal Materials. Published since 1962.

International Organization. Published since 1947.

Journal of Air Law and Commerce. Published since 1930; from 1930 to 1942 as *Journal of Air Law.*

Journal of Public Law. Published since 1952.

LE FUR, LOUIS, and CHKLAVER, GEORGE. *Recueil de textes de droit international public.* Deuxieme edition. Paris: Librairie Dalloz, 1934.

McNAIR, LORD. *International Law Opinions.* 3 vols. Cambridge: Cambridge University Press, 1956.

MOORE, J. B. *A Digest of International Law.* 8 vols. Washington, D.C.: U.S. Government Printing Office, 1906.

MOORE, J. B. *History and Digest of the International Arbitrations to Which the United States Has Been a Party.* 6 vols. Washington, D.C.: U.S. Government Printing Office, 1898.

MOORE, J. B. *International Adjudications.* 6 vols. New York: Oxford University Press, 1929–1933.

OPPENHEIM, L. *International Law, A Treatise.* 8th ed. of Vol. I and 7th ed. of Vol. II revised by H. Lauterpacht. London: Longmans, Green & Co., Inc., 1955, 1952.

PERMANENT COURT OF INTERNATIONAL JUSTICE. *Collection of Judgments* (Series A) ; *Collection of Judgments, Orders and Advisory Opinions* (Series A/B) ; *Collection of Advisory Opinions* (Series B) . Published between 1923 and 1940.

Reports of International Arbitral Awards. United Nations publication. 15 volumes published to early 1968.

Virginia Journal of International Law. Published since 1961.

WHITEMAN, MARJORIE M. *Digest of International Law.* 5 vols. by early 1968. Washington, D.C.: U.S. Government Printing Office, 1963–65.

WIGMORE, JOHN A. *A Guide to American International Law and Practice.* New York: Matthew Bender and Co., 1943.

World Polity. Published since 1957.

Yearbook of the International Law Commission. Published since 1949.

Texts and Treatises

BRIERLY, J. L. *The Law of Nations.* 5th ed. Oxford: Clarendon Press, 1955; 6th ed. by Sir Humphrey Waldock, 1963.

FENWICK, C. G. *International Law,* 3d and 4th ed. New York: Appleton-Century-Crofts, Inc., 1948, 1965.

GOULD, W. L. *An Introduction to International Law.* New York: Harper & Bros., 1957.

HALL, W. E. *A Treatise on International Law.* 5th ed. by J. B. Atlay. Oxford: Clarendon Press, 1904. (Various editions from 1880 to 1924).

KELSEN, H. *Principles of International Law.* New York: Rinehart and Co., 1952.

KELSEN, H. *Principles of International Law.* 2d ed. by Robert W. Tucker. New York: Holt, Rinehart & Winston, Inc., 1966.

PFANKUCHEN, L. *A Documentary Textbook in International Law.* New York: Farrar and Rinehart, 1940.

SCHUSCHNIGG, K. VON. *International Law: An Introduction to the Law of Peace.* Milwaukee, Wis. Bruce Publishing Co., 1959.

SCHWARZENBERGER, G. *A Manual of International Law.* 3d ed. London: Stevens & Sons Ltd., 1952. (5th ed., 1967).

SCHWARZENBERGER, G. *International Law,* Vol. I. 3d ed. London: Stevens & Sons Ltd., 1957.

STARKE, J. G. *An Introduction to International Law.* 4th ed. London: Butterworth and Co., 1958. (5th ed., 1963).

SVARLIEN, O. *Introduction to the Law of Nations.* New York: McGraw-Hill Book Co., Inc., 1955.

VON GLAHN, GERHARD. *Law among Nations.* New York: The Macmillan Company, 1965.

WHITAKER, URBAN G., JR. *Politics and Power.* New York: Harper & Row, 1964.

WILSON, G. G. *International Law.* 9th ed. New York: Silver, Burdett and Co., 1935.

Casebooks and Case Collections

BISHOP, W. W., JR. *International Law Cases and Materials.* Englewood Cliffs, N.J.: Prentice-Hall, Inc., 1951. (2nd edition, 1962.)

BRIGGS, H. W. *The Law of Nations: Cases, Documents, and Notes.* 2d ed. New York: Appleton-Century-Crofts, 1952.

British International Law Cases, New York: Oceana Publications, 1964–. Five volumes published by early 1968.

COBBETT, P. *Leading Cases and Opinions on International Law.* 6th ed. by W. L. Walker. London: Sweet and Maxwell, 1947.

DICKINSON, E. D. *Cases and Materials on International Law.* Brooklyn: Foundation Press, 1950.

FENWICK, C. G. *Cases on International Law.* 2d ed. Chicago: Callaghan and Co., 1951.

GREEN, L. C. *International Law through Cases.* 2d ed. New York: Frederick A. Praeger, Inc., 1955.

HUDSON, M. O. *Cases and Other Materials on International Law.* 3d ed. St. Paul, Minn.: West Publishing Co., 1951.

JAEGER, H. E., and O'BRIEN, W. V. *International Law. Cases, Text Notes and Other Materials.* Washington, D.C.: Georgetown University Press, 1958.

MANGONE, GERARD J. *The Elements of International Law.* Rev. ed. Homewood, Ill.: The Dorsey Press, 1967.

O'CONNELL, D. P. *International Law.* 2 vols. Dobbs Ferry, New York: Oceana Publications, 1965.

ORFIELD, L. B., and RE, E. D. *Cases and Materials on International Law.* Indianapolis: Bobbs-Merrill Co., 1955.

History, Sources, Doctrine, and Future Prospects

Academy of Sciences of the U.S.S.R., Institute of State and Law. *International Law.* Moscow: Foreign Languages Publishing House, 1961.

AMERICANO, J. *The New Foundation of International Law.* New York: The Macmillan Co., 1947.

BOWETT, D. W. *The Law of International Institutions*. New York: Frederick A. Praeger, Inc., 1963.

BRIERLY, J. L. *The Basis of Obligation in International Law and Other Papers*. Ed. H. Lauterpacht and C. H. M. Waldock. Oxford: Clarendon Press, 1958.

BRIERLY, J. L. *The Outlook for International Law*. Oxford: Clarendon Press, 1944.

CARLSTON, KENNETH S. *Law and Organization in World Society*. Urbana, Ill.: University of Illinois Press, 1962.

COPLIN, WILLIAM D. *The Functions of International Law: An Introduction to the Role of International Law in the Contemporary World*. Chicago: Rand McNally & Co., 1966.

Classics of International Law. (In this series published under the auspices of the Carnegie Institute are some of the works of Belli, Ayala, Grotius, Gentili, Pufendorf, Bynkershoek, Zouch, Rachel, Vattel, Wheaton, Suarez, Vitoria, Textor, and de Lignano.)

CORBETT, P. E. *Law and Society in the Relations of States*. New York: Harcourt, Brace & World, Inc., 1951.

CORBETT, P. E. *The Study of International Law*. Garden City, N.Y.: Doubleday & Co., Inc., 1955.

DEENER, D. R. *The United States Attorneys General and International Law*. The Hague: Martinus Nijhoff, 1957.

DE VISSCHER, C. *Theory and Reality in Public International Law*. Trans. P. E. Corbett. Princeton, N.J.: Princeton University Press, 1957.

FALK, RICHARD A. *et al. Essays on International Jurisdiction*. Columbus, Ohio: State University Press, 1961.

FINCH, G. A. *The Sources of Modern International Law*. Washington, D.C.: Carnegie Endowment, 1937.

GARNER, JAMES W. *Recent Developments in International Law*. Calcutta: University of Calcutta, 1925.

HIGGINS, A. P. *Studies in International Law and Relations*. Cambridge: University Press, 1928.

HIGGINS, ROSALYN. *The Development of International Law through the Political Organs of the United Nations*. New York: Oxford University Press, 1963.

JACOBINI, H. B. *A Study of the Philosophy of International Law as Seen in Works of Latin American Writers*. The Hague: Martinus Nijhoff. 1954.

JENKS, C. W. *The Common Law of Mankind.* New York: Frederick A. Praeger, Inc., 1958.

JESSUP, PHILIP C. *A Modern Law of Nations.* New York: The Macmillan Co., 1948.

JESSUP, PHILIP C. *Transnational Law.* New Haven, Conn.: Yale University Press, 1956.

JESSUP, P. C. *The Use of International Law.* Ann Arbor, Mich.: University of Michigan Law School, 1959.

KAPLAN, M. A., and KATZENBACH, N. deB. *Political Foundations of International Law.* New York: John Wiley & Sons, Inc., 1961.

KEETON, G. W., and SCHWARZENBERGER, G. *Making International Law Work.* London: Stevens & Sons Ltd., 1946.

KELSEN, HANS. *General Theory of Law and State.* Cambridge, Mass.: Harvard University Press, 1945.

KELSEN, HANS. *The Communist Theory of Law.* New York: Frederick A. Praeger, Inc., 1955.

KELSEN, HANS. *What Is Justice? Justice, Law and Politics in the Mirror of Science.* Berkeley: University of California Press, 1957.

KHADDURI, M. *War and Peace in the Law of Islam.* 2d ed. Baltimore: The Johns Hopkins Press, 1955.

KOROWICZ, MAREK ST. *Introduction to International Law.* The Hague: Martinus Nijhoff, 1959.

KRABBE, HUGO. *The Modern Idea of the State.* Trans. with an introduction by G. H. Sabine and W. J. Shepard. New York: D. Appleton Co., 1922.

LARSON, ARTHUR, JENKS, C. W. *et al. Sovereignty within the Law.* Dobbs Ferry, N.Y.: Oceana Publications, Inc., 1965.

LAUTERPACHT, H. *The Function of Law in the International Community.* Oxford: Clarendon Press, 1933.

LIPSKY, G. (ed.) *Law and Politics in the World Community.* Berkeley, Calif.: University of California Press, 1953.

LISKA, G. *International Equilibrium.* Cambridge, Mass.: Harvard University Press, 1957.

LISSITZYN, OLIVER J. *International Law Today and Tomorrow.* Dobbs Ferry, N.Y.: Oceana Publications, Inc., 1965.

McDOUGAL, MYRES S. and FELICIANO, F. P. *Law and Minimum World Public Order.* New Haven, Conn.: Yale University Press, 1961.

McDOUGAL, M. S., and ASSOCIATES. *Studies in World Public Order.*

New Haven, Conn.: Yale University Press, 1960.

MOORE, J. B. *The Collected Papers of John Basset Moore.* 7 vols. New Haven, Conn.: Yale University Press, 1944.

MOORE, J. B. *International Law and Some Current Illusions and Other Essays.* New York: The Macmillan Co., 1924.

NUSSBAUM, A. *A Concise History of the Law of Nations.* 2d ed. New York: The Macmillan Co., 1954.

OPPENHEIM, L. *The Future of International Law.* Oxford: Clarendon Press, 1921.

PHILLIPSON, COLEMAN. *The International Law and Custom of Ancient Greece and Rome.* 2 vols. London: Macmillan and Co., 1911.

RAMUNDO, BERNARD A. and RUSIS, ARMINS. *The Socialist Theory of International Law.* Washington, D.C.: Institute of Sino-Soviet Studies, Series No. 1, George Washington University 1964.

ROSENAU, JAMES N. *International Aspects of Civil Strife.* Princeton, N.J.: Princeton University Press, 1964.

SCELLE, GEORGE. *Precis de droit des gens principes et systematique.* Paris: Librairie du Recueil Sirey, 1932.

SERENI, ANGELO PIERO. *The Italian Conception of International Law.* New York: Columbia University Press, 1943.

STARKE, J. L. *Studies in International Law.* London: Butterworth & Co. (Publishers) Ltd., 1965.

STONE, JULIUS. *Quest for Survival.* Cambridge, Mass.: Harvard University Press, 1961.

SYATAUW, J. J. G. *Some Newly Established Asian States and the Development of International Law.* The Hague: Martinus Nijhoff, 1961.

TRISKA, JAN F. and SLUSSER, ROBERT M. *The Theory Law and Policy of Soviet Treaties.* Stanford, Calif.: Stanford University Press, 1962.

TUNG, L. *China and Some Phases of International Law.* New York: Oxford University Press, 1940.

WESTLAKE, J. *The Collected Papers of John Westlake on Public International Law.* Ed. L. Oppenheim. Cambridge: University Press, 1914.

WRIGHT, Q. *Contemporary International Law: A Balance Sheet.* Garden City, N.Y.: Doubleday & Co., Inc., 1955.

WRIGHT, Q. *Problems of Stability and Progress in International Relations.* Berkeley, Calif.: University of California Press, 1954.

Recognition and Succession

CHEN, J. C. *The International Law of Recognition.* New York: Frederick A. Praeger, Inc., 1951.

HERVEY, J. G. *The Legal Effects of Recognition in International Law.* Philadelphia: University of Pennsylvania Press, 1928.

LAUTERPACHT, H. *Recognition in International Law.* Cambridge, Mass.: Harvard University Press, 1948.

MAREK, K. *Identity and Continuity of States in Public International Law.* Geneve: Librairie E. Droz, 1954.

NEUMANN, W. L. *Recognition of Governments in the Americas.* Washington, D.C.: Foundation for Foreign Affairs, 1947.

O'CONNELL, D. P. *The Law of State Succession.* Cambridge: University Press, 1956.

Rights and Obligations of States

BORCHARD, E. M. *Diplomatic Protection of Citizens Abroad.* New York: Banks Law Publishing Co., 1915.

DICKINSON, E. D. *The Equality of States in International Law.* Cambridge, Mass.: Harvard University Press, 1920.

DUNN, F. S. *The Protection of Nationals.* Baltimore: The Johns Hopkins Press, 1932.

EAGLETON, C. *The Responsibility of States in International Law.* New York: New York University Press, 1928.

FREEMAN, A. V. *The International Responsibility of States for Denial of Justice.* London: Longmans, Green & Co., Inc., 1938.

LAUTERPACHT, H. *International Law and Human Rights.* New York: Frederick A. Praeger, Inc., 1950.

RE, E. D. *Foreign Confiscations in Anglo American Law.* Dobbs Ferry, N.Y.: Oceana Publications, Inc., 1951.

SHEA, D. R. *The Calvo Clause.* Minneapolis, Minn.: University of Minnesota Press, 1955.

THOMAS, A. V. W., and THOMAS, A. J. J. *Non-Intervention: The Law and Its Import in the Americas.* Dallas, Tex.: Southern Methodist University Press, 1956.

WHITEMAN, M. M. *Damages in International Law.* 3 vols. Washington, D.C.: U.S. Government Printing Office, 1937–43.

WORTLEY, B. A. *Expropriation in Public International Law.* Cambridge: University Press, 1959.

Jurisdiction

AHLUWALIA, KULJIT. *The Legal Status, Privileges and Immunities of the Specialized Agencies of the United Nations and Certain Other International Organizations.* The Hague: Martinus Nijhoff, 1964.

BAXTER, R. R. and TRISKA, JAN F. *The Law of International Waterways.* Cambridge, Mass.: Harvard University Press, 1964.

BERBER, F. J. *Rivers in International Law.* London: Stevens & Sons Ltd., 1959.

BOCZEK, B. A. *Flags of Convenience.* Cambridge, Mass.: Harvard University Press, 1962.

BOGGS, S. W. *International Boundaries.* New York: Columbia University Press, 1940.

CHRISTOL, C. Q. *The International Law of Outer Space (International Law Studies* 1962, Vol. LV). Washington, D.C.: U.S. Government Printing Office, 1966.

CLUTE, ROBERT E. *The International Legal Status of Austria 1938–1955.* The Hague: Martinus Nijhoff, 1962.

COLOMBOS, C. J. *The International Law of the Sea.* 4th rev. ed. London: Longmans, Green & Co., Ltd, 1959.

DREIER, J. C. *The Organization of American States and the Hemisphere Crisis.* New York: Harper & Row, 1962.

FALK, RICHARD A. *et al. The Aftermath of Sabbatino.* Dobbs Ferry, N.Y.: Oceana Publications, Inc., 1965.

FAWCETT, J. E. S. *The British Commonwealth in International Law.* London: Stevens & Sons, Ltd., 1963.

FELD, WERNER. *The Court of the European Communities: New Dimension in International Adjudication.* The Hague: Martinus Nijhoff, 1964.

GARCIA-MORA, M. R. *International Law and Asylum as a Human Right.* Washington, D.C. Public Affairs Press, 1956.

HILL, N. L. *Claims to Territory in International Law and Relations.* London: Oxford University Press, 1945.

INTER-AMERICAN INSTITUTE OF INTERNATIONAL LEGAL STUDIES. *The Inter-American System: Its Development and Strengthening.* Dobbs Ferry, N.Y.: Oceana Publications, Inc., 1966.

Jessup, P. C. *The Law of Territorial Waters and Maritime Jurisdiction.* New York: G. A. Jennings, Co., 1927.

Jessup, P. C., and Taubenfeld, H. J. *Controls for Outer Space and the Anarctic Analogy.* New York: Columbia University Press, 1959.

Keller, A. S.; Lissitzyn, O. J.; and Mann, F. J. *Creation of Rights of Sovereignty through Symbolic Acts, 1400–1800.* New York: Columbia University Press, 1938.

Kutner, Luis. *World Habeas Corpus.* Dobbs Ferry, N.Y.: Oceana Publications, Inc., 1962.

Lindley, M. F. *The Acquisition and Government of Backward Territory in International Law.* London: Longmans, Green & Co., Inc., 1926.

Mason, Henry L. *The European Coal and Steel Community, Experiment in Supranationalism.* The Hague: Martinus Nijhoff, 1955.

McDougal, Myres S., Lasswell, Harold D., and Vlasic, Ivan A. *Law and Public Order in Space.* New Haven, Conn.: Yale University Press, 1963.

McDougal, Myres S. and Burke, William T. *The Public Order of the Oceans.* New Haven, Conn.: Yale University Press, 1962.

Mouton, M. W. *The Continental Shelf.* The Hague: Martinus Nijhoff, 1952.

Nussbaum, A. *Principles of Private International Law.* New York: Oxford University Press, 1943.

Papadatos, P. *The Eichmann Trial.* New York; Frederick A. Praeger, Inc., 1964.

Reid, H. D. *International Servitudes in Law and Practice.* Chicago: University of Chicago Press, 1932.

Remec, Peter P. *The Position of the Individual in International Law According to Grotius and Vattel.* The Hague: Martinus Nijhoff, 1960.

Ronning, C. Neal. *Law and Politics in Inter-American Diplomacy.* New York: John Wiley & Sons, Inc., 1963.

Seekler-Hudson, C. *Statelessness with Special Reference to the United States.* Washington, D.C.: American University Graduate School, 1934.

Smedal, G. *Acquisition of Sovereignty over Polar Areas.* Oslo: Dybwad, 1931.

VALI, F. A. *Servitudes of International Law.* 2d ed. New York: Frederick A. Praeger, Inc., 1958.

WEIS, P. *Nationality and Statelessness in International Law.* London: Stevens & Sons Ltd., 1956.

YDIT, M. *International Territories.* Leyden: A. W. Sythoff, 1961.

Treaties

CAMARA, J. S. *The Ratification of International Treaties.* Toronto: Ontario Publishing Co., 1949.

CHANG, YI-TING. *The Interpretation of Treaties by Judicial Tribunals.* New York: Columbia University Press, 1933.

CRANDALL, S. B. *Treaties, Their Making and Enforcement.* 2d ed. Washington, D.C.: John Byrne and Co., 1916.

HILL, C. *The Doctrine of "Rebus Sic Stantibus" in International Law.* Columbia, Mo.: University of Missouri Press, 1934.

HOYT, E. C. *The Unanimity Rule in the Revision of Treaties: A Re-Examination.* The Hague: Martinus Nijhoff, 1959.

MCINTYRE, S. H. *Legal Effect of World War II on Treaties of the United States.* The Hague: Martinus Nijhoff, 1958.

MCNAIR, A. D. *The Law of Treaties—British Practice and Opinions.* New York: Columbia University Press, 1938.

WILCOX, F. O. *The Ratification of International Conventions.* London: George Allen and Unwin Ltd., 1935.

WILSON, R. R. *The International Law Standard of Treaties of the United States.* Cambridge, Mass.: Harvard University Press, 1953.

YU, TSUNE-CHI. *The Interpretation of Treaties.* New York: Columbia University Press, 1927.

Agents

ADAIR, E. R. *The Extraterritoriality of Ambassadors in the Sixteenth and Seventeenth Centuries.* London: Longmans, Green and Co., 1929.

CROSSWELL, C. M. *Protection of International Personnel Abroad: Law and Practice Affecting the Privileges and Immunities of International Organization.* Dobbs Ferry, N.Y.: Oceana Publications, Inc., 1952.

HERSHEY, A. S. *Diplomatic Agents and Immunities.* Washington, D.C.: Government Printing Office, 1919.

PLISCHKE, E. *Conduct of American Diplomacy.* New York: D. Van Nostrand Co., 1950.

PUENTE, J. I. *The Foreign Consul: His Juridical Status in the United States.* Chicago: Burdette J. Smith and Co., 1926.

SATOW, E. *A Guide to Diplomatic Practice,* 4th ed. by Sir N. Bland. London: Longmans, Green & Co., Inc., 1957.

STUART, G. H. *American Diplomatic and Consular Practice.* 2d ed. New York: Appleton-Century-Crofts, 1952.

Modes of Redress Short of War

BUSTAMENTE Y SIRVEN, A. S. *The World Court.* New York: The Macmillan Co., 1926.

CARLSTON, K. S. *The Process of International Arbitration.* New York: Columbia University Press, 1946.

COLBERT, H. S. *Retaliation in International Law.* New York: King's Crown Press, 1948.

HAMBRO, E. *The Case Law of the International Court.* Leyden: A. W. Sijthoff, 1952.

HINDMARSH, A. E. *Force in Peace.* Cambridge, Mass.: Harvard University Press, 1933.

HOGAN, A. E. *Pacific Blockade.* Oxford: Clarendon Press, 1908.

HUDSON, M. O. *By Pacific Means.* New Haven, Conn.: Yale University Press, 1935.

HUDSON, M. O. *The Permanent Court of International Justice, 1920–1943.* New York: The Macmillan Co., 1943.

KELSEN, H. *Peace through Law.* Chapel Hill, N.C.: University of North Carolina, 1944.

LAUTERPACHT, H. *The Development of International Law by the International Court.* New York: Frederick A. Praeger, Inc., 1958.

LISSITZYN, O. J. *The International Court of Justice: Its Role in the Maintenance of International Peace and Security.* New York: Carnegie Endowment, 1951.

RALSTON, J. H. *International Arbitration from Athens to Locarno.* Stanford, Calif.: Stanford University Press, 1929.

ROSENNE, S. *The International Court of Justice: An Essay in Politi-*

.cal and Legal Theory. Leyden: A. W. Sijthoff, 1957.

SIMPSON, J. L. and Fox, H. International Arbitration: Law and Practice. New York: Frederick A. Praeger, Inc., 1959.

STOWELL, E. C. Intervention in International Law. Washington, D.C.: John Byrne and Co., 1921.

War and Neutrality

APPLEMAN, J. A. Military Tribunals and International Crimes. Indianapolis: The Bobbs-Merrill Co., Inc., 1954.

BOWETT, D. W. Self-Defense in International Law. New York: Frederick A. Praeger, Inc., 1958.

CASTRÉN, E. The Present Law of War and Neutrality. Helsinki: Annales Academiae Scientiarum Fennicae (Ser. B, Tom. 85) 1954.

COLOMBOS, J. C. A Treatise on the Law of Prize. 3d ed. London: Longmans, Green & Co., Inc., 1949.

DEPARTMENT OF THE ARMY. Geneva Conventions of 12 August 1949 for the Protection of War Victims. Army Pamphlet No. 20–150. Washington, D.C.: U.S. Government Printing Office, 1950.

DEPARTMENT OF THE ARMY, Law of Land Warefare. F. M. 27–10. Washington, D.C.: U.S. Government Printing Office, 1956. (Also, War Department. Rules of Land Warefare. F. M. 27–10. Washington, D.C.: U.S. Government Printing Office, 1940.)

DOMKE, MARTIN. The Control of Alien Property. New York: Central Book Co., 1947.

DOMKE, MARTIN. Trading with the Enemy in World War II. New York: Central Book Co., 1943.

FLORY, W. E. S. Prisoners of War. Washington, D.C.: American Council on Public Affairs, 1942.

GRABER, D. A. The Development of the Law of Belligerent Occupation 1863–1914. New York: Columbia University Press, 1949.

GREENSPAN, M. The Modern Law of Land Warfare. Berkeley, Calif.: University of California Press, 1959.

GROB, F. The Relativity of War and Peace. New Haven, Conn.: Yale University Press, 1949.

JESSUP, P. C.; DEAK, F.; PHILLIPS, W. A.; REED, A. H.; and TURLINGTON, E. Neutrality Its History, Economics and Law. 4 vols. New York: Columbia University Press, 1935–36.

Materials on the Trial of Former Servicemen of the Japanese Army Charged with Manufacturing and Employing Bacteriological Weapons. Moscow: Foreign Languages Publishing House, 1950.

LATIFI, ALMÀ. *Effects of War on Property.* London: Macmillan and Co., Ltd., 1909.

McNAIR, A. D. *Legal Effects of War.* 3d ed. Cambridge: Cambridge University Press, 1948.

ORVIK, N. *The Decline of Neutrality 1914–41.* Oslo: Tanum, 1953.

PADELFORD, N. J. *International Law and Diplomacy in the Spanish Civil Strife.* New York: The Macmillan Co., 1939.

POMPE, C. A. *Aggressive War An International Crime.* The Hague: Martinus Nijhoff, 1953.

SPAIGHT, J. M. *Air Power and War Rights,* 3d ed. London: Longmans, Green & Co., Inc., 1947.

STONE, J. *Legal Controls of International Conflict.* New York: Rinehart and Co., 1954.

Trial of the Major War Criminals before the International Military Tribunal. Nuremberg: International Military Tribunal, 1947–49. 42 vols.

Trials of War Criminals Before the Nurnburg Military Tribunals Under Control Law No. 10. Washington, D.C.: U.S. Government Printing Office, 1951. 15 vols.

TUCKER, R. W. *The Law of War and Neutrality at Sea.* (Naval War College, International Law Studies, 1955, Vol. XIX; includes in appendix official manual, *Law of Naval Warfare* [Washington, D.C.: U.S. Government Printing Office, 1957]).

WESTLAKE, J. *International Law,* Part II: War. Cambridge: University Press, 1913.

WRIGHT, Q. *A Study of War.* 2 vols. Chicago: University of Chicago Press, 1942.

APPENDIX

Selected Data on Treaty Accessions

THE FOLLOWING EXHIBITS have been adapted from two principal sources, both of which are public documents, and represent the states which have become parties to 46 selected multilateral conventions.

Forty-two of these accords are up to date as of January 1, 1967.[1] The four exceptions include the Genocide Convention and the following three maritime conventions on: The High Seas; The Continental Shelf; and The Territorial Sea and Contiguous Zone.[2] These are up to date as of January 5, 1967.

INTERNATIONAL ORGANIZATIONS AND THE WORLD COURT

Those states which are parties to the Charter of the United Nations with the Statute of the International Court of Justice annexed thereto[3] are shown in Exhibit 1. The Charter was signed at San Francisco, June 26, 1945, and entered into force for the United States on October 24, 1945.

---

[1] From *Treaties in Force; A list of Treaties and Other International Agreements of the United States in Force on January 1, 1967.* (Compiled by the Treaty Affairs Staff, Office of the Legal Adviser, Department of State.) Department of State Publication 8188.

[2] From *Status of Multilateral Conventions in Respect of Which the Secretary General Acts as Depository,* United Nations, 1959 (With revisory inserts through December, 1963). U.N., St/LEG/3, Rev. 1. Additional supplementary inserts apparently revise to January 5, 1967.

[3] 59 Stat. 1031; T.S. 993. Amendment: December 17, 1963 (16 U.S.T. 1134; T.I.A.S. 5857).

389

EXHIBIT 1

United Nations

Afghanistan	Greece	Niger
Albania	Guatemala	Nigeria
Algeria	Guinea	Norway
Argentina	Guyana	Pakistan
Australia	Haiti	Panama
Austria	Honduras	Paraguay
Barbados	Hungary	Peru
Belgium	Iceland	Philippines
Bolivia	India	Poland
Botswana	Indonesia	Portugal
Brazil	Iran	Romania
Bulgaria	Iraq	Rwanda
Burma	Ireland	Saudi Arabia
Burundi	Israel	Senegal
Byelorussian Soviet	Italy	Sierra Leone
Socialist Republic	Ivory Coast	Singapore
Cambodia	Jamaica	Somali Republic
Cameroon	Japan	South Africa
Canada	Jordan	Spain
Central African	Kenya	Sudan
Republic	Kuwait	Sweden
Ceylon	Laos	Syrian Arab Republic
Chad	Lebanon	Tanzania
Chile	Lesotho	Thailand
China	Liberia	Togo
Colombia	Libya	Trinidad and Tobago
Congo (Brazzaville)	Luxembourg	Tunisia
Congo (Kinshasa)	Madagascar	Turkey
Costa Rica	Malawi	Uganda
Cyprus	Malaysia	Ukrainian Soviet
Czechoslovakia	Maldive Islands	Socialist Republic
Dahomey	Mali	Union of Soviet
Denmark	Malta	Socialist Republics
Dominican Republic	Mauritania	United Arab Republic
Ecuador	Mexico	United Kingdom
El Salvador	Mongolian People's	United States
Ethiopia	Republic	Upper Volta
Finland	Morocco	Uruguay
France	Nepal	Venezuela
Gabon	Netherlands	Yemen Arab Republic
Gambia	New Zealand	Yugoslavia
Ghana	Nicaragua	Zambia

All members of the United Nations are ipso facto parties to the Statute of the International Court of Justice[4] and in addition several countries not members of the U.N. have become parties to the Statute pursuant to resolutions adopted by the

---

[4] Article 93 U.N. Charter.

General Assembly.[5] They are Liechtenstein, San Marino, and Switzerland.

A number of countries have accepted the compulsory jurisdiction of the International Court of Justice under article 36 of the Statute of the Court[6] and are listed in Exhibit 2.

EXHIBIT 2

International Court of Justice *

Countries accepting jurisdiction with conditions:

Australia	Israel	Philippines
Belgium	Japan	Portugal
Cambodia	Kenya	Somali
Canada	Liberia	Republic
China	Liechtenstein	South Africa
Colombia	Luxembourg	Sudan
Denmark	Malta	Sweden
Dominican	Mexico	Switzerland
Republic	Netherlands	Turkey
El Salvador	New Zealand	Uganda
Finland	Nigeria	United Arab
France	Norway	Republic
Gambia	Pakistan	United Kingdom
Honduras	Panama	United States
India	Paraguay	

Countries accepting jurisdiction without conditions:

Haiti   Nicaragua   Uruguay   Paraguay

* According to the 1966–67 Yearbook of the Court, Paraguay and Turkey are not signatories, and Malawi is. See International Court of Justice, *Yearbook 1966–1967* (The Hague: J. C. T., 1967), pp. 44–72.

The charter of the Organization of American States was signed at Bogota, April 30, 1948 and entered into force for the United States, on December 13, 1951, subject to a reservation.[7] Signers of the Charter are listed in Exhibit 3.

EXHIBIT 3

Organization of American States

Argentina	Dominican Republic	Nicaragua
Bolivia	Ecuador	Panama
Brazil	El Salvador	Paraguay
Chile	Guatemala	Peru
Colombia	Haiti	United States
Costa Rica	Honduras	Uruguay
Cuba	Mexico	Venezuela

[5] 59 Stat. 1055; T.S. 993.

[6] *Ibid.*

[7] 2 U.S.T. 2394; T.I.A.S. 2361; 119 U.N.T.S .3.

THE RIGHTS AND DUTIES OF STATES

Parties to the convention on the rights and duties of states in the event of civil strife, Habana, February 20, 1928, are listed in the accompanying Exhibit 4. This convention entered into

EXHIBIT 4

Parties to the Habana Convention

Argentina	Dominican Republic	Nicaragua
Bolivia	Ecuador	Panama
Brazil	El Salvador	Paraguay
Colombia	Haiti	Peru
Costa Rica	Honduras	United States
Cuba	Mexico	Uruguay

force for the United States on May 21, 1930, subject to an understanding.[8]

A second convention on the rights and duties of states at Montevideo, December 26, 1933 entered into force for the United States on December 26, 1934, subject to a reservation.[9]

EXHIBIT 5

Parties to the Montevideo Convention

Brazil	Ecuador	Mexico
Chile	El Salvador	Nicaragua
Colombia	Guatemala	Panama
Costa Rica	Haiti	United States
Cuba	Honduras	Venezuela
Dominican Republic		

The following three exhibits relate to the Convention on the Prevention and Punishment of the Crime of Genocide (New York, 1948) in force since January 12, 1952. They show, in addition to the parties to the convention, extensions to territorial application and a tabulation of the reservations and objections to the convention.

---

[8] 46 Stat. 2749; T.S. 814; IV Trenwith 4725; 134 I.N.T.S. 45.

[9] 49 Stat. 3097; T.S. 881; IV Trenwith 4807; 165 I.N.T.S. 19.

EXHIBIT 6

Convention on the Prevention and Punishment of the Crime of Genocide *

State	Territorial Application	Declarations and Reservations	Date of Signature	Date of Receipt of Instrument of Ratification or Accession (a)
Afghanistan				22 March 1956 a
Albania	x			12 May 1955 a
Algeria	x			31 October 1963 a
Argentina	x			5 June 1956 a
Australia	x		11 December 1948	8 July 1949
Austria				19 March 1958 a
Belgium	x		12 December 1949	5 September 1951
Bolivia			11 December 1948	
Brazil			11 December 1948	15 April 1952
Bulgaria	x			21 July 1950 a
Burma	x		30 December 1949	14 March 1956
Burundi				
Byelorussian SSR	x		16 December 1949	11 August 1954
Cambodia				14 October 1950 a
Cameroon				
Canada			28 November 1949	3 September 1952
Central African Republic				
Ceylon				12 October 1950 a
Chad				
Chile			11 December 1948	3 June 1953
China			20 July 1949	19 July 1951
Colombia			12 August 1949	27 October 1959
Congo (Brazzaville)				
Congo (Leopoldville)				31 May 1962 d
Costa Rica				14 October 1950 a
Cuba			28 December 1949	4 March 1953
Cyprus				
Czechoslovakia	x		28 December 1949	21 December 1950
Dahomey				
Denmark			28 September 1949	15 June 1951
Dominican Republic			11 December 1948	
Ecuador			11 December 1948	21 December 1949
El Salvador			27 April 1949	28 September 1950
Ethiopia			11 December 1948	1 July 1949
Federal Republic of Germany				24 November 1954 a
Finland	x			18 December 1959 a
France			11 December 1948	14 October 1950
Gabon				
Ghana				24 December 1958 a
Greece			29 December 1949	8 December 1954
Guatemala			22 June 1949	13 January 1950
Guinea				
Haiti			11 December 1948	14 October 1950
Honduras			22 April 1949	5 March 1952
Hungary	x			7 January 1952 a
Iceland			14 May 1949	29 August 1949
India	x		29 November 1949	27 August 1959
Indonesia				
Iran			8 December 1949	14 August 1956
Iraq				20 January 1959 a
Ireland				
Israel			17 August 1949	9 March 1950
Italy				4 June 1952 a
Ivory Coast				
Jamaica				
Japan				
Jordan				3 April 1950 a

* In force since January 12, 1951.

d Original accession was made by preceding sovereign. The present (successor) has informed the U.N. that it continues to be bound.

EXHIBIT 6—*Continued*

State	Territorial Application	Declarations and Reservations	Date of Signature	Date of Receipt of Instrument of Ratification or Accession (a)
Kenya				
Kuwait				
Laos				8 December 1950 a
Lebanon			30 December 1949	17 December 1953
Liberia			11 December 1948	9 June 1950
Libya				
Liechtenstein				
Luxembourg				
Madagascar				
Malaysia				
Mali				
Mauritania				
Mexico			14 December 1948	22 July 1952
Monaco				30 March 1950 a
Mongolia				5 January 1967 a
Morocco		x		24 January 1958 a
Nepal				
Netherlands				20 June 1966 a
New Zealand			25 November 1949	
Nicaragua				29 January 1952 a
Niger				
Nigeria				
Norway			11 December 1948	22 July 1949
Pakistan			11 December 1948	12 October 1957
Panama			11 December 1948	11 January 1950
Paraguay			11 December 1948	
Peru			11 December 1948	24 February 1960
Philippines		x	11 December 1948	7 July 1950
Poland		x		14 November 1950 a
Portugal				
Republic of Korea				14 October 1950 a
Republic of Viet-Nam				11 August 1950 a
Romania		x		2 November 1950 a
Rwanda				
San Marino				
Saudi Arabia				13 July 1950 a
Senegal				
Sierra Leone				
Somalia				
South Africa				
Spain				
Sudan				
Sweden			30 December 1949	27 May 1952
Switzerland				
Syria				25 June 1955 a
Tanganyika				
Thailand				
Togo				
Trinidad and Tobago				
Tunisia				29 November 1956 a
Turkey				31 July 1950 a
Uganda				
Ukrainian SSR		x	16 December 1949	15 November 1954
Union of Soviet Socialist Republics		x	16 December 1949	3 May 1954
United Arab Republic			12 December 1948	8 February 1952
United Kingdom				
United States of America			11 December 1948	
Upper Volta				14 September 1965 a
Uruguay			11 December 1948	
Venezuela		x		12 July 1960 a
Western Samoa				
Yemen				
Yugoslavia			11 December 1948	29 August 1950

EXHIBIT 7

Convention on the Prevention and Punishment of the Crime of Genocide:
Territorial application

Notification by	Date of Recipt of Notification	Extension to
Australia.......	8 July 1949	All territories for the conduct of whose foreign relations Australia is responsible.
Belgium........	13 March 1952	Belgian Congo and the Trust Territory of Ruanda-Urundi.

EXHIBIT 8

Convention on the Prevention and Punishment of the Crime of Genocide:
Tabulation of reservations and objections thereto

Reserving States	Reservations to Article	Australia	Belgium	Brazil	Ceylon	China	Cuba	Ecuador	Greece	Guatemala	Norway	Republic of Viet-Nam †
						Objecting States*						
Albania	IX and XII					x			x			x
Algeria	VI, IX and XII											
Argentina	IX and XII								x			x
Bulgaria	IX and XII	x	x	x		x	x	x	x	x		x
Burma	VI and VIII					x			x			x
Byelorussian SSR	IX and XII	x	x	x		x	x	x	x	x		x
Czechoslovakia	IX and XII	x	x	x		x	x	x	x	x		x
Finland												x
Hungary	IX and XII					x			x			x
India	IX											x
Morocco	VI and IX											x
Philippines	IV, VI, VII, IX	x		x		x			x		x	x
Poland	IX and XII	x	x	x		x	x	x	x			x
Romania	IX and XII	x	x	x	x	x	x	x	x			x
Ukrainian SSR	IX and XII	x	x	x		x	x	x	x	x		x
USSR	IX and XII	x	x	x		x	x	x	x	x		x
Venezuela	VI, VII and IX											x

* The Government of El Salvador informed the Secretary-General that "The Government of El Salvador does not wish to make objection to the reservations to the Convention made by the Union of Soviet Socialist Republics, Byelorussian Soviet Socialist Republic, Ukrainian Soviet Socialist Republic, Czechoslovakia, Philippines and Bulgaria, but it expresses its complete disagreement with them, in particular those relating to articles IX and XII of the Convention."

† The Government of the Republic of Viet-Nam informed the Secretary-General that ". . . It was the intent of the Government of Viet-Nam in acceding to the Convention for the Prevention and Punishment of the Crime of Genocide, to accept only the text of that Convention as approved on 9 December 1948 in resolution 260 A (III) and voted by the General Assembly of the United Nations at its 179th plenary meeting, and not the reservations submitted by the above-mentioned States or by any other State at the time of signature by their representatives, or of deposit of their instruments of ratification or accession to the Convention."

WARFARE AND NEUTRALITY

The exhibits within this section list the parties to selected conventions regarding various phases of the conduct of warfare and neutrality including several regarding prisoners and civilians and applying to both land and sea hostilities.

EXHIBIT 9

Convention concerning the Rights and Duties of
Neutral Powers in Naval War*

Austria	Haiti	Panama
Belgium	Hungary	Philippines †
Brazil	Japan †	Portugal
China †	Laos	Romania
Denmark	Liberia	Sweden
El Salvador	Luxembourg	Switzerland
Ethiopia	Mexico	Thailand
Finland	Netherlands	Union of Soviet
France	Nicaragua	Socialistic
Germany †	Norway	Republics
Guatemala		United States ‡

* Signed at The Hague, October 18, 1907; entered into force for the United States on February 1, 1910. 36 Stat. 2415; T.S. 545; II Malloy 2352.
  † With reservation.
  ‡ With reservation and understanding.

EXHIBIT 10

Declaration concerning the Discharge of Projectiles and
Explosives from Balloons*

Australia	Haiti	Pakistan
Belgium	India	Panama
Bolivia	Ireland	Philippines
Brazil	Liberia	Portugal
Canada	Luxembourg	South Africa
Ceylon	Netherlands	Switzerland
China	New Zealand	Thailand
El Salvador	Nicaragua	United Kingdom
Ethiopia	Norway	United States
Finland		

* Signed at The Hague, October 18, 1907; entered into force for the United States, November 27, 1909. 36 Stat. 2439; T.S. 546; II Malloy 2366.

EXHIBIT 11

Convention on Maritime Neutrality*

Bolivia	Haiti
Colombia	Nicaragua
Dominican Republic	Panama
Ecuador	United States†

* Signed at Habana, February 20, 1928; entered into force for the United States on March 22, 1932. 47 Stat. 1989; T.S. 845; IV Trenwith 4743; 135 L.N.T.S. 187.

† With reservation.

EXHIBIT 12

Part IV of the Treaty for the Limitation and Reduction of Naval Armament*

Afghanistan	Guatemala	New Zealand
Albania	Haiti	Norway
Australia	Holy See	Panama
Austria	Hungary	Peru
Belgium	India	Poland
Brazil	Indonesia	Saudi Arabia
Bulgaria	Iran	South Africa
Canada	Iraq	Sweden
Costa Rica	Ireland	Switzerland
Czechoslovakia	Italy	Thailand
Denmark	Japan	Turkey
El Salvador	Latvia	Union of Soviet
Estonia	Lithuania	Socialist Republics
Finland	Mexico	United Arab Republic
France	Nepal	United Kingdom
Germany	Netherlands, including	United States
Greece	Surinam and Curacao	Yugoslavia

* Signed at London, April 22, 1930; entered into force for the United States, December 31, 1930. 46 Stat. 2858; T.S. 830; IV Trenwith 5268; 112 L.N.T.S. 65.

All provisions of this treaty with the exception of Part IV, which relates to rules of international law in regard to the operations of submarines or other war vessels with respect to merchant vessels, expired on December 31, 1936. Under the terms of article 23, Part IV "shall remain in force without limit of time."

EXHIBIT 13

Convention Relative to the Protection of Civilian Persons in Time of War*

Afghanistan
Albania[1]
Algeria
Argentina[1]
Australia[1,2]
Barbados[3]
Belgium
Botswana
Brazil[1]
Bulgaria[1]
Burundi[4]
Byelorussian Soviet
  Socialistic Republic[1]
Cambodia
Cameroon
Canada
Central African
  Republic
Ceylon
Chile
China, People's
  Republic[1]
Colombia
Congo (Kinshasa)
Cuba
Cyprus
Czechoslovakia[1]
Dahomey
Denmark
Dominican Republic
Ecuador
El Salvador
Finland
France
Gabon
Gambia
Germany (Federal
  Republic)[5]
Germany (Democratic
  Republic)[1]
Ghana
Greece
Guatemala
Guyana
Haiti

Holy See
Honduras
Hungary[1]
Iceland
India
Indonesia
Iran
Iraq
Ireland
Israel[1]
Italy
Ivory Coast
Jamaica
Japan
Jordan
Kenya
Korea[1]
Korea (Democratic
  Republic)[1]
Kuwait[3]
Laos
Lebanon
Lesotho[3]
Liberia
Libya
Liechtenstein
Luxembourg
Madagascar
Malawi[7]
Malaysia
Mali
Malta[8]
Mauritania
Mexico
Monaco
Mongolian People's
  Republic
Morocco
Nepal
Netherlands[1]
New Zealand[1]
Nicaragua
Niger
Nigeria
Norway

Pakistan[1]
Panama
Paraguay
Peru
Philippines
Poland[1]
Portugal[1]
Romania[1]
Rwanda
San Marino
Saudi Arabia
Senegal
Sierra Leone
Singapore[9]
Somali Republic
South Africa
Spain
Sudan
Sweden
Switzerland
Syrian Arab Republic
Tanzania:
  Tanganyika
  Zanzibar[3]
Thailand
Togo
Trinidad and Tobago
Tunisia
Turkey
Uganda
Ukrainian Soviet
  Socialist Republic[1]
Union of Soviet
  Socialist Republics
United Arab Republic
United Kingdom
United States[6]
Upper Volta
Venezuela
Viet-Nam
Viet-Nam (Democratic
  Republic)[1]
Yugoslavia
Zambia[10]

* Dated at Geneva, August 12, 1949; entered into force for the United States on February 2, 1956.
6 U.S.T. 3516; T.I.A.S. 3365; 75 U.N.T.S. 287.
  [1] With a reservation.

EXHIBIT 14

Convention Relative to the Laying of Automatic Submarine Contact Mines*

Australia †	Germany †	New Zealand †
Austria	Guatemala	Nicaragua
Belgium	Haiti	Norway
Brazil	Hungary	Pakistan †
Canada †	India †	Panama
Ceylon †	Ireland †	Philippines
China	Japan	Romania
Denmark	Laos †	South Africa †
El Salvador	Liberia	Switzerland
Ethiopia	Luxembourg	Thailand †
Finland	Mexico	United Kingdom †
France †	Netherlands	United States

* Signed at The Hague, October 18, 1907; entered into force for the United States on January 26, 1910. 36 Stat. 2332; T.S. 541; II Malloy 2304.

† With reservation.

---

² With a declaration.

³ Included in declaration by the United Kingdom. Continued application has apparently not been determined.

⁴ Included in declaration by Belgium. Continued application has apparently not been determined.

⁵ Applicable to Land Berlin.

⁶ With a declaration and a statement.

⁷ In a note dated November 24, 1964 to the Secretary General of the United Nations, the Prime Minister of Malawi stated that as regards multilateral treaties the Government of Malawi proposes to review each of them individually and to indicate to the depositary in each case what steps it wishes to take in relation to each such instrument—whether by way of confirmation of termination, confirmation of succession or accession. During such interim period of review, any party to a multilateral treaty which has prior to independence, been applied or extended to the former Nyasaland Protectorate may, on a basis of reciprocity, rely as against Malawi on the terms of such treaty.

⁸ In an exchange of letters on December 31, 1964 between the Government of the United Kingdom and the Government of Malta, it was agreed that all obligations and responsibilities of the Government of the United Kingdom which arise from any valid international instrument shall, as from September 21, 1964, be assumed by the Government of Malta insofar as such instruments may be held to have application to Malta. The rights and benefits heretofore enjoyed by the Government of the United Kingdom in virtue of the application of any such international instrument to Malta shall, as from September 21, 1964, be enjoyed by the Government of Malta.

⁹ Art. 13 of the Constitution and Malaysia (Singapore Amendment) Act, 1965 annexed to the Independence of Singapore agreement, 1965, reads in part as follows: "Any treaty, agreement or convention entered into before Singapore Day between the Yang de-Pertuan Agong or the Government of Malaysia and another country or countries, including those deemed to be so by Art. 169 of the Constitution of Malaysia shall in so far as such instruments have application to Singapore, be deemed to be a treaty, agreement or convention between Singapore and that country or countries, and any decision taken by an international organization and accepted before Singapore Day by the Government of the United Kingdom shall in so far as that decision has application to Singapore be deemed to be a decision of an international organization of which Singapore is a member."

¹⁰ In a note dated September 1, 1965 to the Secretary General of the United Nations, the Minister of Foreign Affairs of Zambia stated that "many treaty rights and obligations of the Government of the United Kingdom in respect of Northern Rhodesia were succeeded to by Zambia upon independence by virtue of customary international law. . . . It is desired that it be assumed that each treaty has been legally succeeded to by Zambia and that action be based on this presumption until a decision is reached that it should be regarded as having lapsed. Should the Government of Zambia be of the opinion that it has legally succeeded to a treaty, and wishes to terminate the operation of the treaty, it will in due course give notice of termination in the terms thereof.

EXHIBIT 15

Convention concerning Bombardment by Naval Forces in
Time of War*

Australia†	Guatemala	Panama
Austria	Haiti	Philippines
Belgium	Hungary	Poland
Bolivia	India†	Portugal
Brazil	Ireland†	Romania
Canada†	Japan†	South Africa†
Ceylon†	Laos†	Spain
China	Liberia	Sweden
Cuba	Luxembourg	Switzerland
Denmark	Mexico	Thailand
El Salvador	Netherlands	Union of Soviet
Ethiopia	New Zealand†	Socialist
Finland	Nicaragua	Republics
France†	Norway	United Kingdom†
Germany†	Pakistan†	United States

* Signed at The Hague, October 18, 1907; entered into force for the United
States, January 26, 1910. 36 Stat. 2351; T.S. 542; II Malloy 2314.
† With reservation.

EXHIBIT 16

Convention for the Adaptation to Maritime Warfare of the
Principles of the Geneva Convention of
July 6, 1906*

Austria	Guatemala	Panama
Belgium	Haiti	Philippines
Bolivia	Hungary	Poland
Brazil	Italy	Portugal
China†	Japan	Romania
Cuba	Laos	Spain
Denmark	Latvia	Sweden
El Salvador	Luxembourg	Switzerland
Ethiopia	Mexico	Thailand
Finland	Netherlands	Union of Soviet
France	Nicaragua	Socialist Republics
Germany	Norway	United States

States on January 26, 1910. 36 Stat. 2371; T.S. 543; II Malloy 2326. Super-
seded as between contracting parties by the Convention of August 12, 1949
(T.I.A.S. 3363) for the Amelioration of the Condition of the Wounded, Sick and
Shipwrecked Members of Armed Forces at Sea.
† With reservation.

EXHIBIT 17

Convention Relative to Certain Restrictions with Regard to
the Exercise of the Right of Capture in Naval War*

Australia	Haiti	Pakistan
Austria	Hungary	Panama
Belgium	India	Philippines
Brazil	Ireland	Poland
Canada	Japan	Portugal
Ceylon	Laos	Romania
China	Liberia	South Africa
Denmark	Luxembourg	Spain
El Salvador	Mexico	Sweden
Ethiopia	Netherlands	Switzerland
Finland	New Zealand	Thailand
France	Nicaragua	United Kingdom
Germany	Norway	United States
Guatemala		

* Signed at The Hague, October 18, 1907; entered into force for the United States on January 20, 1910. 36 Stat. 2396; T.S. 544; II Malloy 2341.

EXHIBIT 18

Convention for the Exemption of Hospital Ships, in Time of War,
from the Payment of All Dues and Taxes Imposed for the Benefit of
the State*

Austria	Italy	Portugal
Belgium	Japan	Romania†
China	Korea	Spain
Cuba	Luxembourg	Sweden
Denmark	Mexico	Switzerland
France	Netherlands	Thailand
Germany†	Norway	Turkey
Greece	Peru	Union of Soviet
Guatemala	Poland, including Free	Socialist Republics
Iran	City of Danzig	United States

* Done at The Hague, December 21, 1904; entered into force for the United States on March 26, 1907. 35 Stat. 1834; T.S. 459; II Malloy 2135.
† With reservations.

EXHIBIT 19

Convention Relative to the Opening of Hostilities*

Australia	Haiti	Panama
Austria	Hungary	Philippines
Belgium	India	Poland
Bolivia	Ireland	Portugal
Brazil	Japan	Romania
Canada	Laos	South Africa
Ceylon	Liberia	Spain
China	Luxembourg	Sweden
Denmark	Mexico	Switzerland
El Salvador	Netherlands	Thailand
Ethiopia	New Zealand	Union of Soviet
Finland	Nicaragua	Socialist Republics
France	Norway	United Kingdom
Germany	Pakistan	United States
Guatemala		

* Signed at The Hague, October 18, 1907; entered into force for the United State on January 26, 1910. 36 Stat. 2259; T.S. 538; II Malloy 2259.

EXHIBIT 20

Convention Respecting Laws and Customs of War on Land, and Annexations*

Australia	Germany†	Pakistan
Austria†	Guatemala	Panama
Belgium	Haiti	Philippines
Bolivia	Hungary†	Poland
Brazil	India	Portugal
Canada	Ireland	Romania
Ceylon	Japan†	South Africa
China	Laos	Sweden
Cuba	Liberia	Switzerland
Denmark	Luxembourg	Thailand
Dominican Republic	Mexico	Union of Soviet
El Salvador	Netherlands	Socialist Republics†
Ethiopia	New Zealand	United Kingdom
Finland	Nicaragua	United States
France	Norway	

* Signed at The Hague, October 18, 1907; entered into force for the United States on January 26, 1910. 36 Stat. 2277; T.S. 539; II Malloy 2269.
† With reservations.

EXHIBIT 21

Convention Respecting the Rights and Duties of Neutral
Powers and Persons in Case of War on Land*

Austria	Guatemala	Philippines
Belgium	Haiti	Poland
Bolivia	Hungary	Portugal
Brazil	Japan	Romania
China	Laos	Spain
Cuba	Liberia	Sweden
Denmark	Luxembourg	Switzerland
El Salvador	Mexico	Thailand
Ethiopia	Netherlands	Union of Soviet
Finland	Nicaragua	Socialist Republics
France	Norway	United States
Germany	Panama	

* Signed at The Hague, October 18, 1907; entered into force for the United
States on January 26, 1910. 36 Stat. 2310; T.S. 540; II Malloy 2290.

EXHIBIT 22

Treaty Providing for the Renunciation of War as an Instrument of
National Policy*

Afghanistan	Greece	Paraguay
Albania	Guatemala	Peru
Australia	Haiti	Poland, including
Austria	Honduras	Free City of
Belgium	Hungary	Danzig
Brazil	Iceland	Portugal
Bulgaria	India	Romania
Canada	Iran	Saudi Arabia
Chile	Iraq	South Africa
China	Ireland	Spain
Colombia	Italy	Sweden
Costa Rica	Japan	Switzerland
Cuba	Latvia	Thailand
Czechoslovakia	Liberia	Turkey
Denmark	Lithuania	Union of Soviet
Dominican Republic	Luxembourg	Socialist Republics
Ecuador	Mexico	United Arab Republic
Estonia	Netherlands	United Kingdom
Ethiopia	New Zealand	United States
Finland	Nicaragua	Venezuela
France	Norway	Yugoslavia
Germany	Panama	

* Signed at Paris, August 27, 1928; entered into force for the United States on July 24,
1929. 46 Stat. 2343; T.S. 796; IV Trenwith 5130; 94 L.N.T.S. 57.

AGREEMENTS CONCERNING THE WOUNDED AND SICK AND PRISONERS OF WAR

Data concerning the parties to four conventions are combined in the first exhibit in this section (Exhibit 23). It includes the Convention for the Amelioration of the Condition of the Wounded and Sick in Armed Forces in the Field (1949) ;[10] the Convention for the Amelioration of the Condition of the Wounded, Sick, and Shipwrecked Members of the Armed Forces at Sea (1949) ;[11] Convention for the Amelioration of the Wounded and Sick of Armies in the Field (1929) ;[12] and the Convention for the Amelioration of the Wounded and Sick of Armies in the Field, with Protocol (1906) .[13]

The Geneva Convention Relative to the Treatment of Prisoners of War, 1929,[14] was superseded between contracting parties by the Geneva Convention Relative to the Treatment of Prisoners of war (1949) .[15] Parties to both conventions are combined in Exhibit 24.

---

[10] Dated at Geneva, August 12, 1949; entered into force for the United States, February 2, 1956. 6 U.S.T. 3114; T.I.A.S. 3362; 75 U.N.T.S. 31.

[11] Dated at Geneva, August 12, 1949; entered into force for the United States on February 2, 1956. 6 U.S.T. 3217; T.I.A.S. 3363; 75 U.N.T.S. 85.

[12] Dated at Geneva, July 27, 1929; entered into force for theUnited States on August 4, 1932. 47 Stat. 2074; T.S. 847; IV Trenwith 5209; 118 L.N.T.S. 303. Superseded as between contracting parties by the Convention of 1949 (T.I.A.S. 3362) .

[13] Signed at Geneva, July 6, 1906; entered into force for the United States on August 9, 1907. 35 Stat. 1885; T.S. 464; II Malloy 2183. Superseded as between contracting parties by the Convention of 1929 (T.S. 847) and 1949 (T.I.A.S. 3363) .

[14] Done at Geneva, July 27, 1929; entered into force for the United States on August 4, 1932. 47 Stat. 2021; T.S. 846; IV Trenwith 5224; 118 L.N.T.S. 343.

[15] Done at Geneva, August 12, 1949; entered into force for the United States on February 2, 1956. 6. U.S.T. 3316; T.I.A.S. 3364; 75 U.N.T.S. 135.

EXHIBIT 23

Combined Data of Four (Red Cross Conventions) Concerning Wounded, Sick, or Shipwrecked in Time of War on Land or on the Sea

	1949		1929	1906
	Field	*Sea*		
Afghanistan	x	x		x
Albania	x[1]	x[1]		x
Algeria	x	x		
Argentina	x[1]	x[1]	x	
Australia	x[2]	x[2]	x[1]	
Austria	x	x	x	x
Barbados	x[3]	x[3]		
Belgium	x	x	x	x
Bolivia				x
Botswana	x[4]	x[4]		
Brazil	x	x	x	x
Bulgaria	x[1]	x[1]	x	x
Burma				x
Burundi	x[5]	x[5]		
Byelorussian S.S.R.	x[1]	x[1]		
Cambodia	x	x		
Cameroon	x	x		
Canada	x	x	x[1]	
Central African Rep.	x	x		
Ceylon	x	x		
Chile	x	x	x	x
China				x
China, People's Rep.	x[1]	x[1]		
Colombia	x	x		x
Congo (Kinshasa)	x	x		
Costa Rica				x
Cuba	x	x		x
Cyprus	x	x		
Czechoslovakia	x[1]	x[1]	x	x
Dahomey	x	x		
Denmark	x	x	x	x
Dominican Republic	x	x		x
Ecuador	x	x		x
El Salvador	x	x	x	x
Estonia				x	x
Ethiopia				x	x
Finland	x	x	x	x
France	x	x	x	x
Gabon	x	x		
Gambia	x	x		
Germany	x[6]	x[6]	x	x

EXHIBIT 23—*Continued*

| | 1949 | | | |
	Field	Sea	1929	1906
Germany, Dem. Rep.	x^1	x^1		
Ghana	x	x		
Greece	x	x	x	x
Guatemala	x	x		x
Guyana	x^7	x^7		
Haiti	x	x		x
Holy See	x	x		
Honduras	x	x		x
Hungary	x^1	x^1	x	x
Iceland	x	x		x
India	x	x	x^1	
Indonesia	x	x	x	
Iran	x	x		
Iraq	x	x	x	
Ireland	x	x		
Israel	x^1	x^1	x	
Italy	x	x	x	x
Ivory Coast	x	x		
Jamaica	x	x		
Japan	x	x	x^1	x
Jordan	x	x	x	
Kenya	x	x		
Korea	x	x		
Korea, Dem. Rep.	x^1	x^1		
Kuwait	x^3	x^3		
Laos	x	x		
Latvia			x	x
Lebanon	x	x	x	
Lesotho	x	x		
Liberia	x	x		
Libya	x	x		
Liechtenstein	x	x	x	
Lithuania			x	x
Luxembourg	x	x		x
Madagascar	x	x		
Malawi	x^8	x^8		
Malaysia	x	x		
Mali	x	x		
Malta	x^9	x^9		
Mauritania	x	x		
Mexico	x	x	x	x
Monaco	x	x	x	
Mongolian People's Rep.	x	x		
Morocco	x	x		

EXHIBIT 23—*Continued*

	1949		1929	1906
	Field	Sea		
Nepal	x	x		
Netherlands	x	x	x	x
New Zealand	x	x	x[1]	
Nicaragua	x	x		x
Niger	x	x		
Nigeria	x	x		
Norway	x	x	x	x
Pakistan	x	x	x	
Panama	x	x		
Paraguay	x	x		x
Peru	x	x	x	
Philippines	x	x	x	
Poland	x[1]	x[1]	x	x[10]
Portugal	x[1]	x[1]	x	x
Romania	x[1]	x[1]	x	x
Rwanda	x	x		
San Marino	x	x	x	
Saudi Arabia	x	x		
Senegal	x	x		
Sierra Leone	x	x		
Singapore	x[11]	x[11]		
Somali Republic	x	x		
South Africa	x	x	x	
Spain	x	x	x	x
Sweden	x	x	x	x
Switzerland	x	x	x	x
Sudan	x	x		
Syrian Arab Republic	x	x	x	
Tanzania:	x	x		
Tanganyika				
Zanzibar[3]				
Thailand	x	x	x	x
Togo	x	x		
Trinidad and Tobago	x	x		
Tunisia	x	x		
Turkey	x	x	x	x[1]
Uganda	x	x		
Ukrainian S.S.R.	x[1]	x[1]		
U.S.S.R.	x[1]	x[1]	x	x
United Arab Republic	x	x	x	x[1]
United Kingdom	x[12]	x[12]	x[13,14]	x
United States	x[1,2]	x[12]	x	x
Upper Volta	x	x		
Uruguay				x

EXHIBIT 23—*Continued*

	1949		1929	1906
	Field	*Sea*		
Venezuela........................x	x	x	x
Viet-Nam........................x	x		
Viet-Nam, Dem. Rep.............x¹	x¹		
Yugoslavia......................x¹	x¹	x	x
Zambia.........................x¹⁵	x¹⁵		

¹ With reservation.

² With a statement.

³ Included in declaration by United Kingdom. Continued application has apparently not been determined.

⁴ In a note dated October 6, 1966 to the Secretary General of the United Nations, the President of Botswana stated that the Government of Botswana proposes to review each multilateral treaty individually and to indicate to the depositary in each case what steps it wishes to take in relation to each such instrument—whether by way of confirmation of termination, confirmation of succession or accession. During such interim period of review, any party to a multilateral treaty which has, prior to independence, been applied or extended to the former Bechuanaland Protectorate, may, on a basis of reciprocity, rely as against Botswana on the terms of such treaty.

⁵ Included in declaration by Belgium. Continued application has apparently not been determined.

⁶ Adherence by Federal Republic of Germany, with application to Land Berlin.

⁷ In a note dated June 30, 1966 to the Secretary General of the United Nations, the Prime Minister of Guyana stated that many treaty rights and obligations of the Government of the United Kingdom in respect of British Guiana were succeeded to by Guyana upon independence by virtue of customary international law. . . . It is desired that it be presumed that each treaty has been legally succeeded to by Guyana and that action be based on this presumption until a decision is reached that it should be regarded as having lapsed. Should the Government of Guyana be of the opinion that it has legally succeeded to a treaty and wishes to terminate the operation of the treaty, it will in due course give notice of termination in the terms thereof.

⁸ In a note dated November 24, 1964 to the Secretary General of the United Nations, the Prime Minister of Malawi stated that as regards multilateral treaties the Government of Malawi proposes to review each of them individually and to indicate to the depositary in each case what steps it wishes to take in relation to each such instrument—whether by way of confirmation of termination, confirmation of succession or accession. During such interim period of review, any party to a multilateral treaty which has prior to independence, been applied or extended to the former Nyasaland Protectorate may, on a basis of reciprocity, rely as against Malawi on the terms of such treaty.

⁹ In an exchange of letters on December 31, 1964 between the Government of the United Kingdom and the Government of Malta, it was agreed that all obligations and responsibilities of the Government of the United Kingdom which arise from any valid international instrument shall, as from September 21, 1964, be assumed by the Government of Malta insofar as such instruments may be held to have application to Malta. The rights and benefits heretofore enjoyed by the Government of the United Kingdom in virtue of the application of any such international instrument to Malta shall, as from September 21, 1964, be enjoyed by the Government of Malta.

¹⁰ Including the Free City of Danzig.

¹¹ Art. 13 of the Constitution and Malaysia (Singapore Amendment) Act, 1965 annexed to the Independence of Singapore agreement, 1965, reads in part as follows: "Any treaty, agreement or convention entered into before Singapore Day between the Yang de-Pertuan Agong or the Government of Malaysia and another country or countries, including those deemed to be so by Art. 169 of the Constitution of Malaysia shall in so far as such instruments have application to Singapore, be deemed to be a treaty, agreement or convention between Singapore and that country or countries, and any decision taken by an international organization and accepted before Singapore Day by the Government of Malaysia shall in so far as that decision has application to Singapore be deemed to be a decision of an international organization of which Singapore is a member."

¹² Applicable to all territories for whose international relations the United Kingdom is responsible including Bahrain, Qatar, and the Trucial States.

¹³ With a declaration.

¹⁴ Including all parts of the British Empire not separate members of the League of Nations.

¹⁵ In a note dated September 1, 1965 to the Secretary General of the United Nations, the Minister of Foreign Affairs of Zambia stated that "many treaty rights and obligations of the Government of the United Kingdom in respect of Northern Rhodesia were succeeded to by Zambia upon independence by virtue of customary international law. . . . It is desired that it be assumed that each treaty has been legally succeeded to by Zambia and that action be based on this presumption until a decision is reached that it should be regarded as having lapsed. Should the Government of Zambia be of the opinion that it has legally succeeded to a treaty, and wishes to terminate the operation of the treaty, it will in due course give notice of termination in the terms thereof.

EXHIBIT 24

Conventions Relating to the Treatment of Prisoners of
War

	1949	1929
Afghanistan	x	
Albania	x[1]	
Algeria	x	
Argentina	x[1]	x
Australia	x[2]	x
Austria	x	x
Barbados	x[3]	
Belgium	x	x
Bolivia	x	
Botswana	x	
Brazil	x	x
Bulgaria	x[1]	x
Burma	x	
Burundi	x[4]	
Byelorussian S.S.R.	x[1]	
Cambodia	x	
Cameroon	x	
Canada	x	x
Central African Republic	x	
Ceylon	x	
Chile	x	x
China	x	
China, People's Rep.	x[1]	
Colombia	x	x
Congo (Kinshasa)	x	
Cuba	x	
Cyprus	x	
Czechoslovakia	x[1]	x
Dahomee	x	
Denmark	x	x
Dominican Republic	x	
Ecuador	x	
El Salvador	x	x
Estonia	x	
Finland	x	
France	x	x
Gabon	x	
Gambia	x	
Germany	x[5]	x
[Germany, Dem. Rep.]	x[1]	
Ghana	x	
Greece	x	x
Guatemala	x	
Guyana	x	
Haiti	x	

EXHIBIT 24—*Continued*

	1949	1929
Holy See	x	
Honduras	x	
Hungary	x[1]	x
Iceland	x	
India	x	x
Indonesia	x	x
Iran	x	
Iraq	x	x
Ireland	x	
Israel	x	x
Italy	x[1]	x
Ivory Coast	x	
Jamaica	x	
Japan	x	
Jordan	x	x
Kenya	x	
Korea	x[1]	
[Korea, Dem. Rep.]	x[1]	
Kuwait	x[3]	
Laos	x	
Latvia	x	
Lebanon	x	
Lesotho	x[3]	
Liberia	x	
Libya	x	
Liechtenstein	x	x
Lithuania	x	
Luxembourg	x	
Madagascar	x	
Malawi	x	
Malta	x	
Malaysia	x	
Mali	x	
Mauritania	x	
Mexico	x	x
Monaco	x	x
Mongolian People's Republic	x	
Morocco	x	
Nepal	x	
Netherlands	x	x
New Zealand	x[2]	x
Nicaragua	x	
Niger	x	
Nigeria	x	
Norway	x	x
Pakistan	x	x
Panama	x	
Paraguay	x	

EXHIBIT 24—*Continued*

	1949	1929
Peru	x	
Philippines	x	x
Poland	x[1]	x
Portugal	x[1]	x
Romania	x[1]	x
Rwanda	x	
San Marino	x	
Saudi Arabia	x	
Senegal	x	
Sierra Leone	x	
Singapore	x	
Somali Republic	x	
South Africa	x	x
Spain	x[1]	x
Sudan	x	
Sweden	x	x
Switzerland	x	x
Syrian Arab Republic	x	
Tanzania:	x	
Tanganyika		
Zanzibar[3]		
Thailand	x	x
Togo	x	
Trinidad and Tobago	x	
Tunisia	x	
Turkey	x	x
Uganda	x	
Ukrainian S.S.R.	x[1]	
U.S.S.R.	x[1]	
United Arab Republic	x	x
United Kingdom	x[6]	x[7]
United States	x[2]	x
Upper Volta	x	
Venezuela	x	x
Viet-Nam	x	
[Viet-Nam, Dem. Rep.]	x[1]	
Yugoslavia	x[1]	x
Zambia	x	

[1] With reservation.
[2] With a statement.
[3] Included in declaration by the United Kingdom. Continued application has apparently not been determined.
[4] Included in declaration by Belgium. Continued application has apparently not been determined.
[5] Adherence by Federal Republic of Germany with application to Land Berlin.
[6] Applicable to all territories for whose international relations the United Kingdom is responsible including the British Protected States of Bahrain, Qatar, and the Trucial States.
[7] Including all parts of the British Empire not separate members of the League of Nations.

PACIFIC SETTLEMENT OF DISPUTES

EXHIBIT 25

Convention for the Establishment of International Commissions of Inquiry*

Costa Rica   Nicaragua
Guatemala   United States
Honduras

* Signed at Washington, February 7, 1923; entered into force for the United States, June 13, 1925. 44 Stat. 2070; T.S. 717; IV Trenwith 4677

EXHIBIT 26

Treaty to Avoid or Prevent Conflicts Between the American States*

Brazil   El Salvador   Panama
Chile   Guatemala   Paraguay
Colombia   Haiti   Peru
Costa Rica   Honduras   United States
Cuba   Mexico   Uruguay †
Dominican Republic   Nicaragua   Venezuela
Ecuador

* Signed at Santiago, May 3, 1923; entered into force for the United States, October 8, 1924. 44 Stat. 2527; T.S. 752; IV Trenwith 4691; 33 L.N.T.S. 25.
† With reservation.

EXHIBIT 27

General Treaty of Inter-American Arbitration and Protocol of Progressive Arbitration*

Brazil   El Salvador †   Nicaragua
Chile †   Guatemala †   Panama
Colombia †   Haiti   Peru
Cuba   Honduras †   United States ‡
Dominican Republic † Mexico †   Venezuela †
Ecuador †

* Signed at Washington, January 5, 1929; entered into force for the United States, April 16, 1935. 49 Stat. 3153; T.S. 886; IV Trenwith 4756; 130 L.N.T.S. 135.
† With reservation.
‡ With an understanding.

EXHIBIT 28

General Convention of Inter-American Conciliation*

Brazil	El Salvador	Panama
Chile	Guatemala	Paraguay
Colombia	Haiti	Peru
Cuba	Honduras	United States
Dominican Republic	Mexico	Uruguay
Ecuador	Nicaragua	Venezuela

* Signed at Washington, January 5, 1929; entered into force for the United States, November 15, 1929. 46 Stat. 2209; T.S. 780; IV Trenwith 4763; 100 L.N.T.S. 401.

EXHIBIT 29

Additional Protocol to the General Convention of Inter-American Conciliation*

Chile	Guatemala	Paraguay
Colombia	Honduras	United States
Dominican Republic	Mexico	Venezuela†

* Signed at Montevideo, December 26, 1933; entered into force for the United States, March 10, 1935. 49 Stat. 3185; T.S. 887; IV Trenwith 4798.
† With reservation.

EXHIBIT 30

Anti-War Treaty of Nonaggression and Conciliation*

Argentina	El Salvador†	Paraguay
Brazil	Finland†	Peru†
Bulgaria†	Guatemala	Romania†
Chile†	Haiti	Spain
Colombia†	Honduras†	United States†
Cuba	Mexico	Uruguay
Czechoslovakia†	Nicaragua	Venezuela
Dominican Republic	Panama	Yugoslavia†
Ecuador†		

* Signed at Rio de Janeiro, October 10, 1933; entered into force for the United States, November 13, 1935. 49 Stat. 3363; T.S. 906; IV Trenwith 4793
† With reservation.

EXHIBIT 31

Convention for the Maintenance, Preservation, and Reestablishment of Peace*

Chile	El Salvador	Nicaragua
Colombia	Guatemala	Panama
Costa Rica	Haiti	Paraguay†
Cuba	Honduras†	United States
Dominican Republic	Mexico	Venezuela
Ecuador‡		

* Signed at Buenos Aires, December 23, 1936; entered into force for the United States, August 25, 1937. 51 Stat. 15; T.S. 922; IV Trenwith 4817; 188 L.N.T.S. 9.
† With reservation.
‡ With a declaration.

EXHIBIT 32

Additional Protocol Relative to Nonintervention*

Brazil	Ecuador‡	Mexico
Chile	El Salvador	Nicaragua
Colombia	Guatemala	Panama
Costa Rica	Haiti	United States
Cuba	Honduras	Venezuela
Dominican Republic		

* Signed at Buenos Aires, December 23, 1936; entered into force for the United States, August 27, 1937. 51 Stat. 41; T.S. 923; IV Trenwith 4821; 188 L.N.T.S. 31.
† With reservation.
‡ With a declaration.

EXHIBIT 33

Convention for the Pacific Settlement of International Disputes*

Argentina	France‡	Paraguay‡
Australia	Germany‡	Peru
Austria‡	Greece	Philippines†,‡
Belgium‡	Guatemala‡	Portugal‡
Bolivia‡	Haiti‡	Romania†,‡
Brazil‡	Honduras‡	South Africa
Bulgaria	Hungary‡	Spain‡
Byelorussian Soviet	India	Sweden‡
Socialist Republic‡ §	Iran	Switzerland‡
Cameroon‡	Ireland	Thailand‡
Canada	Italy	Turkey†
Ceylon	Japan‡	Ukrainian Soviet
Chile†	Laos‡	Socialist Republic‡,§
China‡	Luxembourg‡	Union of Soviet
Colombia	Mexico†	Socialist Republics‡,§
Congo (Kinshasa)‡	Netherlands‡	United Kingdom
Cuba‡	New Zealand	United States†,‡
Denmark‡	Nicaragua‡	Upper Volta‡
Dominican Republic‡	Norway‡	Uruguay
Ecuador	Pakistan	Venezuela
El Salvador‡	Panama‡	Yugoslavia†

* Signed at The Hague, July 29, 1899; entered into force for the United States on September 4, 1900. 32 Stat. 1779; TS. 392; II Malloy 2016.
   † With reservation.
   ‡ Replaced as between contracting parties by 1907 Convention on the same subject (T.S. 536).
   § With a statement.

EXHIBIT 34

Convention for the Pacific Settlement of International Disputes*

Austria	Germany	Poland
Belgium	Guatemala	Portugal
Bolivia	Haiti	Romania†
Brazil†	Honduras	Spain
Byelorussian Soviet	Hungary	Sudan
Socialist Republic‡	Israel	Sweden
Cameroon	Japan†	Switzerland†
Congo (Kinshasa)	Laos	Thailand
China	Luxembourg	Uganda
Cuba	Mexico	Ukrainian Soviet
Czechoslavakia	Netherlands	Socialist Republic‡
Denmark	Nicaragua	Union of Soviet
Dominican Republic	Norway	Socialist Republics‡
El Salvador	Panama	United States§‖
Finland	Paraguay	Upper Volta
France	Philippines§‖	

* Signed at The Hague, October 18, 1907; entered into force for the United States on January 26, 1910. 36 Stat. 2199; T.S. 536; II Malloy 2220.
  † With reservation.
  ‡ With a statement.
  § With declaration(s).
  ‖ With an understanding.

EXHIBIT 35

Convention Respecting the Limitation of the Employment
of Force for the Recovery of Contract Debts*

Australia	Haiti	Pakistan
Austria	Hungary	Panama
Canada	India	Philippines§
Ceylon	Ireland	Portugal
China	Japan	South Africa
Denmark	Laos	Spain
El Salvador†	Liberia	Union of Soviet
Finland	Netherlands	Socialist Republics‡
France	New Zealand	United Kingdom
Germany	Nicaragua†	United States§
Guatemala†	Norway	

* Signed at The Hague, October 18, 1907; entered into force for the United States on January 26, 1910. 36 Stat. 2241; T.S. 537; II Malloy 2248.
  † With reservation.
  ‡ With a statement.
  § With an understanding.

EXHIBIT 36

Treaty for the Prevention of Controversies*

Chile	Ecuador	Mexico
Colombia	El Salvador	Nicaragua
Costa Rica	Guatemala †	Panama
Cuba	Haiti	United States
Dominican Republic	Honduras	

* Signed at Buenos Aires, December 23, 1936; entered into force for the United States on July 29, 1937. 51 Stat. 65; T.S. 924; IV Trenwith 4824; 188 L.N.T.S. 53.
† With reservation.

EXHIBIT 37

Inter-American Treaty on Good Offices and Mediation*

Brazil	Dominican Republic	Honduras †
Chile	Ecuador	Mexico
Colombia	El Salvador	Nicaragua
Costa Rica	Guatemala	Panama
Cuba	Haiti	United States

* Signed at Buenos Aires, December 23, 1936; entered into force for the United States on July 29, 1937. 51 Stat. 90; T.S. 925; IV Trenwith 4827; 188 L.N.T.S. 75.
† With reservation.

CONVENTIONS IN REGARD TO OUTER SPACE AND NUCLEAR TESTING

Satellite

EXHIBIT 38

Agreement on Cooperation in Intercontinental Testing in Connection With Experimental Communications Satellites.*

Denmark	Sweden
Norway	United States

* Exchanges of notes at Stockholm, July 5 and 25, 1963, at Oslo, July 8 and September 11, 1963, and at Copenhagen, July 2 and September 14, 1963; entered into force for the United States, September 14, 1963.
14 U.S.T. 1278; T.I.A.S. 5431; 488 U.N.T.S. 121.

EXHIBIT 39

Agreement Establishing Interim Arrangements for a Global
Commercial Communications Satellite System.*

Algeria	Ireland	Philippines
Argentina	Israel	Portugal
Australia	Italy	Saudia Arabia
Austria	Japan	Singapore
Belgium†	Jordan	South Africa
Brazil	Kuwait	Spain
Canada	Lebanon	Sudan
Ceylon	Libya	Sweden
Chile	Liechtenstein	Switzerland
China	Malaysia	Syrian Arab Rep.
Colombia	Mexico	Thailand
Denmark	Monaco	Tunisia
Ethiopia	Morocco	United Arab Republic
France	Netherlands	United Kingdom
Germany, Fed. Rep.	New Zealand	United States
Greece	Nigeria	Vatican City State
India	Norway	Venezuela
Indonesia	Pakistan	Yemen Arab Republic
Iraq		

* Done at Washington, August 20, 1964; entered into force for the United States, August 20, 1964. 15 U.S.T. 1705; T.I.A.S. 5646; 514 U.N.T.S. 26.
  † Provisionally in force.

EXHIBIT 40

Special Agreement

Governments or Entities
Which Are Parties:

Country designating
entity:

Ministry of Posts, Telecommunications, Public Works
and Transportation. . . . . .Algeria
Secretaría de Estado de Communicaciones. . . . . .Argentina
Overseas Telecommunications Commission (Australia). . Australia
Bundesministerium für Verkehr und Elektrizitätswirt-
schaft, Generaldirektion für die Post-und Tele-
graphenverwaltung. . . . . .Austria
Régie des Télégraphes et Téléphones. . . . . .Belgium
National Telecommunications Council. . . . . .Brazil
Canadian Overseas Telecommunication Corp. . . . . .Canada
Permanent Secretary in charge of Ministry of Posts and
Telecommunications. . . . . .Ceylon
Empresa Nacional de Telecommunicaciones S.A. . . . . . . .Chile
Directorate General of Telecommunications. . . . . .China
Colombia
Generaldirektoratet for Post og Telegrafvesenet. . . . . . . .Denmark
Ethiopia
France
Deutsche Bundespost. . . . . .Germany, Fed. Rep
Ministry of Communications, Directorate General of
Telecommunications. . . . . .Greece
India
Dewan Telekomunikasi. . . . . .Indonesia
Ministry of Communications. . . . . .Iraq
An Roinn Poist Agus Telegrafa. .Ireland
Ministry of Posts. . . . . .Israel
Società Telespazio. . . . . .Italy
Kokusai Denshin Denwa Co., Ltd. . . . . .Japan
Ministry of Communications. . . . . .Jordan
Ministry of Post, Telegraphs, and Telephones. . . . . .Kuwait
Lebanon
Libya
Liechtenstein
Director-General, Telecommunications Department. . . . .Malaysia
Department of Communications and Transportation. . . . .Mexico
Monaco
Ministry of Post, Telegraph and Telephone. . . . . .Morocco
Netherlands
Postmaster-General. . . . . .New Zealand
Nigeria
Telegrafstyret. . . . . .Norway
Pakistan
Philippine Communications Satellite Corporation. . . . . . .Philippines
Administração Geral dos Correios, Telégrafos e Telefones. Portugal

EXHIBIT 40—*Continued*

Governments or Entities Which Are Parties:	*Country designating entity:*
Ministry of Communications	Saudi Arabia
Telecommunications Department	Singapore
Department of Posts and Telegraphs	South Africa
Spain	
Department of Posts and Telegraphs	Sudan
Kungl. Telestyrelsen	Sweden
Direction Générale des PTT	Switzerland
Ministry of Communications	Syrian Arab Rep.
Thailand	
Secretariat of State for Post, Telegraph and Telephone	Tunisia
United Arab Republic	
Her Britannic Majesty's Postmaster General	United Kingdom
Communications Satellite Corp.	United States
Vatican City State	
Ministry of Communications	Venezuela
Ministry of Communications	Yemen Arab Rep.

* Done at Washington, August 20, 1964; entered into force for the United States Communications Satellite Corporation on August 20, 1964. 15 U.S.T. 1745; T. I. A. S. 5646; 514 U. N. T. S. 48.

EXHIBIT 41

Supplementary Agreement on Arbitration

Governments or Entities *Which Are Parties:*	*Country designating entity:*
Ministry of Posts, Telecommunications, Public Works and Transportation†..........................	Algeria
Secretaría de Estado de Communicaciones...........	Argentina
Overseas Telecommunications Commission...........	Australia
Bundesministerium für Verkehr und Elektrizitätswirt- schaft, Generaldirektion für die Post-und Telegraph- enverwaltung................................	Austria
Régie des Télégraphes et Téléphones.................	Belgium
National Telecommunications Council...............	Brazil
Canadian Overseas Telecommunication Corp.........	Canada
Permanent Secretary in charge of Ministry of Posts and Telecommunications..........................	Ceylon
Empresa Nacional de Telecommunicaciones S.A........	Chile
Directorate General of Telecommunications...........	China
Colombia	
Generaldirektoratet for Post og Telegrafvesenet.......	Denmark
Ethiopia	
France	
Deutsche Bundespost.............................	Germany, Fed. Rep.
Ministry of Communications, Directorate General of Telecommunications..........................	Greece
India	
Dewan Telekomunikasi...........................	Indonesia
Ministry of Communications......................	Iraq
An Roinn Poist Agus Telegrafa.....................	Ireland
Ministry of Posts...............................	Israel
Società Telespazio..............................	Italy
Kokusai Denshin Denwa Co., Ltd...................	Japan
Ministry of Communications......................	Jordan
Ministry of Post, Telegraphs, and Telephones‡.......	Kuwait
Lebanon	
Libya	
Liechtenstein	
Director-General, Telecommunications Department.....	Malaysia
Department of Communications and Transportation.....	Mexico
Monaco	
Ministry of Post, Telegraph and Telephone...........	Morocco
Netherlands	
Postmaster-General..............................	New Zealand
Nigeria	
Telegrafstyret..................................	Norway
Pakistan	
Philippine Communications Satellite Corp.............	Philippines
Administração Geral dos Correios, Telégrafos e Telefones.	Portugal
Ministry of Communications......................	Saudi Arabia
Telecommunications Department...................	Singapore

EXHIBIT 41—*Continued*

| *Governments or Entities* | *Country designating* |
| *Which Are Parties:* | *entity:* |

Department of Posts and Telegraphs.................South Africa
Spain
Department of Posts and Telegraphs†................Sudan
Kungl. Telestyrelsen.............................Sweden
Direction Générale des PTT......................Switzerland
Ministry of Communications§......................Syrian Arab Rep.
Thailand
Secretariat of State for Post, Telegraph and Telephone†..Tunisia
United Arab Republic
Her Britannic Majesty's Postmaster General...........United Kingdom
Communications Satellite Corp......................United States
Vatican City State
Ministry of Communications.......................Venezuela
Ministry of Communications.......................Yemen Arab Rep.

   * Done at Washington, June 1, 1965; entered into force for the United States Communications Satellite Corporation on November 21, 1966. T.I.A.S. 5646.
    † With a statement.
    ‡ With an understanding.
    § With reservation.

EXHIBIT 42

Treaty Banning Nuclear Weapon Tests in the Atmosphere, in Outer Space and Under Water *

Afghanistan[1]
Australia[1]
Austria[1]
Belgium[1]
Bolivia[2]
Brazil[1]
Bulgaria[1]
Burma[1]
[Byelorussian Soviet Socialist Republic][3]
Canada[1]
Central African Republic[4]
Ceylon[1]
Chad[5]
Chile[6]
China[5]
Congo (Kinshasa)[5]
Cyprus[1]
Czechoslovakia[1]
Dahomey[1]
Denmark[1]
Dominican Republic[1]
Ecuador[1]
El Salvador[1]
Finland[2]
Gabon[1]
Gambia[7]
[German Democratic Republic][8]
Germany, Fed. Rep.[2,9]
Ghana[1]
Greece[1]
Guatemala[5,10]

Honduras[2]
Hungary[1]
Iceland[1]
India[1]
Indonesia[1]
Iran[1]
Iraq[1]
Ireland[1]
Israel[1]
Italy[1]
Ivory Coast[5]
Japan[1]
Jordan[1]
Kenya[4]
Korea[2,10]
Kuwait[1,10]
Laos[1]
Lebanon[1]
Liberia[1]
Luxembourg[1]
Madagascar[5]
Malawi[11]
Malaysia[1]
Malta[11]
Mauritania[1]
Mexico[1]
Mongolia[12]
Morocco[1]
Nepal[1]
Netherlands[1,13]
New Zealand[1]
Nicaragua[1]
Niger[1]
Norway[1]

Panama[5]
Peru[1]
Philippines[1,10]
Poland[1]
Romania[1]
Rwanda[14]
San Marino[1]
Senegal[1]
Sierra Leone[1]
South Africa[15]
Spain[2]
Sudan[1]
Sweden[1]
Switzerland[1]
Syrian Arab Republic[1]
Tanganyika[6]
Thailand[1]
Togo[5]
Trinidad and Tobago[1]
Tunisia[1]
Turkey[1]
Uganda[2]
[Ukrainian Soviet Socialist Republic][3]
Union of Soviet Socialist Republics[1,16]
United Arab Republic[2,10]
United Kingdom[1,16]
United States[1,16]
Venezuela[1]
Western Samoa[1]
Yugoslavia[1]
Zambia[11]

* Done at Moscow, August 5, 1963; entered into force for the United States, October 10, 1963. 14 U.S.T. 1313; T.I.A.S. 5433; 480 U.N.T.S. 43.

[1] Ratification deposited at Washington, London, and Moscow.

[2] Ratification deposited at Washington and London.

[3] With reference to the reported signature and deposit of ratification at Moscow by the Byelorussian Soviet Socialist Republic and the Ukrainian Soviet Socialist Republic, the government of the United States considers those two constituent republics as already covered by the signature and deposit of ratification of the treaty by the Union of Soviet Socialist Republics.

[4] Accession deposited at Washington, London and Moscow.

[5] Ratification deposited at Washington.

[6] Ratification deposited at London.

[7] Notification of succession deposited at Washington and London.

[8] With reference to the reported signature and deposit of ratification at Moscow by the "German Democratic Republic", attention is called to the following statement in a note of August 16, 1963 from the Government of the United States to the Government of the Union of Soviet Socialist Republics: "In as much as the Government of the United States of America does not recognize the 'German Democratic Republic' as a State or as an entity possessing national sovereignty, it does not accept notice of signature in behalf thereof. Bearing in mind, however, the purpose of the treaty, the Government of the United

MARITIME AGREEMENTS

EXHIBIT 43

Convention on Fishing and Conservation of
Living Resources of the High Seas*

Australia	Malawi	Switzerland
Cambodia	Malaysia	Trinidad
Colombia	Mexico	and Tobago
Dominican	Netherlands	Uganda
Republic	Nigeria	United Kingdom†
Finland	Portugal	United States‡
Haiti	Senegal	Upper Volta
Jamaica	Sierra Leone	Venezuela
Madagascar	South Africa	Yugoslavia

* Done at Geneva, April 29, 1958; entered into force for the United States on
March 20, 1966. 17 U.S.T. 138; T.I.A.S. 5969.
† With declaration.
‡ With an understanding.

States of America notes that the East German regime has signified its intention with respect to the matters
dealt with in the treaty." That view was reaffirmed by the Government of the United States in a note
of January 24, 1964 to the Government of the Union of Soviet Socialist Republics in connection with
reported deposit of ratification.
 9 Including Land Berlin.
 10 With a statement.
 11 Notification of succession deposited at Washington, London, and Moscow.
 12 Ratification deposited at London and Moscow.
 13 Including Surinam and Netherlands Antilles.
 14 Ratification deposited at Washington; accession deposited at London.
 15 Accession deposited at Washington and London.
 16 Original Party.

EXHIBIT 44

Convention on the High Seas *

State	Declarations and Reservations	Date of Signature		Date of Receipt of Instrument of Ratification or Accession (a)	
Afghanistan		30 October	1958	28 April	1959
Albania				7 December	1964 a
Algeria					
Argentina		29 April	1958		
Australia		30 October	1958	14 May	1963
Austria		27 October	1958		
Belgium					
Bolivia		17 October	1958		
Brazil					
Bulgaria	x	31 October	1958	31 August	1962
Burma					
Burundi					
Byelorussian SSR	x	30 October	1958	27 February	1961
Cambodia				18 March	1960 a
Cameroon					
Canada		29 April	1958		
Central African Republic				15 October	1962 a
Ceylon		30 October	1958		
Chad					
Chile					
China		29 April	1958		
Colombia		29 April	1958		
Congo (Brazzaville)					
Congo (Leopoldville)					
Costa Rica		29 April	1958		
Cuba		29 April	1958		
Cyprus					
Czechoslovakia	x	30 October	1958	31 August	1961
Dahomey					
Denmark		29 April	1958		
Dominican Republic		29 April	1958	11 August	1964
Ecuador					
El Salvador					
Ethiopia					
Federal Republic of Germany		30 October	1958		
Finland		27 October	1958	16 February	1965
France		30 October	1958		
Gabon					
Ghana		29 April	1958		
Greece					
Guatemala		29 April	1958	27 November	1961
Guinea					
Haiti		29 April	1958	29 March	1960
Holy See (Vatican City)		30 April	1958		
Honduras					
Hungary	x	31 October	1958	6 December	1961
Iceland		29 April	1958		
India					
Indonesia	x	8 May	1958	10 August	1961
Iran	x	28 May	1958		
Iraq					
Ireland		2 October	1958		
Israel	x	29 April	1958	6 September	1961
Italy				17 December	1964 a
Ivory Coast					

EXHIBIT 44—*Continued*

State	Declarations and Reservations	Date of Signature	Date of Receipt of Instrument of Ratification or Accession (a)
Jamaica			8 October 1965 d
Japan			
Jordan			
Kenya			
Kuwait			
Laos			
Lebanon		29 May 1958	
Liberia		27 May 1958	
Libya			
Liechtenstein			
Luxembourg			
Madagascar			31 July 1962 a
Malawi			3 November 1965 a
Malaysia			21 December 1960 a
Mali			
Mauritania			
Mexico			2 August 1966 a
Monaco			
Mongolia			
Morocco			
Nepal		29 April 1958	28 December 1962
Netherlands		31 October 1958	18 February 1966
New Zealand		29 October 1958	
Nicaragua			
Niger			
Nigeria			26 June 1961 d
Norway			
Pakistan		31 October 1958	
Panama		2 May 1958	
Paraguay			
Peru			
Philippines			
Poland	x	31 October 1958	29 June 1962
Portugal		28 October 1958	8 January 1963
Republic of Korea			
Republic of Viet-Nam			
Romania	x	31 October 1958	12 December 1961
Rwanda			
San Marino			
Saudi Arabia			
Senegal			25 April 1961 a
Sierra Leone			13 March 1962 d
Somalia			
South Africa			9 April 1963 a
Spain			
Sudan			
Sweden			
Switzerland		24 May 1958	18 May 1966
Syria			
Tanganyika			
Thailand		29 April 1958	
Togo			
Trinidad and Tobago			11 April 1966 d
Tunisia		30 October 1958	
Turkey			
Uganda			14 September 1964 a
Ukrainian SSR	x	30 October 1958	12 January 1961

EXHIBIT 44—*Continued*

State	Declarations and Reservations	Date of Signature	Date of Receipt of Instrument of Ratification or Accession (a)
Union of Soviet Socialist Republics........................x		30 October 1958	22 November 1960
United Arab Republic............................			
United Kingdom...................x		9 September 1958	14 March 1960
United States of America...................15 September 1958			12 April 1961
Upper Volta......................................			4 October 1965 *a*
Uruguay...............................29 April		1958	
Venezuela..............................30 October		1958	15 August 1961
Western Samoa.................................			
Yemen..			
Yugoslavia.............................29 April		1958	28 January 1966
Zanzibar...			

* In force since September 30, 1962.

EXHIBIT 45

Convention on the Continental Shelf*

State	Declarations and Reservations	Date of Signature	Date of Receipt of Instrument of Ratification or Accession (a)
Afghanistan		30 October 1958	
Albania			7 December 1964 a
Algeria			
Argentina		29 October 1958	
Australia		30 October 1958	14 May 1963
Austria			
Belgium			
Bolivia		17 October 1958	
Brazil			
Bulgaria			31 August 1962 a
Burma			
Burundi			
Byelorussian SSR		31 October 1958	27 February 1961
Cambodia			18 March 1960 a
Cameroon			
Canada		29 April 1958	
Central African Republic			
Ceylon		30 October 1958	
Chad			
Chile		31 October 1958	
China		29 April 1958	
Colombia		29 April 1958	8 January 1962
Congo (Brazzaville)			
Congo (Leopoldville)			
Costa Rica		29 April 1958	
Cuba		29 April 1958	
Cyprus			
Czechoslovakia		31 October 1958	31 August 1961
Dahomey			
Denmark		29 April 1958	12 June 1963
Dominican Republic		29 April 1958	11 August 1964
Ecuador		31 October 1958	
El Salvador			
Ethiopia			
Federal Republic of Germany	x	30 October 1958	
Finland		27 October 1958	16 February 1965
France			14 June 1965 a
Gabon			
Ghana		29 April 1958	
Greece			
Guatemala		29 April 1958	27 November 1961
Guinea			
Haiti		29 April 1958	29 March 1960
Holy See (Vatican City)			
Honduras			
Hungary			
Iceland		29 April 1958	
India			
Indonesia		8 May 1958	
Iran	x	28 May 1958	
Iraq			
Ireland		2 October 1958	
Israel		29 April 1958	6 September 1961
Italy			
Ivory Coast			
Jamaica			8 October 1965 a
Japan			

EXHIBIT 45—*Continued*

State	Declarations and Reservations	Date of Signature	Date of Receipt of Instrument of Ratification or Accession (a)
Jordan			
Kenya			
Kuwait			
Laos			
Lebanon	29 May	1958	
Liberia	27 May	1958	
Libya			
Liechtenstein			
Luxembourg			31 July 1962 a
Madagascar			3 November 1965 a
Malawi			21 December 1960 a
Malaysia			
Mali			19 May 1966 d
Malta			
Mauritania			2 August 1966 a
Mexico			
Monaco			
Mongolia			
Morocco			
Nepal	29 April	1958	
Netherlands	31 October	1958	18 February 1966
New Zealand	29 October	1958	18 January 1965
Nicaragua			
Niger			
Nigeria			
Norway			
Pakistan	31 October	1958	
Panama	2 May	1958	
Paraguay			
Peru	31 October	1958	
Philippines			
Poland	31 October	1958	29 June 1962
Portugal	28 October	1958	8 January 1963
Republic of Korea			
Republic of Viet-Nam			
Romania			12 December 1961 a
Rwanda			
San Marino			
Saudi Arabia			
Senegal			25 April 1961 a
Sierra Leone			
Somalia			9 April 1963 a
South Africa			
Spain			
Sudan			
Sweden	22 October	1958	18 May 1966
Switzerland			
Syria			
Tanganyika			
Thailand	29 April	1958	
Togo			
Trinidad and Tobago			
Tunisia	30 October	1958	
Turkey			
Uganda			14 September 1964 a
Ukrainian SSR	31 October	1958	12 January 1961
Union of Soviet Socialist Republics	31 October	1958	22 November 1960
United Arab Republic			

EXHIBIT 45—*Continued*

State	Declarations and Reservations	Date of Signature	Date of Receipt of Instrument of Ratification or Accession (a)
United Kingdom............................		9 September 1958	11 May 1964
United States of America....................		15 September 1958	12 April 1961
Upper Volta...............................			
Uruguay.................................		29 April 1958	
Venezuela...............................	x	30 October 1958	15 August 1961
Western Samoa............................			
Yemen...................................			
Yugoslavia...............................		29 April 1958	28 January 1966
Zanzibar.................................			

* In force since June 10, 1964.

EXHIBIT 46

Convention on the Territorial Sea and Contiguous Zone*

State	Declarations and Reservations	Date of Signature		Date of Receipt of Instrument of Ratification or Accession (a)	
Afghanistan		30 October	1958		
Albania					
Algeria					
Argentina		29 April	1958		
Australia		30 October	1958	14 May	1963
Austria		27 October	1958		
Belgium					
Bolivia		17 October	1958		
Brazil					
Bulgaria	x	31 October	1958	31 August	1962
Burma					
Burundi					
Byelorussian SSR	x	30 October	1958	27 February	1961
Cambodia				18 March	1960 a
Cameroon					
Canada		29 April	1958		
Central African Republic					
Ceylon		30 October	1958		
Chad					
Chile					
China		29 April	1958		
Colombia	x	29 April	1958		
Congo (Brazzaville)					
Congo (Leopoldville)					
Costa Rica		29 April	1958		
Cuba		29 April	1958		
Cyprus					
Czechoslovakia	x	30 October	1958	31 August	1961
Dahomey					
Denmark		29 April	1958		
Dominican Republic		29 April	1958	11 August	1964
Ecuador					
El Salvador					
Ethiopia					
Federal Republic of Germany		27 October	1958	16 February	1965
Finland		27 October	1958	16 February	1965
France					
Gabon					
Ghana		29 April	1958		
Greece					
Guatemala		29 April	1958		
Guinea					
Haiti		29 April	1958	29 March	1960
Holy See (Vatican City)		30 April	1958		
Honduras					
Hungary	x	31 October	1958	6 December	1961
Iceland		29 April	1958		
India					
Indonesia					
Iran	x	28 May	1958		
Iraq					
Ireland		2 October	1958		
Israel	x	29 April	1958	6 September	1961
Italy				17 December	1964 a
Ivory Coast					

EXHIBIT 46—*Continued*

State	Declarations and Reservations	Date of Signature		Date of Receipt of Instrument of Ratification or Accession (a)	
Jamaica				8 October	1965 d
Japan					
Jordan					
Kenya					
Kuwait					
Laos					
Lebanon					
Liberia		27 May	1958		
Libya					
Liechtenstein					
Luxembourg					
Madagascar		31 July		1962 a	
Malawi		3 November	1965 a		
Malaysia		21 December	1960 a		
Mali					
Malta		19 May		1966 d	
Mauritania					
Mexico		2 August		1966 a	
Monaco					
Mongolia					
Morocco					
Nepal		29 April	1958		
Netherlands		31 October	1958	18 February	1966
New Zealand		29 October	1958		
Nicaragua					
Niger					
Nigeria		26 June		1961 d	
Norway					
Pakistan		31 October	1958		
Panama		2 May	1958		
Paraguay					
Peru					
Philippines					
Poland					
Portugal		28 October	1958	8 January	1963
Republic of Korea					
Republic of Viet-Nam					
Romania	x	31 October	1958	12 December	1961
Rwanda					
San Marino					
Saudi Arabia					
Senegal		25 April		1961 a	
Sierra Leone		13 March		1962 d	
Somalia					
South Africa		9 April		1963 a	
Spain					
Sudan					
Sweden					
Switzerland		22 October	1958	18 May	1966
Syria					
Tanganyika					
Thailand		29 April	1958		
Togo					
Trinidad and Tobago		11 April		1966 d	
Tunisia	x	30 October	1958		
Turkey					
Uganda		14 September	1964 a		
Ukrainian SSR	x	30 October	1958	12 January	1961

EXHIBIT 46—*Continued*

State	Declarations and Reservations	Date of Signature	Date of Receipt of Instrument of Ratification or Accession (a)
Union of Soviet Socialist Republics	x	30 October 1958	22 November 1960
United Arab Republic			
United Kingdom	x	9 September 1958	14 March 1960
United States of America		15 September 1958	12 April 1961
Upper Volta			
Uruguay		29 April 1958	
Venezuela	x	30 October 1958	15 August 1961
Western Samoa			
Yemen			
Yugoslavia		29 April 1958	28 January 1966
Zanzibar			

* In force since September 10, 1964.

Index of Cases

Index

439

This book has been set in 11 and 10 point Baskerville, leaded 2 points. Chapter numbers and titles are in 14 and 18 point Helvetica. The size of the type page is 27 by 43¾ picas.